Nebraska
Symposium on
Motivation
1979

Nebraska Symposium on Motivation, 1979, is Volume 27 in the series on
CURRENT THEORY AND
RESEARCH IN MOTIVATION

University of Nebraska Press
Lincoln/London 1980

Nebraska Symposium on Motivation 1979

Beliefs, Attitudes, and Values

Herbert E. Howe, Jr.	*Series Editor*
Monte M. Page	*Volume Editor*
Carolyn Wood Sherif	*Professor of Psychology The Pennsylvania State University*
Martin Fishbein	*Professor of Psychology University of Illinois at Urbana-Champaign*
Herbert C. Kelman	*Richard Clarke Cabot Professor of Social Ethics Harvard University*
Harry C. Triandis	*Professor of Psychology University of Illinois at Urbana-Champaign*
Milton Rokeach	*Director, Unit on Human Values, and Professor of Sociology and Psychology Washington State University*
M. Brewster Smith	*Professor of Psychology Adlai E. Stevenson College University of California, Santa Cruz*

Preface

Continuing a tradition which has characterized the last several years of the Nebraska Symposium on Motivation, both the fall and spring sessions of the 1978–79 Symposium have dealt with one central issue—for this symposium the issue of Attitudes, Values, and Beliefs. This volume, the twenty-seventh, was edited by Professor Monte Page, without whose enthusiasm, dedication, and skill this volume and the symposium would have been impossible. His excellent job is greatly appreciated.

This Nebraska Symposium on Motivation is dedicated to the memory of Harry K. Wolfe, one of America's early psychologists. A student of Wilhelm Wundt, Professor Wolfe established the first undergraduate laboratory in psychology in America at the University of Nebraska. It is especially appropriate that funds donated to the University of Nebraska Foundation in the memory of this pioneer psychologist by his late student Dr. Cora L. Friedline are used to support the Nebraska Symposium. The editors thank the University of Nebraska Foundation for its support.

HERBERT E. HOWE, JR.
Series Editor

Contents

Introduction

 *T*his year's Nebraska Symposium brought together six of the most eminent social psychologists in the country to discuss an old and central topic of social psychology, the psychology of attitudes. Because attitudes are best conceptualized together with a number of individual difference concepts which, along with attitudes, make up the personality system, the topic was expanded to include beliefs and values. The call that went out to the speakers was to update their thinking and to examine the current state of that area of social psychology which concerns itself with beliefs, attitudes, and values—a charge each speaker responded to in his or her own way.

 Carolyn Wood Sherif began the fall session of the symposium with a paper that consisted of two main parts. The first part may be considered a substantive introduction to the entire symposium; in it she states one of the major themes of the symposium and sets the stage for the later papers of Rokeach and Smith by insisting that the attitude concept cannot be understood apart from personality and the self-system. Asking why the attitude concept was ever considered central for social psychology in the first place, the most important answer she provides is that it helped us deal theoretically with the link between the psychology of the individual and the twin problems of social control and social change. Sherif's position comes through "loud and clear." In much that has recently passed for attitude research, we have lost the original vision of what social psychology should be, and what it was about attitudes that was important. The result has been a trivialization of the attitude field; but the original centrality of the attitude concept for social psychology has not disappeared. Attitudes separated from the rest of the person become aridly academic; attitudes in the context of their function for the self-system become central for understanding the person-society relationship.

In the second part of her paper Sherif discusses her own version of a social-psychological theory where the concept of attitude is of central importance. She puts in perspective the "Social Judgment–Involvement Theory" on which she and Muzafer Sherif have been working for many years. Those familiar with that point of view will be pleased to see this theoretical up-date and report on recent research, while those unfamiliar with the approach should be challenged to read further in this area.

Under the title of "A Theory of Reasoned Action," Martin Fishbein presents the theory of social behavior which he has developed in recent years. His paper presents several sharp contrasts with that of Sherif. Fishbein believes in parsimony; his mission is to predict action and, given these goals, his theory reasonably follows. The attitude concept is not central, although it is important. We must view attitude in the context of the belief, attitude, intention, and behavior sequence or series. "Traditional attitudes" are "external variables" in Fishbein's system, and what is important in predicting action is what he calls "attitude toward the behavior." Because considerations of personality and values do not add to the goal of prediction, they are external to his theory. But while the contrast between Fishbein and several of the other authors in this symposium is sharp, there is a similarity at another level. Like all of the other contributors, Fishbein is dissatisfied with the arid triviality of much of the social psychology of attitudes during the fifties and sixties. His solution is to revitalize the attitude concept in some exciting and practical ways by linking it with the concepts of belief and intention.

Herbert Kelman was the third speaker at the fall session. Those familiar with the themes associated with Kelman's name over the years in the attitude area will recognize some of the concepts (compliance, identification, and internalization) that he utilizes, and some of the basic questions of the author (e.g., of what functional utility are attitudes?). Drawing on his recent experiences in the mid-East and discussing some of his recent research, Kelman re-examines his past work on attitudes and carries it beyond past formulations. He reminds us that attitudes and action are in a dynamic-reciprocal relationship and thus rounds out our grasp of the nature of attitudes.

The first speaker at the spring session of the symposium was Harry Triandis. In a wide-ranging paper he attempts a "conscious move toward synthesis" in social psychological theory. He does this through a set of heuristic theoretical equations (one discussion session participant accused him of being "neo-Hullian" in this regard, and he did not strenuously object), flow charts, and numerous definitions and hypotheses. Triandis has added some dimensions of breadth and depth that are indispensable to the total picture presented in this volume. Of particular note in this regard is his relating of the notion of "subjective culture" to the attitude area.

It was especially gratifying to see the second speaker at the spring session, Milton Rokeach, stand up and deliver his first major address since recovering from a serious illness. More than anyone else, Rokeach has argued for the inclusion of values in our understanding of social attitudes. It is clear that I have taken Rokeach's advice in the organization of this symposium, even to the point of borrowing one of his phrases (beliefs, attitudes, and values) for the volume subtitle. If the wave of the future in attitude psychology is (as I hope it will be) to recognize that attitudes must be understood in the broader context of personality, values, and selfhood on the one hand, and in the more specific context of beliefs and intentions on the other, then Rokeach has been prophetic. He delivered a particularly lucid, dynamic, and forward-looking address, the flavor of which is also maintained in the written version.

Rokeach focuses on the core of some of the major contemporary issues in the attitude area. Some high points are his discussion of the attitudes and behavior controversy (which is also touched upon by some of the other authors in this volume), his discussion of attitudes and causal attributions, and his resurrection of the belief-congruence controversy. On this latter issue Rokeach "came out swinging." As an interesting sidelight, we may note that both Triandis and Dienstbier were present at this session of the symposium, a situation which made for some lively discussions.

The final speaker was M. Brewster Smith, whose paper on "Attitudes, Values, and Selfhood" capped off the symposium. Here we have a long-standing contributor to attitude theory, now vitally interested in the broader issues of personality and selfhood, bringing the two together in a coherent perspective. Smith's paper will no doubt be disquieting for some traditional social psychologists. He puts the field of social psychology in perspective even as he focuses more specifically upon the attitude concept. He points out the futility of trying to understand attitudes apart from their broader context as an aspect of personality and experiences of selfhood. His paper is a clarion call for a social psychology of the future which is true to the humanistic visions and traditions which had so much to do with the rise of social psychology in the first place.

Within this volume, we cover the entire range of psychological concerns that can be considered in a social psychology of attitudes. If one hypothesizes a theoretical funnel necessary for a complete account of the attitude area, Fishbein focuses upon the narrow end, the end closest to specific acts. Triandis, Sherif, and Kelman range further up the broadening stem of this funnel until we reach Rokeach, whose central focus is upon values but who encompasses the total length of the funnel from action to personality. And finally there is Smith, who focuses upon the person and selfhood and thus outlines the wide upper rim of our funnel. If all of these critics of the status quo in attitude theory were combined to achieve a total picture, the sequence of concepts would proceed from self, to values, to attitudes, to beliefs, to intentions, and finally to behavior or action.

At the fall session, just prior to the introduction of his wife and long-time collaborator, I read the following dedication: "To Muzafer Sherif, pioneer, innovator, and enthusiast, for the social psychology of beliefs, attitudes, and values"—a fitting dedication to the man who exemplifies the spirit of this year's Symposium and who, many years ago, introduced me to the topic and inspired me to a long-time interest in the social psychology of beliefs, attitudes, and values. Being volume editor this year has been a very rewarding experience. I wish to thank Herb Howe and the Symposium committee for giving me this opportunity, and to thank each of the authors for his or her dedication to this task. It was no small feat to bring this extraordinary group of psychologists together, and perhaps only in the context of the tradition of the Nebraska Symposium was it possible. I am confident that the efforts of all of us this year in reassessing an old traditional concept have resulted in something of value for the future of social psychology.

MONTE M. PAGE

Social Values, Attitudes, and Involvement of the Self

Carolyn Wood Sherif[1]

The Pennsylvania State University

*T*he overarching problem in social psychology is the psychological relationship between the human individual and the social environment. That social environment includes places for work and living, objects invested with value, and other persons, as well as their positions in the organized schemes for activities and interpersonal interchange that are summed up in sociological concepts such as group, family, institution, status hierarchy, social class, gender, race, ethnicity, nation, and so on. Social objects and the social structuring of persons and of activities are never neutral in human societies. The social values and the beliefs supporting their use and opposing their change are constituents of human culture—complex, varied, and differentiated. Human cultures also invest value in the physical world, above and beyond the foodstuffs and liquids essential to life.

This overarching problem of the human individual–society relationship can be approached at different levels of analysis. Each level implies a different unit of analysis in theory and research. Social psychology is in the peculiar position of focusing upon the human individual's psychological functioning and behavior, attempting to relate the individual unit of analysis to social structure and social values, i.e., to sociological units of analysis that subsume single

1. Readers have called my attention to the occasional use of the first-person collective pronoun in this chapter. It reflects collaboration since 1945 with Muzafer Sherif. Readers of his earlier work (Sherif, 1936) will recognize the continuity in development of the theory and research presented here, as well as modifications responsive to research findings. In addition to associates whose research is presented here, I thank the following colleagues for constructive criticism of the text: Charles Korte, Monte Page, Muzafer Sherif, R. Lance Shotland, and J. Diedrick Snoek.

individuals. There are many avenues toward exploring these relationships.

One avenue is the study of those social perceptions involving judgment, i.e., comparing, categorizing, choosing—symbolically and in action. Perception and judgment are traditionally included in psychological processes labeled "cognitive," that is, "knowing" about the world. When the objects compared, categorized, or chosen are socially valued, judgment is both cognitive and evaluative, inevitably and whether the individual is aware of it or not.

However, human individuals offer evaluative judgments at the drop of a hat, every day, whether asked for them or not. They also frequently reverse or revise such opinions. Those social judgments or opinions that evoke conceptual distinctiveness, suggesting the need for a psychological concept such as attitude, exhibit a pattern over time and across specific situations. Thus, patterns of social judgment have been a focus of our study aimed at uncovering the structure of an attitude.

Very early, we discovered that every major theoretical statement and empirical generalization about attitudes in psychological functioning and action contained a qualification. I began to collect the terms of such qualification. Some of the terms suggested a geometric concept of psychological organization, for example, attitude "centrality" vs. "peripherality." Some qualifications referred to "connectedness" with other attitudes, or suggested hierarchical organization, e.g., the "priority" of various attitudes. Regardless of the specific term, the literature is full of generalizations about attitude functioning qualified by the phrase "depending on . . . ." The qualification then concerns how *central*, how high in *priority*, how *connected*, how *important*, how *salient*, how *intense*, how *meaningful*, how *relevant*, how *involving*, how *personal* or *personalized* the attitude is.

Such qualifications about attitudes relate to significant issues, including how certain, confident, persistent, motivated, disappointed, frustrated, or gratified a person becomes in ongoing events. They pertain to the entire issue of when an individual's behavior is coherently patterned in terms of consistent directionality toward or away, for or against, positively or negatively, relative to other persons, social objects, groups, institutions, ideas, etc. In short, the qualifications are integral to an adequate psychology of human attitudes, not an afterthought to be studied when other problems are settled.

In recent years, such qualifying terms have been used in the literature as though everyone surely understood what they meant. True, there have been passing discussions on whether "involvement" should be classified according to what one is involved *in*, whether involvement and object importance are the same or different, whether self-ratings of confidence or certainty in judgment might not be more useful than ratings of object importance, etc. However, such technical discussions seldom ask the obvious question: "Importance, centrality, relevance, meaningfulness, salience, involvement, intensity, for *whom*?"

The obvious answer is "for the person, of course." But what *about* the person? His toes? Her elbow? The qualifications make very little sense unless they refer to the organization of self-defining past experiences that establish psychological relationships with objects, persons, situations, and other environmental events. Such psychological organization can be referred to as a self-system. In the interests of parsimony, all such qualifications to statements about attitudes can be subsumed as special problems arising from involvement of self in ongoing psychological processes and activity. Indeed, it is my counter-thesis that attitude research which reveals nothing about the human self-system contributes little to those intellectual and practical issues that gave rise to the attitude concept in social psychology.

A concept like the self-system produces shudders of horror in some colleagues. For some, the term violates a lifetime attempt to avoid conceptions smacking of a metaphysical past. For others, "self-system" equals "self-concept," a term that has dominated the literature. I am not referring here to the "self-concept" as currently used, which translates readily into "self-esteem." Therefore, I need not discuss issues in its use, which include overreliance on correlated self-ratings, social desirability effects, and the relativity of self-esteem to situational contexts and standards.

Fortunately, at least one other author in this volume has shared the concern that the study of human psychology becomes a collection of fragments without a conception of the self-system (Smith, 1968). While I will offer a conception later, it is not my aim to discuss all possible directions where it proves useful. Rather, I will make the modest attempt to show that we keep bumping into something like self in research on human cognition and that the encounters are critical for understanding the attitude–social value relationship.

The term "involvement," which is widely used in current literature, has no meaningful referent apart from a conception of a self-system, whose constituents may be implicated in ongoing psychological processes or be evoked in situational episodes. When "involvement" is invoked as a psychological variable abstracted from the self or from ongoing situations, it is meaningless. It is an abbreviation of the term "ego involvement," which was introduced into the psychological literature by Muzafer Sherif (1936). Sherif and Cantril (1947) made it abundantly clear that the term did not refer to a Freudian or neo-Freudian ego, and, in fact includes phenomena segregated to a "super-ego." However, I fear that over forty years of denial is enough. Like them I would prefer a neutral term. They suggested "x" instead of "ego" or "self," which they used interchangeably. I hesitate to repeat that suggestion, in fear of the remote possibility that the term X-involvement might catch on. Therefore, I will speak of involvement of self or of personal involvement.

I will consider first the issue of why, historically, the attitude concept received the accolades it has for being a "central" concept in social psychology. Some of the reasons have bearing on the centrality of the attitude concept in social-psychological theories. Others do not. Conceptual confusion as well as discontinuities between writing about attitudes and measuring them are parts of the picture. Then theory and research on social judgment will be discussed as they bear most directly on the question of what value-attitude research can reveal about the human self-system. There I am constrained by circumstances to concentrate on our own research with students and colleagues.

WHY DID ATTITUDE BECOME AN IMPORTANT CONCEPT?

Widely hailed as "central" and "indispensable" in social psychology, the attitude concept was called into question during the last decade or so. The criticisms led to self-examination, considerable research, and sharpened conceptualizations. Social psychologists have rediscovered wheels that they should have known had to be under the cart that carried the attitude concept. Some of the confusion, the self-castigation, and the discontinuities can be clarified by asking why the attitude concept came to be regarded as "central" in social psychology in the first place.

At the risk of oversimplifying and selective interpretation, I will discuss three major sets of reasons. One is theoretical, namely, the origin of the attitude concept in dealing with major problems of the psychological relationships between the individual, social structure, and culture, including social values. The second set concerns the relationship between theory and attitude measurement technology, particularly as technology provided an alleged "scientific basis" for the thriving commercial venture known as the public opinion survey. The third set pertains to social psychology's post–World War II experiences in trying to gain respectability and a voice in academia, with the aid of subsidies to attitude research from government, private foundations, and business.

I. Attitude as Central in Theory

The earlier social-psychological literature introduced the attitude concept, or its British counterpart of "sentiment," to forge a psychological linkage with two broad problems of social philosophy and, more recently, the social sciences. The first is the broad problem of "social control." How, short of constant threat of force and coercion, do human societies or groups within them manage to maintain conformity to their status criteria, norms for conduct, ideologies, and other social values? The second concerns those social changes sufficiently compelling to alter social values, as well as those changes initiated by groups within society toward reform or recasting social institutions, i.e., social movements. If societies can effectively control their members, how do individuals ever change?

The development of the attitude concept in social psychology may be contrasted with alternative treatments of the social control problem. Consider the treatment by classical political philosophers in the British liberal tradition. Their abstract "man" was endowed both with an individualistic hedonism and a rational mind (Elshtain, 1979). Forced to function as a "social atom" by a society aggregated to serve specific instrumental goals, on one hand, and "group interests," on the other, this rational "man" behaved through calculations that recognized social realities, in the form of rewards and punishments limiting the pursuit of hedonism. In such a philosophical tradition, social control is possible because human cognition learns to replicate the social scheme. The individual's behavior is rational as long as that xerox copy controls the calculation of hedonistic pursuits.

However, when subjective desires, preferences, or biases slosh over to spoil the xerox copy of society's scheme, the individual is said to be "irrational." Thus, conformity to the existing scheme is rational, under cognitive control, while nonconformity is irrational, requiring the full force of constraining laws and institutions. It follows that change is also an irrational process.

The attitude concept came into social psychology with alternative views on the psychological problems of social control—views that did not split the human being into a rational knowing mind and a body with unruly, irrational preferences. With all of his faults for the modern reader, McDougall (1908) insisted that "sentiment" (his term for the attitude concept) always had cognitive, affective, and conative sides, joined in purposive action, not stored in separate compartments. Thomas and Znaniecki (1918), who did use the attitude term, formulated their problem as that of the relationship between "subject," or individual consciousness, and social value or "object." Interested in Polish immigrants to the United States, far removed from the social control system of their peasant culture, they touched a problem at the core of the attitude concept. Why does the subject-object relationship dominate in the absence of coercive or reward power from society?

In short, the attitude concept came into social psychology to deal with those problems of social control expressed by the term "internalization" or (to use Piaget's word) "interiorization" of social values. As Kelman (1958) reminded us many years later, the contrast between "compliance" to immediate normative demands or social constraints and "internalization" is not trivial psychologically. The latter is not merely learning what is expected. The evidence for "internalization" is that individuals conform willingly, self-regulating their own actions in the absence of situational demands, at times eagerly initiating actions that promote social values and volunteering as watchdogs to bark at nonconformity. Nor can the larger problem of social control be reduced to societal determinism achieved through force, coercion, and reward power, as Collins and Raven (1969) reminded us. Their list of sources for social power include many that presume a human individual already actively pursuing activities wherein social values are both means and ends.

For F. C. Bartlett (1932), individual attitudes related to cultural values contributed to organized mental schema for the individual's active construction and reconstruction of past events. Following formulations by Thomas, Bartlett, and Piaget, Sherif (1936) made attitude a central concept in social-psychological theory that linked the study of individual functioning with the study of social values. Social values were to be understood through sociological study of social life, including social objects, moral rules, and other normative social data. He called sociological study of values essential "but merely a beginning" in the study of attitudes. Within the sociological framework, he characterized the psychological issues as follows: study of the progressive "interiorization" of social values by the child during development; study of the role of attitudes in psychological functioning and activity; and study of individual differences in intensity of attachment, desire to conform, and mode of affective expression. All three issues were seen as central to the psychological problems associated with social control and social change.

The insistence upon sociocultural study as prerequisite to adequate study of attitude formation and functioning was not out of context in a social psychology of the 1930s. Its pioneers in attitude research had devoted their greatest energy to studying varied psychological manifestations of the racist values and institutions in U.S. society. Surely I need only mention the pioneering works of Bogardus (1925), Allport and Katz (1931), Katz and Braly (1932), and Horowitz (1936). Their reports on social distance and exclusion, on prejudiced beliefs and unfavorable attributions to subordinated groups by "educated" college students, on the prejudices of white toward black children, make very little sense apart from the context of institutional discrimination, immigration laws, and legal restrictions for minorities in society at that time. Similarly, the work of Otto Klineberg (1940) was already showing the value of cross-cultural data for understanding interpersonal and group-related attitudes.

Yet there were and still are social psychologists who regard the suggestion for preliminary study of social values and social structure as clear evidence that the speaker is not a *psychologist*. Today, such critics often prefer to be called *psychological* social psychologists, as though unsure of their identity. They have not begun to grapple with the problem that the early apostle of individualism in social psychology, F. H. Allport, came to see as the "master problem" in social psychology, viz. the individual–social unit relationship (Allport, 1962). As critics have correctly charged (Brooks & Johnson, 1978), any psychologist has to be concerned with the environment, with the stimulus side of the stimulus-organism-behavior formula. As a result of neglect of the properties of the social environment, psychology has witnessed the rise of movements labeled "environmental psychology," "ecological psychology," "organizational psychology" and "cultural psychology." Whether adopting the banner of behaviorism or of cognitive psychology, the self-appointed *psychologicial* social psychologist has had to be reminded that the "master problem" will not evaporate.

The other side of the social control coin, as noted earlier, is the problem of social change. On the psychological level, the problems include those changes in attitude sufficient in magnitude and direction to represent changing allegiances. Sociologists in recent years have engaged in considerable self-castigation for neglecting social change in their enthusiasm for equilibrium models of social systems. Such enthusiasm does appear passing strange when one looks about the world or at our own society over the past few decades; but social psychologists were equally engrossed in equilibrium models of the psychological system, with equal shortsightedness. Nevertheless, a case can be made that earlier the attitude concept came into social psychology to deal with relevant issues of social change.

Interestingly, the pioneers in developing attitude measurement were, in every instance, interested in attitude change, some being advocates of social reform. Bogardus (1967), whose forty years' study of social distance among groups in the United States is a singular contribution, eagerly documented changes in the face of discouraging similarities over the period. Thurstone and his students (1929) quickly put their new scales to work in studying the impact of motion pictures in producing what would probably be called now the "polarization" of attitudes. The early Likert attitude tests (Likert, 1932) were devised in the context of studies with Gardner Murphy, whose interest in social reform was well known.

Shortly, the Likert format was put to use by T. M. Newcomb (1943) in memorable research on the first classes of Bennington College women. Their conservative upbringings were confronted with progressive sociopolitical values, as well as the intellectual challenge from their faculty. Subsequently, Newcomb traced the individual patterns of attitude maintenance or change in terms of the women's varying statuses and reference groups within and outside of the college. Following up over twenty-five years (Newcomb, Koenig, Flacks, & Warwick, 1967), he showed the continuity of the college-adopted values or their decay, in terms of life decisions in occupation and marriage. Women who chose occupations and mates harmonious with the Bennington values maintained their political perspectives, while those who gravitated toward reference persons and groups within their conservative class backgrounds left Bennington values behind.

In the last decade before his too-early death, the work of Kurt Lewin and his associates (1948, 1965) was devoted to problems of social change, wherein the individual level of analysis was linked with social interaction through participation in collective decisions. Further, attitude change was assessed through changed behaviors.

Nor should it be forgotten that the three naturalistic experiments in summer camps by M. Sherif and colleagues (with C. Sherif, 1953; with White and Harvey, 1955; with Harvey, White, Hood, and C. Sherif, 1961) were explicitly designed as a model linking the problems of social change and individual attitude change. Initially, the social changes were the ecological conditions in which the campers interacted, first to form groups and later in the dealings between the two groups. The conditions in which campers from similar backgrounds met fostered new social units (groups), created by the participants collectively. In each, group norms regulating interactions among the individuals, legitimizing power relations among them, and defining valued objects and places were born together with individual attitudes of preference for associates, loyalty, respect, and attachment to the group and its members.

When the two groups chose to compete in games, the social conditions for the competitions introduced by the researchers pitted them repeatedly in a winner-take-all outcome. During the festering intergroup conflicts that ensued, individual attitudes toward the other group members (including derogatory attributions to them) converged toward new norms for conduct, including social distance and organized aggression. Finally, the superordinate goals which cumulatively reduced the intergroup conflict were initially changes in the social ecology, viz., compelling environmental problems faced by both groups that could not be dealt with separately. But the changes in intergroup conduct involved slow, cumulative changes both in normative patterns and in individual attitudes, as erstwhile enemies became potential friends. The distinction between normative change and attitude change essential to their accomplishment was clear in reactions to individual variations, particularly when one person lagged behind or exceeded the normative mode at a given time.

From such traditions in the study of attitude change, it is not a long step, conceptually or practically, to the study of individual nonconformists in a society who join collectively to voice protests and their attacks on some or many aspects of the social system, including its relevant values. Problems of attitudes and their change abound at every step in the formation, the recruitment, and the propaganda attempts of social movements. The conflict between prevailing social values and individual attitudes, themselves often in the process of changing, is joined in the dynamics of forming new social values, norms, and practices. New groups form, whose members attempt to win adherents, as well as to exert whatever social power their numbers and resources permit (M. Sherif & Sherif, 1956, 1969; C. W. Sherif, 1976).

To summarize, the attitude concept became "central" for social psychology in part because it served as a conceptual link in dealing with psychological problems posed by the twin enigmas of social control and social change.

II. Attitude Technology as Central in Social Psychology's Growth

It is claimed that attitude measurement developed with little relationship to attitude theory. I shall attempt to show that such claims are not entirely true. Developers of attitude measurement did have theories, albeit different theories; but the utilization of technology has become divorced from theory over the years. The divorce developed over time in a society where measurement of any kind is regarded as prestigious. Attitude measurement in academia bolstered the claim of being "scientific" and also provided a basis for allegedly scientific assessment enterprises outside academe, including the commercial public opinion survey or poll.

The first attitude measurement technique, the Bogardus social distance scale (1925), certainly did have contact with theory. Inspired by Park's concept that the hierarchical structure of racial and ethnic groups would be reflected in graded role relationships considered intimate, socially distant, or exclusionary, the resulting scale permitted the collection of both normative social data and patterns of individual attitudes (e.g., Bogardus, 1925, 1967; Hartley, 1946). The fact that its original items need modification when transferred to another society, e.g., Greece (Triandis & Triandis, 1965), or as society changes, is entirely in accord with that theoretical basis. The later attempt by Guttman (1947) to generalize the cumulative property of the Bogardus scale to other social values on a sheerly technical basis worked well enough when social values were, indeed, hierarchically organized. But the technique produces only a few scaleable items within a narrow and unrepresentative segment when the full range is not cumulative, as Festinger (1947) pointed out years ago.

Close on Bogardus's heels, Thurstone (1929) developed a model for attitude tests that also had a theoretical basis, this time borrowed from psychophysics. Unwittingly, perhaps, Thurstone and his collaborators began the scaling procedure with sociological methods (viz. culling newspapers, publications, statements by members of diverse groups) to obtain a pool of items representing the entire range of valued beliefs on a topic, such as the deity, crime, or the status of Negroes. Also, like a sociologist, he then set about determining whether or not there was social consensus on the positions of the beliefs, with respect to their favorableness-unfavorableness to the object of study.

But, like a good psychophysicist, he accepted the division of mind into rational cognitive and irrational emotional or affective compartments. Thus he also assumed that, if he so instructed them, the judges who determined consensus could put aside their own attitudes, which were affective, in making judgments, which were cognitive (Thurstone & Chave, 1929). He defined their attitudes as *affective* predispositions, as do Fishbein and Ajzen (1975) more recently. The split was in accord with Thurstone's theory and his assumptions. Such a definition of attitude implies the mind-body split or the tradition of Faculties of Mind that is otherwise passé in modern psychology.

The scale that emerged from Thurstone's procedures had certain advantages that subsequent attitude tests do not share. Based on consensual judgments of the relative positions or order of beliefs, in terms of their favorableness-unfavorableness toward the object, a Thurstone scale is singular in permitting the researcher to speak of relative "extremity" or "moderateness" of attitude *position*. With the exception of modified techniques developed much later in our research, Thurstone's scales are the only ones used with any frequency that permit locating an individual's most preferred position toward a social object within a range from one extreme through increasingly moderate positions to the other extreme. (For example, reference to "moderateness" on a Likert or semantic differential scale refers to moderate agreement or disagreement with extreme beliefs or attributes, not to a "moderate" position or to moderate beliefs about the objects.)

Once he had obtained consensual judgments on the range of beliefs, Thurstone then presented a selected list graded from one extreme to the other, asking subjects to indicate which of the ordered statements they agreed with. For him, this agreement exercised the less rational, affective predisposition that he called "attitude."

One major disadvantage of Thurstone's technique was that it yielded no indication of the degree or intensity of the affect it allegedly measured. Further, its assumption that judges could put aside their affect during the process of constructing the attitude test is unwarranted, both theoretically and empirically. A long line of research started by Sherif and Hovland over a quarter of a century ago shows clearly that partisans on opposite sides of a social issue who are strongly committed to their opposing positions reach very different consensus on the location of beliefs between the extreme positions on that issue, even though their ordering of those beliefs are highly correlated. Their judgments on beliefs also differ from consensus reached by individuals with moderate positions on the same issue, even when all are instructed to put aside their own attitudes and make objective judgments (M. Sherif & Hovland, 1961; C. W. Sherif, M. Sherif, & Nebergall, 1965; Selltiz, Edrich, & Cook, 1965; Zavalloni & Cook, 1965; Eiser & Stroebe, 1972; C. W. Sherif, 1976). The differences have been found on a variety of issues. They are found with paired comparison and ratio scaling methods as well as with the categorization method first used by Thurstone (M. Sherif & C. W. Sherif, 1969; Fraser & Stacey, 1973; Dawes, Singer, & Lemons, 1972).

In the present context, the issue is not whether Thurstone techniques for scaling beliefs can be used profitably (which they can), but whether a theory of human psychology is viable that bifurcates the mind into a rational compartment for cognition and an irrational compartment for affect or attitude. The issue is empirical and practical as well. In social psychology, such assumptions amount to regarding the judgments and the *in*actions of individuals with slight personal involvement on a social issue as more "rational" than the judgments and actions of those who are highly involved in it. Such a view, it would seem, would also assign rationality to the status quo.

In plain truth, criticism of the Thurstone scaling technique is a tempest in the academic teapot, for it has seldom been used outside academia and is less frequently employed within it, mainly because it takes time. The Likert format, developed in part as a time saver, followed the model of psychometric testing, wherein items are chosen on the basis of their discrimination between polarized groups and hence are typically extreme. The person's attitude is represented by summing ratings that indicate degrees of agreement-disagreement with the polarized beliefs. The Semantic Differential rose from Osgood's theoretical rationale for studying the connotations of abstract concepts. Degrees of agreement with the preferred bipolar adjectives as applied to the concept are summed across adjectives to indicate attitude, the adjectives being evaluative ones.

The interpretation of extreme scores on either technique is relatively straightforward, though equating extreme scores with "attitude intensity" has been challenged (Ehrlich, 1973). Intermediate scores are difficult to interpret. Like the "middles" on similarly constructed tests of personality variables, they are often excluded from research designs in attitude study for this reason. A moderate score on either test need not indicate acceptance of a moderate position toward the attitude object, between extreme positions. Such moderate positions are not represented in the items of either test. One can attain a "moderate" test score by extreme ratings on both sides, moderate ratings on one or both sides, or by consistent use of an "uncertain" option.

The interpretation of Semantic Differential ratings is also in some disrepute, with Triandis and Fishbein equating ratings on the evaluative factor scale with "affect" and Ehrlich terming them the "cognitive" component of attitude. Certainly, there is room for argument. Rating scales like the Semantic Differential are often used in studies of stereotyped attribution to groups and the genders (e.g., Broverman et al., 1972). I would propose, of course, that both cognition and affect are involved in such ratings.

Each of the major techniques for attitude assessment developed in academia has been profitably used in studying attitudes through carefully planned research. What amazes the surveyor of attitude literature is the great gap between such well-planned studies, technical writing on measurement, and actual practice in the bulk of social-psychological research purporting to have something to do with attitudes. Shaw and Wright (1967) surveyed available attitude tests and their use some years back, standing aghast at what they found. Fishbein and Ajzen's documentation of more recent practices (1975), notably the use of single questions, one or two ratings, suggests that improvement is slow.

How did such casualness about assessing attitudes come into social psychology? The answer would be incomplete without including the great popularity and commercial success of public opinion polls in this country. Without the existence of attitude tests in academia, I doubt that allegedly "scientific" surveys on public attitudes and opinions could have staked their claims so firmly. But once they had, and as long as they spent enough time and money supplementing survey results with forecasts from past elections to come close in predicting national presidential elections, the impact on new generations in academia could hardly be avoided. Any "scientific basis" for their sometimes casual questions on issues other than national elections has long been questioned, yet nothing succeeds like commercial success. A leading pollster stated on public television during the last presidential election that the only scientific basis for survey research lay in sampling theory. This admission came at a time when the polls were having difficulty in that quarter as well. Avoidance and turn-downs by potential interviewees became so frequent that the American Statistical Association called a conference to discuss the problem (*ASA Footnotes*, 1974), and major survey research institutes started to check out the use of telephones for interviews.

Despite these misfortunes, many social psychologists seem to have grown into a world where a person's attitude was equated with verbal responses on one or two questions or rating scales, a common practice in public opinion polls. Conceptual confusion became rampant. We started hearing strange arguments about whether "attitude" related to "behavior," about whether "attitude" caused "behavior," or "behavior" caused "attitude." LaPiere's 1934 article was used in support of a divorce between "attitudes" and "behavior."

LaPiere had compared the actual reception of a Chinese couple accompanied by an occidental couple in hotels and restaurants with the negative replies by businessmen to a letter subsequently inquiring whether they would "accept members of the Chinese race" in their establishment. The two sets of responses did not correspond. The reported findings are seriously flawed as a basis to test any proposition, but they have served as an inkblot for theoretical speculations, including those divorcing the study of attitude from the study of action. LaPiere's own main point was forgotten.

A moment's reading of the article shows that LaPiere was in fact warning against the dangers in using "a verbal response to a symbolic situation" as a "reflection of a 'social attitude'"—a practice he characterized as "to entirely disregard the definition commonly given for . . . 'attitude'" (p. 237). In fact, he concluded with the reasonable advice that a person's attitude "must, in the main, be derived from a study of human behavior in actual social situations" (p. 237).

It is ironic that such advice has had to be repeated in social psychology of the last decade. The need shows how exclusively social psychologists had come to equate the study of attitudes with verbal tests and, even more dangerously, with one or two responses to improvised questions or rating scales. To understand that trend, we must mention some other developments within social psychology.

III. Social Psychology's Upward Strivings in Academia

Especially after World War II, the once small and socially marginal groups of psychologists and sociologists who called themselves social psychologists began to find themselves more respectable. Joined by others trained originally in laboratory or clinic, social psychologists found government agencies, foundations, and businesses more interested in supporting their research. There was considerable interest in attitude research, for a variety of reasons. These surely include the prestige of measurement in our society. Also there was then a conviction that major problems like war, racial hatreds, and national strife begin in the "minds of men." Shortly, "winning hearts and minds" was seen in large measure as a matter of changing people's attitudes to conform to one's own. Attitude change research appeared "relevant" to all of these assumptions.

Faced with the growing interest and eager for financial support, social psychology had its first hope for gaining respectability and even prestige in its parent disciplines. How does a poor country cousin become acceptable to more prestigeful relatives? Money is not enough. One must also learn to act properly, even to imitate their ways. Psychology at the time was becoming more self-consciously "scientific" than it had been, claiming that its scientific aura shed light on the training of thousands of new clinical psychologists needed to handle distress brought by the war and its aftermath in a rapidly changing society.

Social psychology sought to share and to contribute to that aura. It began to adopt the philosophy and history of science then fashionable among its loftiest experimental psychologists, which was, in turn, what the logical positivists said the gloriously successful physical sciences had been doing. Laboratory experimentation was the method of respect. Operational definitions, value-free aloofness, and mathematical models were means to gain prestige.

During the postwar period, social psychology broke its traditional interest in human development, which had occupied half of the thousand pages in Murphy, Murphy, and Newcomb's prewar *Experimental Social Psychology* (1937). Interest in cultural anthropology was left to "those culture-personality people." Kurt Lewin's ahistorical position was interpreted as license to ignore the historical and institutional significance of the laboratory and the personal history of subjects, excepting that operationally defined by the researcher's measurements. His interest in group dynamics was redefined until a typical experiment on social interaction involved subjects in isolation booths with earphones and buttons to communicate.

In this context, attitudes were not only "that which is measurable by my attitude scale," as Triandis remarked (1967, p. 228), but even "anything I define them to be." Literally, attitude and attitude change were "measured" by a check or two on a rating scale, indicating judgments on similarity of geometric forms, on such statements as "The Bonda fossil was a bird," on the attractiveness of a dull laboratory task or the experimenter, on the frequency of tooth brushing or number of hours of sleep needed.

Social values were not to be involved in such allegedly objective research, but of course they were all over the place. To gain the highest prestige, a social psychologist became sophisticated in matters of research design, statistical analysis, or mathematical modeling, and refrained from talking about social values, especially about controversial social issues. It was considered scientifically proper, not at all demeaning, and good English to report a study of college women in a journal, referring to the subjects with the masculine pronoun. It was all right to study attitude change, since the research was well supported. This pursuit quickly became confined to elaborately designed experiments in which a college sophomore read, heard, or wrote something on a topic of slight interest. An inexhaustible supply of high prestige-low prestige, credible-incredible sources, attractive-unattractive, similar-dissimilar sources of influence was manufactured.

Absurd controversies ensued over whether "attitude" and "behavior" are related. Some revealed a primitive mentality that confused concepts with data and inference with observation. There was lack of awareness of the cultural and social values that pervade even the simplest social situation, including laboratory or classroom. Finally, the controversies disregarded the question of why a concept like attitude had ever crept into social psychology in the first place. It had crept in to deal on the individual level of analysis with issues raised by the broad problems of social control and social change. These are real problems that cannot be defined out of existence.

CHARACTERIZATION OF THE SOCIAL VALUE-ATTITUDE RELATIONSHIP

Fishbein and Ajzen (1975) performed a useful service by pointing to the ambiguities in differing definitions of the attitude concept. They warned that any definition which fails to make explicit its assumptions about the human organism and about the social situations in which the person is studied is bound to contain multiple ambiguities (p. 6). Their warning is a challenge to start by clarifying the conception of the social situations in which attitudes are studied.

Any research situation where data are collected (including the laboratory, interview, or observation post) is a social situation. Any social situation has structural properties that can be and should be studied prior to and independently of the particular individuals from whom psychological data are to be collected (M. Sherif & C. W. Sherif, 1956, 1969; C. W. Sherif, 1976). Thanks to several converging trends in social psychology in recent years, we know a good deal more about social situations than we did twenty-five years ago: We have the writings of "environmental psychologists," ecological psychologists, the diverse research and writing on the "social psychology of the research situation," and the slow but cumulative attempts to delineate structural properties of social situations.

Any social situation is more complex than classical training in psychology would lead one to believe. It consists of interrelated sets of factors pertaining to the location and its facilities, to the tasks and activities there conducted or initiated, and to the people present other than the individual to be studied, including their number; homogeneity-heterogeneity with respect to various social classifications (e.g., gender, age, social class, race, etc.); their pre-existing relationships with one another and with the individuals being studied.

Each aspect of a social situation is loaded with cultural and social values, whether the investigator recognizes them or not. Such value loadings in all major aspects of social situations affect the individual's behavior. Needless to say, it is often the researcher who becomes focal in a research situation, a researcher whose superior status and valued scientific aura can produce the results of Milgram's studies on obedience (1974) when located in appropriately "scientific" settings with impressive equipment and highly structured activities.

It follows that the optimal social situations in which to study whether or not an individual has an attitude will lack structure in some degree with respect to the social value of interest. They will minimize those conditions characterized as "demand character," in this case any situational structure that demands a particular kind of response and precludes not responding. Failure to observe this simple principle has produced study after study in which we literally cannot know whether or not the individual has an attitude. Our research participants ordinarily cooperate, give a rating, pass an opinion on what we ask them in an interview, and leave nothing blank on an attitude test, as instructed. If they refuse, their forms or interview are discarded.

Converse (1970) began to write of "non-attitudes" in dealing with some of the resulting data. Peterson and Dutton (1975) have made the earth-shaking proposition that an individual's behavior in situations involving a possible attitude object will not be influenced by attitude if he or she has no attitude toward it. The need to state such a proposition reveals a great deal about researchers, but also about the highly structured situations where they have studied attitudes. If the individual responds at all, the response is taken as evidence of attitude.

Attributing an attitude to an individual does imply assumptions about the human individual and about human development. It requires evidence beyond one or a few responses in a single social situation. I will spell out our assumptions.

An attitude is a cognitive-affective-motivational structure or schema, formed through interactions with the environment. The schema relates the person psychologically *in some degree* to a domain of objects and specific representatives therein through categorizations of that domain, beliefs about them, and attributions to them that are selectively biased for or against, positively or negatively, toward or away from objects in the different categories. An attitude is inferred from behaviors (verbal or nonverbal), without which we can never know whether a person has an attitude. The behaviors are coherently or consistently patterned in the respects noted, each indicating the person's directional orientations toward or against (favorable or unfavorable) specified members within the domain.

Like most definitions, this one states that attitudes are learned and that they are not temporally fleeting or situationally specific "sets" or expectations. Like many, it states that the behaviors from which attitude is inferred cohere across situations or over time in affective directionality. Unlike some, however, it insists that attitude is a psychological structure or schema, not to be identified with a single behavior or single measurement of response. Further, it states that the structure or schema is inseparably cognitive-affective-motivational.

The sources and degrees of affectivity-motivation of a social attitude derive from the social values in the environment and from the person's experiences while interacting with that environment during development. The formation of the psychological relationship (subject-object) includes the individual's categorizations of the objects, beliefs about them, and attributions to them. When the objects are invested with social value by reference persons and groups and when the person has a psychological relationship with the objects, the process of social judgment will always be both cognitive and affective in some degree. As we shall see, determining the *degree* of that psychological relatedness may be as important as the issue of whether or not the person has an attitude. Further, the degree or extent of the psychological relatedness is incompletely understood through inquiring only about the "intensity" of affect, only about the person's beliefs, or only about the attributional process.

Finally, an attitude includes both being for, or favorably inclined toward something within the specified domain, and being against, or unfavorably inclined toward others within the same domain. The a priori decision to study only what the person favors or only what the person is against appears to us an arbitrary, if sometimes necessary decision by the researcher. A person who is anti-Polish is *for* someone else. A person who is pro-life is against abortion, and one who is pro-abortion is against restrictive legislation.

The issue of whether attitudes are "general" or "specific" becomes an empirical issue, depending upon the cultural classification and the individual's own classification of the particular domain of objects. The issue concerns the extent and the degree of the individual's psychological relationship with the domain. For example, attitudes toward specific situations may be highly abstract to the person who has never participated in any of them or cannnot relate self to them. Nor is there anything inherently specific about behaviors, as objects of attitudes. For example, opening a door for a woman can be conceived by an equalitarian man as a specific act of courtesy, but by a woman as symbolic of protective subordination of women to men for centuries. Conversely, attitudes toward beliefs and practices concerning a deity can be both general and highly specific to an individual deeply immersed in a religious reference group. These are empiricial issues central to attitude study, for they pertain to the individual's psychological relationship to the object domain. They should not be decided a priori by cultural convention that categorizes all beliefs as abstract, hence psychologically remote, and all events or actions as proximal, hence psychologically concrete or specific.

Certain implications for fruitful paths in attitude study follow this characterization, including the importance of studying the process of social judgment. The individual's own categories relating him or her to the domain of social objects are a focus for study, not to be assumed on either a logical or cultural basis. It also follows that exploration should not stop, as some traditional assessment techniques do, with discovery of what the individual accepts, agrees with, or believes about some of the objects. Like Rokeach (1968), we have found it equally significant to discover what the person does not accept, does not believe, or objects to.

SOCIAL JUDGMENT-INVOLVEMENT THEORY

The study of human judgment may be basic in understanding social attitudes from several viewpoints: A judgment process is implicated in dealings with the environment, whether physical or social, when an individual discriminates among objects or persons, compares, labels, or categorizes them. As one of the more developed research areas in psychology, it is a rich source for analyzing determinants of coherently or consistently patterned behaviors, i.e., judgment outcomes. Finally, opinions (evaluative judgments) compose much of the existing data base for inferences about attitudes.

Classic laboratory research on judgment (psychophysics) concentrated on relationships between the physical properties of objects and regularities in their judgment. Judgments in different contexts were analyzed to assess environmental (stimulus) regulation of cognition as well as important properties of cognitive processing itself. The latter were inferred, in particular, by comparing systematic (rather than random) variations in judgments relative to different arrangements or situational contexts for the objects-to-be-judged.

Such research led to the generalization that human judgment is a behavioral outcome of psychological processes wherein the object-to-be-judged is discriminated, compared, and categorized within a frame of reference (system of relationships) composed of others immediately present and previously experienced by the individual (M. Sherif, 1936). The properties of objects that can be unequivocally defined and measured, independent of the experiencing individual, are judged differently in different frames of reference, for example according to the range, order, or relative frequencies of objects previously presented (Volkmann, 1951) or the background and illumination in which the object appears (Helson, 1964).

A second generalization is that the object relationships (e.g., physical properties and differences) in the frame of reference are seldom pooled in psychological processing randomly or equally (as in arithmetic averaging). In other words, the physical values assigned to components need not "register" with absolute or equal weights in the judgment outcome, the occasions when they may being special cases. Thus, there is an empirical problem of discovering their relative weightings in the judgment outcome.

An object relationship in the frame of reference that limits or regulates the effects of others is said to "anchor" the frame of reference (hence function as an "anchor" in judgment). For example, stimuli at both ends of a continuum or early and late in a temporal sequence, a frequently presented exemplar of a judgment category, an explicitly labeled standard, or a clearcut geometric pattern can anchor judgments of other stimuli present. Those same objects are judged differently when so presented than they are in a frame of reference lacking such anchors (Helson, 1964; M. Sherif & Hovland, 1961; Volkmann, 1951).

Anchoring effects are indicated by systematic variations in judgments rendered in differing frames of reference. Assimilation-contrast effects in judgment are among such variations which are of particular interest in social judgments, as we shall see. These re-

ciprocal and complementary variations in judgment within different frames of reference, or by different individuals in the same
situational context, are defined as (a) minimization of difference
relative to an anchor (*assimilation*) and (b) exaggeration of difference relative to an anchor (*contrast*).

Past experiences with an object domain, including the set of
categories formed to deal with it, can anchor the frame of reference
in an ongoing judgment situation, an established finding both in
psychophysical and social judgment. Volkmann's emphasis (1951)
on the range of prior experiences in defining a psychological reference scale or "perspective" for the individual's judgments is an
example. Similarly, Helson's application of his adaptation-level
formula (1964) assigned varying weights to past experiences, at
times through the "background" term and at others in the "residual"
term. (Regrettably, he occasionally identified "adaptation level"
with attitude, a disservice to the former concept and a misplacement
of the latter in his formula.)

Social judgment-involvement theory developed from the fore-
going generalizations on psychophysical judgment, as an analogy
that recognized important differences between psycho*physical* and
psycho*social* judgment (M. Sherif & Cantril, 1947; M. Sherif &
C. W. Sherif, 1956, 1967, 1969; M. Sherif & Hovland, 1961; C. W.
Sherif, M. Sherif, & Nebergall, 1965; C. W. Sherif, 1963, 1976; C. W.
Sherif, Kelly, Rogers, Sarup, & Tittler, 1973). What, in brief, are the
differences?

First, the physical properties of social objects are seldom sufficient, in themselves, for establishing a basis for analyzing judgments
of social objects. Even when their physical properties can be
measured (e.g., weight, size, numerosity), the individual attends
selectively to their social value, classification, or ordering, which
need not vary directly with those physical properties (Tajfel, 1969).
In order to have a basis for analyzing environmental (stimulus)
control in social judgment, the researcher has to study the cultural
and structural values of the objects to be judged, independently,
and prior to the study of individual judgment.

Second, objects of social judgment are seldom "neutral" for the
individual. Unlike lines, weights, or geometric forms, social objects
are frequently linked (affectively-motivationally-cognitively) to significant past experiences and to future anticipations.

Third, if an attitude (as defined earlier) has been formed on the
basis of past experiences, the individual has a set of categories for

classifying the object domain that are simultaneously evaluative, incorporate beliefs about the objects, and attribute positive or negative qualities to them. In fact, depending on what is judged, the individual may classify the self as belonging in one of those categories, but not in others.

Finally, the complexity and the multivariate, symbolic character of much of the social environment permits alternative interpretations and modes of behavior more frequently than the typical psychophysical experiment. As in any judgment situation, the relative contributions of environmental (situational, stimulus) and psychological determinants (e.g., past experiences, including attitudes) vary with the degree of objective structure in the judgment situation (as assessed independent of the judgments being studied). Social objects and situations vary in the degree to which alternative interpretations and modes of responding are defined, but the role of past experiences in their judgment is invariably an issue. The effects of past experiences are manifested at the maximum when situational structure is minimal.

Thus, the possible effects of attitude in social judgment will be most marked when (a) the object to be judged is ambiguous in some respect and (b) anchors for judgment in the situation (e.g., standards or instructions limiting response) are lacking. But when does an attitude (as defined here) become an anchor for judgment? According to the theory, anchoring effects of attitude in social judgment are (c) proportional to the degree in which the self system becomes involved in psychological processing of the situation.

What is meant by involvement of the self? The self is defined as a system of interrelated sets of attitudes, not typically integrated but varying in priority or importance to the person, formed during life experiences in relation to the individual's own body, its parts, its conscious experiences, and distinguishing them from others'; in relation to other persons in various capacities or role-status (power) relationships, and within social classification schemes (e.g., gender, race); in relation to family and other groups, institutions, status systems, beliefs, and ideologies; to other social objects—in short, to experienced aspects of the environment (M. Sherif & Cantril, 1947).

What becomes "involved" are attitudes varying in priority in the self system. "Involvement" refers to their implication in psychological processing of ongoing activities in specific situations. For example, "self-regulated" activity is involving, in some degree.

Discovering the priorities of particular attitudes in the self system is an empirical problem that, of course, concerns the history of individual lives. As Triandis has re-emphasized, lives are bounded by their sociocultural contexts. During development, attitudes are formed toward the particular individual's reference persons and groups, with their status criteria, norms, and ideologies reflecting on individual worth. Thus the problem of priorities cannot be solved in a social vacuum. Such priorities vary during individual development and life history.

They also vary according to situational contexts that may implicate the person's self regard, respect, or worth at the time in ways not dictated by a particular attitude. In other words, degree of involvement associated with a particular attitude is not necessarily a fixed quantity, but in part depends upon the frame of reference in a situation. People have been known to stake everything on an argument or activity whose priority is not high except when challenged in that situation.

Attitudes high in priority will be highly involving anchors for social judgments in relevant situations, however, affecting the process in predictable ways. High involvement may override the effects of situationally provided anchors (e.g., comparison standards, instructions at variance with the individual's own categories, the opinions of others). Less important or less self-defining attitudes may become anchors as circumstances, information, or the actions of others implicate other aspects of self, challenging an individual's worth, sense of decency, or future opportunity, for example. At the other extreme, an attitude tangential in the self system or unrelated to it will be highly susceptible to the impact of the situation, especially to explicit standards and the opinions of significant others.

The anchoring effects of attitude become significant in social judgments when the objects-to-be-judged differ from those already categorized by the individual as acceptable, agreeable, self defining, even ideal. Proportional to the degree of involvement, the theory predicts systematic variations in judgments even when the person is not asked to reveal what is acceptable or agreeable.

The most general prediction is that discrepancies near acceptable categories will be assimilated to them, while increasingly discrepant objects-to-be-judged will be increasingly contrasted to them. However, there is no basis for assuming that attitude structures consist simply of binary categories (what is acceptable and what is not) or, indeed, that all attitides have structure throughout the entire object domain. Such assumptions are as unwarranted as attitude measurement which automatically equates attitude with a point on a continuum, or an arithmetic average, or a single acceptable category.

Instead, it becomes necessary to inquire into the categorical-affective structure of individual attitudes and into their relationship to priorities in the self system. The theory proposes that object discrepancies associated with assimilation-contrast effects in judgment are experienced as discrepancies relative to those attitude structures. If so, the interplay between attitudes, situational anchors, and contexts in producing systematic differences in social judgment can be traced only when attitude structure is specified. Such differences bear on important social-psychological problems, including the conditions for social consensus, polarization, and conflict. I turn now to the problem of specifying the structures of attitudes relative to an object domain, which are most parsimoniously conceived as varying latitudes in that domain for acceptance, rejection, and noncommitment.

ATTITUDE STRUCTURE

We started over a quarter of a century ago toward new approaches to attitude study, not with the intent of replacing methods already available, but of expanding the scope of investigation in directions indicated. Very early, we were struck with the restrictiveness of most traditional techniques of attitude assessment which, for the researcher's convenience, insist upon a response by the individual to every item presented for evaluation. The first attempt to eliminate this restrictiveness was made by Muzafer Sherif and Ed Volkart in 1948 with a simple list of ordered beliefs about the "closed shop" issue.

The "method of ordered alternatives" starts by standardizing a set of belief statements covering the range of positions actually being expressed on a controversial issue. Judges rank order the belief statements from one extreme position to the other, with increasingly moderate statements from each extreme, and an undecided statement in the middle. The standardization requires consensual judgments on the order of the eleven statements. Since I shall refer to her research later, let me illustrate with the ordered alternatives used by Helen Kearney (1975) in research on the issue of legalized abortion.

A. A Constitutional Amendment guaranteeing the right to life of the unborn is absolutely necessary; legal abortion should never be available.
B. To protect the rights of the unborn baby legal abortion should not be available.
C. To protect the right to life of unborn children, legal abortion should be available only if childbirth would cause the woman's death.
D. To protect the rights of unborn children, legal abortion should require the consent of the husband (or parents, if the woman is a minor) and be performed only in case of rape or incest, thus severely limiting the number of abortions performed.
E. To protect the rights of unborn children, legal abortion should require the consent of the husband (or parents, if the woman is a minor) and be performed only if childbirth could impair the woman's health, thus somewhat limiting the number of abortions performed.
F. It is difficult to decide whether the rights of the unborn or of the woman are more important in formulating laws regarding abortion.
G. A legal abortion should be available during the first 3 months of pregnancy, but not after.
H. A legal abortion should be available during the first 6 months of pregnancy, but not after.
I. A legal abortion should be available during the first 6 months of pregnancy, but after that time only if the woman's life or health would be endangered by a birth.
J. The law should allow the woman to control her own body by permitting a legal abortion upon her request.
K. Abortion on demand and paid by the state should be guaranteed by law to any woman when she asks for it; without this protection, she is a slave to the state through compulsory pregnancy.

The individual receives these statements in a booklet, the statements being repeated on each of four pages. On the first page, the instruction is to select the *one* statement that comes closest "to your own position." On the second, the option is provided to indicate another statement or statements that are also acceptable to the person. On the third, the instruction is to cross out the one statement which is "most objectionable from your point of view." On the final page, another option is provided, that of indicating another statement or other statements "objectionable from your point of view." To follow instructions, the individual has only to accept one statement on the first page, and reject one statement on the third page. Thus, there is leeway in how many others are accepted or rejected, and in how many statements are not marked in any way. (The four-page format is used to allow this leeway, since the individual is not confronted by a single form containing all responses.)

The technique is convenient for introducing three concepts for studying the structure of individual attitudes:

1. The latitude of acceptance, which consists of the person's most acceptable position plus others accepted.
2. The latitude of rejection, which consists of the person's most objectionable position plus others rejected.
3. The latitude of noncommitment, which consists of those positions that the person neither accepts nor rejects.

As it has turned out, the relative widths of these three latitudes, i.e., the relative frequencies of statements included in them, are related to the degree of personal involvement in the attitude-object domain. The relationships hold when the latitudes are determined by an entirely different technique, the Own Categories method, in which the person classifies a larger number of attitude objects before being questioned about their acceptability. These two methods have been used in studying a wide variety of social issues and social objects, the latter including toys, clothing, hair styles, money, the names of ethnic groups, social behaviors, and supermarkets.

Certain conditions common to all of our research using these concepts and methods need to be specified. In every case, the research starts with study of the entire range of objects, beliefs, or actions, to determine the most extreme representatives culturally available and to insure that the domain is structured sociologically, i.e., includes different social values consensually upheld by actual groups or social categories of people in society. We have dealt chiefly with bipolar domains, as typified by intergroup controversies or the adoption of contrasting values by different groups or social categories, such as the two genders. Some of the object domains, however, represent in-group norms, where members of the group contrast the ideal and acceptable behaviors with intolerable or deviating behaviors.

As noted, consensus about the order of objects or subclasses of objects between the extremes is checked by judges instructed to attend only to their rank order. The Own Categories technique deliberately includes many individual items judged with high variability in pretests, for reasons to be specified later. We make no assumptions about the "psychological distance" between adjacent objects. Nor do we assume anything about the order being "cumulative," in Guttman's sense. To the contrary, we have found that evaluative judgments by personally involved individuals are typically noncumulative. For example, an individual adopting an extreme position on a controversial issue typically does not evaluate all more moderate positions on the same side as acceptable. Nor does accepting a position on one side of an issue necessarily imply rejecting all positions on the other side.

With these basic stipulations about method and definitions, I will summarize major research findings that demonstrate the differential structure of attitudes involving the self in varying degrees, and effects of such structure in social judgment and action.

Attitude Structures with Varying Involvement of Self

The findings on attitude structure, obtained by two different methods and on a variety of attitudes, may be summarized as follows: *The greater the involvement of self with a position on one or the other side of a bipolar issue, the wider the latitude of rejection relative to the combined width of acceptable and noncommittal latitudes.* For a highly involved person, the latitude of rejection engulfs more than half of the object domain, and noncommitment all but disappears. Conversely, the individual lightly implicated in the object domain exhibits a huge latitude of noncommitment, regardless of the positions accepted or rejected. (Evidence is summarized in M. Sherif & Hovland, 1961; C. W. Sherif, M. Sherif, & Nebergall, 1965; M. Sherif & C. W. Sherif, 1967, 1969; C. W. Sherif, 1963, 1976; C. W. Sherif et al., 1973).

How do we know that these demonstrated variations in attitude structure are indeed associated with differential involvement of self, and not solely with situational or other psychological variables? First, the "construct validity" of the latitudes and their relationships has been demonstrated through significant correlations for the frequencies of acceptance, rejection, and noncommitment utilizing the

Method of Ordered Alternatives and the free-sort method (the Own Categories technique) (Rogers, 1978). It is noteworthy that the highest correlations were for the relative frequencies in the latitudes of rejection and noncommitment, particularly for persons whose public actions on the issue of legalized abortion, pro or con, indicated high involvement in the issue. The frequencies of acceptances or agreements obtained by the two methods were significantly correlated, but the coefficient was quite low ($r = .15$). For unselected individuals, not publicly active on the issue, only the size of the latitude of noncommitment was significantly correlated across methods. In short, lightly involved people are *less* consistent across methods and situations than more involved people, as would be expected (cf. Markus, 1977).

Second, most of the research that I shall describe started with sociological study of groups of individuals who take one side or the other of a value-laden issue. We have independently ascertained that the attitude objects were significant in group life. Individuals selected for study were active in group activities. Thus, the research has always included samples whose involvement was validated by behavioral criteria. Typically, the latitudes of such individuals were compared to those of unselected samples, usually student volunteers.

In the earliest research, criterion samples for high involvement were selected from groups known to take extreme stands on a social issue, a "natural" correlation since individuals advocating moderation less frequently organize or make themselves visible (M. Sherif & Hovland, 1961, and C. W. Sherif, M. Sherif, and Nebergall, 1965, summarize the early research). The latitudes of acceptance, rejection, and noncommitment were then compared for individuals choosing each position on the issue as most acceptable.

The average frequencies of items included in the three latitudes by persons choosing each of nine positions as most acceptable were plotted, with the nine positions used as the baseline. The curve on average frequency of rejections resembed the U-shaped relationship between extremity of attitude position and intensity, as measured by how strongly individuals reported upholding their attitudes (Cantril, 1946). The latitude of noncommitment was more nearly a bell-shaped curve, its modal frequencies being for individuals accepting attitude positions that were moderate and uncertain in the middle. The frequency of items accepted was equivalent across all attitude positions, with a suggestive dip toward lower frequency for individuals finding the uncertain middle of the range most acceptable. That dip turned out to reflect a sizable minority of "uncertain" subjects who were not at all uncertain about what they rejected. They rejected almost everything on both sides of the issue (C. W. Sherif, M. Sherif, & Nebergall, 1965), hence they could accept only one or two positions in the middle. This finding, plus the homogeneity of variances at other own positions, led to the attempt to distinguish personal involvement from extremity of attitude position. It must be added, however, that the two are frequently correlated through group processes arising to emphasize polar positions.

Differential Involvement with Comparable Attitude Positions

An obvious objection to comparing latitudes for persons finding different attitude positions acceptable is that they may differ in a host of other ways as well. One way to clarify attitude structures associated with differential involvement is to study individuals who uphold the same positions, belong to the same groups, but vary in their known relationship to those groups. Sarup (in C. W. Sherif et al., 1973) selected two samples of Indian students in the United States, both with favorable attitudes toward India and both rating it as the most desirable place to live and to pursue their chosen professions. They differed with respect to their frequency and regularity in reading Indian papers and journals, attending meetings and cultural events on Indian life, etc. as determined by observations over time.

Asking the students to serve as judges of belief statements about India to be used on a projected study of the "brain drain" from India, Sarup presented fifty belief statements about India's present and future. Each individual classified the statements in terms of their favorableness-unfavorableness to India, constructing as few or as many categories as needed for the task. This is the standard Own Categories instruction, which resembles the Thurstone judgment task with the exception that no set number of categories or distribution of judgments is prescribed in instructions. The statements had been prestandardized by an independent sample of judges using standard Thurstone instructions but specifying the use of five categories. As is typical, the variances of judgments for extremely favorable and unfavorable statements by the standardization sample were smaller than the variances for statements intermediate to the extremes (Edwards, 1946). The fifty statements categorized by the students included a large proportion of those with large variances in the standardization study, since such statements are likely to be categorized differently by different individuals. Would the differential categorizations vary systematically according to degree of involvement with India?

After the Indian students had generated their own categorizations for the statements, Sarup asked each to indicate any piles of statements that were acceptable or objectionable to them personally. The number of beliefs in acceptable and objectionable categories defined the latitudes of acceptance and rejection, while the noncommittal latitude was simply the frequency of statements in categories neither accepted nor rejected. On the average, committed nationalists rejected 30 of the 50 statements, whereas the less active students rejected only about 15. The less active were noncommittal on 13 statements, whereas the committed nationalists, on the average, were noncommittal on only about 4. The committed nationalists accepted only 16 of the 50 statements, whereas the less involved accepted about 22. All of these comparisons were highly significant statistically. They were in accord with the proposition that the structure of attitudes for individuals upholding the same positions and belonging to the same sociological category differ as predicted, according to the criterion of their active involvement with their reference group.

Sarup also confirmed what previous research had shown about the categorizations of highly and less involved individuals, namely that the highly involved use significantly *fewer* categories than the less involved in slicing the same domain. I shall return to this generalization later, namely, that fewer categories and higher involvement go together.

Extending the logic of Sarup's study, Shaffer (1974) compared the latitudes of members of a campus evangelical group according to their status in three hierarchical levels of the group and according to the relative importance of two of the group's major values, viz., the importance of evangelism and the concept of "one way" to salvation. The most acceptable positions on both values at all status levels were within the three most extreme favorable positions on the Method of Ordered Alternatives. Their latitudes of acceptance did not differ significantly on the evangelism norm and only trivially on the "one-way" norm. For both norms, however, members of higher status in the group exhibited significantly larger latitudes of rejection and less noncommitment than members of lower status. In short, individuals endorsing extreme positions on two different value domains exhibited differential attitude structure indicating more and less involvement in those domains. Those with higher status manifested greater involvement in the values than those of lower status in the group.

Both of the studies cited, as well as research by Kelly and by Kearney to be summarized later, show that attitude structure does differentiate individuals endorsing comparable value positions but differing in manifest commitment to those positions.

Is Structure Dependent on Attitude Favorableness-Unfavorableness?

Another reasonable question is whether the attitude structures we have studied are specific to pro or to anti position-taking. Both ends of the bipolarity have been singled out for special treatments, with some authors suggesting that "anti" attitudes have special properties (e.g., G. W. Allport, 1954; Moscovici, 1963) and others that only people with favorable positions toward an object exhibit pronounced bias in judgment (e.g., Eiser & Stroebe, 1972). I do not doubt that either may be the case under given historical circumstances.

However, the issue at hand is whether our findings on attitude structure are confined to attitudes upholding a pro or favorable view or to an anti or unfavorable view. The answer is that they are not. In studies on partisans of different candidates in presidential elections (M. Sherif & Hovland, 1961; C. W. Sherif, M. Sherif, & Nebergall, 1965), and of partisans on both sides of the abortion issue (Kearney, 1975; Rogers, 1978), we have obtained data on the relative sizes of the latitudes for partisans on both sides of the issue that form mirror images. The latitudes of acceptance, rejection, and noncommitment of partisans on one side mirror those of partisans on the other side. The widths of the respective latitudes do not differ.

Certainly, such complementarity need not be so. The most serious evidence to the contrary lies in data reported by Hovland and Sherif (1952) and replicated by several other investigators on the judgments of pro- and anti-Negro judges in Thurstone scaling studies during the 1950s in the United States. Predicted bias (assimilation-contrast) effects in the judgments of those with extreme, highly involved positions were much more pronounced by pro- than by anti-black subjects. Unfortunately, those data were obtained before the exploration of attitude structure began, and attitudes were assessed by Likert and other conventional methods. Therefore, any generalization about the structures of pro and anti attitudes in that early research is speculative. For this and other reasons, the use of those replicated findings on variations in judgment according to the person's attitude position for a broad generalization that favorable attitudes are fundamentally different from anti or unfavorable attitudes appears unwarranted.

In the first place, Vaughn (reported in C. W. Sherif, M. Sherif, & Nebergall, 1965) showed that anti-Mexican attitudes in south Texas produced judgment distributions of belief statements about Mexican-Americans that were a mirror image of those obtained by Hovland and Sherif for pro-black judges. In other words, using Thurstone instructions, the anti-Mexican judges assimilated anti-Mexican statements and contrasted pro-Mexican statements, whereas the pro-black judges had assimilated pro-black statements and contrasted anti-black statements. Anti-Mexican judges who were given the same statements with the Own Categories procedure used significantly fewer categories (85 per cent using three or fewer) than students in north Texas, where there were few Mexican-Americans and little involvement in the issue. Over 90 per cent of the north Texas students used four or more categories. For some reason, these published data have been ignored.

Second, Eiser (1971) made an excellent point in his study of "restrictive" vs. pro-drug attitudes in England when he remarked that the normative climate would surely affect the degree of manifest involvement by individuals in their own positions. To be anti-Negro on a college campus in the 1950s was contrary to those norms on campus strongly advocated by liberal students and faculty. Similarly, to favor restriction of drugs (anti-drugs) was contrary to student norms in England in the late 1960s. In both cases, individuals endorsing positions contrary to the dominant normative climate did not make judgments reflecting their bias as clearly as did their counterparts on the dominant side, namely those pro-Negro in the 1950s and anti-drug-restriction (pro-drugs) in the 1960s.

Eiser and Stroebe (1972) prefer to interpret such data in terms of (1) a contrast effect (exaggeration of difference) between statements with which the person agrees and those with which the person disagrees, which may be modified by (2) a reluctance to agree when the judgment language used in the research is negatively evaluated by social norms of dominant groups in the individual's social milieu. In still more recent research, Eiser and Osmon (1978) have emphasized the "semantic features of the response language" in judgment to the point that the entire issue in earlier research appears to be a matter of self-presentation by judges to the researchers. Such a reduction of the issues ignores the fact that judges in the earlier research were not asked to agree or disagree with the statements, but only to judge them objectively as to favorableness-unfavorableness. It neglects the fact that highly involved judges, pro- (Sherif and Hovland) or con- (Vaughan), used fewer categories when allowed to generate their own.

As noted below, the "semantic features of response language" are not an idle issue, either psychologically or sociologically; however, the earlier results cannot be explained entirely as artifacts of "response language." Nor is there adequate evidence for definitive support of an alternative view, namely that for historical and personal reasons the anti- subjects in the early research on the status of blacks and on the drug issue in England were simply less personally involved in the issue. Such an alternative is feasible if we assume that individuals who see their own positions opposed by an active dominant group while social support for their own positions declines may very well minimize that particular issue, i.e., "forget about it" as a personal concern.

In any event, it is misleading to suggest that individuals on the unpopular side of an issue, pro or con, invariably want to characterize their own views in language acceptable to the other side. Diab (1967) found pro-Arab unity and anti-Arab unity Lebanese quite willing to characterize themselves in terms obnoxious to the other side. In fact, he found them quite willing to characterize themselves as holding extreme positions on the issue, contrary to the norm of moderation which Eiser and Osmon (1978) propose as general, following Aristotle. In short, semantic features of response language are not divorced from historical intergroup processes.

Indeed, the characterization of attitudes as pro or anti by researchers need not correspond to the characterizations employed by partisans on opposite sides, each of whom may develop their own preferred terminology. For example, I have referred to pro- and anti-abortion attitudes. Two studies (Kearney, 1975; Rogers, 1978) have found that the two sides mirror one another's latitudes, but characterize their own acceptable positions in different terms. Pro-choice is the preferred term for those who could be called pro-abortion, while pro-life is the preferred term for those who could be called anti-abortion. This controversy is particularly interesting from the present viewpoint, since both sides emerged as actively partisan groups during a fairly recent change in laws pertaining to abortion in the United States, the pro-life groups after the Supreme Court decision legalizing abortion, at a time when pro-choice advocates thought that their battle was won. Now both sides are presenting their side of the issue to the public as the positive, favorable side. Their nip-and-tuck struggle is reflected in high involvement on both sides.

I would maintain that every attitude is, in one sense, both pro and anti. By endorsing one side, the individual is also objecting to the other. However, empirical study of the structures of attitudes on different sides of public and private controversies will continue to hold many interesting research problems. Meanwhile, there is no necessary reason that pro or anti attitudes be singled out as special cases with inherently different structures for our generalizations about personal involvement.

Is It Possible To Be Highly Involved in a Moderate Position?

We have seen that individuals adopting the same extreme positions vary in their attitude structure; however, that finding does not satisfactorily deal with the alternative explanation that only extreme attitudes exhibit the patterns I have described. Certainly, there are several sociological and psychological reasons why such might be the case. First, U.S. society has been characterized many times as one of moderation, compromise, or consensus. Whether or not the description is accurate, the normative climate created by the description makes it more likely than chance that those who actually do adopt and publicly uphold extreme positions may be unusual as individuals and as groups. I am not suggesting that individuals with extreme views are necessarily maladjusted or even nonconforming. To the contrary, they may be very conforming and "adjusted" to their particular reference groups (cf. Elms, 1972). They are, however, nonconforming to normative pressure to be moderate, compromising, and consensual. Particularly in political life, public commitment to extreme positions in the United States entails a process over time that would be expected to produce higher involvement, if only from the awareness that the majority does not agree.

These circumstances make it difficult to test the proposition that attitude structure is independent of extremity or moderateness of attitude position. The best evidence available to us that it can be is the following:

1. In several studies (C. W. Sherif, M. Sherif, & Nebergall, 1965) on political elections, some respondents to the Method of Ordered Alternatives have chosen an "undecided" alternative between Republican and Democratic options, but have exhibited enormous latitudes of rejection and little noncommitment, a pattern typical of the highly involved person. Beck and Nebergall (in M. Sherif and C. W. Sherif, 1969) were able to show that the inactive, apathetic "undecided" individual on an election displayed an enormous latitude of noncommitment, while those who were "undecided" about the election, but engaging in political activity nonetheless, exhibited attitude structures typical of the highly involved. The same contrast was found between active and inactive persons whose most acceptable position merely "leaned" to one side or the other. The active "leaners" exhibited high involvement, through large latitudes of rejection and little noncommitment, while the inactive "leaners" rejected little and had huge latitudes of noncommitment. Phifer (1970) reported a similar comparison on mild supporters and mild opponents of capital punishment. If contemporary trends of low voter turnout and distrust of government officials continue, we would expect to see more and more individuals who can endorse only an undecided or a moderate position on political issues, but who vehemently reject the political candidates and alternative policies presented to them. In short, we believe that it is possible to be either "undecided" or "moderate" on an issue and to exhibit attitude structure typical of the highly involved person. Like the apathetic voter, such an involved "undecided" or moderate is unlikely to vote, but for entirely different reasons.

2. Finally, varying attitude structures have been found in attitude research where "extremity" vs. "moderation" would be difficult to pose as an issue. Such research includes adolescents' own categorizations of the cost of a winter coat, of social behaviors, and of ethnic groups (C. W. Sherif, 1961, 1963); and adolescents' categoriza-

tions of clothing and hair styles, as well as their plans for the future (Kelly, in C. W. Sherif et al., 1973). In no case did these adolescents favor extreme positions or objects. The relative importance of the object class to their peers was independently determined, either by a preliminary survey (C. W. Sherif, 1961) or by 14 months' observation in their natural setting (Kelly, in C. W. Sherif et al., 1973). In all of these cases, the latitude of noncommitment was significantly smaller for the more important than for the less significant objects. The latitudes of rejection did not differ significantly in these latter studies, which did not focus on bipolar issues (e.g., clothing vs. no clothing).

Therefore, we currently conclude that the structures described are not unique to extreme attitudes. Low noncommitment characterizes the more involved and high noncommitment the less involved in all cases. The large latitude of rejection characterizing high involvement in bipolar issues is not confined to those taking extreme positions, but does appear to require the existence of others upholding widely discrepant views, to which one's own position is frequently compared. In short, the attitude structure cannot be fully understood apart from the social processes in which it arises and functions. A great deal more research is needed on these topics, since it could clarify important sociological and psychological phenomena.

Does Attitude Structure Reflect General Personal Dispositions?

A final issue about attitude structures as related to personal involvement concerns the possibility that differential structures may chiefly reflect individual differences in cognitive style or personality that affect all of the person's categorizations and evaluations.

In a constrained social situation, there is little doubt that an individual responding to several attitude assessment techniques exhibits more consistency than chance allows. Each of the assessment techniques I have described contains, however, some lack of structure. The Method of Ordered Alternatives is a direct, confrontive technique, but the individual is required to make only two responses, the most acceptable and the most objectionable. Hence, the relative sizes of the latitudes are not constrained by circumstances other than the limited number of alternatives available. The Own Categories technique requires the individual to contribute even greater structure, including the number of categories to be used. The question is: Do individuals, in fact, exhibit consistency in the relative widths or sizes of their latitudes of acceptance, rejection, and noncommitment across different attitude domains? If so, it could be maintained that a personal disposition to categorize in a certain way was being revealed.

Available evidence for a personal disposition or categorical style is not compelling; however, there is evidence for consistency when the topics being categorized are related in an ideology supported by the individual. For example, using issues entirely unrelated from the viewpoint of a dominant ideology, Eagly and Telaak (1972) reported no significant correlations among subjects' latitudes of acceptance or rejection on different issues; but when Larson (1971) studied Mormon students' ratings of three issues selected to vary from highly involving to less involving—namely, Communism, liquor by the drink, and an issue concerning television—he did obtain significant results. Since the ideology of the Mormon church strongly opposes Communism and liquor by the drink, it is not surprising that latitudes of rejection on these two issues were significantly correlated, or that both were related to responses on the Rokeach Dogmatism scale, which includes items congenial to the same ideology. Nor is it surprising that attitudes on the television issue, on which the church took no stand, bore no relation to the others. It is interesting, however, that the latitudes of rejection on the three issues were increasingly larger from the television issue through the liquor issue to the Communism issue.

While Larson's study found no significant relationship between the same individuals' latitude of rejection and a measure of cognitive complexity, other studies have reported such a relationship. Such relationships appear when comparisons are made among different individuals on one selected issue, hence the interpretation depends on the validity of the cognitive complexity measure in indicating a generalized cognitive "style." Unfortunately, tests of cognitive complexity used in the several studies do not correlate significantly (Eiser & Stroebe, 1972, p. 108). Indeed, it seems reasonable that cognitive complexity, if it is a generalized personal variable, might be related to categorizations of different issues on the Own Categories technique. At present, however, adequate tests of this proposition do not exist. An adequate test would require comparison of categorizations by the same individuals for a wide variety of object domains with scores on valid tests of cognitive complexity.

On the other hand, a repeated measures design that has the same individuals categorizing different sets of objects known by pretesting to differ in degree of personal involvement for the subjects can suggest the relative significance of personal styles in categorizing and of varying personal involvement. Two early studies with the Own Categories technique (C. W. Sherif, 1961; Glixman, 1965) reported low positive correlations between the numbers of categories used by the same individuals performing three or four sorting tasks at the same session, the correlation coefficients being about .35. This is not surprising, but accounts for very little of the variance. Both studies reported significant differences in the number of categories used for the different sets of objects, the numbers increasing with less personally involving objects. Likewise, the widths of categories differentially evaluated were significantly different.

Another early study (Reich & Sherif in C. W. Sherif et al., 1965) showed fewer categories generated by highly involved women than by less involved women matched for age and education. Kelly (in C. W. Sherif et al., 1973) reported significant differences in number of categories and latitudes of noncommitment exhibited by the same adolescent girls sorting items pertaining to group norms of known and different importance in their reference groups. Earlier, I mentioned Shaffer's findings on differential latitudes by the same individuals for issues of varying normative emphasis in a religious group.

Finally, Rogers (1978) secured latitudes of acceptance, rejection, and noncommitment on issues of abortion, space flights, and bilingualism in Canada from individuals in Georgia chosen to be highly pro or con on the abortion issue, as well as unselected students. The latitudes varied as predicted on the issues, rejection being significantly greater on the abortion issue among partisans and lower among unselected subjects. Rejections on the space and bilingualism issues were comparable for abortion partisans and unselected subjects, as would be predicted on the basis of their lower involvement in these issues. Noncommitment also differentiated among the issues and the groups reliably. If the partisans on either side of the abortion issue differed from unselected students chiefly in terms of cognitive complexity, this pattern of results could not have been obtained.

In conclusion, there is certainly a possibility that attitude structure varies according to other personal variables, such as cognitive complexity; but evidence that it does is equivocal. Latitudes on different issues should be significantly correlated when the issues are ideologically related in the individuals' reference groups, and there is some evidence for this proposition. However, there is also sufficient evidence that the relative sizes of the latitudes differ significantly in terms of the same person's relative involvement in different issues that are not ideologically related or that are assigned differential importance in the individual's reference group.

DEVELOPMENT OF CATEGORICAL SCHEMA VARYING IN SELF-IMPLICATION

If, as we believe, the structure of an individual's attitude reveals something of the self-system, it is logical to expect that the development of a categorical schema defining self will differ in predictable fashion from one that is less self-implicating. Fortunately, we know a little about developmental trends in attitude formation, particularly self-other attitudes defining racial identity. The data from Horowitz's pioneering research (1936) onward are consistent in indicating low correlations across measures and situations for very small children and increasingly higher intercorrelations after about 4 to 6 years of age. We know a great deal more about children's classifications of laboratory stimuli deliberately prepared to eliminate meaningful or personal implications, e.g., geometric shapes and colors.

That literature reports a general sequence in the development of children's classifications, starting with "graphic" collections of objects up to about age 5, wherein objects are collected on the basis of spatial, perceptual, and associative similarities, with little overall plan for classification. According to Inhelder and Piaget (1964), a transition period around ages 5 to 7 or so is followed by "true classification" wherein an overall plan and consistent criteria guide the child's categorizations. Thus, the number of categories used by the child, their contents, and the reasons given for classification change from early to later childhood. Fewer categories are used with age, and the contents resemble sociolinguistic conventions more closely. Those authors warned, however, that children's classifications of "thematic materials" may not always conform to these theoretical expectations.

One "theme" central in self-definition is gender, and one set of thematic materials used frequently in the study of gender identity is toys. Another equally familiar set of thematic materials for children that are far less implicating of self is household furniture. A comparison of children's categorizations of the two sets of thematic materials permits a particularly interesting test of Inhelder and Piaget's warning, and, simultaneously, of the expectation that the development of self-implicating categories will differ from that of categories more tangentially related to developing self-definitions.

Escovar (1975) performed such a comparison with boys and girls ages 4 to 5, 6 to 7, and 8 to 9 years old in rural central Pennsylvania. The children were assigned randomly in each age group to classify pictures either of toys or household objects. The household objects were to be sorted so that those in each pile "belonged together," while toys were sorted so that those in each pile belonged together in terms of "how good they are to play with." The objects in each set (28 in each) had been standardized, on the basis of adult judgments on the typical location of household objects and on the "masculinity-femininity" of the toys. For example, six toys had been consensually judged by adults as "most feminine" and six as "most masculine," with more moderately gendered toys and with neutral toys in between.

Table 1 shows the average number of categories used by children in different age groups in sorting the household objects and toys. There were no significant gender differences in this respect. In classifying household objects, the children used significantly fewer categories with age, as the developmental literature would predict.

Table 1
Mean numbers of categories used by children of different ages (Boys and girls combined, adapted from Escovar, 1975)

Age	N	Household Objects M	Toys M
4–5	40	10.8	3.2
6–7	40	8.9	2.8
8–9	40	6.9	3.6

Analysis of the contents of the categories through cluster analysis and the children's reasons for their groupings showed that these changes were accompanied by increasingly conventional placements of the household objects, for reasons pertaining to the arrangement of a house. The single and interesting gender difference was the placement of a wooden gun cabinet, which older girls classified with living room furniture but older boys classified with bedroom objects.

The average number of categories used for toys did not change significantly with age nor differ with gender. Further, significantly fewer categories were used for toys that "belonged together" than for household objects at every age. Using adult judgments classifying the toys as masculine or feminine, Escovar found statistically significant age trends, which were most marked for the boys, toward increasing acceptance of own-gender toys and increasing rejection of other-gender toys. At least in rural central Pennsylvania, 4- to 5-year-old boys did not consistently accept "masculine" toys or reject "feminine" toys. Both boys and girls accepted increasingly more toys classified by adults as "gender appropriate" with age and increasingly rejected those judged appropriate for the other gender, with the boys becoming more conventional than the girls by ages 8 to 9.

To the extent that toy preferences and rejections are related to other indicators of gender identity (self as boy or girl), Escovar's data confirm the growing literature showing that those attitudes related to one's own gender and evaluation of the other gender develop toward conventional classifications prevailing in the social milieu. From the perspective of attitude theory, they show that attitudes defining self develop fewer categories and a structure that differs from categorical schema for equally familiar but less involving object domains.

As such, they are pertinent to those theories of cognitive development that see the beginnings of gender identity in the child's categorizations of self and others. If so, such theories of gender identity will have to confront the issue of the degree to which different gender-related schema are self-defining. The issue is critical. The literature from the 1940s to the present is consistent with the proposition that schema highly defining of self are related to differential processing of relevant events and to behavioral coherence across situations and time (M. Sherif & Cantril, 1947; M. Sherif & C. W.

Sherif, 1953, 1969; C. W. Sherif et al., 1973; Bem & Allen, 1974; Markus, 1977).

SOCIAL JUDGMENTS, INTENTIONS, AND ACTIONS

Exploration of attitude structure and its development would be an esoteric exercise if that structure bore no relationship to what individuals intend to do and actually do in other circumstances. Earlier, I referred to Shaffer's study comparing the attitude structures of members with varying status in a religious group to norms of varying significance in group life. In a subsequent quasi-experimental design, Shaffer (1974) found that the lower status members also made fewer public commitments than higher status members for evangelism and for recruitment of new members to weekly meetings. All members made fewer commitments to activities regarded by the group as less important (recruitment to meetings) than to the more important activity (personal evangelism). Their differential involvement, as exhibited in the different structure of attitudes by members with different status, was the psychological linkage for his conclusion that "when attitudes related to overt behavior were positive and relatively homogeneous, the commitment to perform overt behavior by reference group members was best predicted by his or her social location in the group and the relative importance of the norm governing that behavior" (p. 75).

The attitude measures in that research were obtained several weeks prior to asking for commitment to specific actions. The lower status, less-involved members made fewer commitments than those of middle or high status and reported fewer evangelistic contacts later. Since these contacts involved target persons of differing acquaintance and differing sympathy with evangelism, it is particularly interesting that frequency of commitment to evangelize declined with the targets' decreasing sympathy for the group's values, especially for the less important norm of bringing people to weekly group meetings. A major difference between the commitments of the more and less involved members lay in whether or not they named specific individuals as their targets for evangelical activity. More involved members named such targets significantly more often and also reported more follow-up contacts than less-involved members.

Important as Shaffer's research is in linking attitude-value problems to the workings of the individual's reference group, there is the possible objection that status in a group consists of much more than personal involvement and that, therefore, the link to commitment and to action is confounded. To such objections, Merrilea Kelly's research on attitude, commitment, and action in attending a meeting related to the attitude will be more convincing. She studied unrelated individuals.

Kelly (in C. W. Sherif et al., 1973) made extensive surveys in 1969 of students' rankings of issues as having personal importance to them. Choosing three issues that were the most consensually ranked as of high, moderate, or less importance, she then assessed attitudes on those issues. Later, individuals randomly assigned to one of three samples were invited to attend a meeting on one of the three issues. Contrary to what might have been expected on a college campus in 1969 and early 1970, none of the issues pertained to the war or directly to national issues. The issue of highest importance to students was personal-social adjustment, and the meeting related to it was a T-group session. That of intermediate importance concerned the status of blacks on campus, while the least important concerned academic issues. Meetings to discuss the latter two were also arranged.

The attitudes of the students were all favorable to the issues, namely improved personal adjustment, improved status for blacks on campus, and improved academic life. Using both Likert-type scales and the Own Categories method, Kelly found no relationship between commitment to attend the meeting or actual attendance and extremity of favorable attitude. However, the Own Categories data did support the ordering of the issues according to involvement, viz., the latitudes of rejection and noncommitment varied as would be predicted from high to lower involvement in the three issues.

With no obligation or reward for attending the meetings, Kelly asked two questions: (1) Would the students' stated intentions to attend a meeting and their actual attendance be related to their degree of personal involvement in the issue? (2) Would the consistency among attitude, stated intention, and actual attendance vary with degree of personal involvement in the issue? Her test was made at a particularly demanding time, as it was the spring of the Cambodian invasion when the particular campus studied reached its

Table 2
Percentages with consistent and inconsistent attitudes, intentions, and actions on issues of varying personal involvement (Adapted from Kelly in C.W. Sherif et al., 1973)

	Issue		
	Highly Involving (Adjustment) (N = 60) %	Moderately Involving (Black Rights) (N = 68) %	Less Involving (Academic) (N = 60) %
Consistent attitudes, intentions, actions	63.33	48.51	38.33
Consistent negative intentions and no action, inconsistent with attitude	28.33	47.06	53.33
Consistent attitudes and intentions, no action	8.33	4.42	8.33

$\chi^2 = 12.74$, $df = 4$, $p < .01$, one-tailed test.

peak of ferment. Many competing activities and group discussions were springing up all over. Kelly held one round of meetings, then called those who had committed themselves to attend but did not. She announced another meeting on the same topic, asking for their intentions with regard to that meeting as well. The data summarize the successive waves of intentions and attendances.

As the percentages in Table 2 show, the total percentages committing themselves to attend and actually attending a meeting differed significantly, with higher proportions from the first meeting onward on the most involving topic. The proportions of students whose intentions were not to attend a meeting, despite favorable attitudes, increased from the more to the less involving topics. The proportions who were inconsistent by declaring their intentions to attend two meetings, but failing to appear at either, were small and comparable across all three topics.

Kelly's findings support the emphasis placed by several authors (e.g., Fishbein & Ajzen, 1975; Kiesler, 1971; Triandis, 1970) on the importance of public commitment or intentions for whether or not an action is taken. However, they also show that the question of whether such intentions are favorable to the action and consistent with attitudes is related to the degree of personal involvement in the topic or issue. In this context, it is interesting that recent research applying the Fishbein-Ajzen formula for predicting intentions and actions has reported better predictions for those individuals who were highly involved than for those who were less involved (Bennett & Harrell, 1975).

In reviewing two dozen studies of relationships between attitudes and specific actions related to those attitudes, Peterson and Dutton (1975) found only four that considered what they called "centrality" or "ego-involvement" in the attitude object. Only a third of the studies included some self-rating of "intensity" of feeling, a correlated indicator of personal involvement. Calling attention to the "long-standing discontinuity between theory and research," wherein conceptual analysis of attitudes typically contains qualifications which are seldom assessed in research, they proposed that few theoretical statements about attitudes can be tested until variations in personal involvement are systematically considered in actual research practice.

ASSIMILATION-CONTRAST EFFECTS IN REACTIONS TO ATTITUDE OBJECTS

The process whereby individuals with attitudes varying in personal involvement judge or compare objects in the attitude domain is perhaps best understood through the Own Categories procedure.

In the Own Categories procedure, the individual faces the range of the domain of attitude objects. While he or she attends closely to the task of distinguishing among the numerous objects and grouping them by their features, the process of comparison is also relative to an internal anchor, viz., the acceptable latitude. To the degree that the individual is highly involved in the object domain, judgments of specific objects are made relative to that internal anchor, even though the instructions call for judgments of the objects, not for the individual's agreements or acceptances and rejections.

The effects of an internal anchor on judgments need be considered no more mysterious or "irrational" than those that occur in judgments of physical objects or their properties, such as their weight, length, or intensity. One class of such systematic errors was traditionally labeled a "contrast effect," meaning an exaggeration of differences. For example, after lifting a series of heavy boxes, a moderately heavy box seems light. The same box lifted after a series of empty boxes will seem unusually heavy.

The psychophysical literature is also replete with references to errors in which differences are minimized, though a variety of specific terms is used in referring to them (e.g., central tendency effect, halo effect, negative halo effect, and even "reversal of classical contrast"). More recently, the familiar term "assimilation" has been used to refer to all such errors minimizing differences (M. Sherif & C. W. Sherif, 1956; M. Sherif & Hovland, 1961; Helson, 1964).

As Helson (1964) also emphasized, assimilation and contrast effects are not discrete processes or phenomena, but complementary. Assimilating something usually involves contrasting something else. Emphasizing the differences between objects placed in different categories means emphasizing similarities among objects placed in the same category (Bruner, 1957; Tajfel, 1969; Taylor, Fiske, Etcoff, & Ruderman, 1978). With the added assumption that the most acceptable categories serve as an anchor in judgment for the entire range of a domain, the findings from the Own Categories Procedure become clear. This assumption is necessary since assimilation effects occur for items that are not otherwise classified together (e.g., when only acceptable items are presented). As I reported some years ago (1961, 1963), individuals make finer distinctions when classifying objects that lie wholly within their acceptable latitudes than when classifying the entire range, including objects that are rejected. In the latter case, the otherwise "different" objects are classified together as acceptable.

Using the acceptable latitude as anchor, the highly involved individual assimilates neighboring objects but contrasts those increasingly discrepant from the anchor. When the acceptable objects are somewhat extreme, the result is a series of contrast effects for items increasingly different from the anchor—their differences from the acceptable latitude being emphasized. Thus objects "intermediate" for the uninvolved judge, and even for an involved judge who is instructed to use, say, five categories, are categorized together as similar and objectionable when the involved judge generates the categories. The outcome is the use of few categories and a bipolar distribution of objects into categories, the broadest category being rejected (M. Sherif & Hovland, 1953). In two separate studies (La Fave & Sherif, 1968; Rogers, 1978) such assimilation-contrast effects on intermediate items with the Own Categories procedure have been demonstrated. When highly involved and less involved judges are pooled, the result is strikingly greater variances for the judgments of intermediate than for the most extreme items.

The less-involved judge attends more closely to the stimulus properties of the objects, thereby requiring a longer decision time (Reich & Sherif, in C. W. Sherif et al., 1965) and also requiring significantly more categories to sort the same stimulus domain. Other research using a prescribed number of categories (for example, eleven) shows that judges with moderate attitude positions and probably less involvement in the issue tend to assimilate items over a wide range, thereby giving less extreme judgments on extreme items than a highly involved judge (Eiser & Stroebe, 1972, summarizing research by several authors). The greater bipolarity of extreme items exhibited in the average judgments by highly involved judges with extreme positions is consistent with their assimilation of items at one end toward their own extreme positions and their contrast of items at the opposite extreme.

To suggest that the less-involved judge is more "rational" because the judgment process is less affected by attitude, or that the highly involved judge errs through irrationality, is to misunderstand both the judgment process and the nature of attitudes. Attitudes are cognitive as well as affective affairs. The involved person is judging as cognitively as the less involved. Determination of which is the "better" or more "rational" judge can ultimately be made only by turning away from the judges toward the actual social life and events that occur there, not inside of heads.

Assimilation-Contrast in Locating Communication

As an example, consider appraisals made immediately following the Bakke decision by the U.S. Supreme Court on affirmative action by the University of California Medical School at Davis in June 1978. Perhaps the most accurate appraisals of that decision were made by a constitutional lawyer, who after reading the three 5–4 decisions, characterized the text as "an onion," each layer peeling off but revealing no pith. Others referred to them as a "mixed bag." Consider now the appraisals made by moderate and strong proponents of affirmative action. Moderates, including the Attorney General whose public position favored affirmative action, said of the decision that "affirmative action is enhanced." Strong proponents, on the other hand, declared the Court action a "watershed" comparable to the Plessy vs. Ferguson decision which had affirmed segregation. The Reverend Jesse Jackson was explicit in placing the decision in the same category as a recent California vote limiting property taxes, the decision granting Nazis the right to march in Skokie, and a Ku Klux Klan march in Mississippi.

On the other side, opponents of affirmative action displayed similar disagreement in appraising the decisions. A moderately conservative newspaper announced the decision in the headline "Supreme Court Bars Quotas," a conclusion not contained in the decision but widely echoed by affirmative action opponents. The more extreme opponents disagreed: to them the decision was a temporizing move to delay complete dismantling of affirmative action machinery. In short, the more extreme proponents and the opponents were both emphasizing the differences between their own positions and that of the decisions—a contrast effect. The moderates on both sides were assimilating the decision toward their own positions, thereby seeing it as affirming their own positions.

Hovland, Harvey, and Sherif (1957) plotted such judgments of an ambiguous communication which diverged in varying extent from individuals' own positions on both sides on the issue, with a baseline which represented the judges' own position on the issue. The function resembled an angular S parallel to the baseline.

Such research requires judgments on the same message by large numbers of individuals with positions on the issue varying from one extreme to the other. Subsequent attempts to repeat the procedures using different issues, messages, and populations were less than satisfying, but they have provided some important implications. Sherif (in M. Sherif & Hovland, 1961) presented a communication with entirely balanced arguments on both sides of the 1956 presidential election campaign, with no conclusion supporting either candidate. The expectation was that judgments of the message would depend upon the discrepancy between an individual's position and the dead-center message, with moderates assimilating it and extremists contrasting it. Contrary to expectations, the only trend was for moderate and extreme partisans on both sides to assimilate the dead-center message toward their own position.

Meanwhile, Manis (1960) reported assimilation of neutral opinion statements about college fraternities by pro- and anti-fraternity students. We tried another dead-center message during the 1960 presidential campaign and again found an increasing assimilation effect with increasing discrepancy of the individuals' own positions from the dead-center message. Such assimilation was even more pronounced in judgments of "which candidate had the edge in the debates" staged between Nixon and Kennedy in 1960 (C. W. Sherif et al., 1965). The more extreme the individuals' support of either candidate the greater was their rating that their own candidate had the edge.

In short, there is considerable evidence that a genuinely balanced communication giving equal time to both sides is typically assimilated by partisans on both sides, increasingly so with increasing discrepancies between their own position and the dead-center, balanced communication. We believe that the explanation lies in the complementarity of assimilation-contrast effects. The listener contrasts the arguments of the opponent to those on "my side." The result is assimilation of the arguments on the preferred side of the issue to the individual's own position, even though they are discrepant from it. The overall judgment of the two-sided communication is, therefore, that it favors one's own side, with the tacit assumption that other listeners will also experience the contrast between the two viewpoints.

However, the same balanced message that ends in mild support for one side or the other is judged quite differently. During the 1960 presidential election, such a mildly Republican message was judged by partisans on both sides exactly as predicted, i.e., assimilated by moderates on both sides but contrasted by extreme partisans on both sides (C. W. Sherif et al., 1965). The differences in their judgments were statistically significant. Another large sample heard the same message but with a mildly Democratic conclusion. The distribution of their judgments was rectilinear—flat, no differences. There we were with all those data, signifying nothing.

It was then, post hoc but with an objective criterion, that we started looking at the issue of how involved the judges were in their own positions. We had found that, on the average, ardent active partisans rejected five of nine positions on the outcome of the election. Therefore, we arbitrarily divided the sample of those who had heard the moderately Democratic message into those who were highly involved, by that criterion, and those who were less involved. Lo and behold, we had two different and statistically significant functions for the judgments by more and less involved individuals. The less involved judges increasingly assimilated the message toward their own position as the message diverged from it. The more involved supporters on both sides contrasted the same message, increasingly with greater discrepancies between their own position and the message (C. W. Sherif et al., 1965). Ironically, it was the less involved listeners who were engaging in "wish fulfillment," hearing the message as resembling their own position. The more involved, increasingly with the discrepancy, saw the same message as more opposed to their own position.

Owing to the varying numbers of individuals upholding different positions, the confound between extremity of position and involvement, and the many other ways individuals upholding different positions might differ, we abandoned this design to look more closely at the effects of varying involvement on reactions to communications by individuals with comparable positions on the issue.

Assimilation-Contrast Effects with Varying Involvement of Self

The social controversy between proponents and opponents of liberalized abortion laws proved to be a good testing ground for examining personal involvement in reactions to communications. The issue was daily in the papers. Organized groups had formed on both sides. It seemed reasonable to expect that individuals were also adopting polarized positions. Helen Kearney (1975) first undertook a field study of groups on both sides of the issue. Using the Method of Ordered Alternatives presented earlier, she found that members in each group typically chose statements next to their extreme as most acceptable, also accepted one or two other statements on that side, but rejected 7 of the 11 ranked positions presented to them, on the average. They also reported high levels of activity on the abortion issue.

This field study was invaluable in several ways, as we shall see. One was that Kearney could state what the structure of attitudes for active partisans on both sides looked like, hence what structures could be considered as high, moderately, or less involving.

From a large pool of volunteer college students, Kearney then selected 152 women, all of whom endorsed as most acceptable one of the three most extreme pro-choice positions (favoring abortion). Although she had wanted to study both pro-choice and pro-life attitudes, there were too few pro-life students to be included. Further, the criterion adopted for personal involvement eliminated male undergraduates, since too few were at all involved in the issue, according to the criterion. The criterion was that individuals who had rejected five or more positions were classified as moderately involved, whereas those rejecting fewer than five positions were classified as low in involvement.

At a second session, each woman read a moderately pro-life communication, supporting a position actually being introduced by pro-life partisans into the state legislature, namely that abortion should be permitted only when the mother's life was endangered and only then with permission of spouse or parent. For half of the women, this message was preceded by an extremely pro-life message, advocating a national constitutional convention to outlaw abortion. The other half read an irrelevant message. Half of the women in each of these conditions were exposed beforehand to procedures intended to make the issue, the chronology of events, and the partisan groups on each side as salient as possible. In this situationally involving condition, each woman also wrote a statement of her own position and signed her name to it. After reading the moderate pro-life message, each judged its position on a linear scale and rated the message in a variety of ways.

Statistical analysis of the judgments showed strong effects for the difference in personal involvement in the issue and for the effect of reading the message in the context of an extremely pro-life message, compared with an irrelevant message (Table 3). This latter effect was in contrast to that in the field study, where the presentation of a message moderately opposed to the partisans' own positions in the context of an extremely opposed message had no significant effect on the partisans' judgments. Overall, the procedures to increase the salience of the issue and the individual's position did not produce a statistically significant difference; however, those procedures did interact significantly with the level of personal involvement, as we shall see.

Table 3

Mean judgments of position advocated in moderate pro-life message by women with differing involvement in different experimental conditions (adapted from Kearney, 1975)

	Attitudes: Pro-Choice	
	Moderate Involvement	Low Involvement
No Situational Involvement		
Irrelevant context	8.68[c]	5.91
Opposed end anchor	7.10	4.99[a]
Situational Involvement		
Irrelevant context	7.54[c]	7.75[c]
Opposed end anchor	6.18	5.41[a]

Pro-life extreme = 11
Pro-choice extreme = 0   Scale midpoint = 5.5

c = contrast
a = assimilation

Significant effects (ANOVA)
  Involvement: $F(1, 144) = 12.98, p < .0005$
  Message context: $F(1, 144) = 15.67, p < .0002$
  Involvement × Situational involvement: $F(1, 144) = 7.82, p < .006$

Kearney found that the moderately involved women contrasted the moderate communication, as had their highly involved counterparts in the field study. The introduction of the extremely pro-life message reduced this contrast effect significantly, particularly when it was coupled with the preceding sober reminder of the course of events and group alignments. By comparison, the less involved women showed no contrast effect when they were not reminded of the importance of the issue. Further, when the moderate pro-life message appeared in the context of an extremely pro-life message, the less involved women assimilated the moderate message to their own side of the issue ($M = 4.99$). In effect, pro-choice but lightly involved women in this condition were saying that requirements for proof of a threat to the mother's health and permission of spouse or guardian were moderately pro-abortion, at a time when the U.S.

Supreme Court had ruled to permit abortion during the first two trimesters.

However, women with low involvement who were reminded of the importance of the issue, then judged the moderate pro-life message in an irrelevant context, exhibited a contrast effect, as did the more involved women. The introduction of an extremely pro-life message again produced assimilation.

In summary, we can now say a good deal more about assimilation-contrast effects in judgments of messages that are discrepant from the person's own position and with which there are varying levels of involvement. Given some ambiguity as to the message's position and moderate discrepancy from the individual's own position, the highly involved partisans on either side use their own positions as the main anchor for judgment, contrasting the message to it, exaggerating the difference, and expressing strong dislike for the moderate message. The introduction of a situational anchor, in the form of a truly extreme and opposed message, has no significant effect in reducing the contrast effect. A moderately involved person with similar attitude position reacts similarly, but does attend to the introduction of a situational anchor by reducing the contrast effect slightly, but significantly.

The less involved individuals are not as consistent. If aroused beforehand by procedures situationally heightening the significance of the issue and their own position, their judgments and reactions to the message resemble those of a more involved person. The reduction of contrast is greater when an opposed end anchor is available. But without such situational arousal, less involved persons actually assimilate the message to their own side of the issue and like it better than any of the other judges, despite the fact that all had endorsed similar positions as most acceptable.

Self as Anchor in Assimilation-Contrast Effects

The findings reviewed above clarify why uninvolved or little involved individuals find the reactions of highly involved partisans puzzling, and, at times, disagreeable. They also help in understanding why, as Sereno and Mortenson (1969) reported, less involved individuals find it easier to agree with others having different opinions, agreeing more often and more quickly than highly involved persons discussing the same issue. Being more attentive to situational standards than to their own positions, the less involved individual more readily assimilates opposing arguments and agrees with them.

Other findings clarify, in turn, the reasons why extreme partisans on both sides of an issue see the other side as engaging in more extreme arguments than they themselves are (Dawes, Singer, & Lemons, 1972). In Dawes et al.'s interesting study of Hawks and Doves on the Viet Nam war, paired comparison judgments for extremity of Hawk and Dove arguments revealed that the other side was seen as more extreme than one's own. Small wonder, when the highly involved partisans in Kearney's study regarded even a moderate message opposed to their own stand as near the extreme opposite end of the scale, while adopting the next to the extreme on their own side as more acceptable. Both are contrast effects. Similarly, when Hawks and Doves were asked to compose arguments representing the other side of the war issue, their productions were so extreme as to be disclaimed by those to whom they were attributed. Of course, it may be argued that the greater extremity attributed to the opposition reflects a cultural norm sanctioning extremity; but it cannot be claimed that either Hawks or Doves regarded their own views as "moderate," a claim belied by the positions they accepted. A simple contrast effect relative to their own respective positions on the issue explains the findings most parsimoniously, as Dawes et al. suggest.

One alternative account of the Hawk and Dove findings and of all such contrast effects is that people invariably accentuate the difference between positions with which they disagree and those with which they agree (Eiser & Stroebe, 1972). Of course such a generalization is descriptive but in no way leads to clarification of why this should be so. Unfortunately, this alternative cannot explain another set of findings: why or under what circumstances people would assimilate to their own side and agree with a position that was formerly in their latitude of noncommitment or even slightly within their latitude of rejection (Peterson & Koulack, 1969).

It would seem that a more adequate psychology of the self is needed before we can begin to speak of a theory of social judgment. The formulation that accommodates all of the findings to date has to deal with both assimilation and contrast effects, the generation of varying numbers of categories by individuals differing in involvement, and the conditions under which a given message will be seen as falling within or near a category with which the person agrees and within or near a category with which the person disagrees. While such conditions include the degree of personal involvement, they also depend upon situational structure, including the presence or absence of other standards and, most certainly, the structure of the task required by a researcher. However, we would predict that the less involved individuals will be more responsive to such situational variations, as they have been in previous research.

The differential structure of attitudes according to the degree of their self implication bears on the question of when and how a discrepancy is recognized between a message and the individual's position on an issue. Such discrepancies are not absolute but relative to the individual's attitude structure. Hence, the issue of whether or not a discrepant message or action arouses personal discomfiture, conflict, or dissonance depends upon the individual's attitude structure.

CONCLUSION

The attitude concept came into social psychology as a tool in dealing with certain psychological issues raised by the twin sociological problems of social control and social change. Specifically, the questions concerned, on one hand, the self-regulation of experience and action along the lines of established social values in the absence of coercion or specifically hedonistic rewards and, on the other, the formation or adoption of new social values by individuals. The social-psychological problems raised by the concept include attitude formation, the role of attitudes in psychological processing, individual as well as group differences in attachment to social values, and problems of attitude change. Clearly, social psychology has only begun to tackle these social-psychological problems adequately. Each problem implies a clear preliminary perspective on the social environment, both on its more enduring social values and structure and on the structural properties of situations where attitudes are studied. All imply study of social interactions with reference persons and groups, concomitant with psychological processes in attitude formation, functioning, and change.

Unless we are to remain in the jungle of confusing research data and tangled discussions that characterize much of the literature, we must strike out on paths other than the circles of fruitless past controversies. One such path leads to the structural properties of attitudes. The study of social judgment, and especially social categorization, offers a vehicle for proceeding on that path. However, it is unreasonable to assume that all social judgment is regulated by attitudes. Hence, the first step in any attitude research must affirm whether the individual has formed an attitude in the first place, or is in the process of doing so.

In studying the patterns of social judgment, we have found significant variations according to the extent to which an attitude has become self-defining for the individual. Specifically, greater involvement of self is reflected in categorizations of bipolar domains with disproportionately wider categories for rejected objects than for accepted ones, and little noncommitment. Little personal involvement is invariably reflected in a wide latitude of noncommitment. Our preliminary efforts suggest that it is feasible to incorporate the relative widths of acceptable, objectionable, and noncommittal categories into a ratio index of personal involvement in a domain.

The consequences of the varying involvement of self in an attitude are numerous and significant. The more involved individual, when asked to delineate the attitude domain objectively, generating the categories for this purpose, sees the need for fewer categories. The resulting category widths are disproportionately unequal, reflecting contrast effects which exaggerate differences between ambiguous objects somewhat discrepant from the acceptable latitude and hence place them in objectionable categories. Such a contrast effect is pronounced in judgment of single communications that are both somewhat ambiguous as to location and moderately discrepant from the person's latitude of acceptance.

If such accentuation of differences between acceptable and objectionable objects were the only effect of high involvement, our account could be quite simple and straightforward; however, it is not. The highly involved person is more impervious than those moderately or less involved to situational standards introduced to locate an object's position relative to the extremes, continuing to use his or her own acceptable latitude as an internal anchor for judgment. On the other hand, a highly involved individual is also more likely than others to commit self to action, to act, and to respond consistently to appeals to act in line with the attitude. In general, the involved person exhibits other judgments and behaviors more coherent with attitude directionality than a less involved person.

The less involved individual generates more categories in sizing up the object domain, being noncommittal toward a broader range of objects. Accentuation of differences between acceptable and objectionable objects occurs when the person is reminded, situationally, of the importance of the attitude. Otherwise, however, the less involved individual is inclined to assimilate a discrepant message that is located somewhat ambiguously on the opposite side of the issue. Its position is pulled toward his or her own side, especially when an opposing extreme standard is provided situationally. It is also liked more. As these variations in assimilation-contrast effects suggest, the less involved person simply does not judge or behave as consistently from one situation to the next, over time.

It is the less involved person, therefore, who is more prone to be swayed by situational appeals or constraints. However, it is also the less involved person who is less likely to act voluntarily in ways that expose self to novel or contrary views. Less likely to be consistent in stating intentions congruent with acceptable positions and less likely to commit self to action, the less involved person is, ironically, both more subject to inertia and more likely to comply with situational standards once into a new situation. It should be clear that involvement of self is not a fixed or static mechanism, but a process always involving interactions of person with the situation.

Our findings suggest that future efforts in attitude research should always attempt to specify the relative degree of the person's involvement in the value domain as well as the relative position of acceptable objects within a range of positions, i.e., extremity-moderateness of differentiable positions toward the attitude object. It is not sufficient to know only how strongly they agree or disagree with the extreme positions. The findings do not suggest that being more or less involved in one attitude domain necessarily implies more or less involvement in another, though attitudes relevant to the ideology of a reference group would be expected to cohere. Our findings suggest that even within the normative system of a group, differential involvement of self occurs among individuals, relative to their status and to the particular value emphasis of that group.

We infer from our findings that the dynamics of attitude change may be quite different in matters that are highly involving for the individual and those less involving. The latter may change within a relatively short time period filled with appeals, personal and prestigeful urgings, or striking events that are both discrepant and mobilizing for the person. On least involving matters, such changes may occur with little internal conflict or dissonance, for the self is slightly affected. On the other hand, moving away from cherished personal positions and beloved hostilities may require a series of drastic events over time: recognition of a world beginning to crumble, or betrayal by those whose trust and understanding has affirmed one's personal investment in the cherished values. Highly involved people do change, but we should not expect that the experienced dissonance or the conflicts engendered with others who still maintain the values are brief, smooth, or easy. Losing an old and dear part of oneself never is a simple matter. The thousands of individuals whose lives have been touched by profound social changes or who have themselves participated in a developing social movement toward change tell us that their attitude changes have involved changing themselves.

REFERENCES

Allport, F. H. A structuronomic conception of behavior: individual and collective: 1. Structural theory and the master problem in social psychology. *Journal of Abnormal and Social Psychology*, 1962, **64**, 3–30.

Allport, F. H., & Katz, D. *Students' attitudes*. Syracuse, NY.: Craftsman Press, 1931.

Allport, G. W. *The nature of prejudice*. Reading, MA.: Addison-Wesley, 1954.

ASA Footnotes. Survey research problems getting worse, study shows. Washington, D. C.: American Sociological Association, 1974, **2**(5), 2.

Bartlett, F. C. *Remembering: A study in experimental and social psychology*. New York: Cambridge University Press, 1932.

Bem, D. J., & Allen, A. On predicting some of the people some of the time: The search for cross-situational consistencies in behavior. *Psychological Review*, 1974, **81**, 506–520.

Bennett, P. D., & Harrell, G. D. The role of confidence in understanding and predicting buyers' attitudes and purchase intentions. *Journal of Consumer Behavior*, 1975, **2**, 110–117.

Bogardus, E. S. Measuring social distance. *Journal of Applied Sociology*, 1925, **9**, 299–308.

Bogardus, E. S. *A forty year racial distance study*. Los Angeles: University of Southern California, 1967.

Brooks, G. P., & Johnson, R. W. Floyd Allport and the master problem in social psychology. *Psychological Reports*, 1978, **42**, 295–308.

Broverman, I. K., Vogel, S. R., Broverman, D. M., Clarkson, F. E., & Rosenkrantz, P. S. Sex-role stereotypes: A current appraisal. *Journal of Social Issues*, 1972, **28**(2), 54–78.

Bruner, J. S. On perceptual readiness. *Psychological Review*, 1957, **64**, 123–152.

Cantril, H. The intensity of an attitude. *Journal of Abnormal and Social Psychology*, 1946, **41**, 129–135.

Collins, B. E., & Raven, B. H. Group structure: Attraction, coalitions, communication, and power. In G. Lindzey & E. Aronson (Eds.), *The handbook of social psychology* (Vol. 4). Reading, MA.: Addison-Wesley, 1969.

Converse, P. E. Attitudes and nonattitudes: Continuation of a dialogue. In E. R. Tufte (Ed.), *The quantitative analysis of social problems*. Reading, MA.: Addison-Wesley, 1970.

Dawes, R. M., Singer, D., & Lemons, F. An experimental analysis of contrast effect and its implications for intergroup communication and indirect assessment of attitude. *Journal of Personality and Social Psychology*, 1972, **21**, 281–295.

Diab, L. N. Measurement of social attitudes: Problems and prospects. In C. W. Sherif & M. Sherif (Eds.), *Attitude, ego-involvement and change*. New York: Wiley, 1967.

Eagly, A. H., & Telaak, K. Width of the latitude of acceptance as a determinant of attitude change. *Journal of Personality and Social Psychology*, 1972, **23**, 388–397.

Edwards, A. L. A critique of "neutral" items in attitude scales constructed by the method of equal appearing intervals. *Psychological Review*, 1946, **53**, 159–169.

Ehrlich, H. J. *The social psychology of prejudice*. New York: Wiley, 1973.

Eiser, J. R. Enhancement of contrast in the absolute judgment of attitude statements. *Journal of Personality and Social Psychology*, 1971, **17**, 1–10.

Eiser, J. R., & Osmon, B. E. Judgmental perspective and value connotations of response scale labels. *Journal of Personality and Social Psychology*, 1978, **36**, 491–497.

Eiser, J. R., & Stoebe, W. *Categorization and social judgment*. London: Academic Press, 1972.

Elms, A. C. *Social psychology and social relevance*. Boston: Little, Brown, 1972.

Elshtain, J. B. Methodological sophistication and conceptual confusion: A critique of mainstream political inquiry on women, politics and values. In

J. Sherman & E. T. Beck (Eds.), *The prism of sex*. Madison: University of Wisconsin Press, 1979.

Escovar, L. *Categorization of social stimuli by young children: A study of social cognitive development*. Unpublished doctoral dissertation, Pennsylvania State University, 1975.

Festinger, L. The treatment of qualitative data by scale analyses. *Psychological Bulletin*, 1947, **44**, 149–161.

Fishbein, M., & Ajzen, I. *Belief, attitude, intention and behavior: An introduction to theory and research*. Reading, MA.: Addison-Wesley, 1975.

Fraser, C., & Stacey, B.C. A psychophysical investigation of the influence of attitude on the judgment of social stimuli. *British Journal of Clinical and Social Psychology*, 1973, **12**, 337–352.

Glixman, A. R. Categorizing behavior as a function of meaning domain. *Journal of Personality and Social Psychology*, 1965, **2**, 370–377.

Guttman, L. The Cornell technique for scale construction. *Educational and Psychological Measurement*, 1947, **7**, 247–280.

Hartley, E. L. *Problems in prejudice*. New York: King's Crown Press, 1946.

Helson, H. *Adaptation-level theory*. New York: Harper & Row, 1964.

Horowitz, E. L. The development of attitudes toward Negroes. *Archives of Psychology*, 1936, No. 194.

Hovland, C. I., Harvey, O. J., & Sherif, M. Assimilation and contrast effects in communication and attitude change. *Journal of Abnormal and Social Psychology*, 1957, **55**, 242–252.

Hovland, C. I., & Sherif, M. Judgmental phenomena and scales of attitude measurement: Item displacement in Thurstone scales. *Journal of Abnormal and Social Psychology*, 1952, **47**, 822–832.

Inhelder, B., & Piaget, J. *The early growth of logic in the child. Classification and seriation*. New York: Harper & Row, 1964.

Katz, D., & Braly, K. Racial stereotypes of one hundred college students. *Journal of Abnormal and Social Psychology*, 1932, **28**, 280–290.

Kearney, H. R. *Personal involvement and communication context in social judgment of a controversial social issue*. Unpublished doctoral dissertation, Pennsylvania State University, 1975.

Kelman, H. C. Compliance, identification, and internalization: Three processes of attitude change. *Journal of Conflict Resolution*, 1958, **2**, 51–60.

Kiesler, C. A. *The psychology of commitment: Experiments linking behavior to belief*. New York: Academic Press, 1971.

Klineberg, O. *Social psychology*. New York: Holt, 1940.

La Fave, L., & Sherif, M. Reference scales and placement of items with the Own Categories technique. *Journal of Social Psychology*, 1968, **76**, 75–82.

LaPiere, R. T. Attitudes vs. actions. *Social Forces*, 1934, **13**, 230–237.

Larson, K. S. Affectivity, cognitive style and social judgment. *Journal of Personality and Social Psychology*, 1971, **19**, 119–123.

Lewin, K. *Resolving social conflicts*. New York: Harper & Row, 1948.

Lewin, K. Group decision and social change. In H. Proshansky & B. Seidenberg (Eds.), *Basic studies in social psychology*. New York: Holt, Rinehart & Winston, 1965.

Likert, R. A technique for measuring attitudes. *Archives of Psychology*, 1932, No. 140.

Manis, M. The interpretation of opinion statements as a function of recipient attitude. *Journal of Abnormal and Social Psychology*, 1960, **60**, 340–344.

Markus, H. Self-schemata and processing information about the self. *Journal of Personality and Social Psychology*, 1977, **35**, 63–78.

McDougall, W. *An introduction to social psychology*. London: Methuen, 1908.

Milgram, S. *Studies on obedience*. New York: Harper & Row, 1974.

Moscovici, S. Attitudes and opinions. In P. F. Farnsworth, O. McNemar, & Q. McNemar (Eds.), *Annual review of psychology*. Palo Alto: Stanford University Press, 1963.

Murphy, G., Murphy, L. B., & Newcomb, T. M. *Experimental social psychology*. New York: Harper & Row, 1937.

Newcomb, T. M. *Personality and social change*. New York: Holt, Rinehart & Winston, 1943.

Newcomb, T. M., Koenig, L. E., Flacks, R., & Warwick, D. P. *Persistence and change: Bennington College and its students after twenty-five years*. New York: Wiley, 1967.

Peterson, K. K., & Dutton, J. E. Centrality, extremity, intensity. Neglected variables in research on attitude-behavior consistency. *Social Forces*, 1975, **54**, 393–414.

Peterson, P. D., & Koulack, D. Attitude change as a function of latitudes of acceptance and rejection. *Journal of Personality and Social Psychology*, 1969, **11**, 309–311.

Phifer, M. K. *Influence of the process of discrimination in the selection of items for an attitude scale*. Unpublished doctoral dissertation, University of Oklahoma, 1970.

Rogers, L. *The influence of ego-involvement on attitude structures for issues of varying degrees of personal relevance*. Unpublished doctoral dissertation, Pennsylvania State University, 1978.

Rokeach, M. A theory of organization and change within value-attitude systems. *Journal of Social Issues*, 1968, **24**, 13–33.

Selltiz, C., Edrich, H., & Cook, S. W. Ratings of favorableness of statements about a social group as an indicator of attitude towards the group. *Journal of Personality and Social Psychology*, 1965, **2**, 408–415.

Sereno, K. K., & Mortenson, C. D. The effects of ego-involved attitudes on conflict negotiations in dyads. *Speech Monographs*, 1969, **36**, 8–12.

Shaffer, L. S. *Group structure, importance of norms and situational thresholds as factors in attitude-related behavior*. Unpublished doctoral dissertation, Pennsylvania State University, 1974.

Shaw, M. E., & Wright, J. M. *Scales for the measurement of attitudes.* New York: McGraw-Hill, 1967.

Sherif, C. W. *Established reference scales and series effects in social judgment.* Unpublished doctoral dissertation, University of Texas, Austin, 1961.

Sherif, C. W. Social categorization as a function of latitude of acceptance and series range. *Journal of Abnormal and Social Psychology,* 1963, **67**, 148–156.

Sherif, C. W. *Orientation in social psychology.* New York: Harper & Row, 1976.

Sherif, C. W., Kelly, M., Rodgers, H. L., Jr., Sarup, G., & Tittler, B. I. Personal involvement, social judgment and action. *Journal of Personality and Social Psychology,* 1973, **27**, 311–328.

Sherif, C. W., Sherif, M., & Nebergall, R. E. *Attitude and attitude change: The social judgment-involvement approach.* Philadelphia: W. B. Saunders, 1965.

Sherif, M. *The psychology of social norms.* New York: Harper & Row, 1936.

Sherif, M., & Cantril, H. *The psychology of ego-involvements.* New York: Wiley, 1947.

Sherif, M., Harvey, O. J., White, B. J., Hood, W. R., & Sherif, C. W. *Intergroup conflict and cooperation. The Robbers Cave Experiment.* Norman, OK.: Institute of Group Relations, 1961.

Sherif, M., & Hovland, C. I. Judgmental phenomena and scales of attitude measurement: Placement of items with individual choice of number of categories. *Journal of Abnormal and Social Psychology,* 1953, **48**, 135–141.

Sherif, M., & Hovland, C. I. *Social judgment, assimilation and contrast effects in communication and attitude change.* New Haven: Yale University Press, 1961.

Sherif, M., & Sherif, C. W. *Groups in harmony and tension.* New York: Harper & Row, 1953.

Sherif, M., & Sherif, C. W. *An outline of social psychology.* New York: Harper & Row, 1956.

Sherif, M., & Sherif, C. W. Attitude as the individual's own categories: The social judgment-involvement approach to attitude and attitude change. In C. W. Sherif & M. Sherif (Eds.), *Attitude, ego-involvement and change.* New York: Wiley, 1967.

Sherif, M., & Sherif, C. W. *Social psychology.* New York: Harper & Row, 1969.

Sherif, M., White, B. J., & Harvey, O. J. Status in experimentally produced groups. *American Journal of Sociology,* 1955, **60**, 370–379.

Smith, M. B. *Social psychology and human values.* Chicago: Aldine, 1968.

Tajfel, H. Social and cultural factors in perception. In G. Lindzey & E. Aronson (Eds.), *The handbook of social psychology* (Vol. 3). Reading, MA.: Addison-Wesley, 1969.

Taylor, S. E., Fiske, S. T., Etcoff, N. L., & Ruderman, A. J. Categorical and contextual bases of person memory and stereotyping. *Journal of Personality and Social Psychology,* 1978, **36**, 778–793.

Thomas, W. I., & Znaniecki, F. *The Polish peasant in Europe and America.* Chicago: University of Chicago Press, 1918.

Thurstone, L. L. Theory of attitude measurement. *Psychological Review,* 1929, **36**, 222–241.

Thurstone, L. L., & Chave, E. J. *The measurement of attitude.* Chicago: University of Chicago Press, 1929.

Triandis, H. C. Toward an analysis of interpersonal attitudes. In C. W. Sherif & M. Sherif (Eds.), *Attitude, ego-involvement, and change.* New York: Wiley, 1967.

Triandis, H. C. *Attitude and attitude change.* New York: Wiley, 1970.

Triandis, H. C., & Triandis, L. M. Some studies of social distance. In I. Steiner & M. Fishbein (Eds.), *Current studies in social psychology.* New York: Holt, Rinehart & Winston, 1965.

Volkmann, J. Scales of judgment and their implication for social psychology. In J. H. Rohrer & M. Sherif (Eds.), *Social psychology at the crossroads.* New York: Harper & Row, 1951.

Zavalloni, M., & Cook, S. W. Influence of judges' attitudes on ratings of favorableness of statements about a social group. *Journal of Personality and Social Psychology,* 1965, **1**, 43–54.

A Theory of Reasoned Action: Some Applications and Implications

M. Fishbein

University of Illinois at Urbana-Champaign

Why do people behave the way they do? The answers to this question have ranged far and wide, representing almost every aspect of psychological theory and research. We have heard about primary and secondary drives, incentives, conscious and unconscious processes, and biochemical, biological, physiological, cognitive, and affective bases for behavior. If nothing else we have learned of the complexity of motivational constructs and we have seen more than enough evidence to indicate that there is a plethora of factors underlying human behavior that act, react, and interact in strange and mysterious ways. And, to make matters even worse, it appears that the factors underlying one behavior are very different from those underlying another behavior. Indeed, we have seen a movement away from comprehensive formal theories of behavior to particularistic empirical approaches that seem to focus on special processes or concepts that are deemed relevant for the particular behavior or class of behaviors under investigation.

But do we really need different theories to explain different behaviors? Are the processes underlying aggressive behaviors really so different from those underlying altruistic or affiliative behaviors? Similarly, are the processes underlying political behavior so different from those underlying consumer behavior or family planning behavior that we have to develop totally different theories to account for phenomena in each of these domains?

There is little question that different types of theories are required for different levels of analysis. Moreover, even at a given level of analysis, the substantive explanations for different actions will vary considerably. I would like to suggest, however, that at least at the individual level of analysis it is possible to predict and explain most human behavior (irrespective of the label it is given) by reference to a relatively small number of concepts embedded within a theoretical framework. I strongly believe that our field will continue to advance only if we now turn away from mini theories and unique explanations of different behaviors and return to more comprehensive, and hopefully more formal, theories of behavior.

For the past ten years my colleagues and I have been attempting to develop this type of theory. Although the theory has remained nameless, I think it can best be referred to as a theory of reasoned action, since it is based on the assumption that humans are rational animals that systematically utilize or process the information available to them. While we do not assume that a person's information is either complete or veridical, the theory of reasoned action does assume that the information is used in a reasonable way to arrive at a behavioral decision.

I want to make it clear that the theory is neither complete nor necessarily correct. It has already been revised and refined many times and as attempts are made to apply it to new behavioral domains, additional changes will be necessary. But even in its present, preliminary form, I think it is useful. Not only does it provide a systematic approach for investigating behavior in a large variety of domains, but it also helps to explain apparent inconsistencies in empirical results and thus it serves an organizing and integrating function. Moreover, as I will demonstrate, the theory of reasoned action can serve as a diagnostic tool for identifying factors that distinguish between performers and nonperformers of any given action as well as for identifying the loci of effects of a large number of demographic and individual difference variables. Since this theory has been spelled out in detail elsewhere (see, e.g., Fishbein & Ajzen, 1975), I will provide just a brief overview of the theory as it is presently formulated.

A THEORY OF REASONED ACTION

The ultimate goal of the theory is to predict and understand an individual's behavior. The first step toward this goal is to identify and measure the behavior of interest. Unfortunately, this step is not as simple as has often been assumed, and I will discuss some of the problems involved in defining behavioral criteria later in this paper.

Once a behavioral criterion has been clearly defined, however, the theory of reasoned action is quite straightforward. It assumes that most behaviors of social relevance are under volitional control and, consistent with this assumption, it views a person's intention to perform (or not to perform) the behavior as the immediate determinant of that behavior.

In a sense, then, we are suggesting that behaviors are not really difficult to predict. For example, to predict whether an individual will buy Crest toothpaste, the simplest and probably most efficient thing to do is to ask whether he or she intends to do so. This does not mean that there will always be a perfect relationship between intention and behavior. However, barring unforeseen events, a person will usually act in accordance with his or her intention.

Since our goal is to understand human behavior, not merely to predict it, the second step in our analysis requires that we identify the determinants of intentions. According to the theory of reasoned action, a person's intention is a function of two basic determinants, one personal in nature and the other reflecting social influence. The personal factor is the individual's positive or negative evaluation of performing the behavior; this factor may be termed *attitude toward the behavior*. The second determinant of intention is the person's perception of the social pressures put on him or her to perform or not perform the behavior in question. Since it deals with perceived prescriptions, this factor will be termed *subjective norm*. Generally speaking, people will intend to perform a behavior when they evaluate it positively and when they believe that important others think they should perform it.

So far I have said little that does not conform to common sense, but even at this simple level the analysis raises some interesting questions. Consider the case of two women who hold positive attitudes toward using birth-control pills and who perceive social pressures not to use the pill. What will be their intentions in this situation of conflict between attitude toward the behavior and subjective norm? To answer such questions, we need to know the relative importance of the attitudinal and normative factors as determinants of intentions. Our theory assumes that the relative importance of these factors depends in part on the intention under investigation. For some intentions, attitudinal considerations may be more important than normative considerations while for other intentions normative considerations may predominate. Frequently, both factors are important determinants. In addition, the relative weights of the attitudinal and normative factors may vary from one person to another.

The assignment of relative weights to the two determinants of intention greatly increases the explanatory value of the theory. Let us return to the above example and imagine that one woman intended to use birth-control pills while the other did not intend to do so. Since the two women held identical attitudes and subjective norms, their differing intentions could not be explained in terms of these factors alone. However, the different intentions would follow if the first woman's intention was determined primarily by attitudinal considerations and the second woman's intention was primarily under the control of her subjective norm.

For many practical purposes, this level of explanation may be sufficient. It is possible to predict and gain some understanding of a person's intention by measuring his or her attitude toward performing the behavior, his or her subjective norm, and the relative weights of these two components. However, for a more complete understanding of intentions it is necessary to explain why people hold certain attitudes and subjective norms. The theory of reasoned action also attempts to answer these questions.

According to the theory, attitudes are a function of beliefs. Generally speaking, a person who believes that performing a given behavior will lead to mostly positive outcomes will hold a favorable attitude toward performing the behavior, while a person who believes that performing the behavior will lead to mostly negative outcomes will hold an unfavorable attitude. The beliefs that underlie a person's attitude toward the behavior will be termed *behavioral beliefs*.

Subjective norms are also a function of beliefs, but beliefs of a different kind, namely, the person's beliefs that specific individuals or groups think he should or should not perform the behavior. If the person believes that most of these referents think he should perform the behavior, the perceived social pressure to perform it will increase the more he is motivated to comply with each of the referents. Conversely, if he believes that most referents are opposed to his performing the behavior, his perception of social pressure not to perform the behavior will increase with his motivation to comply. The beliefs underlying a person's subjective norms will be termed *normative beliefs*.

Figure 1 summarizes our discussion up to this point. The figure shows how behavior can be explained in terms of a limited number

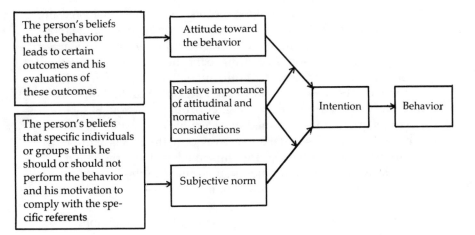

Note: Arrows indicate the direction of influence.

Figure 1. Factors Determining a Person's Behavior

of concepts. Through a series of intervening constructs it traces the causes of behavior back to the person's beliefs. Each successive step in this sequence from behavior to beliefs provides a more comprehensive account of the factors underlying the behavior—that is, each step represents a different level of explanation for a person's behavior. At the most global level, behavior is assumed to be determined by intention. At the next level, these intentions are themselves explained in terms of attitudes toward the behavior and subjective norms. The third level explains these attitudes and subjective norms in terms of beliefs about the consequences of performing the behavior and about the normative expectations of relevant referents. In the final analysis, then, a person's behavior is explained by reference to his or her beliefs. Since a person's beliefs represent the information (be it correct or incorrect) one has about one's world, it follows that a person's behavior is ultimately determined by this information.

Prediction versus Understanding

As we move from behavior to intention, from intention to attitude toward the behavior and subjective norm, and from these two components to the underlying beliefs, we can gain increasing understanding of the factors determining the behavior under consideration. However, this gain in understanding is not accompanied by improved prediction. According to the theory of reasoned action, intention is the immediate determinant of behavior and thus allows us to predict behavior. It follows that knowing the intention's determinants will not improve the accuracy of our prediction. Similarly, a person's intention is assumed to reflect his or her attitude toward the behavior and his or her subjective norm; the effects of these two components on behavior are thus mediated by the intention. Measuring the two components in addition to the intention provides for better understanding, but it cannot improve prediction of the behavior.

Similar considerations apply to the prediction of intentions. Measures of attitudes toward the behavior and of subjective norms provide all the information needed to predict the intention. Assessing the beliefs underlying these two components may help us understand the basis for the intention. However, since the effects of these beliefs are mediated by the attitudinal and normative components, they will make no independent contribution to the prediction of the intention.

Hypotheses Linking Beliefs to Behavior

Our argument that behavior is ultimately determined by beliefs should not be taken to mean that there is a direct link between beliefs and behavior. Beliefs influence attitudes and subjective norms; these two components influence intentions; and intentions influence behavior. Although we postulate relations between these variables, they are neither identical nor interchangeable. That is, from a theoretical point of view we expect certain relations to hold, but as I will show later, there are a variety of reasons why they may not obtain in practice.

The theory of reasoned action, then, consists essentially of a series of hypotheses linking beliefs to behavior, with each hypothesis requiring empirical verification. Clearly, if a measure of intention is found to be unrelated to the behavioral criterion, it would be foolish to try to understand the behavior by investigating the determinants of the intention. Similarly, only when a measure of attitude can first be shown to serve as a determinant of intention does it pay to investigate the beliefs that underlie the attitude. Finally, a given set of beliefs are of explanatory value only if they can, in fact, be shown to be related to the attitude or subjective norm that underlies the intention and ultimately the behavior under investigation.

This discussion should make it clear that it is inappropriate to use beliefs in an attempt to directly predict intentions or behavior. Similarly, it is inappropriate to go directly from attitudes and subjective norms to behavior.[1] Such attempts are meaningful only when the intervening relations have first been empirically demonstrated. In this paper I will illustrate some of these points and at the same time discuss some of the things we have been forced to consider in our attempts to apply the theory of reasoned action in various content areas. More specifically, I will discuss three general issues:

1. The relation between intentions and behavior,
2. The relations among behavioral beliefs, attitudes and intention, and
3. The role of external variables.

Within each of these broad topics, I will try to show how the theory of reasoned action has guided our research and has forced us to reconsider some basic psychological assumptions.

THE INTENTION—BEHAVIOR RELATIONSHIP

Can intentions be said to predict behavior when in many cases people express intentions yet fail to carry them out? Some of the intentions that come readily to mind are intentions to succeed on an exam, to lose weight, to diet, to exercise, to practice family planning, to have (or not have) a child in the next N years, to quit smoking or to quit drinking. Although it is true that many of these things cannot be predicted from intentions, it is equally true that many of these

1. For a more detailed discussion of this issue, see Fishbein & Ajzen (1976).

things are not behaviors. Succeeding on an exam, losing weight, and having a child are not behaviors but rather they are outcomes that may or may not result from the performance of one or more behaviors. Similarly, dieting, exercising, or practicing family planning are also not behaviors. In these cases we are dealing with behavioral categories that may be inferred from the observation of one or more behaviors. That is, you cannot directly observe somebody dieting or exercising or practicing family planning. What you can observe is whether or not the person engages in certain behaviors that you assume are valid indicants of these behavioral categories. It is perhaps worth noting that most of the "behaviors" that psychologists have been interested in are not directly observable behaviors at all, but are, in fact, behavioral categories. For example, aggression, altruism, and prejudice are all inferred from the observation of specific acts that one chooses to label as instances of these more general categories.

Behaviors versus Outcomes

People have sometimes failed to distinguish between behaviors and occurrences that may be the outcomes of those behaviors. Success on exams and weight reduction have often been used as behavioral criteria yet, as I indicated above, neither of these criteria is a measure of behavior. Success on exams is a possible outcome of such specific actions as attending lectures, reading books, memorizing materials, or even copying answers from another person's test paper. Similarly, losing weight may be the result of such actions as eating low calorie foods, skipping meals, or jogging two miles a day.

It should be obvious that many different actions may lead to the same outcome. More important, outcomes such as passing an exam or weight reduction may also be influenced by factors other than the person's own behavior. The exam's difficulty level or a clerical error may determine success or failure on the exam, and loss of weight may sometimes be due to physiological factors like metabolic rate or prolonged illness rather than to any particular actions performed by the individual. Clearly, in order to predict and understand outcomes, it will often be necessary to consider the effects of such nonbehavioral factors in addition to the person's actions per se.

Good examples of this problem can be found in industrial settings where management is concerned with understanding and predicting productivity and sales. Since we are dealing here with outcomes rather than behaviors it is necessary to consider factors other than the behaviors of employees (to predict productivity) or consumers (to predict sales). These other factors may include such things as technology, availability of resources, efficiency of subcontractors, effective distribution, and availability of the product.

The above discussion should make it clear that a person's intention to achieve a certain outcome (or reach a certain goal) need not be related to attainment of that outcome. Although the intention to achieve an outcome may energize and direct a person's actions, there is no guarantee that the actions selected are the most appropriate for attaining the outcome or, even if appropriate, that the outcome in question will follow directly from those actions.

Single Actions versus Behavioral Categories

People often treat inferences from behaviors as if they were themselves behaviors. For example, in discussing behaviors leading to success on an exam or weight reduction, investigators often refer to studying, cheating, dieting, and exercising instead of listing specific actions such as reading books or jogging. Unfortunately, as I indicated earlier, such general terms represent inferences from one or more specific behaviors. More important, these general terms describe a class or category of behaviors rather than any single action.

Behavior categories can refer to a relatively narrow range of behaviors such as raising funds for a political candidate, dieting, and exercising, or to a broader range, such as helping a candidate's campaign, maintaining one's health, and participating in recreational activities. Perhaps the broadest range of behaviors is considered when we are interested in all positive or negative behaviors with respect to some object or person.

As noted above, behavioral categories cannot be directly observed. Instead they are inferred from specific actions assumed to be instances of the general behavioral category. For example, dieting must be inferred from such behaviors as eating, drinking, or taking diet pills. Similarly, raising funds for a political candidate is inferred from such specific actions as making face-to-face requests for contributions, asking for contributions on the telephone, sponsoring a fundraising dinner, sending out invitations to a fundraising dinner, placing a political advertisement in a newspaper, etc.

Since a general behavioral category is comprised of many different specific actions, observation of a single act will rarely provide an adequate measure of the category in question. In fact, when measuring only one or two specific actions, it is probably more appropriate to refer to the specific acts than to a general behavioral category.

Not only are one or two specific actions too small a sample to represent the general category, but more often than one would like, the particular action or actions selected may not be valid indicants of the intended category. In fact, this problem is encountered irrespective of the number of specific actions under consideration. It is not clear, for example, whether drinking coffee without sugar is a valid indication of dieting—the behavioral category which it is assumed to represent. Many individuals drink their coffee without sugar simply because they like it that way, not because they are on a diet. Eating or not eating low calorie foods may appear to be a more adequate measure of "dieting." On closer examination, however, it becomes obvious that this action is also not sufficient evidence for the general class: A person who eats low calorie foods may also be found to snack between meals and drink large quantities of beer. Similarly, a person who does not eat low calorie foods may avoid snacks between meals and eat only two meals a day. Clearly, to obtain an adequate measure of a behavioral category such as dieting it is necessary to observe a *set* of specific actions and in some way combine these observations to arrive at a general measure.

Computation of a simple index can be illustrated with respect to dieting. Table 1 shows 10 specific actions that were selected as indicants of this behavioral category. The first step is to decide for each action whether a person who performs it is $(+1)$ or is not (-1) on a dietary program. These values appear in front of each action in Table 1. The respondent's performance $(+1)$ or nonperformance (-1) of each action is then recorded. Hypothetical performance data for two respondents are shown in Table 1. For example, it can be seen that Respondent A snacks between meals and does not drink coffee without sugar while Respondent B drinks coffee without sugar but does not snack between meals.

For each action, a score is computed by multiplying the action's value by the respondent's performance. The resulting score takes on a value of $+1$ whenever the respondent's behavior indicates that he or she is on a diet and a score of -1 when it indicates that he or she is not on a diet (see Table 1). For example, since Respondent A snacks

Table 1
Computations of an index for dieting behavior

Value	Specific Action	Respondent A Performance	Score	Respondent B Performance	Score
−1	Snack between meals	+1	−1	−1	+1
−1	Eat ice cream	+1	−1	−1	+1
+1	Drink coffee without sugar	−1	−1	+1	+1
+1	Drink low calorie beverages	−1	−1	−1	−1
+1	Eat only two meals a day	+1	+1	−1	−1
−1	Eat starchy food	+1	−1	−1	+1
−1	Have a dessert with dinner	+1	−1	−1	+1
−1	Drink beer	+1	−1	+1	−1
+1	Take diet pills	−1	−1	−1	−1
−1	Eat bread	−1	+1	−1	+1
	Dieting index:		−6		+2

between meals, the score for this action is a −1. In contrast, Respondent B does not snack between meals and therefore receives a score of +1 for this act. The general index of dieting is computed by summing the scores for the set of specific actions. It can be seen in Table 1 that Respondent A has a lower dieting index (−6) than Respondent B (+2). Clearly, the higher a person's score on the dieting index, the more dieting behavior that person displays.

These considerations suggest a difference between single actions and behavioral categories that is worth noting. Whereas it is reasonable to ask whether a person does or does not eat bread, it may not be very meaningful to ask this question with respect to being on a diet. As we have seen, people vary in terms of the degree to which they diet, and classifying an individual as being on a diet or not is an arbitrary decision. For example, it would be possible to decide that a person is on a diet if he or she performs at least one dieting behavior (i.e., if the person has any score other than −10). Alternatively the person could be classified as a "dieter" if his or her score is greater than zero, or if the score is at least +4. Because of this problem it is preferable to use the score provided by the index as a quantitative measure of the behavioral category.[2]

The above discussion points out why intentions to engage in behavioral categories cannot be expected to lead to accurate prediction. Not only may the term referring to the behavioral category mean different things to different people, but the way in which the investigator defines and measures his or her behavioral criterion will also influence the intention-behavioral category relationship. Thus, for example, although a person's intention to diet may be a good predictor of that person's self-report of whether or not he or she dieted, it may be unrelated to the particular index of dieting behavior constructed by the investigator.

This does not mean that behavioral categories cannot be predicted from intentions. The basic problem here is that what the respondent means by exercising or dieting, for example, may not correspond to what the investigator means by these terms. One simple of way of eliminating this ambiguity is to ask the respondent to indicate his or her intentions to engage in each of the behaviors that comprise the behavioral category. Then, in a manner similar to that used in constructing the behavioral index, these individual intentions can be used to construct an intentional index. This intentional index should permit good prediction of the behavioral index. In addition, each separate intention should serve to predict the corresponding behavior.

Intention-Behavior Correspondence

Indeed, as I have pointed out elsewhere (see Fishbein, 1973; Ajzen & Fishbein, 1977, 1980), whether one is discussing single actions or behavioral categories, one of the most crucial factors influencing

2. Note that among the set of specific actions comprising the index, there may be some that are really not very good indicants of the general behavioral category. For example, we mentioned earlier that drinking coffee without sugar may provide little information about dieting. Formal procedures adapted from standard attitude scaling methods (e.g., Likert, Thurstone, or Guttman scaling) can be used to eliminate such inappropriate observations. However, if you have selected a relatively large number of specific acts (perhaps 10 or more) that appear to be relevant for the general behavioral category, an index based on the total set of these behaviors will usually provide an adequate measure of the general action under consideration (see Fishbein & Ajzen, 1974).

the size of an obtained intention-behavior relationship is the degree of *correspondence* between the intentional measure and the behavioral criterion. Although they are often overlooked, it is important to realize that every behavioral criterion involves four elements: the *action* itself, the *target* toward which the action is directed, the *context* in which the action occurs, and the *time* at which the action occurs. Each of these elements may be very specific or very general. In other words, a behavioral criterion may be constructed at any level of generality. Correspondence refers to the degree to which the four elements defining the behavioral criterion are also used to define the behavioral intention.

As we saw above, behavioral categories refer to a class of behaviors rather than a single action. Thus, the corresponding intention must refer to the same class of behaviors. However, when the label used to describe the class means different things to different people, correspondence is obtained only by constructing an intentional index that parallels the behavioral criterion.

It is also possible to develop behavioral criteria that generalize across the target, context and time elements. What we often tend to forget is that a behavioral criterion is defined by the observational procedures used to measure it. For example, you may be interested in measuring whether or not people buy beer, and you may decide to observe this buying behavior in a local supermarket. The criterion you actually obtain is a measure of whether the person buys (action) beer (target) *in that supermarket* (context) during the (time) period in which you conducted your observations. It is not a measure of beer-buying behavior that is either context- or time-free.

This problem tends to arise because a single action is always performed with respect to a given target, in a given context, and at a given point in time. Although we often are interested in the performance of a given action with respect to a given target, we usually have little interest in a specific context or a specific point in time. For example, in considering whether a person drinks Falstaff, you may not care where or when he drinks it. It follows that in order to construct such a general criterion you will have to consider all contexts in which the behavior may reasonably occur and you will have to make your observations over a reasonable period of time.

The fact that an investigator's behavioral criterion does not always represent what he thinks he is measuring can perhaps best be illustrated by looking at laboratory research on racial discrimination. To obtain an appropriate measure of an individual's discriminatory behavior with respect to, say, blacks, we would have to observe the extent to which he performed different actions falling within the behavioral category of "discrimination," and these observations would have to be made with respect to a representative sample of black individuals, in a variety of contexts, and over a reasonable period of time.

In marked contrast, in the typical laboratory study, the investigator creates a situation where he can observe whether the subject performs a particular behavior with respect to one or two black individuals. The behavioral criterion is thus not discrimination toward blacks but rather the performance of a single action (e.g., administration of electrical shocks), with respect to a specific target (a particular black individual), in a given context (e.g., a "learning experiment"), within a limited time period.

It is time that we recognize the fact that most of our research has focused on one or two behaviors that, more often than not, are very inadequate measures of the behavioral categories they are supposed to represent. If we really want to study concepts such as discrimination, prejudice, aggression, altruism, or any other behavioral category, we will either have to directly observe our respondents performing or not performing a variety of behaviors with respect to different targets in various contexts during a reasonable time period or rely on self-reports. Since direct behavioral observation is often impossible and always time-consuming and costly, our options are rather limited. I personally feel that the insistence of many investigators on direct behavioral observation, at least with respect to concepts like aggression, prejudice, and altruism, has not only been inappropriate, but that it has actually impeded rather than advanced scientific knowledge.

To summarize briefly, then, I have argued that many of the more obvious "failures" of intentions to predict behavior are not really tests of the intention-behavior relationship but rather merely reflections of the fact that we have often failed to distinguish between single behaviors, behavioral categories, and outcomes. While specific actions should be predictable from corresponding intentions, there is no reason to assume that general intentions to engage in a behavioral category or to attain certain outcomes will be predictive of measures of performance in those categories or of achievement of the outcome in question. Many of these points are illustrated in a study conducted at the University of Massachusetts in Amherst (see Sejwacz, Ajzen, & Fishbein, in press).

Predicting weight loss. The study investigated loss of weight among 88 college women over a two-month time period. At the first session, the women completed a questionnaire assessing a variety of intentions and they were individually weighed by the experimenter. More specifically, the women were asked to indicate their intentions to: (1) lose weight during the next two months, (b) to adhere to a diet to lose weight during the next two months, (c) to engage in physical activity to lose weight during the next two months, and (d) to engage in each of several specific dieting behaviors and physical activities during the next two months. These latter measures were used to construct *indices* of intentions to diet and to engage in physical activity during the next two months.

At the end of the two-month period, the 88 women were again individually weighed by the experimenter and they were asked to indicate the extent to which they had performed each of the specific dieting behaviors and physical activities in the course of the preceding two months. Following procedures like those described earlier, these self-reports were used to derive an index of dieting and an index of physical activity during the two months in question.[3] Thus we had measures of the extent to which each respondent dieted and engaged in physical activity during a two-month period as well as a measure of the actual amount of weight she lost (or gained) in the course of that time period.

The relations among the various intentions, the intentional indices, the behavioral indices, and the weight-loss outcome are summarized in Figure 2. Note first that although dieting behavior was significantly related to actual weight loss ($r = .42$), engaging in physical activities had little, if any, influence on the amount of weight the women lost or gained ($r = .14$). More important, although general intentions to diet and to engage in physical activities were significantly related to dieting behavior ($= .40$) and to physical

3. In addition, 45 of the respondents were asked to complete the same behavior inventory on a weekly basis. Dieting and physical activity indices were computed for each week, and the final measures of behavior were obtained by averaging these weekly scores. These measures of behavior were highly related ($r = .88$) to the measures obtained at the end of the two-month period, suggesting that the retrospective behavioral reports reflected the behaviors performed during the preceding weeks accurately. Since the weekly schedules were completed by only part of the sample, the results below will be discussed in terms of the retrospective reports of behavior which are available for all respondents. Analysis of the weekly reports led to the same conclusions.

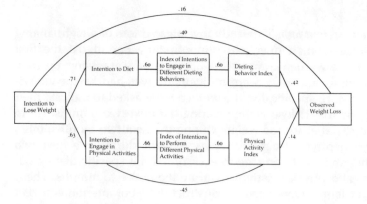

Figure 2. An analysis of intentions and behaviors influencing weight loss.

activities (*r* = .45), both of these correlations were significantly lower than those between the intentional indices and the behavioral indices (*r* = .60 for both dieting and physical activity). Moreover, although the intention to lose weight is strongly related to the general intention to diet (*r* = .71) and to the general intention to engage in physical activities (*r* = .63), it is not related to actual weight loss (*r* = .16).

Finally, although not indicated in the figure, only the specific behavioral intentions were systematically related to the performance or nonperformance of each of the behaviors comprising the behavioral indices. Thus, despite the fact that there appears to be a directive influence of intentions to achieve outcomes on performance, such intentions cannot be expected to predict the outcome itself or the particular behaviors one performs in the attempt to attain that outcome. Similarly, although the general intention to perform a class of behaviors may influence the number of different behaviors one intends to, and actually does, perform, these general intentions cannot be expected to systematically or consistently predict performance or nonperformance of a particular behavior that is an instance of the behavioral category in question. As I indicated earlier, one can only expect accurate prediction when the intentional measure corresponds directly to the behavioral criterion.

Predicting smoking and nonsmoking behaviors. What about drinking or smoking? These are, in fact, behaviors, and we all know people who have intended to quit smoking but have been unable to do so. Isn't this a "true" example of the failure of intentions to predict behavior? In point of fact, it turns out that intentions are highly accurate predictors of smoking behavior. In retrospect, this finding is not as surprising as it may first appear. Suppose you randomly selected 100 people and asked them if they intended to smoke. Approximately 70% of these people will be nonsmokers and almost all of them will have nonsmoking intentions. Similarly, a substantial majority of the smokers will say they intend to smoke. As you can imagine, if you observe these respondent's behavior one week, one month, two months, or even six or more months later, you will find that very few (if any) of the nonsmokers have become smokers and that most smokers have continued to smoke. Overall, then, you would find a very strong relationship between smoking intentions and smoking behaviors.

However, this does not really answer the question of the relationship between quitting intentions and quitting behavior. Before attempting to answer this question there is something I should point out. If you ask cigarette smokers if they intend to quit, over 60% will answer in the affirmative. However, if you ask these same smokers whether they intend to quit *in the next week*, less than 5% will answer "Yes." Clearly then, correspondence in the time element of the intentional measure and the behavioral observation is a crucial factor in assessing the relationship between smoking intentions and actual smoking behavior.

In order to investigate the relationship between intentions to quit and actual quitting, 25 young women smokers were asked to indicate their intentions to quit smoking *in the next two months* on the following scale:

I intend to quit smoking cigarettes in the next two months
likely   :   :   :   :   :   :   unlikely

Sixteen women reported that they intended to quit, six said they did not intend to quit, and the remaining three were uncertain. Two months later, the women were recontacted and asked to report their current smoking status. Table 2 shows the obtained relation between the women's intentions and their self-reports of behavior.

It can be seen that there was no relationship between quitting intentions and behavior; in fact, predictive accuracy was slightly less than the 50% expected by chance alone. While such a result may appear discouraging, it was not unexpected. What we often forget is that the performance of any behavior reflects a *decision* on the part of the individual. The term decision implies a choice among two or more alternatives. It must be realized that quitting is not the only behavioral alternative available to smokers. In fact, as I have pointed out elsewhere (see Fishbein, Note 1) current smokers have at least four alternatives available to them: (1) they can continue smoking at the same rate; (2) they can increase their smoking; (3) they can decrease their smoking; or (4) they can quit smoking. According to almost all decision theories, all of a person's alternatives must be considered if one wishes to predict that person's ultimate choice. To put this in the context of intentions, we would expect the person to choose that alternative toward which he or she has the strongest intention.

In order to test this notion, the 25 young women smokers were also asked to indicate, on seven-place *likely-unlikely* scales, their intentions to: (a) continue smoking at the same rate during the next two months; (b) increase their smoking during the next two months; and (c) decrease their smoking during the next two months. Not surprisingly, none of the women intended to increase their smoking, but many expressed intentions to continue smoking at the same rate or to decrease.

Let us now reconsider the 16 smokers who said they intended to quit (i.e., who checked the "likely" side of the quitting intention scale). As can be seen in Table 3, only two of these women had stronger intentions to quit than to either continue smoking at the

Table 2

Prediction of quitting (N = 25)

Intention to Quit in Next 2 Months	Behavior	
	Continue Smoking	Quit
Y	10	6
?	2	1
N	4	2
	16	9

Table 3
Analysis of those intending to quit (N = 16)

	Behavior	
	Continue Smoking	Quit
$I_Q > I_C$ or I_D	0	2
$I_Q = I_C$ or I_D	5	4
$I_Q < I_C$ or I_D	5	0
	10	6

same rate or to decrease their smoking, and both of these women did in fact quit. In contrast, five of the women had stronger intentions to decrease or to continue at the same rate than to quit, and all five of these women continued smoking. The remaining nine women reported equally strong intentions to quit *and* to continue at the same rate or to decrease; five of these women continued smoking and four quit.

Thus, although a person's intention to perform a given behavior is the best *single* predictor of whether or not the person will perform the behavior in question, it will often be necessary to consider a person's intentions with respect to all of his or her available alternatives in order to accurately predict the person's actual behavioral choice.

Generally speaking, when a person is confronted with two mutually exclusive and exhaustive alternatives, knowledge of one of the two intentions will usually be sufficient for predicting the person's choice. Thus, for example, if smokers are asked their intentions to *both* smoke and not smoke, either of these intentions provide quite accurate predictions of their smoking behavior. In keeping with the notion of *choice*, however, the difference between the two intentions results in a slightly more accurate prediction of the person's actual smoking or nonsmoking behavior.

Moreover, when more than two alternatives are available or when the individual does not view the alternatives presented as being mutually exclusive and exhaustive, knowledge of any one intention will not provide highly accurate behavioral prediction. The latter is clearly the case with smokers who do not view quitting and decreasing as mutually exclusive alternatives. Even more important, non-smokers apparently do not view continuing not to smoke and trying a cigarette as mutually exclusive. Although this has important implications for smoking prevention programs, a discussion of these implications is beyond the scope of the present paper. (See, however, Fishbein, Note 1).

To summarize briefly, then: intentions do predict behaviors, but it is important to distinguish between behaviors, behavioral categories, and outcomes. Additionally, it should be recognized that every behavior represents a decision, and accurate behavioral prediction will often require a consideration of the person's intentions with respect to all the behavioral alternatives that the person perceives as available. While I am convinced that there are some behaviors that cannot be predicted from intentions, I can honestly report that I have not yet been able to find them.

BELIEFS, ATTITUDES AND INTENTIONS

The second problem I would like to discuss concerns the relations among behavioral beliefs, attitudes, and intentions. According to the theory of reasoned action, knowledge of behavioral beliefs and outcome evaluations in addition to attitudes should increase understanding but not prediction of intention. Unfortunately, as I indicated earlier, there have been enough empirical findings contrary to this hypothesis that I feel it is worth commenting on. While it is true that such findings could indicate that the theory is wrong, we have discovered that findings of this type have actually served to increase our confidence in the theory.

First, recall that, theoretically, attitudes are viewed as a function of beliefs. Thus, if were were able to tap and accurately measure all of a person's salient behavioral beliefs and outcome evaluations, the indirect measure of attitude based on these beliefs and outcome evaluations (Σbe) should be perfectly correlated with a direct valid measure of attitude (Ao). Thus, the direct (Ao) and indirect measures (Σbe) would be interchangeable. Since there is always some error of measurement, it is conceivable that, on at least some occasions, the indirect measure could be more reliable and valid than a direct measure of the same attitude.

In fact, if one assumes that the theory is "true," then a finding that Σbe is more highly correlated with intention than Ao can only mean that (a) the two measures are interchangeable or (b) that there is something wrong with the direct measure. If neither of these hypotheses were correct, we would have to conclude that the theory was wrong.

Many of the "contradictory" findings have turned out to be nothing more than a case of two equally valid and thus interchangeable attitude measures. The more interesting cases, however, are those where the direct and indirect measures are only moderately correlated, but where the indirect measure provides better behavioral prediction than the direct measure. Analyses of these findings have indicated that in almost every case, the problem is one of correspondence. More specifically, what we have found is that the indirect measure corresponds exactly to the behavioral intention, while the direct measure does not. For example, in market research one is often concerned with predicting a person's intention to buy a given product. What has frequently happened is that the investigator has measured beliefs about *buying that product*, but the direct measure of attitude is toward the product *per se*. Thus, while the indirect measure corresponds exactly to the intention, the direct measure does not correspond in the *action* component. Often, the problem is somewhat more subtle in that the lack of correspondence is with respect to context or time. For example, one may be interested in predicting a person's intention to buy a given brand in *the next week* and may measure beliefs about buying that brand in the next week. In this case, lack of correspondence would occur if one measured attitude toward "buying the brand" in general. Thus, by assuming that the theory is correct, we have often been able to discover that the direct measure of attitude has involved an inappropriate "object" (i.e., an object that does not correspond exactly to the intention in question).

Perhaps the most interesting case is when beliefs, attitude, and intention all correspond perfectly. According to the theory of reasoned action, if the indirect measure is not highly correlated with the direct measure but is a better predictor of intention than the direct measure, the latter measure must be less valid than the former. Since this, as well as several other points, are well illustrated in a study of smoking we recently conducted (Fishbein, Loken, Roberts, & Chung, Note 2), let me describe the study in some detail.

Before doing this, however, I think it would be helpful to put the smoking problem into some perspective.

To date there have been well over 10,000 studies attempting to identify the psychological and sociological factors that underlie a person's smoking decision. A review of this literature (Fishbein, Note 1) made it abundantly clear that, at the present time, there is relatively little that is actually known about the basis for (or the determinants of) a given smoking decision. Despite the enormous amount of research on smoking that has been conducted, all we now know is that there are a virtual plethora of factors that have been found to be related to various smoking behaviors at one time or another. Unfortunately theorists and researchers in the smoking area have been unable to develop an empirically supported, systematic theory of smoking that can account for people's decisions to start, continue, or stop smoking. There is, however a general consensus that:

A. Different factors underlie different smoking decisions, i.e., the factors underlying the initiation of smoking are different from those underlying the maintenance or continuance of smoking, which in turn are different from those underlying the cessation of smoking.

B. There are a large number of factors underlying any given smoking decision.

C. With respect to any given behavior (e.g., continuing to smoke), the factors influencing one person's decision to continue may be very different from the factors that influence this same decision in another person.

As the Advisory Committee to the Surgeon General put it, "there is no single cause or explanation of smoking . . . . Smokers may start, continue, and discontinue smoking in response to different inner needs and external influences, social and other." (*Smoking and Health*, 1964, p. 376). Perhaps as a result of this conclusion, it has often been argued that because of "the diversity of needs which impel different persons to smoke . . . no general rule concerning efforts to persuade people not to smoke, or to give up smoking, will be valid or effective . . . . No single approach will be satisfactory for more than a minority of individuals . . . ." (Larson & Silvette, 1968, p. 304).

Despite this pessimistic outlook, it seemed to me that the theory of reasoned action was directly applicable to cigarette smoking. According to the theory, different factors (e.g., different beliefs) *should* underlie different smoking decisions, and two people making the same smoking decision could have arrived at this decision on the basis of very different sets of beliefs. Even more important, as we saw above, a person's smoking or nonsmoking behavior could be predicted from his or her intentions, and there was no reason to believe that these intentions were different from any other intentions.

Personal versus General Measures

However, in reviewing the smoking literature I became aware of an important distinction that has frequently been overlooked—namely, a distinction between general and personal beliefs. Consider, for example, the following two statements: (1) Smoking is harmful to health, and (2) My smoking is (would be) harmful to my health. It seems reasonable to assume that although nonsmokers would be equally likely to agree with both of these statements, smokers would be significantly more likely to agree with the former than with the latter. Yet almost all research in the smoking area (as well as in most other areas I have been able to check) have utilized questionnaires written in a general rather than a personalized format. And this is true not only of beliefs, but of attitudes as well. For example, attitudes have not been measured toward "My smoking" but toward "Smoking" in general. Let me again emphasize that this is not just true of research on smoking. To the best of my knowledge almost all surveys and public opinion polls assess general rather than personal beliefs and attitudes. It is important to note that this distinction is theoretical as well as methodological. According to the theory of reasoned action, it is a person's beliefs about, and attitude toward, his or her *own performance* of the behavior that are directly relevant to the formation of intentions. Although a person may believe that "smoking is harmful to health," this should have little or no influence on the person's smoking decision if he or she also believes that "*My* smoking is *not* harmful to *my* health."

In order to test these notions, as well as to explore the importance of considering beliefs and attitudes with respect to all behavioral alternatives rather than any given alternative, 192 young college women were asked to complete a rather lengthy questionnaire. Among other things, the women indicated their intentions to smoke (I_S) and to not smoke (I_{NS}); their attitudes toward "smoking" (A_{S_G}),

Table 4

Prediction of differential intention ($I_S - I_{NS}$) from attitude

	Personal	General
A_S	.371	.438
A_{NS}	−.464	−.303
$A_S - A_{NS}$	.469	.400

"not smoking" (A_{NS_G}), "My smoking" (A_{S_p}) and "My not smoking" (A_{NS_p}); and their beliefs that "smoking," "not smoking," "my smoking" and "my not smoking" would lead to each of 16 outcomes (e.g., "keep weight down," "relieve tension," "breathing problems"). In addition, the women evaluated each of the 16 outcomes.[4] All the above measures were obtained on single seven-place bipolar scales; *likely-unlikely* was used to measure beliefs and intentions, and *good-bad* was used as the measure of attitudes and outcome evaluations.

Since, as indicated above, the difference in intentions was found to be the best predictor of the women's actual smoking (or not smoking) behavior, we first attempted to predict the differential intention score ($I_s - I_{NS}$) from the direct measures of attitude obtained at both the personal and general level. In Table 4 it can be seen that we obtained some negtive evidence for both of our hypotheses. First, the attitude toward "smoking" was a somewhat better predictor of the differential intention than was the attitude toward "My smoking," and second, the general attitude toward smoking was a somewhat better predictor than was the difference between the general attitudes toward "smoking" and "not smoking" ($A_S - A_{NS}$). Although the remaining data in Table 4 are consistent with expectations, the overall pattern of results was rather discouraging.

Note, too, that although all the correlations in Table 4 are significant, they are only of moderate magnitude. While this is not necessarily problematic (recall that intentions may also be determined by subjective norms), the consideration of subjective norms in addition

4. The 16 outcomes were identified in an independent elicitation study. They represent the 16 most frequent responses to questions concerning the advantages and disadvantages of one's own smoking and not smoking. The importance of such elicitations will be discussed below.

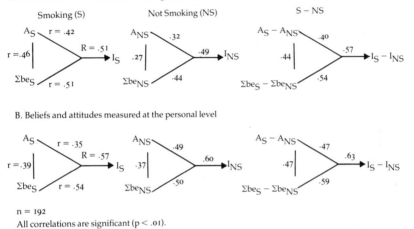

Figure 3. Relations among beliefs, attitudes, and intentions

to the direct attitude measures did not improve prediction. But the worst (or the best) was yet to come. Figure 3 shows the obtained zero-order and multiple correlations among beliefs, attitudes, and intentions. It can be seen that irrespective of whether beliefs and attitudes were measured at the personal or general level, and irrespective of whether the criterion was the intention to smoke (I_S), the intention to not smoke (I_{NS}), or the differential intention ($I_S - I_{NS}$), the data consistently produced only low to moderate correlations between direct (A_B) and indirect (Σbe) measures. More important, the indirect measure was always more highly correlated with the intentions than was the direct measure. Moreover, consideration of both measures significantly improved prediction (above the highest zero-order correlation) in almost every case. Although these latter findings are clearly contrary to my theory, they nevertheless gave us some encouragement.

Attitudes, Affect, and Evaluation

Before discussing this in more detail, I should note that the findings in Figure 3 are entirely consistent with Triandis's model for the prediction of intentions (see his paper in this volume). That is, according to Triandis, both affect and the value of perceived consequences contribute to intentions. More specifically, while both he and I agree that beliefs about performing a behavior determine the person's *evaluation* of the behavior, he has argued that this cognitively based evaluation (i.e., Σbe) differs from a person's *affective* response to the behavior. That is, he essentially distinguishes between evaluation and affect, and he views affect as a noncognitive, classically conditioned emotional response. In the context of the present experiment, then, one could view the direct measure as assessing affect (A) and the indirect measure as assessing evaluation (Σbe). Viewed in this light, the data in Figure 3 could be interpreted as indicating that smoking (or nonsmoking) intentions are influenced more heavily by "evaluative" than "affective" considerations.

In contrast to Triandis's position, however, I do not feel that a distinction between affect and evaluation is warranted or useful. First, it seems to me that the decision to call a given measure evaluation or affect is purely arbitrary. Second, it is usually impossible to distinguish empirically between these two concepts.[5] Third, and perhaps most important, I simply do not believe that there are noncognitive attitudinal responses (be they called attitude, affect, or evaluation). Thus, as I stated above, I view what Triandis calls the cognitive component of attitude (i.e., Σbe) as the basis for what he considers to be the affective component.

While this position may seem somewhat strange given the data in Figure 3, it should be recalled that from my point of view, the data can be interpreted in two ways: either the theory of reasoned action is wrong *or* the direct measure of attitude is *less* valid than the indirect measure. Let us thus consider the direct measure in more detail. Recall that attitude was measured on a single, seven-place "good-bad" scale. Although in retrospect I can see how foolish this was, at the time we designed the study it seemed quite reasonable.

5. Indeed, when direct and indirect measures are found to be highly correlated, it could either be argued that affect and evaluation are highly correlated in this situation *or* that the direct measure was actually tapping evaluation and not affect. Because of this methodological problem, Triandis has been attempting to develop a "pure" measure of affect.

In all of our previous research we had found that a valid measure of attitude could be obtained by using a semantic differential comprised of a set of empirically determined evaluative scales. Even more important, we found that the evaluative dimension was always marked by a "good-bad" scale, and that use of the single "good-bad" scale did as well as, if not better than, the full, multi-item semantic differential. Thus I slipped into the habit of using a single "good-bad" scale as my measure of attitude, particularly when respondents were asked to make a large number of other judgments. The above findings, however, suggested that "good-bad" was not an appropriate measure of evaluation in this content domain. To put this somewhat differently, the above findings suggested that despite all our previous evidence for the validity of using a single good-bad scale, we were encountering what Osgood, Suci, and Tannenbaum (1957) have called a concept-scale interaction such that, at least with respect to smoking concepts, "good-bad" was tapping something other than evaluation.

In order to test this notion, a new sample of 62 young women were asked to rate "My smoking cigarettes" on a 12-item semantic differential (see Chung & Fishbein, Note 3). Table 35 presents the Varimax rotated factor structure. Note first that "good-bad" did not

Table 5
Ratings of "My smoking cigarettes" Orthogonal Factors (78.6% of Variance)

	I	II	III
Enjoyable	.92	.19	−.13
Satisfying	.91	.22	−.12
Pleasant	.85	.24	−.34
Healthy	.16	.91	−.22
Beneficial	.16	.84	−.23
Good	.33	.75	−.24
Wise	.26	.71	−.31
Right	.07	.27	−.88
Clean	.33	.35	−.68
Sophisticated	.54	−.23	−.64
Attractive	.49	.36	−.57
Nice	.64	.34	−.43
% Variance	38.9%	34.0%	27.1%

load on the first factor. Indeed, in contrast to being evaluative or attitudinal (i.e., enjoyable, satisfying, pleasant), "good-bad" appears to be denoting a health dimension (healthy, beneficial, wise).

At this point, a short digression is necessary. Clearly, the labeling of factors is arbitrary, and different investigators may interpret the same results in different ways. Some—including Triandis—would call the first dimension "affect" and the second "evaluation." Fortunately, however, these two sets of labels have very different and testable theoretical implications.

Consider first the relations among the two factors and the young women's intentions to smoke cigarettes. If you adopt Triandis's position and view the first factor as affect and the second as evaluation, all relations among these variables are equally acceptable. That is, from Triandis's point of view either affect, evaluation, or both may contribute to intentions. Moreover, although consideration of both Factor I and Factor II should lead to better prediction than consideration of either factor in isolation, the Triandis model does not require that an increment in predictability be obtained.

If you adopt my position and view the first dimension as a measure of attitude (toward "My smoking") and the second dimension as a measure of a health belief (e.g., "My smoking cigarettes is bad for my health"), you would predict that Factor I would be more highly correlated with the intention to smoke than would Factor II. Moreover, since health beliefs should already be incorporated into one's attitude toward his or her own smoking, considering both factors should not improve prediction above that obtained on the basis of Factor I alone.

In order to test these notions, two scores were computed for each respondent by summing over the three scales with the highest loadings on each factor. Consistent with the theory of reasoned action, the score based on Factor I (i.e., attitude) had a significantly higher correlation with the intention to smoke ($r = .80$) than did the score based on Factor II (i.e., the Health belief, $r = .48$). In addition, regressing the intention on both Factor I and Factor II scores did not improve prediction ($R = .80$). Indeed, only the standardized regression weight of the attitude score was significant ($\beta = .74$ and $.12$ for Factor I and Factor II respectively).

Although the above findings support my view, they do not provide conclusive evidence since they are also consistent with Triandis's position. A direct test of the two approaches is possible, however, when one considers the relations among the two factors and an indirect measure of the attitude toward "My smoking cigarettes." According to the theory of reasoned action, attitudes are a function of behavioral beliefs and outcome evaluations. Thus, an indirect measure of attitude based on these underlying cognitions (i.e., Σbe) should be highly correlated with a direct measure of that attitude (.e., Factor I). Although the theory makes no prediction about the size of a correlation between a belief dimension (Factor II) and an attitude estimate that incorporates beliefs representing the dimension, the theory would predict that Σbe will be more highly correlated with a valid direct measure of the corresponding attitude than with a measure referring to a health belief. From the point of view of Triandis's model, however, exactly the opposite would be predicted. That is, since affect is viewed as a noncognitive classically conditioned emotional response, viewing Factor I as affect implies it should essentially be unrelated to the value of perceived consequences (i.e., Σbe). However, this cognitively based measure should be strongly related to a direct measure of evaluation (i.e., Factor II).

In order to test this hypothesis, the 62 women filled out part of the same questionnaire that was used in the initial study. More specifically, since we measured only the women's attitudes toward "My smoking cigarettes," only personalized beliefs and outcome evaluations with respect to this concept were obtained. The responses to these items were then used to compute indirect estimates of attitude toward "My smoking cigarettes" (Σbe), and this indirect estimate of attitude was correlated with the two factor scores described above. Consistent with the theory of reasoned action and with the notion that Factor I should be viewed as evaluative or attitudinal, Σbe was more highly correlated with the score based on Factor I ($r = .58$) than with the score based on Factor II ($r = .48$). Although the difference between these correlations is not significant, the findings make it clear that irrespective of the label it is given (i.e., attitude, affect or evaluation), Factor I *cannot* be viewed as being unrelated to an underlying cognitive structure.

Taken as a whole, I hope the above analyses have demonstrated that the Factors in Table 5 can most appropriately be labeled as attitude and Health (rather than as affect and evaluation). Given this interpretation, it can now be seen that, at least in the context of smoking, "good-bad" does not serve as a valid measure of attitude. Thus, rather than questioning the theory of reasoned action, the results displayed in Figure 3 merely indicate the invalidity of the attitude measure that was used. In fact, as can be seen in Figure 4, when a valid, empirically determined instrument is used to assess attitude directly, the relations among beliefs, attitudes, and intentions are entirely consistent with the theory of reasoned action. That is, Figure 4 shows that, in contrast to our previous findings (see the data set in the lower left hand panel of Figure 3 for a direct comparison), we now obtain a strong correlation ($r = .80$) between the direct measure of attitude toward "My smoking cigarettes" and the young women's intentions to smoke cigarettes. In addition, we now find a relatively strong relationship ($r = .58$) between the direct and indirect measures of attitude, and—consistent with theoretical expectations—consideration of the indirect measure (i.e., Σbe) in addition to the direct measure does *not* improve prediction ($R = .81$). Indeed, only the direct measure receives a significant weight in the regression equation ($\beta = .73$ and $.13$ for the direct and indirect measures respectively).

To summarize briefly, I have tried to show that when appropriate measures are used, the theoretical relations among beliefs, attitudes, and intentions that are specified by the theory of reasoned action are consistently supported. At least to date, empirical results that appear contrary to the theory have not disproved the theory, but instead they have served to increase our confidence in the theory by allowing us to identify inappropriate or invalid measures of attitude.

Figure 4. Relations among young women's beliefs about "My smoking cigarettes," their attitudes toward "My smoking cigarettes" and their intentions to smoke cigarettes

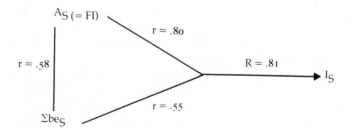

A_S (= FI)

$r = .80$

$r = .58$

$R = .81$

I_S

$r = .55$

Σbe_S

$n = 62$

Before concluding this section, I would like to say a bit more about the distinction between measurements at the personal and general levels, as well as about the utility of considering beliefs and attitudes with respect to more than a single alternative. Recall that in our initial tests of these notions, the findings were essentially negative (see Table 4). In light of our above discussion, however, we can see that the measure of attitude used in the analyses was not valid. But there is no reason to assume that this was also true of the indirect measure. Looking at Figure 4 and the lower left hand panel of Figure 3, it can be seen that the correlations between the indirect measures and intentions were virtually identical in the two studies ($r = .54$ and .55 in Studies 1 and 2 respectively). This finding, in conjunction with the finding that the indirect measure did permit relatively accurate prediction of the valid direct attitude measure used in Study 2 ($r = .58$), provides some support for the validity of the indirect measure. Thus we retested the hypotheses using the indirect measures (Σbe).

In Table 6 it can be seen that the estimates of attitude based on personalized beliefs consistently yielded better prediction of the differential intentions than did identical estimates based on general beliefs. In addition, better prediction was obtained by considering beliefs about *both* smoking *and* not smoking than by considering beliefs about either of the alternatives in isolation. As expected, the estimate of the differential attitude ($\Sigma be_S - \Sigma be_{NS}$) based on personal beliefs led to significantly better prediction of the differential intention ($r = .586$) than did the estimates based on general beliefs about either smoking ($r = .518$) *or* not smoking ($r = -.445$). Although some of the comparisons in Table 6 do not reach statistical significance, the overall pattern of results provide support for both hypotheses.

Table 6
Prediction of differential intention ($I_S - I_{NS}$) from attitude estimates (Σbe)

	Personal	General
Σbe_S	.553	.518
Σbe_{NS}	−.501	−.445
$\Sigma be_S - \Sigma be_{NS}$	.586	.539

Even stronger support for these hypotheses is obtained if one considers individual beliefs. Although a complete discussion of these findings is beyond the scope of the present paper (they will be reported in Fishbein, Loken, Roberts, and Chung, Note 2), a few general points can be made. First, with respect to many beliefs about smoking and about nonsmoking, we found highly significant interactions between smoking status (i.e., smokers vs. nonsmokers) and level of measurement (i.e., personal vs. general). For example, while nonsmokers are as likely to believe that their own smoking would lead to their having breathing problems as they are to believe that smoking (in general) leads to breathing problems, smokers are significantly less likely to believe the former (personalized belief) than the latter. Similarly, while smokers believe that *their own* not smoking will cause them to gain weight to the same extent they believe that not smoking (in general) leads to weight gain, nonsmokers are significantly more certain that their own not smoking will *not* affect their weight than they are that not smoking (in general) will not lead to weight gain. As the above examples illustrate, the exact nature of the interaction depends, in part, upon whether the belief is about smoking or not smoking *and* upon whether the outcome being considered is positive or negative. Generally speaking, smokers are less likely to personalize information linking smoking to negative consequences and not smoking to positive consequences, while nonsmokers are less likely to personalize information about the benefits of smoking or the disadvantages of not smoking. However, if one considers any given consequence (e.g., relieves tension), all the above generalizations may not hold. That is, the smoking status by level of measurement interaction may occur with respect to both the belief about smoking and the belief about not smoking, or with respect to only one or to neither of these two beliefs.[6] Thus, only by considering beliefs about *both* smoking *and* not smoking (i.e., by considering the difference between these two beliefs) can one be assured of identifying important differences between smokers and nonsmokers.

The above findings point out that in order to predict and fully understand behavior in some content domains, it will be necessary to (a) consider a person's beliefs, attitudes, and intentions with

6. The four-way interaction between smoking status (smoker vs. nonsmoker), level of measurement (personal vs. general), type of belief (smoking vs. not smoking), and outcome evaluation (positive vs. negative) was significant.

Figure 5. Prediction of differential intentions from estimated attitudes and subjective norms

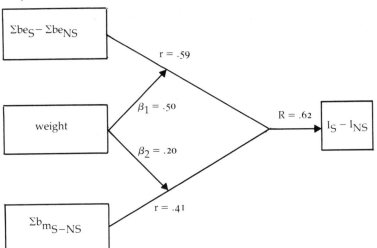

respect to all the person's available alternatives[7] and (b) assess beliefs and attitudes at a personal rather than a general level. When such considerations are taken into account, one can accurately predict and explain young women's smoking (or not smoking) behaviors.

Factors underlying smoking behavior. As we saw earlier, whether or not women will smoke can be very accurately predicted from the differences in the women's intentions to smoke and not smoke cigarettes. Moreover, as can be seen in Figure 5, these differential intentions can, in turn, be predicted with considerable accuracy ($R = .62$) from a consideration of the women's behavioral beliefs, outcome evaluations, normative beliefs, and motivations to comply.[8] Note, however, that at least for this sample of young women,

---

7. One can often reduce the size of the available set by providing the respondent with a pair of mutually exclusive and exhaustive alternatives.

8. Theoretically, the intention is a function of attitudes and subjective norms. However, since it was shown that Σbe was a valid estimate of attitude, and since we also found that Σbm was a valid estimate of subjective norms (i.e., the correlation between Σbm and SN was .57, df = 190, $p < .001$), we are able to use these estimates in the prediction equation. It must be noted, however, that even given valid indirect measures, this level of analysis will often reduce predictability. Fortunately this is more than compensated for by an increase in understanding.

Table 7

Average differential behavioral beliefs, outcome evaluations, and products for women who intend and do not intend to smoke (N = 186)

| Outcomes | $b_S - b_{NS}$ | | |
	I_S (36)	I_{NS} (150)	
Harmful to health	4.53	5.37	**
Increase cancer	4.33	5.34	**
Breathing problems	3.89	4.90	**
Offensive to others	2.81	4.65	**
Bad breath	3.44	5.09	**
Bad odor on clothes	3.67	5.26	**
Increase dependency	4.78	4.93	
Expensive	4.17	5.05	**
Relieves tension	2.75	−.48	**
Relaxing	2.94	−1.40	**
Helps concentrate	.44	−2.29	**
Helps interact	1.28	−1.65	**
Acceptance by peers	−.39	−2.03	**
Something to do with hands	3.75	1.35	**
Keep weight down	1.00	−3.37	**
Pleasant taste experience	.14	−4.76	**

** = difference between I_S and I_{NS} significant at .01 level.

the differential smoking intention is more strongly influenced by attitudinal ($\beta = .50$) than by normative ($\beta = .20$) considerations.

Thus, in attempting to explain why some women intend to smoke ($I_S > I_{ns}$) while others do not ($I_{ns} > I_s$), we should first consider their personal beliefs about smoking and not smoking as well as their evaluations of the outcomes they associate with engaging in these two behaviors. Table 7 shows the mean differential beliefs ($b_s - b_{ns}$), outcome evaluations (e), and the differential belief-evaluation products ($be_s - be_{ns}$) for women with intentions to smoke ($I_s > I_{NS}$) and to not smoke ($I_{NS} > I_s$) cigarettes.

Perhaps the first thing to note in Table 7 are the beliefs themselves. According to the theory of reasoned action, attitudes are a

e_i			$be_S - be_{NS}$		
I_S	I_{NS}		I_S	I_{NS}	
−2.17	−2.71	**	−9.44	−14.62	**
−1.94	−2.75	**	−10.38	−14.97	**
−2.33	−2.75	**	−9.06	−13.52	**
−2.14	−2.65	**	−6.11	−12.52	**
−2.50	−2.51		−8.44	−12.82	**
−1.83	−2.52	**	−6.72	−13.39	**
−2.08	−2.88	**	−10.00	−14.31	**
−.86	−.79		−3.53	−4.09	
2.31	2.47		6.39	−1.17	**
2.56	2.51		7.92	−3.55	**
2.31	2.21		1.42	−5.41	**
2.08	2.12		3.47	−3.51	**
1.67	1.57		−.56	−3.22	**
.58	.65		2.86	1.63	
2.72	2.50		2.75	−8.45	**
2.13	2.03		.44	−9.41	**

function of salient beliefs, and thus one cannot simply sit down and construct a list of beliefs. Instead, it is necessary to first identify those beliefs that are most salient for (i.e., occur with the greatest frequency in) the population under consideration. Thus, prior to conducting the study, an independent sample of young women were asked to tell us what they believed were (or would be) the advantages and disadvantages of their own smoking and not smoking. Table 7 shows only those beliefs that were elicited most frequently in response to these questions.[9]

9. The beliefs are not ordered in terms of frequency in Table 7. Rather, they have been grouped to illustrate various positive and negative outcomes.

What is perhaps most striking is the small number of beliefs that refer to the health consequences of smoking or not smoking. Although many health outcomes may be incorporated within the belief that "My smoking is harmful to my health," it was still surprising to find little or no mention of such things as coronary heart disease, life expectancy, or premature or stillborn births. Equally surprising were the relatively large number of beliefs referring directly or indirectly to interpersonal relations (e.g., offensive to others, bad breath, helps me interact, gives me something to do with my hands). Indeed, even without further analysis, these findings make it clear that young women's smoking decisions are not based primarily on health considerations. Let us consider these beliefs and outcome evaluations in somewhat more detail.

Turning first to the evaluations, it can be seen that both intenders and nonintenders were in general agreement about which outcomes were good (+) and which were bad (−). With respect to six of the eight negative outcomes, however, intenders were significantly *less* negative than nonintenders. Thus, for example, although intenders felt that "being harmful to health" and "being offensive to others" were "bad," they did not view these outcomes as negatively as did the nonintenders. In marked contrast, there were no significant differences between intenders and nonintenders with respect to any of the positive outcomes (e.g., tension relief, acceptance by peers, and having a pleasant taste experience).

The major differences between intenders and nonintenders occur with respect to differential beliefs. Recall that all beliefs were scored from +3 (likely) to −3 (unlikely). The difference scores can thus range from +6 to −6, with positive scores indicating that the women believed that the outcome was more likely to be a result of their smoking than of their not smoking and negative scores indicating the opposite. Ignoring for a moment the magnitude of the difference scores, it can be seen that although all the young women believed that smoking was more likely to lead to each of the eight negative consequences than was not smoking, they differed markedly in their differential beliefs about the positive consequences. More specifically, while intenders believed that their smoking would be more likely to lead to seven of the eight positive outcomes than their not smoking, nonintenders believed they would be more likely to attain seven of the eight positive outcomes by not smoking.

When the magnitude of the differential beliefs is taken into account, intenders and nonintenders are found to differ significantly with respect to almost every outcome, be it positive or negative. For example, although all the women believed that their smoking was more likely to lead to negative health consequences than their not smoking, intenders believe this significantly *less* than do nonintenders. Given this finding and the previous finding that intenders evaluate health consequences less negatively than do nonintenders, it follows that these health beliefs make a significantly more negative contribution to the differential attitudes of nonintenders than of intenders (see the last two columns of Table 7). Thus despite the fact that almost all the women recognize some of the negative health consequences of smoking, the findings in the first three rows of Table 7 make it clear that health considerations still play an important role in influencing the women's smoking or not smoking behaviors. In fact, with the exception of beliefs about the relative cost of smoking, all the beliefs considered were found to make significantly different contributions to the differential attitudes of intenders and nonintenders.

To summarize, young women appear to consider many different factors in arriving at their decisions to smoke or not to smoke cigarettes. In addition to considering the effects of smoking and not smoking on a limited number of health outcomes, the women take into account the effects of smoking and not smoking on others (e.g., will it offend them, will I be more or less likely to be accepted?), as well as upon themselves (e.g., will these behaviors lead to bad breath, to weight gain, or to tension relief? Will I be more relaxed or better able to interact in social situations?). Finally, they also consider questions of cost and habituation.

Although all the young women believe that their smoking is more likely to lead to the negative consequences than is their nonsmoking, some women hold these differential beliefs more strongly than others. Generally speaking, the more strongly a woman holds these beliefs, the less likely she is to be (or to become) a smoker.

More important, many women believe that most of the positive outcomes enumerated above are more likely to be attained by smoking than by not smoking, while others believe these same positive outcomes are more likely to be achieved by not smoking than by smoking. Not surprisingly, the first group of women are likely to be (or become) smokers, while women in the second group are very unlikely to make this decision.

To put this most simply, some women apparently believe that the benefits of smoking (relative to not smoking) outweigh the risks while others see little or no benefits and many risks. These differential beliefs lead to positive differential smoking attitudes in the former group and negative differential smoking attitudes in the latter group.[10] Given that differential smoking intentions (and hence, actual smoking behavior) is more under attitudinal than normative control, the women in the first group are very likely to be (or to become) smokers, while those in the latter group are very likely to be (or to become) nonsmokers.[11]

Viewed in this light, it can be seen that a woman's smoking decision follows quite *reasonably* from her salient beliefs and outcome evaluations. While one may question the values that some women place on certain outcomes or the accuracy of some of their beliefs, a decision to smoke is actually quite *reasonable* if the decision maker believes that the net effects of smoking are more positive than the net effects of not smoking.

Notice that this explanation of smoking behavior is based solely on a consideration of the women's behavioral beliefs and outcome evaluations.[12] In fact, throughout this paper, I have said nothing about the kinds of variables that most social psychologists consider in their attempts to predict and explain human behavior. That is, I have not even mentioned such things as demographic variables, personality traits, or more traditional attitudes such as attitudes toward people, policies, or institutions. Let us now turn to a brief consideration of these variables and the role they play in predicting and explaining human behavior.

---

10. It is interesting to note that very similar findings are obtained with respect to attitudes toward the use of nuclear power. That is, while both PRO and ANTI groups believe there are many risks associated with using nuclear power, the ANTI group holds these beliefs more strongly than the PRO group. While the PRO group believes these risks are outweighed by the economic and technological benefits of using nuclear power, the ANTI group does not (see Otway & Fishbein, 1977).

11. While normative considerations also were found to influence the young women's smoking decisions, they play a relatively minor role and will not be considered in the present paper. However, it should be noted that when one finds that normative beliefs and motivations to comply can accurately predict subjective norms *and* that subjective norms are important determinants of the intention under consideration, it is appropriate to examine the normative component by using an analysis similar to the one used to explore the attitudinal component.

12. See Footnote 11.

THE ROLE OF EXTERNAL VARIABLES

According to the theory of reasoned action, any behavior can be predicted from intentions and can ultimately be explained by reference to a person's behavioral beliefs, outcome evaluations, normative beliefs, and motivations to comply. In fact, one advantage of the theory is that it enables us to identify which of these four variables contributes most to behavioral differences. As we all know, however, there are an almost infinite number of other variables that are often found to be related to overt behavior. Although the theory does not deny the importance of such "external" variables, it does question the assumption that variables of this type are *directly* related to behavior and can thus be used as explanatory constructs.

To put this somewhat differently, a person does not perform a given behavior *because* she is a woman or educated or altruistic or religious or in favor of "zero population growth." Instead, she ultimately performs the behavior *because* she believes that its performance will lead to more "good" than "bad" consequences and/or *because* she believes that most of her important others (i.e., the individuals or groups she most wants to comply with) think she should perform that behavior. If one accepts this view, the role of external variables becomes clear; as can be seen in Figure 6, external variables influence behavior only *indirectly*, by influencing the attitudinal and normative considerations that ultimately determine behavior.

This conception of the role of external variables has several very important implications. First, external variables represent, in a sense, a fourth level of explanation. That is, they may provide some insight into why people differ in their behavioral beliefs, outcome evaluations, normative beliefs, or motivations to comply. Recall, however, that as one moves from right to left in Figure 6, one increases understanding but not prediction. Thus, assessing external variables *in addition to* beliefs, outcome evaluations, and motivations to comply may help one to understand variations in these variables, but it should not improve prediction of attitudes, subjective norms, intentions, or behaviors, Similarly, assessing external variables in addition to attitudes and subjective norms should not improve prediction of intentions or behaviors. Generally speaking, once one has validly assessed the determinants of a given

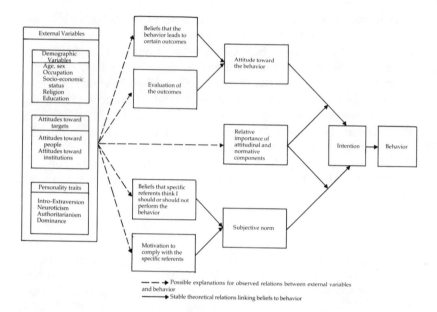

Figure 6. Indirect effects of external variables on behavior

variable, one cannot improve prediction by also assessing more distal variables.

At the same time, however, if one does find a relationship between the variable in question and some distal variable, one should be able to identify the way in which the distal variable indirectly affects that variable. That is, if a distal variable is related to the variable in question, it must also be related to one or more of the determinants of that variable. For example, one should be able to identify the intervening variables that link external variables to attitudes, subjective norms, intentions, or behaviors.

To put this somewhat differently, there are many different ways in which a relation between an external variable and a given behavior may be mediated. As can be seen in Figure 6, external variables can have their effect on behavioral beliefs, outcome evaluations, normative beliefs, motivations to comply, or the relative weights a person places on the attitudinal and normative components as determinants of his or her intention.

Another advantage of the theory of reasoned action is that it allows one to identify the locus (or loci) of effect of any external variable vis-a-vis a given behavior. More important, it allows us to explain *why* a given external variable was (*or was not*) related to a given behavior. Thus it becomes possible to account for many apparent inconsistencies in the literature. For example, suppose altruism is found to be related to whether or not a person donates blood but not to whether or not he stops at the scene of an accident. Moreover, let us suppose that both of these behaviors were found to be primarily under attitudinal control, and that in both cases the primary difference between those who did and those who did not perform these behaviors was with respect to behavioral beliefs.

Clearly, one could find that while altruistic and nonaltruistic people systematically differed in their beliefs about donating their blood, they did not differ in their beliefs about stopping at the scene of an accident. Indeed, if one stops to think about it, there is little reason to assume that a given external variable will be systematically related to a number of different behaviors even though they may all be in the same behavioral category. For example, in any given election, liberals and conservatives may differ in their beliefs about the advantages and disadvantages of voting for a given candidate, but not in their beliefs about voting per se. Similarly, upper and lower class parents may differ in their beliefs about sending their children to college, but not in their beliefs about sending their children to primary school.

Note too, that even though an external variable may be systematically related to one (or more) of the potential determinants of a given behavior, this is no guarantee that the external variable will have an indirect influence on the behavior. For example, although introverts and extroverts may differ in their motivations to comply with a given set of referents, this does not mean that they will have different subjective norms. Moreover, even if they did have different subjective norms, they could still arrive at similar intentions since the intention may be primarily under attitudinal control.

Prediction of Child-Bearing Intentions

Many of the above points are illustrated in a recent study that investigated the influence of work-related variables on married women's intentions to have a child in the next three years (Loken & Fishbein, Note 4). Although many different factors have been assumed to influence women's childbearing intentions, one of the more persistent relationships that has been found in population research is that between family size and female employment. For example, several investigators have found that working women have fewer children than nonworking women and that women who intend to work intend to have fewer children than women who do not have such occupational intentions (e.g., Blake, 1965; Farley, 1970; Hoffman & Hoffman, 1973). Given these findings, we wished to examine this relationship in more detail. More specifically, we wanted to know how occupational variables influenced a woman's childbearing intentions.

Earlier research by Jaccard and Davidson (1975; Davidson & Jaccard, 1976) had demonstrated that women's intentions to have a child in the next two years were primarily determined by, and could be very accurately predicted from, their attitudes to their having a child in the next two years. Moreover, these attitudes were them-selves found to be accurately predicted from a knowledge of the women's behavioral beliefs and outcome evaluations. According to the theory of reasoned action, then, the finding that occupational variables are related to such childbearing intentions implies that occupational variables are related to these behavioral beliefs and/or outcome evaluations. In addition, as we argued above, another implication of the theory is that the consideration of these occupa-tional variables, in addition to the variables specified by the theory, should not improve prediction of the childbearing intention.

In order to test these notions, 100 childless married women who were between the ages of 20 and 38 were asked to fill out a self completion questionnaire.[13] This instrument assessed all of the variables relevant to the theory of reasoned action (i.e., the intention to have a child in the next three years, corresponding attitudes and subjective norms, and corresponding behavioral beliefs, outcome evaluations, normative beliefs, and motivations to comply) as well as a number of external variables such as intentions to have a career, intentions to work full time in the next three years, fear of failure, religiosity, occupational status, and attitudes toward work.

Consistent with the theory of reasoned action and the earlier findings of Jaccard and Davidson, Figure 7 shows that the women's intentions to have a child in the next three years were very accu-

---

13. Following standardized procedures (see Ajzen & Fishbein, 1980), the ques-tionnaire was based on the results of an independent elicitation study which identi-fied the salient behavioral and normative beliefs of the population in question.

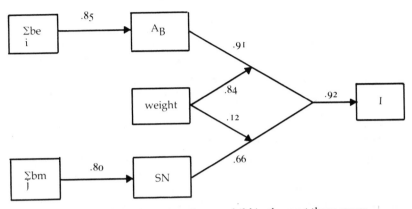

Figure 7. Prediction of intention to have a child in the next three years

rately predicted from their corresponding attitudes and subjective norms ($R = .92$) and that these variables were, in turn, predicted with considerable accuracy from salient beliefs, outcome evaluations, and motivations to comply. Moreover, as can be seen in Figure 7, attitudinal considerations were much more important determinants of the women's intention than were normative ones ($\beta = .84$ and $.12$, for attitudes and norms respectively).

Given these findings, we can investigate the determinants of the attitudinal component in more detail in order to identify those beliefs and/or outcome evaluations that most strongly discriminated between intenders and nonintenders.[14] As can be seen in Table 8, women who do and do not intend to have a child in the next three years differ with respect to both behavioral beliefs *and* outcome evaluations. Generally speaking, if a woman believed that having a child in the next three years would fulfill her family life and make her marriage stronger without restricting her freedom or creating a financial or emotional strain, she intended to have a child. On the other hand, if she believed that having a child in the next three years would restrict her freedom, leave less time for her own goals and plans, and create financial problems without either strengthening her marriage or fulfilling her family life, she did not intend to have a child.

14. Since normative considerations played only a minor role in determining intentions, the analysis of normative beliefs and motivations to comply will not be reported in the present paper.

Table 8

Mean beliefs, evaluations, and belief evaluation products for women intending and not intending to have a child within the next three years

	Mean Belief	
	Intenders	Nonintenders
Having a child I could not afford	−1.63	1.11**
Having a child while at a good age	2.56	1.19**
Too much of an emotional strain	−2.17	.27**
A restriction on my freedom	−.40	1.22**
Stronger marriage	.86	−1.57**
Fulfillment of my family life	1.90	−1.24**
An added responsibility	2.30	2.46
Having less time for my own goals and plans	.65	2.00**

*p < .05
**p < .01

Moreover, the more a woman valued having a child at a good age and the more she valued an added responsibility, the stronger was her intention to have a child in the next three years. In contrast, the more strongly she felt about having her freedom restricted or having less time to pursue her own goals and plans, the stronger was her intention to not have a child.

Given the above findings, and particularly the high multiple correlation between these childbearing intentions and the women's attitudes and subjective norms ($R = .92$), it should come as no surprise to find that the consideration of external variables in addition to attitudes and subjective norms did not appreciably improve prediction. Indeed, the highest multiple correlation obtained from regressing an external variable, in addition to attitudes and subjective norms on the intention, was only .93. Nevertheless, many of the external variables were found to be significantly related to the intention to have a child in the next three years. For example, consistent with previous findings, women who intended to pursue a career and/or to work full time during the next three years were significantly less likely to intend to have a child than women who did not have such occupational intentions ($r = −.42$ and $−.50$ for career and

Mean Evaluation		Mean Be Product	
Intenders	Nonintenders	Intenders	Nonintenders
−2.06	−2.51**	3.46	−2.57**
2.71	1.68**	7.13	2.95**
−1.89	−2.24	4.86	−.97**
−1.00	−2.00**	.22	−3.32**
2.22	1.92	2.37	−3.62**
2.40	1.70**	5.33	−1.41**
1.16	−1.49**	3.57	−4.14**
−.83	−2.08**	−.56	−5.41**

full time work intentions respectively). Among the other external variables that were significantly related to the intention to have a child in the next three years were the women's attitudes toward working ($r = -.32$), their beliefs about the negative consequences of achieving success ($r = -.32$), their intended family size ($r = .59$), their religiosity ($r = .39$), their age ($r = -.25$), and their husband's age ($r = -.23$). In marked contrast, personality variables such as need for achievement and self-esteem and various job-related measures such as number of years in present job, satisfaction with work, and income were not found to significantly influence the women's childbearing intentions.

Although a complete analysis of all the external variables is beyond the scope of the present paper, two general points should be made. First, every external variable that was significantly related to the intention to have a child in the next three years was also significantly related to the women's attitudes toward their having a child in that time period. In contrast, external variables that were *not* significantly related to the attitude were also unrelated to the intention. Second, every external variable that was significantly related to the women's attitudes (or subjective norms) was also found to be related to one or more of the behavioral beliefs or outcome evaluations underlying that attitude (or to one or more of the normative beliefs or motivations to comply underlying the subjective norm). Although other external variables also influenced one or two beliefs or outcome evaluations (or motivations to comply), this influence was not carried through to the attitudinal (or normative) level. For example, women with high need for achievement were more likely to believe that their having a child in the next three years would restrict their freedom ($r = .33$) and give them less time to pursue their own goals ($r = .26$) than were women with low need for achievement. Despite this, need for achievement was unrelated to the women's attitudes ($r = -.10$), and it was thus also unrelated to their intention to have a child ($r = -.16$).

Given these general findings, let us now consider in more detail the relations between women's intentions to work full time and their intentions to have a child. As we saw above, there was a relatively strong negative relationship between these two variables ($r = -.50$). Given the knowledge that intentions to have a child in the next three years is primarily determined by attitudinal considerations, and knowing that the women's attitudes were very accurately predicted from their salient behavioral beliefs and outcome evaluations ($r = .85$), we can now determine the exact manner in which intentions to work full time indirectly influence the women's childbearing intentions. Table 9 shows the relations between the intention to work full time and each of the eight behavioral beliefs and outcome evaluations that underlie the women's childbearing intentions.

It can be seen that the intention to work is significantly related to six of the eight behavioral beliefs and five of the eight outcome evaluations. More specifically, in comparison to women who do not intend to work full time in the next three years, the women with full time working intentions are significantly *more* likely to believe that having a child in the next three years would mean having a child they cannot afford, would mean having less time for their own plans and goals, and would be too much of an emotional strain. Moreover, they are *less* likely to believe that having a child in the next three years would mean having a child while they are at a good age, would strengthen their marriages, or would fulfill their family life. Finally, these women also place less positive value on having a child at a good age and fulfilling family life and more negative value on having a child they cannot afford, having less time for personal goals, and having an added responsibility. As we saw earlier (see

Table 9
Relationships between the intention to work full time in the next three years and the behavioral beliefs and outcome evaluations underlying women's intentions to have a child in the next three years (N = 100)

Outcome	Belief	Outcome Evaluations
Having a child I could not afford	.38**	−.21*
Having a child while at a good age	−.24*	−.22*
Too much of an emotional strain	.43**	−.06
A restriction on my freedom	.13	−.16
Stronger marriage	−.29**	−.15
Fulfillment of my family life	−.41**	−.30**
An added responsibility	.00	−.46**
Having less time for my own goals and plans	.26**	−.26**

* p < .05
** p < .01

Table 8), this is exactly the pattern of beliefs and outcome evaluations that should lead to unfavorable attitudes toward having a child in the next three years and thus to negative childbearing intentions. Consistent with this, the correlation between the intention to work full time and the attitude toward having a child in the next three years is −.45.

It should be clear that similar analyses could be conducted for any of the other external variables that were considered. In addition, when normative considerations are found to be important determinants of the intentions under consideration, a parallel analysis can be carried out to investigate the relationships between the external variable and the normative beliefs and motivations to comply that underlie the subjective norm. For example, Figure 8 summarizes the relationships between six external variables and the women's behavioral beliefs (b_i), outcome evaluations (e_i), normative beliefs (b_j), and motivations to comply (m_j). Four of these external variables were significantly related to the women's intention to have a child (i.e., A, B, C, & D in Figure 8), while two (E & F) were not. In each display, the highest zero order correlations as well as the number of

A. Intention to Work Full Time (r = −.50*)

B. Religiosity (r = .39*)

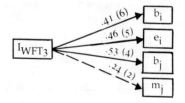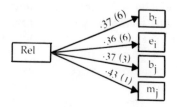

C. Beliefs about Achieving Success (r = .32*)

D. Husband's Age (r = −.32*)

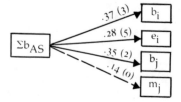

E. Factor II—Self Esteem (r = −.08)

F. Satisfaction with work (r = .10)

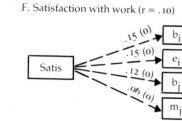

————— significant ————— not significant

Figure 8. Relations between selected external variables and behavioral beliefs, outcome evaluations, normative beliefs, and motivation to comply

significant relations between the external variable and each type of underlying variable can be seen. Thus, for example, we have already seen that the intention to work full time in the next three years was related to six of the eight behavioral beliefs and five of the eight outcome evaluations. Figure 8A shows that this external variable was also related to four of five salient normative beliefs (with the single highest correlation = .53) and two of the five motivations to comply.

Looking at the remaining displays in Figure 8, it can be seen that whenever the external variable was significantly related to the women's childbearing intentions, it was also related to several of the underlying determinants of that intention (Figures 8A, B, C, and D). In contrast, when the external variable was unrelated to the intention, it had little, if any, effect on the women's beliefs, outcome evaluations, or motivations to comply. Finally, it can also be seen that the locus of effect of one external variable can be quite different from that of another. For example, while husband's age influences the intention to have a child primarily through normative and behavioral beliefs, the women's beliefs about achieving success appears to have its influence primarily through behavioral beliefs and outcome evaluations.

To summarize briefly, this section has tried to show how the theory of reasoned action provides a framework for analyzing the impact of demographic variables, personality traits, traditional attitudes, and other individual difference variables on human behavior. More specifically we have tried to demonstrate that such "external" variables influence behavior only indirectly by influencing the beliefs, outcome evaluations, and motivations to comply that ultimately underlie a person's intention to perform (and hence his or her actual performance of) a given behavior.

SOME CONCLUDING COMMENTS

I began this paper by suggesting that rather than continuing to develop completely different theories to predict and understand behavior in different content domains, psychologists should again try to develop more general and comprehensive theories of behavior. In keeping with this suggestion, I have tried to show how a limited number of constructs, embedded within a theoretical network, can be used to predict and explain various human behaviors. More specifically, I have outlined a theory of reasoned action, and I have tried to show its applications and implications in several behavioral domains. In addition, I have tried to answer some of the questions that have been raised by the theory. From my own perspective, I think the most valuable aspect of the theory of reasoned action has been its ability to raise and to answer such questions. While some of these questions have come from critics of the theory, others have come as a result of our attempts to apply the theory in new or different content domains.

For example, if it were not for people questioning our assumption that intentions are the best single predictors of behavior, it is unlikely that we would have found it necessary to distinguish among single acts, behavioral categories, and outcomes. I also doubt that we would have recognized the importance of viewing every action as a *decision* on the part of the actor.

Similarly, if we had not attempted to test the theory's applicability in the area of cigarette smoking, it is unlikely that we would have found it necessary to distinguish between general and personal beliefs, or that we would have discovered that a single "good-bad" scale is not always a valid measure of attitude.

More important, despite its apparent simplicity and common-sense qualities, the theory of reasoned action questions many of our most cherished psychological assumptions. First, it suggests that behavior can be easily and accurately predicted. Second, it implies that there are no necessary or direct relations between traditional attitudes (e.g., toward people, objects, institutions, or policies) and any given action, and it suggests that one can predict and explain that action without reference to such attitudes or to demographic or personality variables. In fact, the notion that there is one and only one attitude that is directly relevant to any given behavior is so alien to most social psychological thinking it is almost heresy. Yet, as I have tried to show, once one has measured the attitude toward the behavior in question (and the corresponding subjective norm), one cannot improve prediction by measuring other attitudes, or by considering personality traits or demographic variables. In fact, in and of themselves, such external variables can tell us very little about *why* a person does or does not perform a given behavior.

Although I recognize that these are strong words, I do feel that they are justified. At the same time, however, I want to make it clear that I am not suggesting that "external" variables are unimportant or that they should be ignored. Although people's actions are ultimately based on their beliefs, outcome evaluations, and motivations to comply, people differ greatly with respect to these underlying variables. It is therefore very important to identify those factors that contribute to differences in beliefs, outcome evaluations, and motivations to comply. And it is here that analyses of external variables can make their greatest contributions. Thus, rather than ignoring external variables, I see the theory of reasoned action as providing a framework in which to more appropriately study these variables.

In fact, what I have tried to show throughout this paper is the utility of having a general theory of behavior. Not only can this type of theory guide research, but it can also serve to organize and integrate research findings that appear to be inconsistent. As I said at the beginning of this paper, I believe that there is not only a place, but also a need, for such comprehensive theories in psychology.

REFERENCE NOTES

1. Fishbein, M. *Consumer beliefs and behavior with respect to cigarette smoking: A critical analysis of the public literature.* Report prepared for the staff of the Federal Trade Commission, submitted to Congress, October 1977.
2. Fishbein, M., Loken, B., Roberts, S., & Chung, J. *Are young women "informed" about cigarette smoking?* In preparation, University of Illinois, 1979.
3. Chung, J., & Fishbein, M. *Predicting young women's intention to smoke: Some implications for attitude measurement.* Paper presented at a meeting of the Midwestern Psychological Association, May 1979.
4. Loken, B., & Fishbein, M. *An analysis of the effects of occupational variables on childbearing intentions.* Unpublished paper, University of Illinois, 1979.

REFERENCES

Ajzen, I., & Fishbein, M. Attitude-behavior relations: A theoretical analysis and review of empirical research. *Psychological Bulletin,* 1977, **84**, 888–918.
Ajzen, I., & Fishbein, M. *Understanding attitudes and predicting social behavior.* Englewood Cliffs, NJ: Prentice-Hall, 1980.
Blake, J. Demographic science and redirection of population policy. *Journal of Chronic Diseases,* 1965, **18**, 1181–1200.
Davidson, A. R., & Jaccard, J. J. Social-psychological determinants of fertility intentions. In S. H. Newman & V. D. Thompson (Eds.), *Population psychology: Research and education issues.* Washington, D.C.: Government Printing House, 1976. DHEW Publ. No. (NIH) 76–574.
Farley, J. Graduate women: Career aspirations and desired family size. *American Psychologist,* 1970, **25**, 1099–1100.

Fishbein, M. The prediction of behaviors from attitudinal variables. In C. D. Mortensen & K. K. Sereno (Eds.), *Advances in communication research*. New York: Harper & Row, 1973.

Fishbein, M., & Ajzen, I. Attitudes toward objects as predictors of single and multiple behavioral criteria. *Psychological Review*, 1974, **81**, 59–74.

Fishbein, M., & Ajzen, I. *Belief, attitude, intentions and behavior: An introduction to theory and research*. Boston: Addison-Wesley, 1975.

Fishbein, M., & Ajzen, I. Misconceptions about the Fishbein model: Reflections on a study by Songer-Nocks. *Journal of Experimental Social Psychology*, 1976, **12**, 579–584.

Hoffman, L. W., & Hoffman, M. S. The value of children to parents. In J. T. Fawcett (Ed.), *Psychological perspectives on population*. New York: Basic Books, 1973.

Jaccard, J. J., & Davidson, A. R. A comparison of two models of social behavior: Results of a survey sample. *Sociometry*, 1975, **38**, 491–517.

Larson, P. S., & Silvette, H. *Tobacco, experimental and clinical studies, Supplement I*. Baltimore: Williams & Wilkins, 1968.

Osgood, C. E., Suci, G. J., & Tannenbaum, P. H. *The measurement of meaning*. Urbana: University of Illinois Press, 1957.

Otway, H. J., & Fishbein, M. *The determinants of attitude formation: An application to nuclear power*. RM-77-80, International Institute for Applied Systems Analysis, Laxenburg, Austria, 1977.

Sejwacz, D., Ajzen, I., & Fishbein, M. Predicting and understanding weight loss: Intentions, behaviors, and outcomes. In I. Ajzen & M. Fishbein, *Understanding attitudes and predicting social behavior*. Englewood Cliffs, NJ: Prentice-Hall, 1980.

Smoking and health: Report of the Advisory Committee to the Surgeon General of the Public Health Service. U.S. Dept. of Health, Education, and Welfare. Public Health Service Document No. 1103. Washington, D.C.: U.S. Government Printing Office, 1964.

The Role of Action in Attitude Change

Herbert C. Kelman
Harvard University

*T*he relationship of action to attitude change has been a central and recurrent theme in my work ever since my doctoral dissertation (Kelman, 1953). I have written several theoretical papers on this issue over the years (Kelman, 1962a, 1974a, 1974b, 1978), and during the 1960s several colleagues and I were engaged in an experimental program on the relationship of discrepant action and attitude change.[1] Some of the results of this program are described in Kelman and Baron (1974), but most of the experiments are still unpublished.[2] The relationship between action and attitude change has also entered importantly into my work in various applied contexts, including psychotherapy (Kelman, 1963), international exchange (Kelman, 1962b, 1975), and conflict resolution (Kelman, 1972; Kelman & Cohen, 1979). I therefore welcome the opportunity, provided by the Nebraska Symposium, to draw together some of my ideas in this area and to distill some of the generalizations that have emerged from my work. I am particularly intrigued with noting some of the continuities and changes in my thinking over the years, as I have moved back and forth between experimental and applied work. It is

1. The research was supported by grants from the National Institute of Mental Health, which are gratefully acknowledged.

2. A series of papers reporting these experiments have been written and will eventually be published in a book by Kelman, Baron, Sheposh, and Lubalin (Note 1). In addition to these four authors, contributors to the volume include Nancy Adler, Nina Rossomando, Eugene Johnson, James M. Dabbs, Kent S. Crawford, and Martin S. Greenberg. I want to take this occasion to thank these colleagues for their stimulating ideas, their creative work, their personal friendship, and their boundless patience.

exciting to observe the way these two lines of activity inform and stimulate each other and thus contribute to theoretical refinement.

The purpose of this paper, then, is to develop a general view of the relationship between action and attitude change, as I now visualize it. It is presented in the spirit of a work-in-progress—as an attempt to bring together a variety of observations and generalizations and to discover what they add up to.

The biases that I bring to this analysis will become abundantly clear as I go along. Let me, however, state them briefly at the outset.

(1) I view attitude as a dynamic process, rather than as a static entity or stable equilibrium point. Attitudes are constantly shifting and changing as people interact with the attitude object and with their social environment. This view contrasts with that implicit in many criticisms of the attitude concept which point to the frequent finding of low relationships between measures of attitude and behavior. Such criticisms tend to conceive of attitudes in static rather than dynamic terms.

(2) I take social interaction as the starting point of my analysis and look at attitudes in that context. Attitudes flow from social interaction and evolve in the course of it. In turn, attitudes feed into social interaction and help to guide the interaction process.

(3) I view attitudes as links between individuals and the various collectivities to which they belong. Attitudes are shared, to varying degrees, within relevant collectivities. The formation, expression, and functioning of attitudes simultaneously represent both individual and collective processes.

(4) I assume that the behavior of individuals within any given situation can best be understood in functional terms. That is, I see individuals as seeking to achieve a variety of goals within that situation, as coping with environmental forces that have a bearing on these goals, and as processing information in relation to these concerns. This functional view provides the framework for analyzing attitudes, actions, and the relations between them. A functional analysis of attitude-action discrepancy contrasts, in many important ways, with an analysis derived from consistency models, particularly as exemplified by dissonance theory.

(5) As a further elaboration of a functional view, I regard the individual as oriented not only toward defense and equilibrium, but also toward growth, new learning, self-development, and self-utilization. This view suggests the possibility that the relationship between action and attitude change may represent not only a

reactive process, but also an active one. That is, action may not only precipitate attitude change, but it may also represent a step in an active effort to transform one's attitudes.

THE BASIC PROPOSITION

The basic proposition to be argued in this paper is that significant attitude change always occurs in the context of action.

In speaking of *action*, I refer to overt behavior that produces some change in the environment and has real-life consequences for the actor. There are various other criteria that come to mind when one thinks of an action, although I would not include them as defining characteristics. Thus, I would be more inclined to speak of action insofar as the behavior is public and irreversible and insofar as it represents an active involvement and long-term commitment. All these conditions enhance the "action-character" of the behavior by strengthening the two defining characteristics. That is, the more public, irreversible, active, and committing the behavior is, the greater the change it produces in the environment and the more real-life consequences it has for the actor. An anonymous, one-time donation to an organization represents an action. But when the donation is public, or when it involves a commitment to solicit matching donations from others, or when it takes the form of a binding pledge to contribute a certain percentage of one's income to the organization, then the action is clearly stronger—or "more of an action." It is nontrivial actions of this kind—that is, actions characterized by active participation, public commitment, and important real-life consequences—that I have in mind as the usual context for significant attitude change.

The statement that significant attitude change always occurs in the context of action clearly does not represent a formal proposition, to be subjected to empirical test. It is hedged in by the requirements that the attitude change be "significant" and that the action be nontrivial. Although the word "always" may sound daring, I can easily handle exceptions by declaring the attitude change to be insignificant or the action to be trivial. Needless to say, for purposes of empirical testing this proposition would have to be broken down into a series of much more specific conditional statements. For the moment, however, my purpose is not to propose specific hypotheses, but to develop a general framework for understanding major attitude changes in the real world. I shall try to argue that such changes are particularly likely to occur when people are involved in action vis-à-vis the attitude object.

The types of action that may provide the context for attitude change vary widely. Social-psychological research on the relationship between action and attitude change (particularly in the dissonance tradition) has generally been restricted to a single paradigm: the individual engages in a discrepant or counterattitudinal action and, as a consequence of that action, an attitude-change process is set into motion. In this paradigm, the impetus for action comes from the outside—that is, it is unrelated to the person's attitudes. Moreover, attitude change is a post-action phenomenon, designed to justify or explain the action that has already been taken. In my view, this is only one of a number of possible ways in which action may be related to attitude change. My discussion is not confined to counterattitudinal actions, nor to actions that entirely precede the onset of a change process. A logical distinction can be made between four types of action, each of which may provide a context for attitude change (see Table 1):

(1) *Response to situational demands.* People may engage in action vis-à-vis an object for a variety of reasons—such as situational demands, role requirements, or social pressures—that are largely unrelated to their initial attitudes toward that object. Indeed, oftentimes the action may be counterattitudinal. This is the kind of action that is involved in the typical forced compliance experiment, popularized by dissonance theory. Such actions, for the reasons postu-

Table 1

Types of action that may provide context for attitude change

| | | Source of Action | |
		Social forces	Personal attitudes
Timing of Action	Prior to Change process	Response to situational demands	Manifestation of attitude
	In midst of change process	Adherence to new policy	Testing of new attitude

lated by dissonance theory or other theoretical orientations, may create the conditions for subsequent attitude change.

(2) *Adherence to new policy.* Changes in social policy may set into motion a process of behavioral and attitudinal change. In keeping with the new policy, individuals may engage in novel actions vis-à-vis the attitude object and these in turn may create the conditions for attitude change. Research on desegregation (Allport, 1954; Saenger, 1953) provides illustrations of the conduciveness of this type of action to attitude change in the direction of acceptance of the new policy.

(3) *Manifestation of attitude.* Not surprisingly, people often engage in actions vis-à-vis an object that flow directly from their attitudes toward that object. For example, someone favorably disposed toward the field of medicine may decide to go to medical school. This action, in turn, may expose the individual to new experiences and information leading to attitude change. The change may take the form of increased commitment or greater differentiation, but it may also take the form of a reassessment of the object or even an abandonment of the initially favorable attitude.

(4) *Testing of new attitude.* Individuals may be engaged in a process of incipient attitude change—a process of reconsidering or reexamining their attitudes toward a particular object. As part of that process, they may engage in some novel action vis-à-vis the object, perhaps by way of testing out a new relationship. This action, in turn, may help to crystallize their new attitudes and to advance the change process that had already begun prior to the action.

This classification of types of action is not meant to represent a formal scheme, nor would I suggest that the four types necessarily occur in pure form. In the real world, the four categories summarized in Table 1 often blend together. I shall bring in examples of these different types of action as I go along, indicating the ways in which they may lead to attitude change. For the moment, however, my purpose is merely to point to the range of phenomena I have in mind when I propose that attitude change occurs in the context of action. In doing so, I have also tried to suggest that action can best be viewed as part of the process of attitude change—as expression of that process, or instigation of that process, or typically a combination of the two.

AN ILLUSTRATION

Having defined my domain in rather abstract terms, let me now offer a concrete example of the role of action in attitude change, in order to provide an intuitive sense of the phenomena with which I am concerned. I take my example from the Arab-Israeli conflict, on which my research has concentrated during the past few years. Specifically, I shall look at the reaction of the Israeli public to the visit of President Sadat to Jerusalem in November, 1977. I was in Israel at the time of that visit and then almost immediately went on to Egypt, where I spent the next few weeks. Thus, I was directly involved in the events that I describe, with all of the advantages and disadvantages entailed by such involvement.

The reaction of the Israeli public can certainly be described as a variety of intense action. Although much of the action was symbolic in nature, it was characterized by almost total participation of many individuals in a large number of public, collective activities. Once firm plans for Sadat's arrival were announced, the entire country was gripped by a holiday mood. It is not enough to speak of enthusiasm and excitement; words like joy, euphoria, and exultation seem more appropriate.

The reaction can best be described as a combination of solemnity and celebration. On the one hand, there was a widespread feeling that a momentous, historical event was about to take place, one that represented a major turning point in the Arab-Israeli conflict. In this spirit, some compared Sadat's landing in Jerusalem to the first landing of spacemen on the moon. On the other hand, the reaction was festive, joyous, and even lighthearted. When the news of the visit was first announced, spontaneous dancing broke out in one of the main squares of Jerusalem; instead of restoring traffic, the police apparently joined in. Another example of lightheartedness was the following advertisement that appeared in the *Jerusalem Post*: "Magnificent 14-room house. Prestige neighborhood. Terms negotiable. Suitable for Egyptian Embassy."

One of the most interesting reactions was the great interest shown by the media and the public in the Egyptian national symbols, the flag and the anthem. There was much concern about the unavailability of Egyptian flags in Israel. Eventually, flags were brought in from New York and Cairo. In the meantime, however, a Jerusalem flagmaker began working around the clock making Egyptian flags.

He took a chance and began the process even before Sadat's official announcement. His story was featured on TV and in the press. A conductor of the military band, who did not have the notes of the Egyptian national anthem. He taped what he guessed (correctly) to be the anthem from Radio Cairo, transcribed it, and began rehearsing his band. By the time the notes arrived from Cairo and New York, confirming his own transcription, he already had the head-start he needed. These incidents were of such special interest to the Israeli public, it seems to me—generating both playful amusement and a sense of awe—because they symbolized concretely the enormity of the step that President Sadat had taken.

When the Egyptian advance party arrived at the outskirts of Jerusalem, they were greeted by a large crowd that had spontaneously gathered to clap, cheer, and shout welcome. The evening of Sadat's arrival, the *Jerusalem Post* came out with a special edition, with words of welcome—in Arabic and English—in large red letters on the front page, and with a facsimile of the Egyptian national flag, suitable for display, on the back. The roads that the motorcade from the airport would be following were lined with Egyptian flags (which by now had obviously been imported and produced in sufficient numbers) alternating with Israeli flags. There was a large, spontaneous outpouring of crowds all along the route—representing all ages and social classes—waiting to clap, cheer, and wave their flags as the official cars drove by.

I was in Jerusalem that evening. I mingled with the crowds in front of the King David Hotel and then proceeded to the home of friends in order to watch the arrival ceremonies on TV. As it happened, my friends lived on a quiet residential street that was on the route of the official motorcade and I thus had an opportunity to observe people's reactions close by. The crowds on this street were not particularly dense—although they filled out just a few minutes before the motorcade arrived. People were obviously following events on TV and they started pouring to the streets and to their balconies as soon as they heard that the motorcade was approaching their neighborhood. The atmosphere was expectant and festive. Policemen in shiny new uniforms were stationed along the street, but they were friendly and relaxed, sharing in the general holiday spirit. Women brought them tea and biscuits, underlining the sense of solidarity between the public and the police. My friends' little daughter had brought down some flowers and talked about throwing them toward the official cars. Almost casually, a policeman advised her and her mother not to throw anything, because it might make the soldiers above us nervous. Looking up, we saw for the first time that soldiers, with their guns drawn, were stationed on the roofs. Clearly, security was tight, but the atmosphere was joyous and relaxed. When the cars finally passed, they were greeted with cheers and clapping. Some of the people near me recited the blessing which is said on Jewish holidays and special joyous occasions, thanking the Lord for having "kept us alive and sustained us and brought us to this day."

At no point during the entire period surrounding the President's visit did I come across any expression of hostility toward Egypt—which is quite amazing, considering the relationship between the two countries over the past three decades. I did hear an occasional expression of skepticism, but no hostility. Indeed, such reactions would have seemed strange and totally out of keeping with the mood of friendship and cordiality that prevailed. Beyond that, I saw no sign of reticence or reserve about expressing cordiality. The question of whether it is proper and loyal to respond with such warmth to the representatives of what was technically an enemy nation did not seem to cross anyone's mind; there was a general assumption that these positive sentiments were shared throughout, by both citizens and officials. Israelis visibly and without hesitation took delight in the Egyptian flag, in the Egyptian anthem, in the Egyptian presence. Along with the spontaneous enthusiasm shown by the population, there was an apparent desire—again quite spontaneous—to make a good impression on the visitors by communicating the people's welcome of the visitors, desire for peace, and appreciation for President Sadat's initiative.

There is no question that the immediate changes in attitude produced by this event were large and significant. An early opinion poll showed that ninety percent of the Israeli public (compared to some forty percent prior to the Sadat visit) believed that Egypt really wanted peace with Israel, and that eighty percent thought that the chances for an overall peace settlement with the Arab world had improved. To be sure, these enormous changes did not maintain themselves. There was considerable backsliding in Israeli public opinion as the Egyptian-Israeli negotiations proceeded and ran into repeated difficulties. Moreover, there is no clear indication that these changes have generalized beyond the specific Egyptian-Israeli relationship. That is, there is no evidence of a major shift in public opinion toward other Arab parties (particularly the Palestinians) and toward other issues (such as withdrawal from the West Bank and Gaza and acceptance of a Palestinian state). Nevertheless, the changes in attitude—at the level of elites as well as the general public—were of sufficient magnitude to support the Israeli government in making substantial concessions on the Egyptian front and in signing a peace agreement. Furthermore, it is my impression that the Sadat visit and the subsequent events have produced a fundamental shift in Israeli attitudes, which will manifest itself as negotiations on the Palestinian issue and other remaining issues proceed. These broader changes have not occurred at the level of near unanimity that characterized the immediate changes brought about by Sadat's visit, but—for at least a large segment of the Israeli population—attitudes toward the Arab-Israeli conflict have undergone a major transformation. The evolution of attitudes on specific issues will depend on external events and pressures, as well as the internal debate and political process. I would predict, however, that the reassessment of attitudes set in motion by Sadat's initiative will have a major impact on Israeli reactions to these emerging issues.

Even if the changes turn out to be less far-reaching than I am predicting, there is little doubt that Sadat's visit produced significant changes in attitudes, which have not been totally dissipated by subsequent events, and which have contributed to a major restructuring of the political, diplomatic, and military situation. These changes were mediated and enhanced by the high degree of active, positive, and collective participation of the Israeli public in the Sadat visit. Thus, the event illustrates my thesis that significant attitude change occurs in the context of action.

To explain the attitude change, one could draw on the principles of cognitive dissonance. In this view, the positive actions in the face of the negative attitudes toward Egypt aroused a high level of dissonance, which was then reduced by bringing the attitudes into line with the actions. Such an explanation, however, is out of keeping with the joyous, festive mood of the occasion; there was certainly no visible evidence that people were experiencing dissonance. (Feelings of "dissonance" did develop in subsequent months, but these were associated with a tendency to revert to earlier more negative attitudes.) Furthermore, a dissonance explanation ignores the fact that the action did not simply come out of nowhere. It took place in a larger context, which both gave meaning to the action itself and provided the conditions for the development and crystalization of new attitudes. Three elements of the larger context are particularly noteworthy:

(1) The action occurred in response to a major, dramatic event, which in itself created a new psychological situation, providing the necessity, possibility, and incentive for reconsidering earlier attitudes. It provided the necessity for change by confronting people with a clear disconfirmation of the strongly held expectation that no Arab would ever accept Israel. It provided the possibility for change by generating trust and thus reducing the perceived risk of new attitudes and policies. It provided the incentive for change by creating a concrete vision of a possible and highly desirable future. In short, the event itself introduced a great deal of new information conducive to attitude change. What the action did was to make this event, with all of its implications, more salient, more personal, and more palpable. It created motivations and opportunities to consider the new information and to work through its implications for people's earlier attitudes.

(2) The action was part of a collective response, widely shared within the community. Moreover, this collective response represented an expression of official policy, which gave it complete legitimacy in the eyes of the participants.

(3) The action was consistent with an element of attitudes toward the Mid-East conflict that was latent within the Israeli public. It gave expression to a collective yearning for peace and acceptance, which was an underlying theme of the Israeli ethos, but which had been suppressed by a pervasive pessimism. In short, I am assuming that the positive attitude was already there, waiting to be released. By the same token, actions congruent with such attitudes—actions expressing friendship and displaying diplomatic niceties—were already part of the cognitive repertoire of Israelis. In addition to this general readiness for new attitudes, it should also be noted that a process of incipient attitude change toward Egypt in particular had already been under way for some time. Increasingly, Israelis had begun to differentiate between Egyptians and other Arabs, which introduced another element of readiness for attitude change.

In sum, I am proposing that public action in response to Sadat's visit contributed to attitude change by bringing the motivational and informational forces of the event into salience in a concrete and

emotionally gripping way; by creating socially shared and legit-
imized experiences and commitments; and by bringing certain
latent dimensions of the attitude—certain readinesses for change—
to the fore. These features of the situation illustrate several of the
themes of my analysis, to which I shall now turn in a more systematic fashion.

CONDITIONS FOR ATTITUDE CHANGE

Before exploring the role of action in attitude change, I want to
specify some of the basic conditions for attitude change—that is, the
circumstances under which attitude change is most likely to occur. I
shall then proceed, in the next section, to show why an action
situation is most likely to provide these conditions.

The conditions favorable to attitude change are linked to what I
see as three central features of attitudes: (1) attitudes are functionally based; (2) attitudes are socially shared; and (3) attitudes
represent a range of commitment to the attitude object.

The Functional Basis of Attitudes

From the perspective of the individual, attitudes can be seen as a
product of the individual's efforts to process information about an
object in a particular motivational context. This view is generally
consistent with a functional approach to attitude (Katz, 1960; Smith,
Bruner, & White, 1956).

Attitudes are formed in the course of a person's interaction with
the attitude object. This interaction may be direct or indirect. Direct
interaction refers to interaction with the object itself. When the
object is another person or another group—i.e., when we are
dealing with interpersonal or intergroup attitudes—then direct
interaction is in effect social interaction with the other person or
with representatives of the other group. Indirect interaction refers to
interactions about the object through other persons or communication media.

In the course of such interaction, whether direct or indirect,
information about the object is transmitted to and processed by the
individual. The way in which the information is processed is a

function of the motivational context in which the interaction occurs. That is, the attitude we form is grounded in the particular functional significance that the situation has for us—the goals we are pursuing, the values we are hoping to maximize, the coping processes in which we are engaged. The motivational context in which the attitude is formed determines the nature of the resulting attitude—i.e., the motivational basis of the attitude and the attitude system of which it becomes a part—and hence the conditions under which we are likely to act on this attitude in one or another way, as well as the conditions under which the attitude is likely to change.

This view of attitudes implies that their functioning is a dynamic process. They develop out of our interaction with an object in a particular motivational and informational context. As we continue to interact with the object (directly or indirectly), our attitudes are tested, exposed to new information, sometimes filled out and shored up, and sometimes changed. Attitude formation and change is thus a continually ongoing process. In principle, attitudes should be developing and changing whenever we are exposed to new experiences and information; in practice, changes are usually quite slow and gradual. This follows from the fact that our attitudes, once established, help to shape the experiences we have with the attitude object. They affect the kind of information to which we are exposed, the way in which we organize that information, and often (as in interpersonal attitudes) the way in which the attitude object itself behaves. Thus an attitude, by its very functioning (quite apart from any special motivations to maintain it), tends to create the conditions for its own confirmation and to minimize the opportunities for its disconfirmation.

In short, then, as we interact with an object toward which we have established an attitude, we are subject to two competing sets of forces. On the one hand, the new information to which we are exposed produces forces toward change. On the other hand, the existing attitude creates forces toward stability—not only in the form of motivated resistances to change (which, of course, do arise insofar as the attitude has functional significance for us), but also and primarily in the form of confirmatory experiences that are inherent in the day-to-day functioning of attitudes. Which of these two sets of forces will prevail on any given occasion—or what balance between them is achieved—depends on the nature of the existing attitude, of the new information to which we are exposed, and of the situation in which the interaction occurs. In general, however, it can be said that both stability and change are part of the essential nature of attitudes.

Attitude change processes are most likely to be set into motion when we are sharply confronted with a discrepancy between an attitude and some item of new information. Discrepant information is not enough, however, since, as we well know, there are many ways of neutralizing the discrepancy short of attitude change. The discrepancy must be sufficiently strong and clear so it cannot be readily assimilated to a pre-existing structure. For example, a clear disconfirmation of a strongly held expectation, as was provided by Sadat's visit to Jerusalem, would meet this requirement. Furthermore, the discrepancy must be challenging, in the sense that it raises serious questions about the quality of our coping with the environment or our ability to achieve our goals. Discrepant information may also be challenging in the sense that it offers new opportunities for enhancing our goals, as exemplified by the vision of the future that Sadat's visit created in the minds of Israelis. Assuming that we are confronted with information that is clearly discrepant, as well as challenging, the likelihood of attitude change will also depend on our receptivity to that information. That is, the situation must generate the necessary motivation to attend to this information and to grapple with it. Such motivation may derive either from the norms of the situation or from the nature of our personal involvement with the attitude object.

The psychotherapy situation provides a good example of the possibilities of bringing together these conditions for change. Psychotherapy provides opportunities for the occurrence of "corrective emotional experiences" (Alexander & French, 1946). Such experiences are based on the manifestation, within the therapy session, of some of the attitudes and behavior patterns that create conflict and distress in patients' real-life relationships. Typically, these attitudes and patterns manifest themselves in the ways in which patients interact with the therapist or, in group psychotherapy, with other patients (Frank & Ascher, 1951). The reactions of the therapist or of fellow-patients may constitute clear disconfirmations of strongly held expectations, or they may demonstrate the ineffectiveness of the patient's interpersonal behavior. Thus, the interactions in the therapy session provide the raw material for confronting patients with distorted, inappropriate, or self-defeating aspects of their attitudes. What is unique about the therapy situation is that it is governed by the strong norm to analyze feelings and reactions as they occur, thus forcing the patient to grapple with the discrepant information. The essence of a corrective emotional experience is the examination of one's attitudes and behavior patterns simultaneously with their actual manifestation at a real-life level of emotional intensity (Kelman, 1963). A similar process may be conducive to insight and attitude change at the intergroup level in the course of problem-solving workshops aimed at conflict resolution. The "here and now" interactions between the parties may provide concrete, emotionally gripping, and incontrovertible illustrations of attitudes that exacerbate and perpetuate the conflict between the two groups represented in the workshop. Such experiences, coupled with norms that encourage their analysis as they occur, may serve as a basis for attitude change (Kelman, 1972; Cohen, Kelman, Miller, & Smith, 1977).

Another example of the confluence of informational and motivational factors conducive to attitude change can be taken from international exchange experiences. Foreign visitors are most likely to develop favorable attitudes toward the host country if they are involved in an ongoing positive relationship with nationals of that country. A case in point would be participation in a cooperative project, in which they play an integral role and which they find professionally rewarding (Kelman, 1962b, 1975). Such experiences often expose visitors to new information about the host society that is particularly convincing and likely to break down earlier stereotypes. They have opportunities to observe members of the host society in contexts that are important and meaningful to themselves, and some of the characteristics of host nationals become visible to them in a concrete, immediate way. They come to know aspects of the host society through direct, personally involving experiences. At the same time, their personal positive involvement with members of the host society in mutually rewarding activities creates special motivations to see the host country in a favorable light. The knowledge that they have participated in positive interactions with nationals of the host country, and that they themselves have engaged in friendly, cooperative behavior toward them, is likely to increase their receptivity to new information that calls for a restructuring of attitudes.

In sum, one of the conditions most conducive to attitude change toward an object is the *simultaneous* presence of genuinely new and challenging information about that object and of the motivation to receive that information and grapple with it. That motivation, as my two examples were designed to illustrate, may be based in situational norms that require us to consider the information, or in personal experiences that impel us to search for or at least be open to certain kinds of new information.

The Shared Character of Attitudes

An attitude is simultaneously a personal disposition and a societal product. Attitude, in my view, always has a societal referent. Each individual's attitude is a product of social interaction, which we share to a greater or lesser extent with other members of our diverse groups, organizations, and communities. An individual's attitude is not necessarily a carbon copy of the attitudes held by fellow group members; there is often considerable variation in the manifestation of a particular attitude among the members of a group. Nevertheless, when we talk about a social attitude, we refer to a disposition that acquires a large part of its meaning from its shared character within a collectivity. In that sense, aggregate attitudes represent a system property; the attitudes of particular individuals (or subgroups) represent variants of that system property.

Within a collectivity, different attitudes differ in the degree to which there is room for variability. Certain attitudes are so closely linked to group goals, or group identity, or concerns for group survival, that there are strong pressures toward uniformity and little tolerance for deviation. Others are seen as matters of individual taste and preference, or as issues for debate within the collectivity, or as legitimate expressions of differing subgroup interests.

Within the individual, attitudes differ in how individualized they are—that is, to what degree they have been transformed, in the process of acquisition and development, from being primarily components of a social (or role) system to being components of a personal (or value) system. In this connection, the theoretical distinction between three processes of social influence—compliance, identification, and internalization—that I have proposed in earlier writings (Kelman, 1958, 1961, 1974b), may be of some relevance. A disposition acquired through compliance is essentially a tendency to give a particular verbal response rather than an attitude per se; a disposition acquired through identification is an attitude that functions primarily as part of the requirements associated with a particular role; and a disposition acquired through internalization is an attitude which, although rooted in shared values, allows the individual to make independent assessments of social demands. These different kinds of dispositions represent different kinds of relationships of the individual to the social system, yielding different degrees of flexibility and independence. Yet all of them derive their meaning from the fact that they are shared with other members of a collectivity.

The nature of the attitude as initially held by the individual—that is, the place it occupies within the individual and within the collectivity—determines the conditions under which it is likely to change. In all cases, however, attitude change typically involves a process of interaction within a group or society. It is through social interaction, in the context of the larger social system, that we explore new information and its implications, compare our views with those of others, become aware of new possibilities, communicate new expectations to one another, and test out what is legitimate and what is normative.

In short, attitude change is typically rooted in some process of communication within a group. The terms of this communication process are frequently set by various political authorities or opinion leaders. In the course of this process, individuals stimulate each other, reinforce each other, test out their own views, and compare themselves with others. As a result, new shared definitions of problems, new social norms, and new attitudes arise. The attitude change process, whether it takes place at the level of compliance, identification, or internalization, is likely to evolve to a significant degree out of such social interaction.

Attitude as a Range of Commitment

Many attitude theorists now assume that an attitude represents a range, rather than just a point on a scale. In this spirit, I propose that, for each individual, a given attitude represents a *range of commitment*. This concept clearly overlaps with the concept of latitude of acceptance (Sherif & Hovland, 1961), except that it is concerned with action potential rather than with judgments. One might think of a person's range of commitment as the range of relationships with or actions toward the object that the person finds acceptable, just as latitude of acceptance refers to the range of positions on an issue that a person finds acceptable.

It is important to keep in mind that the range of commitment may cross the zero point—that is, our range of possible relationships with a particular object may include both positive and negative associations and actions, both approach and avoidance tendencies.[3] My assumption here is that attitude toward an object very often is a resultant of conflicting approach and avoidance components—an issue to be discussed more fully below. In my exploration of attitudes in the Middle East conflict, for example, I have been particularly struck with the extent to which totally contradictory attitudes seem to coexist in the same individual and to emerge under different circumstances. Our standard procedures of attitude measurement miss the ambivalence that so often characterizes attitudes, since they derive a single average score, which defines the person as positive, negative, or neutral. One minimal way of obtaining a better picture of the range of commitment represented by an attitude would be to measure approach and avoidance components separately.

Within a person's range of commitment, one can identify a point representing the modal level of commitment (which is presumably the point to which a person's position on an attitude scale would correspond, if it were possible to devise situation-free attitude measures). The modal point is the best representation of our current equilibrium position—that is, it describes the way we are most likely to relate ourselves to the object under the present set of circumstances. It does not tell us what we would do in all situations, since our behavior vis-à-vis the attitude object fluctuates around the modal point. In some situations, we may display a level of commitment closer to the upper end of our range, in others a level closer to the lower end. The modal point tells us even less about what we might be prepared to do under changing circumstances. The concept of a range of commitment suggests that there may be potential

3. The term "commitment" is somewhat problematic here, because it is generally used to refer to degrees of positive association. For the moment, however, I can find no better term to designate the dimension of attitude that relates to the kinds of actions a person is prepared to take vis-à-vis a particular object. It should be clear, though, that I use commitment here to describe a dimension that goes from active liking or friendliness, through various degrees of approach, indifference, and avoidance, all the way to active hostility.

relationships to the object that are so far out in the range (i.e., so far removed from the modal point in either direction) that they are not likely to be manifested in the course of fluctuations that normally occur from situation to situation. But they may represent latent possibilities that might surface under the appropriate circumstances.

The notion of latent positions at the outer ends of a person's range of commitment has implications for the possibilities of attitude change. Attitude change in this scheme (as distinct from fluctuations around the modal level) would take the form of a shift in one's modal level to another position within the range and/or a shift in the entire range. One can think of the latent positions that are already present within the person's range of commitment as representing a readiness for such shifts, given the proper circumstances. The degree of readiness for a shift, the direction it would take, and the circumstances that might precipitate it may vary as a function of different qualitative factors. The possibility of such a shift to a higher or lower level within the person's range may be largely unconscious, or it may be actively entertained or even desired by the person. For example, we may be willing or even eager to become more actively involved in an organization or profession—to give more of our time to it or to take a leadership role—but the opportunities to do so may not have presented themselves, or other competing forces may have kept us at our present level. Conversely, we may feel ambivalent toward an organization or social group to which we belong, and be willing or even eager to withdraw from it, but the opportunity to do so gracefully in the face of competing considerations may not have arisen. Perhaps the most interesting cases are those in which we are not actively aware of the possibility of shifting toward a now latent attitude position precisely because no opportunities have presented themselves. The absence of opportunities may not only keep us from manifesting certain positions within our range, but it may even keep us from recognizing their existence.

A new event or a new situation may bring to the fore a relationship to the object that has hitherto been latent. I suggested above that Sadat's visit to Jerusalem had precisely that effect on the Israeli public. Typically, an event or experience will have this effect because it presents opportunities or necessities that have not been present before. People may have been ready for this new relationship—in the sense that it was within their range of commitment and part of their potential repertoire—but it had not previously been manifested. Now that it has been activated, it may help to create the conditions for attitude change, producing a shift in the person's range of commitment and establishment of a new modal point.

In sum, one of the conditions most conducive to attitude change is the activation of a latent attitude position already represented within the person's range of commitment. This condition does not assure change; much depends on whether the precipitating event or experience itself marks the beginning of a process of structural change, rather than a temporary, aberrant phenomenon. However, attitude change becomes more likely because an already existing readiness for change has been mobilized.

ACTION AS THE ARENA FOR ATTITUDE CHANGE

The view of attitudes as functionally based, socially shared, and representing a range of commitment places them squarely in an action context. Attitude is not a static psychological entity that can be separated—functionally or temporally—from the flow of action, but rather it is an integral part of action. Attitude and action are linked in a continuing reciprocal process, each generating the other in an endless chain. Action and interaction are the ground on which attitudes are formed, tested, modified, and abandoned. Attitudes are formed in the course of interaction with the object; they are constantly tested and reshaped in interaction with relevant others; and they are characterized by a range of potential action commitments.

I have discussed three situational conditions that enhance the probability of attitude change: the simultaneous presence of new, challenging information about the object and motivation to grapple with that information; the involvement of the person in social interaction with relevant others; and the activation of attitude positions that are already present in the person's repertoire but have hitherto been latent. I shall now argue that these three conditions are most likely to be present in an action situation and that action therefore constitutes the typical arena for attitude change.

(1) Action often provides the context for the simultaneous presence of genuinely new and challenging information about the object and of the motivation to consider that information. This is particularly true for intergroup and interpersonal attitudes, where action takes the form of social *interaction* with the attitude object. There are many kinds of information about another person or group

that we can gather only in the course of interaction with the other. It is only through interaction that we can observe, for example, the other's reaction to what we do, and our own reaction to what the other does.

The examples I gave in the last section illustrate the role of action in bringing together informational and motivational forces conducive to attitude change. Thus, corrective emotional experiences in psychotherapy occur in the context of an action situation. It is because patients are engaged in an active process of interacting with the therapist or fellow patients that the information about their own behavior and its consequences is highly salient and emotionally gripping. At the same time, the motivation to consider this new information derives from the analytic norms governing this action situation. Similarly, the international exchange experiences that, I suggested, are particularly conducive to attitude change occur in the context of an action situation. By virtue of their participation in rewarding joint activities with members of the host society, foreign visitors are likely to be exposed to positive information about that society at a time when they are particularly receptive to finding and noting such information. Their receptivity stems from the fact that they are actively involved in positive associations with the other, which leads them to define themselves as friendly toward the other and to define the other as worthy of that friendliness.

These examples illustrate how confrontation with new and challenging information, as well as motivation to grapple with such information, are particularly likely to occur in an action context. The coming together of these informational and motivational forces in an action situation serves as the occasion for reexamining one's attitudes, thus providing a necessary (though not sufficient) condition for attitude change.

(2) Action links the individual to a relevant collectivity or social network, thus providing another major condition for significant attitude change. Again, of course, the process of collective sharing does not necessarily lead to attitude change; it may just as easily serve to reinforce resistance to change. But where significant change does occur, it is more likely than not to have been shaped by social interaction.

In an action situation, individuals interact directly with other members of their group, organization, community, or society; and they interact indirectly with leaders and opinion makers. It is in the course of such interaction that personal reactions are tested and compared, that a shared interpretation of new events is developed and supported, that new norms are created and enforced, and that new commitments take on a public character. Good illustrations of these processes can be found in the active, public response of Israelis to the visit of President Sadat.

Many factors determine whether the outcome of such interaction processes will actually be attitude change. For example, the probability of change depends on the nature of the event that precipitated the action—the extent to which it is truly dramatic and compelling in character. Another set of factors relates to legitimization processes that bolster the action—the extent to which new interpretations and norms are encouraged by relevant authorities. Where these various factors *are* conducive to change, however, social interaction engendered by active participation provides the conditions for attitude change. Insofar as change is shaped by social interaction, it is particularly likely to take the form of identification, but not exclusively so (Kelman, 1961). Changes at the level of internalization also involve a processing of information that is mediated through social influence.

(3) Action may create the opportunity or necessity to enter into a new kind of relationship with the attitude object. This relationship may represent a degree of association that is within our range of commitment, but which has not previously been manifested. Thus, the action may bring to the fore a component of our attitude that has been latent—a level of commitment that has been quite distant from our modal point. The manifestation of this attitude may then provide a starting point for attitude change. The advantage, of course, is that this starting point is already within our psychological repertoire, so that the usual resistances to change are likely to be reduced—and indeed, internal forces toward change may already be at work.

In some cases, the component of the attitude brought to the fore in the action situation may be one of which we are not actively aware or which we do not consider as a possible position, except under the most hypothetical circumstances. Israeli attitudes toward Egypt, as manifested at the time of Sadat's visit, might be an example here. In these cases, the likelihood of attitude change subsequent to the action would depend heavily on the array of informational, motivational, and social supports that accompany and follow the action. On the other hand, there are some cases in which the action may correspond to a component of the attitude of which we had been quite aware, and which was already close to manifestation. Thus, the action situation may represent an opportunity for us to adopt a new role that we have been anticipating for some time (with more or less ambivalence); or a challenge to make a commitment that we have been toying with but that remained unexpressed because of competing pressures or anxieties; or a deliberate effort to mobilize internal and external supports for a new level of commitment by creating irreversible consequences and social expectations that would prevent us from backsliding. In these cases, we may be ready for change and the action may serve as part of the process of bringing that change into being. Once the action is taken, it helps to sharpen and stabilize the new attitude and to strengthen commitment to it.

ATTITUDES AND THE DEMANDS OF THE ACTION SITUATION

In view of the general nature of attitudes, I have argued that action is the central arena for the occurrence of attitude change. The conditions for attitude change are most likely to be present in an action situation: action may provide for the simultaneous occurrence of new and challenging information about the attitude object and of the motivation to consider that information; action may engulf the individual in social interactions with and around the attitude object; and action may bring to the fore a latent component of the attitude that represents a certain readiness to change. I now want to turn to the question of *how* action brings about attitude change—that is, what are the dynamics of action that make it conducive to attitude change?

Before discussing the dynamics of action, however, let us look at the problem confronting an individual in an action situation. Specifically, I want to look at the role and fate of the individual's initial attitude toward the attitude object. From this point of view, the action situation essentially represents a situation in which the person's attitude toward the object is being put to the test.

It may be helpful to view each action situation as an episode in a continuing socialization process, because this allows us to apply to this problem a social-psychological framework that conceives socialization as a process of negotiation between the socializee and "society" (or an organization or institution) as represented by the socializing agent. Each party to the negotiation makes its own demands, which jointly determine the socialization outcome. Within this framework, each specific action situation can be viewed as one in which both the individual actor and the situation make certain demands. One of the demands of the individuals is to act out—or to act in accordance with—their attitudes. To oversimplify, as a first approximation, the individuals' attitudes represent *their* contribution to the negotiated outcome. It is their preferred basis for action if the choice were entirely theirs. The attitudes have to compete with situational demands, which are essentially of two kinds: social-structural demands, that is, the requirements of the larger social system (the organization, the society) in whose context this episode occurs; and interaction demands, that is, the requirements of the immediate microsystem in which the individual participates.

These two kinds of situational demands are nicely illustrated in the classical study by LaPiere (1934), in which respondents to a mailed questionnaire indicated that they would not serve Chinese guests in their hotels or restaurants, even though they had actually served a Chinese couple who had presented themselves in their establishments earlier. Though this study is cited as a dramatic illustration of the lack of correspondence between attitudes and actions, it really contrasts two behavioral responses in two very differently structured social situations, one dominated by social-structural demands and the other by interaction demands (Kelman, 1978). In answering LaPiere's questionnaire, his respondents were acting primarily in their roles of representatives of their organizations facing the larger social system: they were expressing organizational policy in what was essentially a public, official context. In dealing with the Chinese couple in person they were also acting in part as representatives of their organizations: how they acted toward the couple would certainly affect the reputations of their organizations, especially if there were bystanders observing the interaction. Most important, however, they were enacting a role in the microsystem defined by their immediate interaction with the Chinese couple. It would appear that the situational demands— particularly the desire to avoid the embarrassment of turning away a respectable, pleasant, well-behaved couple, presenting themselves as clients expecting to be served—were so strong as to outweigh any other considerations.

LaPiere's striking finding suggests that both of his measurement situations were almost entirely controlled by structural or situational constraints. The questionnaire responses were constrained by organizational policy, which in turn was governed by national norms; the direct responses were constrained by the structure of the immediate situation, which in turn was governed by powerful norms of social interaction. Attitudes toward the Chinese, as an individual difference variable, clearly played no role in determining responses in either situation, as evidenced by the lack of variance in both sets of data. That is, virtually all respondents said they would not serve Chinese, and virtually all in fact did serve the Chinese couple. This finding has some interesting implications for the nature of these attitudes at the time, but they are quite different from the implications drawn in much of the work that took off from LaPiere.

Whatever may have happened in the LaPiere study, in a typical action situation we can postulate two sets of competing demands: those of the individual actors, as represented by their attitudes, and those of the situation, representing the requirements of the larger social system and of the immediate interaction. If the person's attitude is in some way incongruent with these situational requirements, it must negotiate with them in producing the action outcome. Clearly, under the circumstances, we can never expect literal correspondence between attitude and action. The degree of correspondence always depends on the relative strengths of the competing demands from the individual and from the situation.

So far, I have been treating attitude as the individual's contribution to the negotiated outcome. But, as I indicated above, this is merely an oversimplified first approximation, insofar as it implies that attitudes can be treated as strictly individual dispositions. In the view of attitudes I have presented, they always have a social referent, are products of social interaction, and are shared with other members of relevant collectivities. Thus, the attitude itself reflects a social as well as an individual contribution.[4]

Keeping in mind its socially shared character, how does a particular attitude function in an action situation? This depends on the

4. By the same token, it should be noted that the situational demands cannot be viewed as entirely structural in origin. They also reflect an individual contribution, since structural requirements are mediated by the individual's definition of the situation. Since definitions of the situation are often subject to considerable individual differences, our ability to predict behavior in a given situation—or, more precisely, the impact of situational requirements relative to the impact of the person's own attitude—is greatly enhanced by our knowledge of that person's definition of the situation (Kelman, 1978).

structure of that attitude within the relevant collectivity and within the individual, as described earlier. At the level of the collectivity, the domain to which an attitude belongs determines the way it functions. In a domain that is closely linked to group goals, group identity, and concern for group survival, action is likely to be controlled to a high degree by situational demands; individual attitudes, insofar as they deviate from the group norm, are often overpowered by these demands. On the other hand, attitudes in a domain defined as open to personal preference or subgroup interests are more likely to compete on an equal footing with situational demands. Similarly, at the individual level, the nature of the attitude (i.e., the type of relationship of the individual to the social system that it represents) determines the probability that it will be expressed—or translated into action—in a particular social situation. Compliance-based dispositions are by definition controlled by situational demands, whereas internalized attitudes offer the strongest competition to such demands. Attitudes based on identification are intermediate, in that they are likely to be expressed to the extent that situational demands and role requirements bring them into salience. In short, the likelihood that an attitude will be expressed in action varies with the degree of independence that the particular attitude has from the situational demands of the action situation.

In some cases, the situational constraints are so strong that personal attitudes toward the object play almost no part in the action. The two situations used in the LaPiere (1934) study seem to represent such cases. In other cases, action may be entirely determined by the attitude because the situational demands are very flexible, or because they are completely congruent with the attitude, or because the attitude is so powerful. In many cases, however, there is some degree of conflict between these two sets of demands, leading to negotiation between them. The action outcome of this negotiation may be predominantly determined by the attitude, or it may be predominantly determined by the situation, or—as frequently happens—it may represent some kind of compromise between the two.

These negotiations in the action situation lead up to and give form to the action that the person finally takes. The process and outcome of the negotiations, insofar as they involve some degree of conflict between attitudes and situational demands and yield some degree of compromise between the two, are bound to have an impact on the

person's initial attitudes. They are likely to introduce new information and motivation that may strengthen or weaken the attitude,
constrict or expand it, crystallize it, qualify it, or modify it. Thus, the
conduciveness of action to attitude change is directly related to the
problem that the individual confronts in an action situation. It is
now time to turn in detail to the dynamics of the action itself and the
mechanisms of change that it potentially brings into play.

DYNAMICS OF ACTION AND MECHANISMS OF ATTITUDE CHANGE

How does action bring about attitude change? What happens in the
course of action and as a consequence of action that creates forces
toward change? Table 2 summarizes my attempt to answer these
questions.

The columns of Table 2 distinguish between two kinds of processes generated by action—motivational and informational
processes—that are potentially conducive to attitude change. The
rows of the table describe some of the dynamic features of action,
each of which in its own way may generate such motivational and
informational processes. As indicated by the rows of the table, I am
proposing that action has the potentiality of generating motivational
and informational processes conducive to attitude change for the
following reasons: (1) Action reduces the person's psychological
distance from the attitude object; (2) Action requires the person to
make a decision to act and then to perform the action; (3) The action
in itself—that is, the fact that the person has taken this action—
becomes a new datum in the person's life-space that must be taken
into account in contemplating what has transpired; and (4) The
action has real-life consequences for the actor with which she or he
must contend.

All of these features of action are potentially conducive to attitude
change because they help to create or bring into prominence the
conditions for attitude change that I discussed earlier. That is, they
expose us to new information in a context in which we are motivated
to explore it and to consider its implications for our attitudes; they
link us to relevant others through direct interaction or communication of social norms; and they bring to the fore a level of commitment

or a component of the attitude that has previously been latent. Let me proceed to show more specifically how each of the four dynamic features of action identified in Table 2 is potentially conducive to attitude change.[5]

Table 2[*]
Dynamics of action that generate motivational and informational processes potentially conducive to attitude change

| | Processes Generated by Action | |
Dynamics of Action	Motivational	Informational
Action reduces P's psychological distance from attitude object	Dealing with new and latent requirements and opportunities brought to the fore by closer association	Attending to newly salient features of object and of social environment
Action requires P to decide and perform	Meeting task and situa- tional demands	Coding information about object and social expectations relevant to decision and performance
Action itself becomes a new datum entering P's life space	Explanation and justification of action	Definition of object and of self in terms of their interaction
Action has real-life consequences	Anticipation and fulfillment of new commitments and role requirements	Integration of new experiences and ob- servations generated by action

[*]Adapted from Kelman, 1974a, p. 317.

5. The following discussion draws heavily on Kelman, 1974a, although the framework has been expanded and modified in a number of important ways.

Reduced Psychological Distance

Almost by definition, action requires closer association with the attitude object. I refer here essentially to psychological association, although often it may include physical association. It should be noted that action leads to closer association with the object regardless of whether that action is consistent or inconsistent with the initial attitude. Of course, the relationship of the action to the initial attitude has important implications for the nature and effects of the new association. Similarly, the degree to which the action conforms with or deviates from situational demands has implications for the nature and effects of the association.

The reduced psychological distance from the attitude object means that certain kinds of information about the object become more salient (see right-hand column of Table 2). When you are involved in closer association with an object you are forced to attend to characteristics of the object that you might otherwise ignore. The direct observation conveys these characteristics in a more powerful, emotionally more compelling way. When the object is another person or group, action and association typically take the form of social interaction, which provides a unique and particularly salient type of information about the object—namely information about how the other reacts to you and your input. Finally, when the association occurs in a social context, you can also observe the reaction of others to the object and the norms surrounding that object. Clearly, then, there is an array of new information that becomes available to the individual as a direct result of closer association with the object, and this information represents potential inputs for attitude change.

The fact that we are engaged in closer association with an object also creates special motivation to attend to and respond to confirmatory information, i.e., to information congruent with the nature and level of our association. For example, closer association with members of a group toward which we initially held negative or at least highly ambivalent attitudes creates motivation to attend to and process positive information about that group, so that our association can be more pleasant, more productive, and more capable of contributing to the achievement of our goals. Also, the reduced psychological distance may bring out positive components of our attitude that were in fact within our range of commitment but that had remained latent in the absence of direct association. An especially interesting example here comes from those situations in which

we may in fact have desired a closer positive relationship to the
other, but have confronted strong barriers to the establishment of
such a relationship. These barriers may take the form of lack of trust
(as in the initial Israeli attitudes toward Egypt), status differences,
shyness, pride, or cultural taboos about associating with certain
outgroups. In such cases, the action may propel us (by virtue of
situational demands, *faits accomplis*, or what-have-you) into the
closer relationship that we had wanted but could not achieve. That
is, the action has overcome the psychological barriers to closer
association; and now already existing (though heretofore latent)
motivations to continue the association, and to attend to and
process confirmatory information, take over.

It should be noted that reduced psychological distance (as well as
the other features of action to be discussed below) do not necessarily
lead to attitude change. For example, there is no assurance that
closer association with a negatively viewed other will engender
positive attitudes. We may be propelled into a situation in which we
feel even more threatened by the other than we did before. Or the
newly salient information about the other that becomes available to
us through our closer association may confirm our worst stereotypes. In short, closer association brought about by action may well
produce boomerang effects. All that can be said is that the dynamics
of action make it possible for the conditions for attitude change to
manifest themselves, but they do not assure the occurrence of
attitude change.

Requirement to Decide and Perform

When we find ourselves in a situation in which there are strong
demands to take or consider taking an action to which we have
varying degrees of resistance (e.g., to participate in a protest action),
a decision-making process is set into motion. We assess the options
available to us and their respective consequences; we decide
whether or not to engage in the action; and, if the decision is
positive, we determine the nature and extent of our participation
and preview the content of what we will be doing. In the course of
the decision-making, we are likely to think through the issues raised
by the action, to consider appropriate information, and to review
relevant arguments. These efforts, in turn, may involve us in an
active process of reevaluating our position—of reconsidering our

original attitude from the point of view of its implications for our own values and for our relationship to important reference groups. The process of reexamination may provide attitudinal support for the action we have been asked to take and may thus lead to attitude change, in the form of internalization or identification or some combination of the two (Kelman, 1961). In other words, attitude change may emerge from the process of reexamining our attitudes that has been motivated by the situational requirements of the action.

A high degree of choice about the action is particularly conducive to attitude change. If we are undecided, then the greater the choice, the more likely we are—in the process of arriving at the necessary decision and firming it up—to reexamine our attitudes and to marshal forces in support of the action that we finally select. Of course, we may decide against taking the action, and this negative decision would now have considerable attitudinal support. But if we do take the action, it is likely to be accompanied by attitude change. A high degree of choice may facilitate attitude change even when the situational forces are so strong that we experience no indecision: the fact that we were given the choice may force us to find attitudinal support for the action we have already decided to take through a process of active self-persuasion (Kelman, 1962a). Once a decision to act has been made, our motivation to meet the demands of the task in which we have agreed to participate may bring a further process of reexamination of attitudes into play—depending, of course, on the specific nature of the action. For example, once we have agreed to participate in a protest action, preparation of the protest statement requires review of the issues and development of appropriate arguments. If the task is to be carried out effectively, we have to think up supporting arguments and to present them in a convincing way. In the course of engaging in this process, we may become aware of nuances and implications of the issues that we had not considered before and may thus succeed in persuading ourselves. This is one reason for the potential effectiveness of role playing in producing attitude change, particularly if it requires improvisation (King & Janis, 1956). Though the role playing may be a mere exercise, requiring no commitment on the part of the player, the demands of the task itself may lead us to reconsider our attitudes. In reverse role play among conflicting parties, for example, successful task performance requires each player to consider and present the other party's position from the other's point of view.

The parties may thus gain insights into their adversaries' positions that were not previously available to them, and modify their own views accordingly. In psychotherapy, corrective emotional experiences may be motivated by the patient's desire to do a good job, in keeping with the norms of the situation. In international exchanges, the requirement of effectively carrying out cooperative projects may motivate reexamination of attitudes toward the other group, in order to find positive characteristics congruent with a cooperative relationship.

The motivational processes generated in the action situation are accompanied by informational processes that are similarly conducive to attitude change. In the course of deciding to act and carrying out the action, we process various items of information that have attitudinal relevance. Some of this information is conveyed by the context of the action; some is deliberately sought out by us to help us decide and perform; some is generated by the action itself. We may thus acquire data about the characteristics of the object, about the value implications of various policies, about the distribution of opinions on the issue, and about the expectations held by relevant reference groups. These are the kinds of information that typically enter into the formation of attitudes. Exposure to new information of this variety—under the appropriate motivational circumstances—provides the raw material for attitude change.

Action as a New Datum

Once we have taken action, the action itself becomes a datum with which we have to contend. In other words, action creates a new psychological situation, in which the fact of our action represents a salient element. Contemplation of the action we have taken may raise questions about the meaning of the action, about its implications for our self-image, and about the nature of our ongoing relationship to the object of the action. These musings may generate motivational and informational processes conducive to attitude change. This feature of action, essentially, is the one on which both dissonance (Festinger, 1957; Brehm & Cohen, 1962) and attribution (Bem, 1967) interpretations of forced compliance focus.

On the motivational side, if the action violated certain norms or standards, then the fact that we have taken that action may have negative implications for our self-evaluation. Contemplation of the action may arouse guilt, shame, or some other negative affect, which in turn would generate cognitive efforts to justify the action. The precise nature of the reaction would depend on the form that the action took, the norm that it violated, and the specific motivational system it has thrown out of balance—issues to which I shall return in the next section of this paper. Efforts to explain or justify a discrepant action may bring about attitude change, more or less along the lines proposed by dissonance theory. A morally dissonant act, for example, can be justified if we can convince ourselves that the object we harmed or the cause we betrayed was not worthy of our loyalty; a hedonically dissonant act can be justified if we can convince ourselves that the discrepant action was really enjoyable and profitable (Kelman & Baron, 1974; Kelman, Baron, Sheposh, & Lubalin, Note 1).

Discrepant action is particularly likely to generate justification processes conducive to attitude change to the extent that we have been personally involved in the action. Knowledge that we have acted in a certain way toward an object becomes an important datum in our self-evaluation and in our evaluation of the object if we regard the action as internally motivated and representative of the self. The sense of personal involvement—and hence the probability of attitude change—should be greater if the action is freely chosen, if it requires effort and initiative, and if it represents a complex of interrelated role behaviors within some social system rather than a specific, isolated act (Kelman, 1962a). Contemplation of the action also provides new information—relevant to the definition of the object and to our self-definition—on which attitude change may be based. I always cite, in this connection, the title of the classic collection of children's definitions, *A Hole is to Dig*, because it describes so elegantly our tendency to define objects in terms of the way in which we characteristically act toward them. The action we take toward an object tends to become a salient characteristic of that object. It influences our subsequent interactions with the object and our receptivity to further information about it and thus, eventually, our evaluation of the object. For example, if we have acted in support of a particular policy, we will be inclined to define it in part as a policy that we have supported. This new definition, in turn, may contribute to a new evaluation of it as a policy that is worthy of our support. Such an outcome can be understood in terms of the usual ways in which information is processed, without invoking a special need for consistency. I am simply proposing that our own action toward an object represents one important datum about that object which enters into our evaluation of it.

When the object is another person or group, our own effect on the other—that is, what the other did in response to our actions and especially in response to our influence attempts—becomes a particularly salient item of information about the other. This is largely so because we know—or at least we think we know—what caused the other's actions when they are in response to our initiative. Similarly, the effect the other had on us is also a salient item of information about the other.

The information provided by contemplation of our action also has relevance for our self-definition. In line with a Bemian analysis, if we act toward an object in a certain way, we will (given the proper stimulus conditions) attribute to ourselves the corresponding attitude. Beyond that, if the action touches on central concerns, it will contribute to our more enduring definition of the self. Thus, repeated friendly association with another person will lead us to define ourselves as the other's friend; repeated participation in protests and demonstrations will lead us to define ourselves as activists or radicals. Our conception of the kinds of persons we are, in turn, plays a major role in determining our future actions and interactions. Thus, by being integrated into the person's self-definition, the action-generated attitude gains stability and generality.

Real-life Consequences

Most actions, at least outside of the laboratory, have consequences beyond the immediate situation. They create new realities; they change the social and often the physical environment in which we find ourselves. When taking action, therefore, we prepare ourselves psychologically for its anticipated consequences. At the very least, for example, we can anticipate having to explain and defend our action to others. In preparation for such an eventuality, we may review the issues involved in the action, rehearse the opposing arguments, and reassess our own attitudes toward the object of the action. Out of this process, attitude change may emerge, particularly since we are motivated to find arguments supportive of the action we have taken. If we not only know these arguments, but actually believe them, our ability to offer a comfortable and convincing defense of our action is further enhanced.

The motivation to bring our attitude into line with our action is especially strong if the action commits us to continuing association or public identification with the object and hence, at least implicitly, to future action in support of it. Many simple acts have this consequence—such as buying a product, making a pledge, or allowing our names to be placed on a mailing list. Of special interest, however, are those actions that involve commitment to a new role, such as the act of joining an organization, moving into a new neighborhood, starting a new job, or entering a training program. These actions represent long-term commitments which would be costly to break; they involve us in an extensive set of role relationships; and they often become salient features of our public identities. Under the circumstances, the development and strengthening of appropriate attitudes in preparation for the new role becomes particularly crucial. We are open to and actively search for new information that lends attitudinal support to our action and thus makes our anticipated role performance more effective, more comfortable, and more rewarding. In short, these preparatory processes are likely to facilitate attitude change in the direction of the action taken and of the future actions anticipated (Kelman, 1962a).

Not only the anticipated but also the actual consequences of action generate motivations for attitude change, particularly when the action takes the form of commitment to a new role. The requirements of the new role produce strong forces toward reexamining our attitudes and making them congruent with the expected role performance. Thus, for example, the workers in Lieberman's (1956) study who become foremen have to make choices and take actions in keeping with their new status; effective performance depends on the extent to which they develop the appropriate attitudes. Also, as an integral part of their new roles, they have to defend the position of management, which makes it necessary that they know it and probable that they will adopt it. Of equal importance is the fact that others tend to cast them into the role of spokespersons for management and expect them to take management-oriented positions; such role casting usually has the self-fulfilling effect of binding people into the role so that they become what others expect them to be. To take another example, the white housewives who moved into an interracial housing project in the Deutsch and Collins (1951) study were motivated to reexamine their racial attitudes because they were now involved in regular interaction with black neighbors, because they were called upon to defend their decisions to move into the project, and because they were identified by others as residents in interracial housing. In short, as a consequence of action, we may find ourselves in new roles. Enactment of the role sets into motion various forces conducive to attitude change, not the least of which are the expectations conveyed by others and the tendency of others to attribute certain attitudes to us and to treat us accordingly.

On the informational side, a frequent consequence of action is to provide us with new experiences, which may expose us to new information. The experiences may be in the form of more extensive contact with the attitude object itself. Thus the workers-turned-foremen in Lieberman's study, by virtue of their new roles, have increased contact with management and hence access to new information about it. Since they are open to information supportive of their new roles, it is quite likely that the increased contact will provide them with raw material for attitude change in the direction of management. The white housewives in the Deutsch and Collins study have the opportunity to interact with their black counterparts in daily activities and around common concerns, which represents new experiences for them. Whether such contacts will produce more favorable attitudes depends on what happens in the course of the interaction and how motivated the participants are to receive favorable information. The literature on intergroup contact suggests that contact at least provides the potential for new experiences conducive to attitude change. Favorable change is most likely if the contact meets certain conditions—for example, if it involves equal-status interactions and if it is sanctioned by legitimate authorities (conditions, incidentally, that were met in the Deutsch and Collins study).

Action may also provide us with new social experiences that indirectly yield new information about the object. After taking action in support of a particular group or policy, for example, we may receive praise from others—or at least we may find that the anticipated disapproval is not forthcoming. We may discover that many more people than we expected—at least within our relevant reference groups—agree with the stand we have taken. These new items of information about group consensus and about the social acceptability of our action may contribute to attitude change via the process of identification. In short, as we integrate new experiences consequent to the action—whether these involve direct contact with the object or contact with social norms about it—forces toward attitude change may well be set into motion.

In sum, the analysis of the dynamics of action, as summarized in Table 2, suggests how action potentially creates the conditions necessary for attitude change. By reducing the person's psychological distance from the attitude object, by requiring the person to decide and perform, by entering as a new datum into the person's life-space, and by producing real-life consequences for the person, action brings together informational and motivational processes in ways that may be conducive to attitude change. In and of itself, however, this analysis does not tell us whether, in any given case, change will indeed occur and, if so, what form it will take. In order to make such predictions, we need a functional analysis of the particular case, which takes into account the nature of the attitude, the nature of the action, the nature of the situation in which the action takes place, and the nature of the experiences the person has in the course of the action and subsequent to it.

EFFECTS OF DISCREPANT ACTION

To illustrate the possibilities of a functional analysis of the effects of action on attitude, I shall turn to a special case of action—namely, what has been called discrepant or counterattitudinal action. So far, I have dealt with action broadly, without making any systematic distinctions between actions that are congruent with the person's original attitude and actions that are discrepant from them. In fact, at several points, I have referred to the possibility that an action may be discrepant from some components of the attitude and congruent with others. For the present purposes, however, I shall keep the discussion within the framework of discrepant action, since this has been the primary subject for experimental research in this field, particularly research in the dissonance tradition. The empirical efforts at developing a functional approach to these problems, in which my colleagues and I have been engaged (Kelman, Baron, Sheposh, & Lubalin, Note 1), have similarly concentrated on discrepant action.

The term discrepant action can be used to refer to any action toward an object that is out of keeping (from the actor's own point of view) with the actor's attitude toward that object. In speaking of discrepant action, we usually have in mind actions that in some way "fall short" of the attitude—that is, fail to live up to the level of commitment that the attitude represents. Such failure may occur because actions in line with the attitude appear too costly and difficult, or because they are inhibited by situational pressures, or because their anticipated consequences are too negative, or because competing motives impel the person to follow a different course. Discrepant actions, however, may also take the form of actions that "surpass" the person's attitude—that are at a higher level of commitment than that implied by the attitude. Due to situational pressures or social facilitation, we may act in ways that are more generous, more courageous, or more tolerant than our attitude requires. I shall return to a brief discussion of such "surpassing" actions in a later section of this paper. For now, however, I shall limit the discussion to discrepant action in the more customary sense of action that falls short of the attitude—action that is in some respect "deficient."

Discrepant action is often the occasion for attitude change for the various reasons that have been discussed in the preceding sections. The dynamics of discrepant action (viewed here as a special case of action in general) help to create the conditions that are necessary if attitude change is to occur. Whether or not these conditions will actually lead to change depends on the specific motivational and informational processes that are generated by the action. The occurrence and specific nature of change must be understood, in functional terms, as the outcome of our efforts to process new information in the light of the various motivational forces that the discrepant action has brought into play. This functional view contrasts with the view of attitude change as a reaction to the discrepancy as such, that is, as a way of removing the inconsistency between the action and the initial attitude.

Although a functional analysis does not regard attitude change as merely a way of closing the gap between action and attitude that had been created by the discrepant action, it does concern itself with the existence of this gap as an element in the analysis. I have already alluded to this in my earlier discussion of the dynamics of action, particularly in the discussion of action as a new datum in the person's life-space. In a functional analysis, we would ask what it means to people when they find themselves engaged in (or having engaged in) a particular discrepant action. What are the perceived implications of that action for their various efforts to cope with environmental demands and to achieve their diverse goals? In particular, what implications does this action have for their self-evaluation and for their ability to deal with future events and relationships? Only by knowing what specific dilemmas (if any) the discrepant action has created for individuals and what specific motivational systems it has thrown out of balance can we predict whether attitude change is likely to occur and what form it is likely to take.

Within this perspective, it is probably somewhat misleading to speak of discrepancy between action and *attitude*—i.e., to describe a discrepant action as one that falls short of the person's attitude. To be sure, we are dealing with situations in which the action is somehow inconsistent with the initial attitude (or at least with the person's modal level of commitment). But, given the nature of attitudes and the relationship between attitude and action that I have been expounding, such inconsistencies are not necessarily experienced as deficiencies. They may simply reflect fluctuations in the attitude across different situations or shifts in the attitude in response to new opportunities or necessities. What lends motivational significance to a discrepant act is not discrepancy between action and attitude as such, but discrepancy between action and some kind of *standard* or *expectation*. Thus, for the purposes of a functional analysis, a discrepant action is an action that falls short of social norms, moral values, role expectations, personal standards, or private interests.

The approach to discrepant action that has just been outlined is linked to a general conception of cognitive inconsistency that differs from dissonance theory and certain other consistency models. According to this conception, inconsistency serves primarily as a *signal* rather than as a motive (Kelman & Baron, 1968a). It alerts us to the possibility that our coping mechanisms may not be functioning at their best and that we may not be moving most effectively toward the achievement of our goals. In response, the individual may engage in an active searching process, designed to assess the functional implications of the inconsistency. Whether this process leads to attempts to reduce the inconsistency and what specific mechanisms of inconsistency reduction (or inconsistency maintenance)— including attitude change—are employed, depends on the *specific* functional implications that are revealed (Kelman & Baron, 1968b).

Starting with these assumptions, a functional analysis of discrepant action must focus on the specific content of that action in order to assess its functional implications from the actor's point of view. Thus, a functional approach is based on qualitative distinctions between discrepant actions in terms of the kinds of problems or dilemmas they create for the individual. The nature of the dilemma determines the individual's reaction and hence, among other things, whether or not attitude change will be part of that reaction—and, if it is, what kind of change it will be.

Moral and Hedonic Dilemmas

In some of the research that my colleagues and I have carried out, we distinguish between two kinds of dilemmas that discrepant action might create for the individual: moral dilemmas and hedonic dilemmas (Kelman, Baron, Sheposh, & Lubalin, Note 1). A moral dilemma arises if the person performs an action that violates a moral precept or value. A hedonic dilemma arises if the person performs an action that turns out to be unrewarding, entailing costs that exceed the benefits. We assume that these two kinds of actions have very different motivational implications for the individual and confrontation with them is likely to produce rather different consequences.

Violation of a moral precept or of an important value carries direct implications for central aspects of the person's self-image. Morally discrepant action is likely to arouse guilt and to lead to efforts at expiation or reparation. If opportunities for such resolutions are unavailable to us, we may change our attitudes toward the object in a way that would justify our action. Alternatively, we may strengthen our original attitude as a way of reducing the likelihood of future lapses. In either event, changes are likely to be relatively persistent and to be accompanied by an active search for information in support of the new attitude.

In contrast, hedonically discrepant actions create more transitory and peripheral concerns. To some extent, they may affect our self-esteem, in that they may raise questions about our competence in protecting our own interests. The major reaction, however, is likely to be a sense of inequity due to insufficient rewards for our efforts. If this experience is part of an ongoing relationship or represents a repetitive pattern, then it may set an attitude change process into motion. If it is a relatively isolated event, however, then one way of dealing with the discomfort is by a memorial adjustment: we may remember the experience as more rewarding or less effortful than it was, thus justifying our action. Such a change is likely to be transitory and low in generality.

Variables that affect the arousal and reduction of dissonance, such as reward and effort, can be expected to have differential effects in the two types of situations. Thus, for example, it can be argued that the greater the reward we receive for a morally discrepant action, the greater our guilt and hence the greater the discomfort we experience. The greater the effort involved on our part, the less the psychological discomfort, since effort can serve as a form of expiation. These predictions of the effects of reward and effort are opposite to those made by dissonance theory. On the other hand, for hedonically discrepant actions, we would predict, along with dissonance theory, that discomfort would be greatest under low reward and high effort. Similarly, differential predictions for moral and hedonic dilemmas can be made about the variables that control different mechanisms of resolving these dilemmas, including attitude change.

We carried out several experiments to test the effects of different variables on arousal and resolution of moral and hedonic dilemmas. In one such experiment (Baron, Kelman, Sheposh, & Johnson, Note 2; for a briefer description, see Kelman & Baron, 1974), the independent variable of interest was the attractiveness of the inducing agent (i.e., of the experimenter, who in this case was responsible for inducing the subjects' discrepant action).

The basic design of the experiment can be seen readily from the column and row headings in Table 3. Two types of situations were created experimentally, one conducive to moral dissonance and the other to hedonic dissonance. In each of these, the degree of dissonance arousal and the attractivenenss of the inducing agent were varied. In both situations, the substantive attitude issue concerned government interference with speakers on state campuses—an issue that was a live topic at the time on the campus where the experiment was carried out.

In the moral dissonance situation, the subjects (female undergraduates) conducted an interview on state control over campus speakers with another subject (a male student), who was in fact a confederate giving standardized answers. Subjects were asked to reinforce statements by the interviewee that favored state control— a position contrary to their own. In the course of the interview, they were able to observe the interviewee shifting his statements in the direction of the reinforced position. Thus, the subjects were led to believe that they were actively supporting a position contrary to their own by reinforcing another subject's shift toward that position—a shift that would, presumably, maintain itself outside the

Table 3*
Attitudes toward issue, task, and experiment as a function of degree of dissonance arousal and attractiveness of the inducing agent in moral and hedonic situations

	Moral Dissonance		Hedonic Dissonance	
	A. Attitude toward Central Issue			
	High Arousal	Low Arousal	High Arousal	Low Arousal
Attractive E	4.16	2.67	3.18	2.74
Unattractive E	2.63	2.74	2.92	2.26
	B. Attitude toward Wider Issue			
	High Arousal	Low Arousal	High Arousal	Low Arousal
Attractive E	3.16	2.97	2.87	2.86
Unattractive E	2.71	2.85	2.77	2.85
	C. Attitude toward Task			
	High Arousal	Low Arousal	High Arousal	Low Arousal
Attractive E	4.90	4.32	4.32	4.35
Unattractive E	4.12	4.99	5.20	3.40
	D. Attitude toward Experiment			
	High Arousal	Low Arousal	High Arousal	Low Arousal
Attractive E	5.61	5.25	4.64	4.72
Unattractive E	4.77	5.49	5.54	4.05

Note: N = 9 Ss per cell. The higher the score, the more positive the evaluation.
* From Kelman and Baron, 1974, p. 568. Reprinted from S. Himmelfarb & A. H. Eagly (Eds.), *Readings in Attitude Change* (1974), by permission of John Wiley & Sons, Inc.

laboratory. In the high arousal condition, subjects were required to give more frequent and clearer reinforcements to the discrepant position than in the low arousal condition. We assumed, therefore, that subjects in the high arousal condition would feel greater personal responsibility for the effect they were observing and thus greater guilt for betraying their own attitudes.

In the hedonic dissonance situation, subjects were exposed to the identical substantive information as in the moral dissonance situation. They read each of the questions from the interview and then listened to a recording of the standardized answer given by the confederate in the moral dissonance situation. They were assigned the tedious and uninteresting task of counting and listing various categories of words. In the high arousal condition, this task was made even more unpleasant by including white noise on the tape without, however, interfering with reception of the message.

Attractiveness of the inducing agent was manipulated by two means. Subjects heard the confederate describe the experimenter in highly positive or highly negative terms. In addition, to strengthen the manipulation of the unattractive-agent condition, subjects heard the experimenter in that condition make gratuitously disparaging remarks about the student newspaper. To establish linkage between the inducing agent and the induced action, the experimenter in all conditions mentioned his membership in an organization known to favor state control of campus speakers. Thus, it was clear that he personally favored the action taken by the subjects and that it reflected his own attitudes.

It was hypothesized that under conditions of high arousal of hedonic dissonance, the more *unattractive* the inducing agent, the greater the probability of attitude change toward the *action* and the general *situation*. When confronted with a hedonic dilemma, subjects are concerned about the fact that they have engaged in an unrewarding or unpleasant action. The less justified the action, the greater this concern, and hence the greater the tendency to make up in memory for what was missing in fact. Since the unattractive agent makes for less justification and greater dissonance, he should produce greater attitude change. In other words, with respect to evaluation of the action and the situation, we made a straight dissonance prediction here. On the other hand, we expected no systematic relationship between attractiveness of the agent and attitude toward the object or issue in the hedonic-dilemma situation, since these attitudes are not particularly linked to the pleasantness or unpleasantness of the action.

Under conditions of high arousal of moral dissonance, we hypothesized that the more *attractive* the inducing agent, the greater the probability of attitude change toward the *object* or the *issue*. The assumption here is that, in a moral-dilemma situation, subjects are concerned about the fact that they have violated their values. If they can convince themselves that the issue is not as important as they once thought, or that the other side is really more reasonable than they had believed it to be, then they do not have to feel as guilty any more. This particular dilemma is not especially affected by the attractiveness of the agent. Guilt is not increased because the agent was unattractive, nor is it reduced because the agent was attractive. The agent becomes relevant, however, as a source of inputs into subjects' reexamination of their attitudes toward the issue. It should be recalled that the experimenter made clear that he personally favored the induced action. Thus, he served not only as an inducing agent, but also as a source of communication. The general relationship found in communication studies therefore becomes applicable here: attractive agents are more influential, more likely to produce change in attitude toward the issue in the direction they favor. In short, then, we propose that subjects in the moral-dilemma situation focus on the object of their action, on the issue with which the action was concerned; they are motivated to change their attitudes on this issue as a way of reducing guilt. This change, however, is more likely to occur when it has the support of an attractive rather than an unattractive agent. These considerations have no bearing on attitudes toward the action or the situation, which should therefore not be systematically affected by moral dissonance as such.

These hypotheses were generally borne out, as can be seen from the summary of the main data presented in Table 3. In the hedonic-dissonance situation, under conditions of high arousal, the unattractive agent produced more favorable attitudes toward the task (Table 3C) and toward the experiment (Table 3D) than did the attractive agent, as expected.[6] Attitudes toward the issue, however, were not significantly affected by the attractiveness of the agent under hedonic dissonance. By contrast, under conditions of high arousal of moral dissonance, the attractive agent produced signifi-

6. The reversal under conditions of low arousal of hedonic dissonance was unexpected, as was the reversal under conditions of high arousal of moral dissonance. In both cases, we had expected no systematic differences between the attractive and the unattractive agents. Possible explanations of these unexpected findings are offered in Kelman and Baron, 1974, pp. 571–572.

cantly more favorable attitudes toward the central issue than did the unattractive agent (Table 3A), as predicted. Results for attitude items less directly related to the central issue (Table 3B) show the same pattern, but fall short of statistical significance.

The data on attitudes toward the issue in the moral-dissonance situation (see the left-hand portion of Table 3A) are the most relevant to our general concern in this paper with the role of action in attitude change. Attitude toward the issue (i.e., the object of action) is, of course, what we generally have in mind when we speak of attitude change as a consequence of action. The moral-dissonance situation comes closest, in this experiment, to a situation involving action specifically directed to the attitude object (i.e., the issue of state control of campus speakers), and Table 3A presents the effects of the action on attitudes toward that object. The table shows a clear interaction effect: the upper-left cell, in which high arousal of moral dissonance is combined with an attractive agent, stands out in comparison to the other three cells of the sub-table. In fact, this is the only cell in which the mean value (4.16) represents agreement with a position favoring state control over campus speakers and in which there is evidence that attitude *change* has occurred at all. The means of the other three cells approximate very closely the baseline mean of 2.58 (representing a position against state control over campus speakers), obtained from a control group of 101 subjects drawn from the same population as the experimental subjects. Thus, it appears that only subjects in the high-arousal, attractive-agent condition changed their attitudes in the direction of the discrepant action and adopted a position in favor of state control.

The combination of high arousal of moral dissonance and an attractive source of communication represents a coming together of motivational and informational forces conducive to attitude change. The subjects in this particular condition are motivated to reexamine their attitudes because the guilt generated by their discrepant action leads to efforts to justify it; the information that an attractive source favors a different position on the issue helps them to resolve their moral dilemma by modifying their own attitudes. Thus, these findings are consistent with my earlier argument that action is conducive to attitude change insofar as it provides the context for the simultaneous presence of challenging information and the motivation to consider that information. I would not wish to claim, on the basis of the present findings, that high arousal of moral dissonance—even in combination with strong informational forces—would necessarily lead to attitude change. A great deal depends on the significance of the principles that have been violated and their centrality in the person's daily life, as well as on the alternative mechanisms for reducing guilt and justifying the discrepant action that are available in the particular situation. What the findings do suggest is that morally discrepant action creates motivations for change in attitude toward the object of that action; understanding of these motivations can provide a systematic basis for determining the probability of attitude change, the nature of the change, and the variables controlling the magnitude of change.

My colleagues and I have carried out several other experiments on discrepant action, designed to explore the effects of such variables as effort and incentive on the arousal and resolution of moral and hedonic dissonance (Kelman, Baron, Sheposh, & Lubalin, Note 1). The results have been mixed, confirming some of our hypotheses while leaving others unconfirmed. On the whole, however, they tend to support the logic of the distinction between moral and hedonic dilemmas: specifying the nature of the discrepant action—i.e., the particular standard or expectation from which it deviates and hence the type of dilemma it creates for the individual—helps us predict people's emotional reactions to their own discrepant act, the modes of resolution they are likely to employ, the probability that resolution will involve attitude change (and if it does, which attitudes will be affected), and the variables controlling the strength of arousal and resolution. Further indirect support for the moral-hedonic distinction is suggested by Eagly and Himmelfarb (1978, pp. 533–534) in their review of recent studies of counterattitudinal behavior. A number of studies have shown that the increased attitude change predicted by dissonance theory occurs only when the counterattitudinal behavior leads to aversive or unwanted consequences.[7] The evidence is inconsistent, however, with respect to the reversibility of attitude change if the unwanted consequences are later removed. Eagly and Himmelfarb propose that removal of the unwanted consequences may remove personal responsibility and

---

7. The moral-dissonance situation in our experiment, described above, provides an example of unwanted consequences of discrepant action: the subjects were led to believe that their discrepant action (reinforcing statements by the confederate with which they disagreed) actually had an impact on the confederate's attitudes.

hence reverse the attitude change in situations involving hedonic dissonance, but not in situations involving moral dissonance.

The distinction between moral and hedonic dilemmas was derived on an ad hoc basis rather than through a systematic effort to develop a typology of discrepant actions. We originally came up with it in attempting to reconcile conflicting findings from two parallel experiments (Kelman & Baron, 1974). It also seems to capture some of the central characteristics of various experimental situations created in dissonance studies. As we move from this empirical distinction to a more systematic typology, it may be useful to ask what kinds of standards people deviate from when they engage in morally discrepant as compared to hedonically discrepant actions. I proposed above that it is the discrepancy between action and some kind of standard or expectation that lends motivational significance to a discrepant act. Now, both moral and hedonic dilemmas arise from actions that deviate from certain standards—indeed, more specifically, from certain social norms—but the nature of these standards or norms differs in the two situations. Moral dilemmas arise from actions that violate standards for our *conduct*. These standards are based on social norms—shared, to varying degrees, by the actors themselves—that determine how we are expected to act in different situations. Failures to live up to such expectations usually imply personal shortcomings on the part of the actors, although they can of course be attributed to situational causes. By contrast, hedonic dilemmas involve deviations from standards for the *outcome* of our actions. These standards are based, essentially, on the norm of equity, which leads us to expect outcomes commensurate with our inputs. Discrepancies from such expectations are generally attributed to external circumstances; they do not imply shortcomings on the part of the actors, except insofar as they suggest insufficient wisdom or assertiveness to protect themselves against exploitation. Clearly, moral and hedonic dilemmas represent very different psychological situations: they are generated by actions that deviate from two very different kinds of standards, they have different implications for self-evaluation and future planning, and they set different psychological processes into motion.

Deviation from Standards of Conduct

The category of actions that is exemplified by moral dilemmas—i.e., actions discrepant from standards of conduct—is itself complex and varied. In this section, I shall briefly describe an attempt to develop a more systematic typology of discrepant actions, all of which involve deviations from societal standards of conduct.[8] This typology, then, does not include hedonic dilemmas as such, but it further differentiates the notion of moral dilemma and it introduces an additional variety of actions that deviate from societal standards of conduct.

The scheme, summarized in Table 4, classifies types of discrepant action in terms of the societal standards of conduct from which they depart. The columns of Table 4 distinguish two behavioral dimensions on which the deviation from standards has occurred (respon-

Table 4*
A classification of types of discrepant action in terms of the societal standards from which they depart

| | | Behavioral Dimenson on which P's Departure from Societal Standards has Occurred | |
		Responsibility	Propriety
Source of Standards from which P's Action Has Departed	External rules or norms (compliance-based)	Social fear	Embarrassment
	Role expectations (identification-based)	Guilt	Shame
	Values (internalized)	Regret	Self-disappointment

Note: Cell entries refer to the dominant emotional reactions that each type of discrepant action is hypothesized to arouse.
* From Kelman, 1974b. Reprinted from J. T. Tedeschi (Ed.), *Perspectives on Social Power* (1974), by permission of Aldine Publishing Company.

8. For a fuller discussion of this scheme, see Kelman, 1974b, pp. 149–160.

sibility and propriety); the rows distinguish three sources of the standards of conduct from which the person's action has deviated (external rules, role expectations, and social values); and the cell entries suggest the dominant emotional reactions aroused in the person by each of the six types of deviations.

The two dimensions distinguished in the columns of the table refer to domains of individual conduct that are socially defined and monitored. They are not meant to constitute an inclusive list of such domains of conduct. They do, however, represent two dimensions that are probably of universal concern, although societies may differ in the relative emphasis they place on one or the other. Societies have a definite stake in how their members behave on each of these dimensions and take considerable interest in assuring that members adhere to the standards of conduct governing the domain in question. For each dimension, qualitatively different patterns of socialization and means of social control are utilized.

The left column identifies discrepant actions that deviate from societal standards of responsibility (or morality). Most characteristically, these involve actions that cause harm to others or to society in general (e.g., by wasting valuable resources or failing to do productive work). Actions that are seen as disloyal to a cause or to one's group and failures to stand up for one's principles or beliefs would also come under this rubric. Actions causing harm to one's self (e.g., by excessive use of drugs or alcohol, or by dissipating one's energies) also tend to be treated as departures from standards of responsibility, perhaps because they are seen as wasting human resources on which society might otherwise be able to draw. The domain of responsibility is one in which "society" insists on the right to make members answerable (i.e., responsible) for their actions. The social controls exercised in this area typically include punishment or the threat of punishment, exclusion from "responsible" roles in the society, and disapproval in the form of anger.

The right column identifies discrepant actions that deviate from societal standards of propriety. Typically, these are actions deemed inappropriate (i.e., not "one's own") for someone in the actor's position—or, in many cases, for any adult in the society. They represent a failure to live up to a particular personal image, whether it be a strictly public image, or a self-image, or a self-image dependent on public confirmation. Although people are not accountable for actions in the domain of propriety in the same formal sense as they are in the domain of responsibility, behavior in this domain is also subject to social controls. "Society" has an interest in assuring that its members live up to their images, since the smoothness and predictability of social interaction depends on their doing so. The social controls typically exercised in this domain include ridicule, ostracism, and disapproval in the form of contempt.

The three sources of standards distinguished in the rows of Table 4 are linked to the three processes of social influence described in my earlier writings (Kelman, 1958, 1961). Thus, at the level of the individual, the source of standards refers to the particular influence process by which the person originally adopted the standard (or, to put it differently, by which the person acquired the attitudes) from which the discrepant action now deviates. The first row identifies actions that deviate from compliance-based expectations, the second row identifies actions that deviate from identification-based expectations, and the third row identifies actions that deviate from internalized expectations. At the level of the social system, the three sources of standards refer to three components of the system in which standards might be embedded: external rules, role expectations, and values. The three rows, then, indicate the level (compliance, identification, or internalization) at which the particular societal standards of responsibility or propriety are represented in a given individual's cognitive structure.[9]

Put in more general functional terms, Table 4 classifies discrepant actions according to the *nature of the action* and the *nature of the attitude* toward the object with which the person enters the action situation. Thus, the columns distinguish between actions that are perceived as irresponsible and those perceived as improper. The rows distinguish between actions that deviate from compliance-based, from identification-based, and from internalized attitudes. The latter distinction, as mentioned in earlier sections of this paper, represents differences in the degree to which the person's original attitudes toward the object are individualized and independent of situational demands.

9. I do not assume that a given individual operates only at one of these levels. At which level an individual operates in a particular situation may depend on the particular behavior involved. For example, the same person, within the domain of responsibility, may be complying to the rules of cheating, but may have internalized standards of loyalty to one's friends. Even with respect to the same specific behavior, a person may have adopted standards at different levels; all of these may be elicited at the same time, although one or the other may predominate, depending on the nature of the situation.

Each of the six types of discrepant action distinguished in Table 4 should present a distinct pattern of reaction, predictable from the particular interaction of row and column that it represents. First, a violation of societal standards should arouse qualitatively different concerns and emotional responses in people, depending on the socially defined domain whose standards they violated and the level at which they had originally adopted those standards. (Hypotheses about the different concerns likely to be aroused as a function of the level at which the violated standards had originally been adopted can be derived from the theoretical distinctions between compliance, identification, and internalization. Thus, in the first row of Table 4, one would expect people to be primarily concerned with the way others may react to their deviations; in the second row, with the implications of their deviations for their relationships to groups in which their self-definitions are anchored; and in the third row, with the intrinsic implications of their actions, matched against their personal value systems.) Second, depending on the type of discrepant action involved, people should go about handling the concerns and resolving the dilemmas aroused in different ways. For each cell, then, it should be possible to specify what people are likely to do when they find themselves deviating from societal standards—both to avoid or minimize the consequences of deviation, and to rectify the situation and come to grips with it psychologically.

The dominant emotional reactions aroused in the actor by actions that are socially defined as irresponsible can be described, respectively, as social fear, guilt, and regret (see left column of Table 4).

(1) When societal standards for responsible conduct have been adopted at the level of compliance, the concern created by deviation will focus primarily on the way others will react—i.e., on the social consequences of the discrepant action. People will seek to avoid or minimize punishment and disapproval by covering up, so as to evade discovery; or, if discovered, by denying responsibility for the action; or, failing that, by engaging in maneuvers designed to minimize the severity of the consequences—such as introducing extenuating circumstances in order to reduce their degree of responsibility, or ingratiating themselves with others (perhaps through apology or confession) in order to minimize the punishment to be administered to them.

(2) When standards for responsible conduct are identification-based, the emotional reaction to deviation can best be described as

guilt. The concern created by deviation in this case focuses not on the object that has been harmed or the value that has been violated (as it does in the case of regret, to be described below), but primarily on the actor's relationship to the social system and self-definition within it. The discrepant action has thrown this relationship into question and undermined the actor's self-concept as a well-integrated, securely positioned member of society. The core meaning of this reaction is very well conveyed by the German word *Schuld*, which means both guilt and debt. Through the discrepant action, the person has incurred a debt to those harmed and, most important, to society. However, the actor is not just concerned with being restored to the good graces of others, but with reestablishing his or her own self-definition as a worthy member of society. Though the standards violated are external, they have been introjected (in the Freudian sense) and guilt may therefore create a considerable amount of inner turmoil. One way of dealing with the consequences of deviation is to persuade ourselves that our action was in fact not out of keeping with social expectations. For example, we may conclude that the action was justified, because the person we harmed deserved to be harmed or the cause we abandoned was ill-conceived, or that the action—at least in this form and under these circumstances—is generally considered to be acceptable. To the extent that we can redefine the action along such lines—and especially, find social support for this redefinition—our "debt to society" is cancelled and our guilt reduced. Where such resolutions are unavailable, we must find ways of reinstating ourselves in the social order and reestablishing the desired relationship to it. This can be accomplished through compensation of the victim, by means that are socially defined and often publicly administered, or through other types of expiation and reparation that allow people to pay their "debt to society." In other words, guilt is often reduced through the use of an accounting system that enables people to make up for their deviations and regain their place in society. Confession can also serve as a way of dealing with guilt and restoring our position in society since it represents a form of expiation (in that we humble ourselves), a renewed commitment to the standards that we violated, and a way of separating the transgressing self from the normal self. If people despair of the possibility of reestablishing the desired relationship to the society, their guilt may express itself through varying degrees of self-punishment.

(3) When standards for responsible conduct are internalized and hence integral parts of a personal value system, the concern created by deviation will focus primarily on the object that we have harmed by our discrepant action. From a long-range point of view, we are also likely to be concerned about the implications of the action for our ability to live up to our values. One characteristic reaction in this case is to seek ways of correcting the wrong that has been done—not simply by compensating the injured party according to a socially established formula, but by exploring all necessary steps for counteracting and minimizing the harmful consequences of the action. Another type of reaction is repentance, involving not only remorse for the wrong that has been done, but also a resolution to avoid similar actions in the future. In making such a resolution, we may engage in a process of self-examination in order to understand why we failed to live up to our own values and to determine how we might want to change ourselves.

The dominant emotional reactions aroused in the actor by actions that are socially defined as improper can be described, respectively, as embarrassment, shame, and self-disappointment (see right column of Table 4).

(1) When societal standards for proper conduct are based on compliance, the emotional reaction to deviation can be described as embarrassment. The deviation takes the form of a failure to live up to our self-presentation, by publicly behaving in a way that falls short of the expectations that go with a specific role to which we lay claim or with the general role of an adult in the society (e.g., by showing ourselves to be incompetent, inadequate, clumsy, or socially maladroit). The concern caused by deviation in this case focuses not on our own sense of competence or adequacy, but on our public image—on the possibility that others will react negatively to our behavior and disapprove of us. We may be particularly concerned that others will draw conclusions about our general characteristics from our failure in this specific situation. People seek to minimize disapproval by covering up the discrepant action—by pretending that it did not happen or that it did not mean what it seemed to convey (e.g., they may pretend that they never seriously claimed competence in the task in which they fell short). If failure cannot be denied, they may try to minimize its implications by finding ways of demonstrating that they possess the competence

that has just been thrown into question. Another way of dealing with embarrassment is self-ridicule, which has the effect of disarming others, of showing our own control of the situation, and of communicating that we find the discrepant action funny because it is so uncharacteristic of us.

(2) When standards for proper conduct are identification-based, the emotional reaction to deviation can be described as shame. In this case, failure to live up to our self-presentation exposes what we regard as a possible underlying shortcoming. Concern focuses not merely on our public image—on the way others, in the immediate interaction situation, will react to the deviation—but on the implications of the deviation for a role in which our self-definition is anchored. Our failure raises questions about our embeddedness in the role, our ability to live up to its expectations, and thus our long-term place in the social system. As in the case of guilt, one way of dealing with the consequences of deviation is to persuade ourselves that our action was in fact not inconsistent with role expectations. For example, we may attribute our inadequate performance to external causes, or we may conclude that, under the prevailing circumstances, our performance was in fact acceptable. To the extent that we can redefine the action along such lines and find social support for this redefinition, we have nothing to be ashamed of and our place in the social system is secure. When such resolutions are unavailable, we must find ways of reestablishing our relationship to society, which has been threatened. This can be accomplished through some attempt to compensate for our failing— for example, by achieving success in other aspects of role performance. If people's demands on themselves are excessive and they find it impossible to reestablish the desired relationship to society, their reaction may take the form of self-contempt.

(3) When standards for proper conduct are internalized and rooted in a personal value system, the concern created by deviation will focus primarily on the performance of the task or enactment of the role in which we have fallen short. We are not so much concerned about our social standing or the solidity of our relationship to society as we are disappointed in ourselves—in our inability to live up to our own standards of quality and our own definition of what is required for proper task performance or role enactment. One characteristic reaction to such self-disappointment is to examine our

behavior with an eye to understanding where we have failed and how we might improve in the future. Another possible reaction is reexamination of our standards, in order to see whether we have imposed unrealistic expectations on ourselves, which may lead to a revision of those standards accompanied by a greater degree of self-acceptance.

Given the different dilemmas created by the six types of discrepant action that I have just described and the ways in which people characteristically cope with these dilemmas, what is the likelihood of attitude change in each case? Whether or not attitude change can be expected to occur, the precise nature of that change, and the particular attitudes that are likely to be affected can be derived from a functional analysis of these different situations. Such an analysis would reveal in what way attitude change might emerge from and contribute to people's efforts to deal with the consequences of their discrepant action. I have not developed a systematic set of hypotheses along these lines, but I can illustrate the general logic of the approach.

When the discrepant action involves violation of external rules or compliance-based standards, we would not expect attitude change as a coping mechanism per se, since the concern here is primarily with manipulating the reactions of others rather than with maintaining congruity between action and attitude. The experience itself and the concern it arouses may, however, produce certain changes in attitude toward relevant policies or practices. For example, marijuana users, concerned about discovery, may become more actively committed to the legalization of marijuana, both because their own experience has sensitized them to the issue and because such a policy would protect them from negative sanctions.

When the discrepant action involves violation of role expectations or identification-based standards, we are most likely to find attitude change as a form of retrospeective justification for the action, as postulated by dissonance theory and qualified by our analysis of moral dilemmas. Change may occur in attitudes toward the object or the issue involved in the action; for example, to the extent that we can devalue the person harmed or the cause betrayed by our action, or the task on which our performance fell short, our level of guilt or shame would be reduced. Alternatively, we may change our attitude toward the action itself, persuading ourselves that it was in fact consistent with role requirements, at least under the prevailing circumstances. Such a change may be accompanied by a shift in reference group, bringing a different set of standards into play. In some situations, the opportunity for such attitude changes—justifying the action or making it more acceptable—is not readily available and people must confront the discrepancy between their action and role expectations. In these cases, they may actually change their attitudes in the direction of more favorable evaluation of the object or issue involved in the action; by way of compensating for their deviation, they may develop attitudes marked by exaggerated praise, uncritical loyalty, and ritualized devotion.

When the discrepant action involves violation of values or internalized standards, attitude change may occur as part of a process of self-examination, oriented toward preventing similar deviations or failures in the future. This process may produce a strengthened commitment to the values that have been violated by the discrepant action and to the attitude objects (persons, groups, causes, policies, or activities) linked to those values. It may also produce changes in certain self-attitudes. For example, we may decide that we need to alter our way of life, increase our efforts, or improve our skills in order to avoid repetition of our flawed behavior. Alternatively, we may decide that we have been setting unrealistic standards for ourselves and come to accept our limitations.

Some suggestive evidence for this analysis can be found in a study by Nancy Adler (Note 3), who interviewed women before and after they underwent induced abortions. In the initial interviews, she presented her respondents with three issues, corresponding to the three sources of standards from which the action of having an abortion might deviate: a compliance-based issue ("whether people might think less of you or avoid you if they found out that you had had an abortion"), an identification-based issue ("whether having an abortion is something that a good member of your group—for example, your family, your church, the people you associate with—would do"), and an internalization-based issue ("whether having an abortion violates your beliefs or values"). Respondents were asked to rate the extent of their concern with each of these issues and to indicate on which of the issues their predominant concern about the abortion focused. Prior concerns were then related to the respondents' reactions to their experiences, as reported in the post-abortion interviews.

Hypotheses about emotional and behavioral responses as a function of the nature of prior concern were derived from the scheme described above. These hypotheses received partial support from the data. Adler did not derive or test hypotheses about the amount or nature of attitude change as a function of prior concern. However, some indirect evidence on the different attitudinal effects of the abortion was provided by respondents' hypothetical policy choices, obtained in the post-abortion interviews. Respondents were asked to choose between three hypothetical programs that the State of Massachusetts might adopt: a program designed to increase the *availability of abortion*, a program designed to increase the *acceptance of abortion*, and a program designed to increase the availability and acceptance of *birth control*. Adler predicted that women predominantly concerned about the compliance-based issue would tend to choose the first program, since they would want to change the social environment so that abortion would no longer be negatively sanctioned; women predominantly concerned about the identification-based issue would tend to choose the second program, since they would want to change the acceptability of abortion so that their own relationships with others would not be jeopardized by their actions; and women predominantly concerned about the internalization-based issue would tend to choose the third program, since they would be interested in preventing similar occurrences (unwanted pregnancies necessitating abortion) in the future.

The results were generally consistent with these predictions, as can be seen in Table 5. Women predominantly concerned with the compliance-based issue were most likely to choose programs designed to increase the availability of abortion and they did so more often than women in the other two groups; the differences, however, are very small. For the other two groups, the results are much stronger. Women predominantly concerned with the identification-based issue were most likely to choose programs designed to increase the acceptance of abortion and they clearly picked this option more often than the other groups. By contrast, only one out of 36 women concerned with the internalization-based issue chose a program designed to increase the acceptance of abortion; most often— and clearly more often than the other two groups—these women chose programs designed to encourage the use of birth control and thus avoid resort to abortion. This pattern of findings corresponds nicely to the logic of the distinction between the three types of discrepant action and the different kinds of attitude change they can be expected to elicit.

Table 5*

Cross-tabulation of predominant prior concern and choices of hypothetical program

		Predominant Prior Concern		
		Compliance-Based Issue	Identification-Based Issue	Internalization-Based Issue
Hypo-thetical Program Chosen	Abortion—Availability	7 (41.2%)	4 (36.4%)	14 (38.9%)
	Abortion—Acceptance	4 (23.5%)	5 (45.5%)	1 (2.8%)
	Birth Control	6 (35.3%)	2 (18.2%)	21 (58.3%)
		17	11	36

$$x^2 = 14.29$$
$$df = 4$$
$$p = .007$$

* From Adler, Note 3. Reprinted by permission of the author.

Much more needs to be done to refine and test the present scheme, which attempts to classify the important subset of discrepant actions that involve deviations from societal standards of conduct. To summarize, the scheme distinguishes discrepant actions in terms of the behavioral domain in which standards of conduct were violated (the nature of the action) and the source of the standards from which the action has deviated (the nature of the attitude). The six types of discrepant action thus identified produce different dilemmas for the actor, each characterized by a distinct pattern of emotional reactions to the deviation and of efforts at resolution designed to deal with the consequences of the deviation. These different patterns of reaction, in turn, provide the framework for predicting whether attitude change is a likely mechanism for dealing with the particular dilemma that has been aroused and, if so, which attitudes are likely to be affected and what the nature and durability of the attitude change are likely to be.

Action in Relation to Conflicted Attitudes

Another framework for analyzing the relationship between discrepant action and attitude change, which my colleagues and I have utilized, also starts with distinctions in the nature of the attitude from which the action deviates. However, it further recognizes that our attitudes toward an object are often conflicted, comprising—as I have already emphasized earlier in this paper—both approach and avoidance tendencies. In such cases, of course, we cannot speak unambiguously of attitude-action discrepancy. An action in support of the object, for example, would be discrepant with respect to the avoidance component of the attitude, but congruent with the approach component. The degree to which the person experiences the action as discrepant would depend on the strength of the avoidance component relative to the approach component.

The framework (first described in Kelman, 1962a) focuses on situations of induced action, in which people are caused—through the manipulation of situational forces—to act toward an object in ways they would not otherwise have acted, given the nature of their attitudes toward the object. Specifically, conceiving of our relationships to objects as varying along a dimension of "degree of positive association" (i.e., the degree to which we engage in actions that bring us into contact with the object and that involve active support of it), the framework applies to those situations in which we are somehow induced to take a step further along the dimension of positive association with the object than we were prepared to go (see Figure 1). The question is: under what conditions is such induced action likely to lead to attitude change? The answer, according to the present framework, depends on the slopes of the approach and avoidance gradients with respect to degree of positive association.

Let us assume that the strength of both approach and avoidance tendencies toward the object increases as a direct function of degree of positive association with the object. If one of the gradients is steeper than the other, the two may cross at some point along the dimension of positive association, creating a situation of maximal conflict. There are two ways in which this can happen, with different implications for the probable effect of induced action on attitude change.

The first situation, depicted in Figure 2, is one in which the avoidance gradient is steeper than the approach gradient. In such a

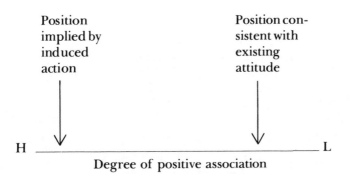

Position
implied by
induced
action

Position con-
sistent with
existing
attitude

H _____ L
Degree of positive association

Figure 1. Induced action as increase in the degree of positive association.

situation, we would normally move up to the point at which the two gradients cross (since approach tendencies outweigh avoidance tendencies in this region), but we would experience conflict once we reached this point. The crossover point represents a stable equilibrium (Miller, 1944): if for any reason we moved beyond this point, we would soon return to it because we would find ourselves in a region in which avoidance outweighed approach. Thus if we have been induced, through temporary situational forces, to take an action that brings us beyond the point of conflict into a region of closer association with the object in which avoidance tendencies come more strongly to the fore, we are not likely to continue the association once the momentary forces have been removed. In other words, induced action propels us into a situation that is increasingly uncomfortable and from which we will escape as soon as possible. Under these circumstances, opportunities for attitude change are likely to be minimal; induction of action, therefore, is not expected to lead to attitude change. Examples fitting this pattern might involve individuals who intellectually accept (or toy with) certain positions or practices that go counter to the norms of their early (now relatively latent) reference groups; once they are induced to act on their intellectual beliefs, however, the contrary norms become salient and cause them to retreat (for more detail, see Kelman, 1962a).

The second situation, depicted in Figure 3, is one in which the approach gradient is steeper than the avoidance gradient. In such a situation, we would normally avoid any association with the object and we would not voluntarily move to the point at which the two

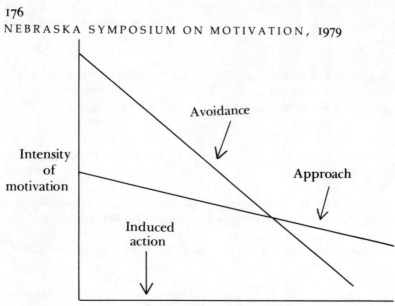

Figure 2. Attitude as a function of degree of positive association: avoidance steeper than approach.

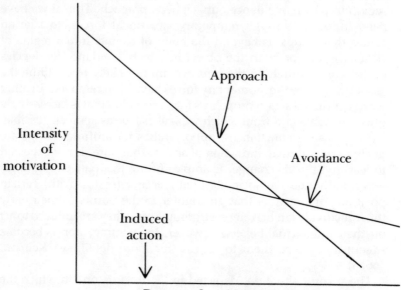

Figure 3. Attitude as a function of degree of positive association: approach steeper than avoidance.

gradients cross (since avoidance tendencies outweigh approach tendencies in this region). If, however, we have been induced by situational forces to take an action that brings us beyond the point of intersection, we find ourselves in a region in which approach tendencies outweigh avoidance tendencies. We should be inclined, therefore, to remain in the situation even after the temporary pressures have been removed, and to continue associating with the object, behaviorally and affectively, thus exposing ourselves to opportunities for attitude change. Induction of action may be more difficult in this situation because of the initial resistance to any degree of positive association; if it is successful, however, it can be expected to lead to attitude change. Examples fitting this pattern might involve individuals who are relatively estranged from certain reference groups and disinclined to enact group-related roles; once they are induced to act out these roles, however, their group identifications become salient and cause them to continue their heightened level of involvement (for more detail, see Kelman, 1962a).

In sum, I have proposed that induced action is more likely to lead to attitude change if the approach component of the attitude is steeper than the avoidance component (Figure 3); it is less likely to lead to attitude change if the avoidance component is steeper than the approach component (Figure 2). The important question then is: what variables determine the steepness of these gradients? One factor that might be involved here is whether the particular attitude (approach or avoidance) is based on identification or internalization (Kelman, 1958, 1961).

To the extent that an attitude is internalized, it can be argued that the gradient of approach or avoidance along the dimension of degree of association should be relatively flat. Since internalized attitudes are integrated with our value system, they should be relatively unaffected by such situational cues as degree of association with the object at the moment. Approach tendencies based on a view of the object as conducive to maximizing our values should remain more or less equal in strength at all levels of association, as should avoidance tendencies based on a view of the object as detrimental to value maximization.

On the other hand, for identification-based attitudes the gradient of approach or avoidance along the dimension of degree of association should be relatively steep. Since identification-based attitudes are tied to our being in the role (i.e., are aspects of role enactment), they should vary considerably as a function of such situational cues as degree of association with the object. Approach or avoidance tendencies toward an object linked to the expectations that circumscribe one of our roles should manifest themselves more strongly under conditions of active association with the object. Both our awareness of role expectations with regard to the object, and the strength of these expectations themselves, increase as the degree of association with the object increases. In short, the manifestation of identification-based attitudes is more dependent on situational cues, and hence varies more sharply with the degree to which the situation brings role requirements into salience—which, in turn, varies with the degree of association with the object. In keeping with this logic, the types of cases I mentioned above as exemplifying the avoidance-steeper-than-approach situation (Figure 2) are ones in which avoidance is based on the person's relationship to important reference groups (i.e., identification-based). Similarly, the types of cases exemplifying the approach-steeper-than-avoidance situation (Figure 3) are ones in which approach is anchored in important reference groups. (In both instances, it should be noted, these attitudes—whether avoidance or approach—are anchored in relatively latent reference groups, i.e., groups that do not constitute the person's key membership groups at the moment.)

These considerations can be summed up in the following hypotheses: (1) Induction of action is more likely to lead to attitude change if the approach component of the person's relationship to the object is identification-based than if it is internalized. (2) Induction of action is more likely to lead to a reversion to the original level of association and less likely to lead to attitude change if the avoidance component of the person's relationship to the object is identification-based than if it is internalized.

Some years ago, we carried out a role-play experiment to test these hypotheses (to be published in Kelman, Baron, Sheposh, & Lubalin, Note 1).[10] The subjects were male and female students in a small denominational junior college, preparing for the ministry or religious instruction. In the first session of the experiment, our purpose was to create attitudes toward a hypothetical organization called the Association for Civic Education (ACE). We told the sub-

10. My collaborators in this experiment were Reuben Baron, Martin S. Greenberg, and John P. Sheposh. I am also grateful to James Heitler for his role in the analysis of the data and to Alice H. Eagly, Kalman J. Kaplan, and Moriah Markus-Kaplan for their helpful comments on the findings of this study.

jects that we were simulating the process of attitude formation by giving them the kinds of information about ACE that people often find in the media when a new organization is established. Each subject then received a "fact sheet" containing two types of information: a series of brief statements about ACE's stand on issues related to several values important to this population (as ascertained in a preliminary study); and a series of nonsubstantive statements evaluating ACE attributed to several reference groups significant to this population (again as ascertained in the preliminary study). Two versions of the fact sheet were distributed, each designed to create a different conflict between values and reference groups (i.e., between internalization-based and identification-based components of the newly created attitudes). For one group of subjects, the items in the fact sheet indicated that ACE was positively evaluated by the relevant reference groups, but that its stands on the issues were negatively related to the subjects' values $(RG + / V -)$. For the second group, the reverse information was provided, indicating negative evaluations by the reference groups, but positive stands with respect to the subjects' values $(RG - / V +)$. Thus, according to our two hypotheses, the first condition was expected to maximize the probability of attitude change as a result of induced action, by creating attitudes with an identification-based approach component and an internalized avoidance component. The second condition was expected to minimize the probability of attitude change by creating attitudes with an identification-based avoidance component and an internalized approach component.

The second session, which was held between one and two weeks later, constituted the induced action situation for the subjects in the experimental conditions (30 males and 28 females).[11] The experimental subjects were assigned to small groups, each consisting of four or five members of the same sex and the same experimental condition. Each group was told that "we would like to study how the attitude formation process is influenced by a person's active involvement in an organization such as ACE." Subjects were asked to play the roles of local district directors of ACE chapters who were

11. About half of the subjects from the first session served as controls in this session. Like the experimental subjects, they were given a retention test and an opportunity to review the ACE fact sheet that they had read in the first session. They did not, however, engage in the induced action. Instead, they did their own reading or studying for fifty minutes and then filled out an attitude questionnaire about ACE. Data for control subjects will not be discussed here.

attending a strategy conference to counteract an anticipated concerted attack on ACE by its opponents. In defense of the organization, they were to formulate at least a dozen suggestions that would help give ACE a more favorable public image. The subjects were given thirty minutes to discuss ideas and plan strategies for this campaign. After the group discussion, subjects—still acting within their assigned roles—wrote individual proposals on how they would implement the recommendations of the conference in their home towns.

On completing the role-play session, subjects answered a questionnaire evaluating the conference (including their own contributions and those of other group members); an attitude questionnaire about ACE identical to one they had filled out at the end of the attitude-formation session; and an open-ended question explaining their attitude toward ACE. A measure of delayed attitude change was obtained about a month after the experimental sessions, when a little over half of the subjects returned to fill out ACE attitude questionnaires for a third time.

Some of the major findings of the study are summarized in Table 6. The mean scores of attitude change (measures I and 2), based on a 14-item semantic differential scale, reveal an unexpected sex difference. For the males, the pattern is entirely consistent with the theoretical predictions: those in the RG + /V − condition show significant attitude change immediately after the induced action, while those in the RG − /V + condition do not. Moreover, the change manifested by the males in the RG + /V − condition maintains itself on the delayed measure of attitude change. For the females, on the other hand, we find a reversal: significant immediate change in the RG − /V + condition, but none in the RG + /V − condition. The change manifested by the females in the RG − /V + condition, however, does not maintain itself; the delayed measure, in fact, shows a more negative evaluation of ACE than the questionnaire administered at the end of the first session.

To gain an understanding of the sex differences in attitude change, we examined the additional data that had been gathered from the experimental subjects. For each subject we had observer ratings of interactions during the group discussion, coder ratings of the written proposal and the open-ended explanation of attitude toward ACE, and self-ratings of the role-play session. In all, these different sources of data provided 52 separate scores per subject, which were subjected to a factor analysis that yielded ten factors.

Table 6
*Conflict study: Comparison between males and females in each experimental
condition*

Conditions:	Reference Groups + Values −		Reference Groups− Values +	
Measures	Males	Females	Males	Females
1. Attitude change toward ACE immediately after action (Semantic Differential)	.73	− .11	.24	.63
2. Delayed attitude change (Semantic Differential)	.71	− .36	.15	− .45
3. Positive involvement in role (observation & self-rating)	2.41	−5.86	3.46	− .91
4. Satisfaction with conference (self-ratings)	.69	− .21	.44	−1.10
5. Active search for support of ACE (in proposal)	−5.37	−4.90	6.77	3.29
6. Attempt to minimize criticism of ACE (in proposal)	−1.06	− .95	− .01	2.26
7. Defensive assertion of closeness to ACE (proposal and ratings)	− .86	− .32	− .95	2.40
8. Perceived goodness of ACE ideals (in proposal)	− .55	−3.68	2.58	1.35
9. Perceived reference group support for ACE (in proposal)	2.19	1.01	−1.60	1.70
10. Indications of conflict toward ACE (in proposal and open-ended question)	1.23	.42	−1.98	.45

Table 6 (measures 3–10) presents mean scores for eight of these factors on which we obtained significant differences between sexes and/or between experimental conditions.

Looking first at the RG + /V − condition, we find a large and highly significant sex difference in positive involvement in the role (measure 3 in Table 6). Women were much more uncomfortable in the role playing and much more dissatisfied with their performance than men. In a similar vein, women expressed less satisfaction with the role-played conference in which they had just participated (measure 4). The difference seems to be related to the relative salience of the approach and avoidance components of the attitude toward ACE for the two sexes. As the men performed the induced action on behalf of ACE, they were cognizant of the reference group support for the organization (9), while they tended to minimize the disparity between ACE goals and their own values (8). By contrast, for the women the disparity between ACE goals and their own values was highly salient (8), while they paid relatively little attention to the reference group support for the organization (9). Thus it seems that the avoidance component loomed larger for the women as they were engaging in the induced action, which contributed to their discomfort and dissatisfaction, whereas the men found it easier to put the avoidance component aside and hence experienced little discomfort in performing their assigned roles. The difference can perhaps be understood in terms of traditional sex role distinctions. Conventional social expectations permit men (particularly in the occupational sphere) a certain amount of role playing, pretending, and cross-situational variability—even at the expense of their own values. Women, on the other hand, traditionally receive less social support for multiple role enactment and are expected to bring a stable and consistent set of values to their various interactions. The women in the experiment, therefore, may have found it difficult to play the assigned role, particularly when it required support for an organization whose goals were inconsistent with their values, while the men took such an assignment in their stride.

These findings suggest that, for the males, the RG + /V − manipulation produced, as expected, an approach-steeper-than-avoidance situation (Figure 3). According to the theoretical model, induced action under these circumstances should strengthen the positive component of the attitude and lead to a relatively stable attitude change. The attitude change data for the men (Table 6, measures 1 and 2) are consistent with the process postulated by the model. By contrast, for the women, the RG + /V − manipulation seems to have produced an avoidance-steeper-than-approach situation (Figure 2). These findings suggest that, contrary to our original hypothesis, an internalized avoidance (or approach) tendency does not necessarily produce a flat gradient. We had assumed that the strength of internalized attitudes, because they are relatively independent of situational cues, would not be significantly affected by degree of association with the object, ignoring the possibility that different evaluations may be attached to different degrees or kinds of association with an attitude object. Thus, for example, if we consider an organization detrimental to our values, we may feel perfectly comfortable about listening to a lecture expounding its views, but we would feel very uncomfortable about publicly defending its programs. This would make for a steep avoidance gradient, not because the attitude is highly dependent on the strength of situational cues, but because the different degrees of association have qualitatively different meanings: listening to the lecture does not represent a betrayal of our values, while actively promoting the organization does. The absence of attitude change among the women in the RG + /V − condition (measures 1 and 2) is consistent with the assumption that they found themselves in an avoidance-steeper-than-approach situation. Induced action under these circumstances should create discomfort and a tendency to escape, thus minimizing the opportunities for attitude change.

In the RG − /V + condition, we again find significant sex differences in degree of comfort with the role-play performance: men showed more positive involvement in their roles (measure 3) and reported greater satisfaction with the conference (4). These differences must be understood, however, in terms of the particular form that the induced action took in this condition. The action gave subjects an excellent opportunity to counteract the lack of reference group support for ACE, since it called for suggestions of steps to improve the organization's public image. Both men and women proposed to undertake an active search for support of ACE, presumably aimed at persuading their reference groups that the organization was worthy of approval, but the men did so to a greater extent than the women (5). We might speculate that, in line with traditional sex role differences, the women felt less comfortable about active efforts to persuade the opposition and less confident that they would succeed in such efforts. Their proposals tended to be more defensive, aiming to minimize criticism of ACE (6). They experienced greater conflict than the men in their attitudes toward ACE (10): they were less emphatic about the congruence of ACE goals with their own values (8) and probably less assured that they could neutralize reference group opposition by their own actions. The women also scored high on a factor that included both items expressing closeness to ACE and items indicating a preference for shortening the role-play session (7). Thus, their reaction seemed to combine a desire to escape from the situation with a recommitment to ACE—both apparent defenses against the pressures they felt in a situation that brought the conflict between values and reference groups into salience. The men gave no evidence of such a conflict, apparently because they felt confident that, through the active efforts spelled out in their proposals, they would be able to overcome the opposition of their reference groups.

These different reactions of the men and women are reflected in the attitude change data. In keeping with our prediction for the $RG-/V+$ condition, the men showed no significant attitude change—but clearly not because of discomfort generated by a steep avoidance gradient, as we had postulated. Rather, it would appear that the action provided no particular reason for them to change their attitudes toward ACE (which were already quite favorable); they chose instead to act on the environment. The women, on the other hand, did experience discomfort and sought to escape from the situation. Yet, unexpectedly, they manifested attitude change. The change, however, appears to have served primarily a defensive function in the action situation—allowing them to declare their commitment to ACE in the face of reference group pressure—as evidenced by the short-lived nature of the change.

In sum, the study suggests that we can gain a better understanding of the relationship between action and attitude change by separating the approach and avoidance components of the attitude and examining their relative salience in the action situation. At the same time, it appears that, contrary to our hypotheses, the steepness of the approach and avoidance gradients is not simply a function of the nature of the attitude (i.e., whether it is based on identification or internalization), nor is it necessarily true that an approach-steeper-than-avoidance situation is more conducive to attitude change than is its opposite. To understand what happens in a given situation, we must look at the way people react to the action itself—what it means to them, how they carry it out, what opportunities it offers them—and these reactions are not entirely predictable from the nature of the initial attitudes. Other variables, including individual difference variables (such as the sex differences observed in the present study) seem to influence these reactions and hence the likelihood and nature of attitude change. Thus in the kind of situation exemplified by our RG + /V − condition, attitude change seems to depend on how comfortably individuals can enter into the action even though it is inconsistent with their values. Those who, for whatever reason, can do so (such as the males in our experiment) may, as a result, have both the motivation and the opportunity to reexamine their attitudes, which may lead to gradual and lasting change (as often happens when an individual adopts a new role; cf. Lieberman, 1956). In the kind of situation exemplified by our RG − /V + condition, the relationship of attitude change to comfort in performing the action may be quite different. Those who feel comfortable because they see the action itself as an opportunity to overcome reference group opposition (such as the males in our experiment) may be able to resolve their conflict without resort to attitude change, while those for whom the action heightens the conflict between values and reference groups (such as the females in our experiment) may display a short-lived shift in attitude as a way of reasserting their values in the face of reference group pressures.

EFFECTS OF "SURPASSING" ACTION

The discussion of action in relation to conflicted attitudes helps to call attention to some of the ambiguities in the concept of discrepant action. Insofar as an attitude toward an object has both an approach and an avoidance component, actions vis-à-vis that object are never unambiguously discrepant. An action supportive of the object may be discrepant with respect to the avoidance component, but perfectly congruent with respect to the approach component. The action may, of course, be experienced as discrepant depending on the relative strength or salience of the two components. Nevertheless, the presence of the two components underlines the possibility that an action, though largely perceived as discrepant, may carry some positive implications from the actor's point of view.

Even an action that is unambiguously discrepant is not necessarily experienced by the individual as a totally negative occurrence, to be avoided, denied, or neutralized at all costs. A discrepant action may provide the occasion for new learning and insight, leading to constructive changes in attitudes, behavior patterns, social relations, or standards. It is important to keep this in mind as a corrective to the tendency to view discrepant action as an aversive, undesirable state of affairs.

As a further corrective, it should be noted that discrepant action may not only have constructive consequences for the actor, but it may actually be viewed—by the actor and/or by observers—as a praiseworthy rather than a blameworthy event. So far I have used "discrepant action" in the customary sense of an action that is deficient, falling short of the person's attitude (or, more precisely, of certain standards). As I indicated at the beginning of the last section, however, discrepant actions may also take the form of actions that surpass the person's attitude. That is, people may act in ways that exceed expectation—that represent, for example, higher levels of generosity, courage, or tolerance than their attitudes require. Technically, such actions could be described as discrepant actions in the sense that they are out of keeping with what would be expected on the basis of the person's attitudes. But, of course, they have very different psychological and social meanings from actions that fall short of expectation. For example, "surpassing" actions should not bring into play such negative emotional reactions as guilt, shame, regret, or self-disappointment, which are aroused by deviations from societal standards of conduct.

Surpassing actions are conducive to attitude change for the same reasons and by the same means that action in general is conducive to attitude change, as discussed in earlier sections of this paper: they bring together motivational and informational processes in ways that create the conditions necessary for change to occur. Surpassing action is of special interest, however, because it provides a particularly clear illustration of an important phenomenon that has been largely ignored in research on the relation between action and attitude change: the role of action as a step in the attitude change process (Kelman, 1974a, pp. 321–324). I indicated at the beginning of the present paper (in the reference to "testing of new attitude" in Table 1 and the surrounding text) that this is one of the phenomena that my discussion is intended to encompass. Much of the discussion, however—particularly in the long section on discrepant action—has looked at the relationship between action and attitude change in a single direction only, focusing on action as instigation of the attitude change process. Let me correct for this imbalance by pointing out, in these concluding paragraphs, that action does not merely precipitate attitude change, but may itself be an integral part of an ongoing attitude change process.

Closer examination of an apparently discrepant action, particularly one that surpasses expectations, may reveal that the action is not completely out of keeping with the actor's attitudes. The action may indeed occur in response to situational demands, to interpersonal pressures, to social facilitation, or to other extraneous influences. This does not necessarily mean, however, that the response is entirely passive and unrelated to the actor's preferences. Instead, the action may reflect an incipient attitude change. Prior to the action, we may already have been moving toward a new attitude, but this attitude had not yet been crystallized and we had not fully committed ourselves to it. Extraneous forces may thus precipitate an action for which we were already partly prepared. The action in turn contributes to attitude change, in the sense that it provides an occasion for us to sharpen the new attitude and commit ourselves to it. In short, as the phenomenon of surpassing action helps us recognize, attitude change in relation to discrepant action need not be an entirely *reactive* process, but may well be an *active* process in which action plays a catalytic role.

This process can be readily understood if we conceive of an attitude as representing a range of commitment, as I proposed earlier in this paper. Within such a framework, it becomes clear that an action can simultaneously flow from an attitude and mediate changes in that attitude. Let us take, for example, a situation in which we support a cause that we generally favor with a financial contribution that surpasses expectation. Using the notion of attitude as range of commitment, we can describe what happens as follows: We find ourselves in a setting (perhaps a rally organized in response to an emergency) that calls for action (in the form of financial contribution) at a level higher than our modal level of commitment, but still within our range. For one or another reason (perhaps because of a combination of high emotional arousal and social pressure), we decide to take the action called for, which thus involves us at least temporarily at a level of commitment higher than our usual level. Having taken the action, we become subject to the various action-generated forces conducive to attitude change, which were discussed earlier; as a result we may manifest change by raising our modal level and our entire range, as well as perhaps by narrowing or widening the range. Thus we have an action that flows from our existing attitudes (even though it goes beyond what we and others would have expected, given our usual level of commitment), yet at the same time contributes to change in these attitudes.

An action situation may prompt us to take actions that surpass our modal level of commitment for a number of reasons, to which I have already alluded (p. 138). It may offer us an opportunity to adopt a new role that we have been anticipating for some time; it may confront us with a challenge to make a commitment that we have been considering but have avoided because of competing pressures or anxieties; or it may provide us with an occasion for deliberate efforts to mobilize internal and external supports for a new level of commitment that we have been seeking. Let me illustrate each of these possibilities and the ways in which they may generate attitude change.

The first possibility would be exemplified by members of an organization who have hitherto been relatively inactive but now accept an invitation to take on leadership roles. Their new roles commit them to actions that far surpass their previous level of commitment. Yet the fact that these particular individuals are selected for leadership is probably not a mere coincidence. Chances are that they were available for this higher level of commitment to the organization, that they had been moving in that direction for some time, that they had been building relevant attitudes in preparation for it—in short, that they had been undergoing a process of anticipatory socialization—but that the opportunity to act on these attitudes had not presented itself. Thus, the invitation to leadership represents an opportunity for them to adopt roles for which they were already prepared. Once they actually enter into the roles, significant further changes in attitude are likely to follow. Organizational leadership calls for a wide range of personally involving and publicly visible actions that generate a variety of new requirements, experiences, and social expectations. As a result, the new attitudes that were evolving before entry into the leadership roles are likely to become reorganized, sharpened, and stabilized at a higher level of commitment.

To exemplify an action situation that confronts a person with a challenge, let us visualize a student from a fairly conservative background whose political views and commitments have been moving in a new direction. She has settled into a generally liberal position, marked by support for various causes but not a high level of personal involvement in them. The possibility of a deeper commitment to some of these causes is within her attitudinal range, but she is not quite ready for it because she is not willing to break entirely with her family and home community, or because she is not prepared to pay the price of higher commitment, or because she has not fully sorted out her ideas on the matter. As often happens, this student may find herself in a situation in which social facilitation or social pressure from her current associates induce her to participate in political action that surpasses her modal level of commitment. This action in turn generates motivational and informational processes that reinforce and facilitate further attitude change, leading to a higher level of commitment. Although situational forces played a major role in inducing the action, she was at least partly ready for it. In fact, she may have had a latent interest in trying out this higher level of commitment but needed the extra push that social pressure provided. Other examples of this process are provided by Allport (1954), in his discussion of conscience-stricken opponents of desegregation who welcomed external pressures, in the form of laws or *faits accomplis*, that constrained them to go along with integration; and by Pettigrew (1961), in his discussion of "latent liberals" in the South who were racially prejudiced for reasons of conformity but quite ready to change once the social norms pointed in the direction of greater tolerance.

The challenge provided by an action situation may be primarily social in nature, as in the above examples, or it may be primarily cognitive. In the latter case, a person's movement to a higher level of commitment is inhibited, not by the existence of cross-pressures, but by failure to make certain cognitive connections. For example, a young man may have serious moral compunctions about war and thus be a latent conscientious objector. He may never have considered taking this position, however, because he was unaware of the existence of this social category and because it never occurred to him that response to the draft law was within a person's domain of moral choice. Once confronted with the possibility of such a position, he may draw the implications of his own values and declare himself a conscientious objector. This action in turn is likely to change his perspective and identity in ways conducive to further attitude change.

The third way in which an action situation may prompt surpassing actions—namely, by providing us with an occasion for deliberate efforts to mobilize internal and external supports for a new level of commitment that we have been seeking—suggests some of the most interesting instances of action as a step in an ongoing process of attitude change. It often happens that people want, with at least some degree of consciousness, to move to a higher level of commitment, but for various reasons (such as cross-pressures or other competing forces) are not quite ready to do so. Examples would be the political activist who wants to engage in more militant action but is reluctant to pay the price it would entail; the religious seeker who would like to make a complete commitment but lacks the faith to take the final leap; or the graduate student who is profoundly interested in a field of study but hesitates to make a life-long commitment to it. In such situations, people may deliberately take actions that are beyond their current levels of commitment. The political activist may decide to engage in an act of civil disobedience; the religious seeker may decide to spend a summer with the sect to which he or she is attracted; the graduate student may accept a research assistantship with the full expectation that the work will be engrossing. These actions do not represent a total commitment, but they do represent identifiable steps in that direction.

To some extent, people may take such steps in order to test their level of commitment, on the assumption that true commitment implies a readiness to take actions of this kind. The action thus provides them an opportunity to demonstrate their commitment to themselves (as well as to others)—or perhaps to determine, once and for all, that they really lack the commitment. What is even more intriguing, however, is that such actions are often taken to bring about a deeper level of commitment. People are at least vaguely aware that by taking such actions they place themselves in situations in which they will gradually be propelled into increasing commitment. The action creates some irreversible consequences. For example, by engaging in an act of civil disobedience, the political activist risks jail, which in turn may greatly limit his or her future opportunities. Furthermore, the action creates expectations in others—in both those who share the action and those who witness it—who will then treat the actor as someone who is fully committed to the cause. By setting up these expectations in others, people make it more difficult for themselves to withdraw, for both practical and psychological reasons. In short, by taking the action people are not only testing and mobilizing their own commitment, but also mobilizing external forces to support a strengthened commitment and to prevent them from backsliding. The array of forces generated by the action thus places the actors in a new psychological and social situation, which facilitates a shift to a higher level of commitment and a stabilization of attitudes that were not yet fully formed prior to the action.

In all of the examples that I have presented, action creates commitment and generates attitude change. Yet, at the same time, the person's readiness for such change is at least partly responsible for the original decision to take the action. Thus, action is both the product and the source of an attitude change process. The examples of self-mobilization are of particular interest since they represent deliberate attempts by people to use action as a vehicle for attitude change. They demonstrate the potential interactions, both between deliberate choice and external constraints, and between action and attitude change. They show most clearly the interplay of attitude and action in a continuing, reciprocal, circular process. Not only are attitudes an integral part of action, but action is an integral part of the development, testing, and crystalization of attitudes.

The observation that action can simultaneously flow from an attitude and mediate changes in that attitude underscores the paradoxical or dialectical character of attitudes, which has been an implicit but recurring theme throughout this paper. Attitudes determine action, yet they are shaped and reshaped by action. Attitudes structure our experiences with objects, yet they emerge out of the experiences we have with these objects. Attitudes give stability to our dealings with the environment, yet they fluctuate over time and across situations. Attitudes constitute the individual's contribution to social relations, yet they evolve in the course of social interaction. Attitudes are unique features of individual personality, yet they represent collective social products. Attitudes sharpen our sensitivity to inconsistency, yet they are riddled with inconsistencies. Attitudes reflect long-term principles and interests, yet they vary with the options and opportunities of the moment.

There is considerable variation—between individuals, between attitudes within a group, between attitudes within an individual—in the degree to which one or the other pole of each of these contradictions predominates. But every attitude, to a greater or lesser degree, contains these contradictions within itself. They are inherent in human existence and the social base of that existence. On the one hand, we need a stable, coherent framework by which our relations to the environment are organized and to which our experiences are assimilated. On the other hand, we need to adapt to the changing realities, necessities, and opportunities that the environment presents. (The fact that we live in society both makes these needs more imperative and helps to meet them.) Attitudes perform an important function in mediating these two sets of needs—a function reflected in the various struggles, at different levels, that characterize attitudes: the struggles between approach and avoidance, between stability and change, between individual and group. They can provide the needed continuity in our relationship to the environment insofar as they are open to change; they can guide action insofar as they in turn are guided by reality.

REFERENCE NOTES

1. Kelman, H. C., Baron, R. M., Sheposh, J. P., & Lubalin, J. S. *Varieties of discrepant action: Toward a functional theory.* Book in preparation, 1979.
2. Baron, R. M., Kelman, H. C., Sheposh, J. P., & Johnson, E. *Attitudinal effects of experimenter attractiveness in situations arousing moral and hedonic dissonance.* Unpublished manuscript, University of Connecticut, 1970. (To be published in the book cited in Note 1.)
3. Adler, N. *Abortion as discrepant action: A test of Kelman's model of reactions to discrepant action.* Unpublished manuscript, University of California, San Francisco, 1975. (To be published in Note 1.)

REFERENCES

Alexander, F., & French, T. M. *Psychoanalytic therapy.* New York: Ronald Press, 1946.
Allport, G. W. *The nature of prejudice.* Cambridge, MA.: Addison-Wesley, 1954.
Bem, D. J. Self-perception: An alternative interpretation of cognitive dissonance phenomena. *Psychological Review,* 1967, **74**, 183–200.
Brehm, J. W., & Cohen, A. R. *Explorations in cognitive dissonance.* New York: Wiley, 1962.
Cohen, S. P., Kelman, H. C., Miller, F. D., & Smith, B. L. Evolving intergroup techniques for conflict resolution: An Israeli-Palestinian pilot workshop. *Journal of Social Issues,* 1977, **33** (1), 165–189.
Deutsch, M., & Collins, M. E. *Interracial housing: A psychological evaluation of a social experiment.* Minneapolis: University of Minnesota Press, 1951.

Eagly, A. H., & Himmelfarb, S. Attitudes and opinions. *Annual Review of Psychology*, 1978, **29**, 517–554.

Festinger, L. *A theory of cognitive dissonance*. Stanford: Stanford University Press, 1957.

Frank, J. D., & Ascher, E. Corrective emotional experiences in group therapy. *American Journal of Psychiatry*, 1951, **108**, 126–131.

Katz, D. The functional approach to attitude change. *Public Opinion Quarterly*, 1960, **24**, 163–204.

Kelman, H. C. Attitude change as a function of response restriction. *Human Relations*, 1953, **6**, 185–214.

Kelman, H. C. Compliance, identification, and internalization: Three processes of attitude change. *Journal of Conflict Resolution*, 1958, **2**, 51–60.

Kelman, H. C. Processes of opinion change. *Public Opinion Quarterly*, 1961, **25**, 57–78.

Kelman, H. C. The induction of action and attitude change. In S. Coopersmith (Ed.), *Personality Research*. Copenhagen: Munksgaard, 1962 (a).

Kelman, H. C. Changing attitudes through international activities. *Journal of Social Issues*, 1962, **18** (1), 68–87. (b)

Kelman, H. C. The role of the group in the induction of therapeutic change. *International Journal of Group Psychotherapy*, 1963, **13**, 399–432.

Kelman, H. C. The problem-solving workshop in conflict resolution. In R. L. Merritt (Ed.), *Communication in international politics*. Urbana: University of Illinois Press, 1972.

Kelman, H. C. Attitudes are alive and well and gainfully employed in the sphere of action. *American Psychologist*, 1974, **29**, 310–324. (a)

Kelman, H. C. Social influence and linkages between the individual and the social system: Further thoughts on the processes of compliance, identification, and internalization. In J. T. Tedeschi (Ed.), *Perspectives on social power*. Chicago: Aldine, 1974. (b)

Kelman, H. C. International interchanges: Some contributions from theories of attitude change. *Studies in Comparative International Development*, 1975, **10** (1), 83–99.

Kelman, H. C. Attitude and behavior: A social-psychological problem. In J. M. Yinger and S. J. Cutler (Eds.), *Major social issues: A multidisciplinary view*. New York: Free Press, 1978.

Kelman, H. C., & Baron, R. M. Inconsistency as a psychological signal. In R. P. Abelson, E. Aronson, W. J. McGuire, T. M. Newcomb, M. J. Rosenberg, & P. H. Tannenbaum (Eds.), *Theories of cognitive consistency: A sourcebook*. Chicago: Rand McNally, 1968. (a)

Kelman, H. C., & Baron, R. M. Determinants of modes of resolving inconsistency dilemmas: A functional analysis. In R. P. Abelson, E. Aronson, W. J. McGuire, T. M. Newcomb, M. J. Rosenberg, & P. H. Tannenbaum

(Eds.), *Theories of cognitive consistency: A sourcebook*. Chicago: Rand McNally, 1968. (b)

Kelman, H. C., & Baron, R. M. Moral and hedonic dissonance: A functional analysis of the relationship between discrepant action and attitude change. In S. Himmelfarb & A. H. Eagly (Eds.), *Readings in attitude change*. New York: Wiley, 1974.

Kelman, H. C., & Cohen, S. P. Reduction of international conflict: An interactional approach. In G. W. Austin & S. Worchel (Eds.), *The social psychology of intergroup relations*. Monterey, CA.: Brooks/Cole, 1979.

King, B. T., & Janis, I. L. Comparison of the effectiveness of improvised versus nonimprovised role-playing in producing opinion changes. *Human Relations*, 1956, **9**, 177–186.

LaPiere, R. T. Attitudes vs. actions. *Social Forces*, 1934, **13**, 230–237.

Lieberman, S. The effects of changes in roles on the attitudes of role occupants. *Human Relations*, 1956, **9**, 385–402.

Miller, N. E. Experimental studies of conflict. In J. McV. Hunt (Ed.), *Personality and the behavior disorders* (Vol. 1). New York: Ronald Press, 1944.

Pettigrew, T. F. Social psychology and desegregation research. *American Psychologist*, 1961, **16**, 105–112.

Saenger, G. *The social psychology of prejudice*. New York: Harper, 1953.

Sherif, M., & Hovland, C. I. *Social judgment: Assimilation and contrast effects in communication and attitude change*. New Haven: Yale University Press, 1961.

Smith, M. B., Bruner, J. S., & White, R. W. *Opinions and personality*. New York: Wiley, 1956.

Values, Attitudes, and Interpersonal Behavior

Harry C. Triandis[1]

University of Illinois,
Urbana-Champaign

*I*n recent years many areas of psychology have been experiencing centrifugal forces of fragmentation into minor research areas. As researchers become more and more focused on specialized topics, other psychologists find their work irrelevant. The sheer number of variables that might be investigated by psychologists is so large that in some ways fragmentation is inevitable. But as more and more psychologists become active researchers, trying to do something original, the centrifugal forces are likely to increase unless we begin constructing cohesive theoretical frameworks which will provide centripetal forces. This paper is conceived as an effort in that direction, a conscious move toward synthesis. Its focus is the relationship of attitudes, values, and other acquiried behavioral dispositions (Campbell, 1963) to action or behavior. An attempt will be made to present a theoretical framework which will pull together relationships involving these concepts.

Obviously, this kind of theoretical work must consist of networks of interrelated hypotheses. As Poincaré (1905) noted many years ago, reasonable hypotheses summarizing the state of knowledge at one point in time, even if they prove incorrect at a later point in time, serve a very useful function. In many cases, he argues, an incorrect hypothesis is even more useful than one that appears convincingly correct, because when we find evidence that it is incorrect we change our mind much more drastically than when we find evidence that supports our hypotheses.

1. I am grateful for useful comments received from John Adamopoulos, John Berry, David Brinberg, Andy Davidson, Jack Feldman, Fred Kanfer, and Roy Roper.

In this paper, then, I will try to do what I have just advocated: present a network of interrelated hypotheses around the constructs of attitude and behavior, placing them in the broadest possible context. The first section of the paper will define a rather long list of concepts. An attempt will be made to indicate not only what is meant by a concept, but also what relationships the concept may have or not have with other concepts, and what kinds of dimensions of variation are likely to emerge when studying the particular concept. Evidence will be presented, when available, to support the theoretical statements. Methods of operationalization of each concept will be described, to make sure that the concepts presented are not incapable of being subjected to research.

However, it is necessary to distinguish a theoretical construct from its methods of operationalization. The theoretical construct may include logical relationships, some of which are a matter of definition. As Smedslund (1978) has argued, there are many propositions in psychology that follow from the definitions of terms, and in those cases empirical testing is unnecessary, just as it is unnecessary to test the Pythagorian theorem of Euclidean geometry by measuring the sides of right-angled triangles, squaring, and adding. Once the axioms of Euclidean geometry are accepted, the theorem follows logically. If the empirical test does not support the theorem, this indicates that the measurements are deficient, or the axioms are wrong.

A number of controversies in social psychology are due to the unclear distinction between empirically testable propositions and propositions that are true by definition. Most relevant to our present topic is the controversy about the relationship of attitudes and behavior. If attitudes are defined as "predispositions to behavior," then a relationship exists by definition; no empirical test is needed. If attitudes are defined as "affect toward an object," then an empirical test *is* needed. Given the particular definition of attitude, there are numerous ways in which the construct can be operationalized and measured. Each of these methods of operationalization may be fallible, that is, it may not be valid. Unless the researcher has established the validity of a measure, it is incorrect to use this index to measure the theoretical construct, since it is quite possible that the measure is reflecting something quite different from what the researcher thinks it measures. This implies that if attitude is defined as a "predisposition to respond," a measure of attitude is *invalid unless it is shown to predict behavor*. If the definition is that an attitude is the affect toward the attitude object, then some additional measures of affect—physiological, or a parallel way of measuring the results of the affective response—are necessary to establish convergent validity. One of the reasons I prefer the first to the second definition of attitude is that physiological measures are traditionally of low reliability and validity for the assessment of attitudes.

In any case, the strategy that I advocate requires *multimethod measurement* of each construct (Campbell & Fiske, 1959) and convergent operations (Garner, Hake, & Eriksen, 1956) to distinguish one concept from another. Most of the research in the attitude-behavior controversy does not follow this strategy; rather than using multiple measures of attitudes and behavior and checking the relationships between the common variance of the first and second sets of measures, it typically has relied on single measures.

Considering that there is a literature that shows profound and substantial interrelationships of attitudes and behavior,[2] it is unlikely that attitudes are completely unrelated to behavior. When studies are reported where no relationship has been found, one must be suspicious about the methodology—e.g., the reliability of the attitude and behavior measures. So I think it is not fruitful to explore *whether* there is a relationship; rather, I propose to indicate the conditions under which either strong or weak relationships between verbal attitudes and behavior are likely to be observed.

In what follows I will distinguish a logical proposition from a proposition requiring empirical testing by calling the first a theorem. A theorem is deducible from the logical definitions offered in the body of the paper.

The second section of the paper will present a theoretical network consisting of theorems and propositions (relationships that require testing). Under each theorem or proposition I will present, when possible, a summary of the research that has already been done that is consistent with the proposition.

---

2. The study by Newton and Newton (1950) is a good example. Mothers who had positive attitudes about breast feeding had success rates of 74%, while mothers who had negative attitudes had success rates of only 26%, success being indexed by having enough milk on the fifth day not to require a bottle.

OUTLINE OF THEORETICAL FRAMEWORK

One of the problems in the social sciences is that different disciplines have their favorite variables, measure them in their own particular ways, and generate bodies of literature that have no links among themselves. Thus social psychologists measure attitudes through survey methods, anthropologists study kinship systems, roles and norms in different cultures, and psychologists study behavior in animals, the clinic, the field, or the laboratory. If the information collected by anthropologists is to become useful to psychologists (and vice versa), some links must be established. The framework that is presented here is an attempt to provide such links. It includes variables that are general and abstract enough to be relevant to any investigation, in any culture. Thus whether the data are acts, paper-and-pencil responses, surveys, laboratory or field observations, the framework can be used.

Figure 1 presents the framework. *Behavior* is seen as having objective *consequences* (that occur "out there" in the real world) which are *interpreted* (occur inside the person). As a result of these interpretations, the person feels *reinforced*. Reinforcement affects the *perceived consequences* of the behavior in two ways: it changes the *perceived probabilities* that the behavior will have particular consequences and it changes the *value of these consequences*. These probabilities and values, in turn, constitute one of the determinants of *behavioral intentions* to behave, which are one of the determinants of behavior. *Habits* and *relevant arousal* are also determinants of behavior. But even when the intentions are high, the habits well established, and the arousal optimal, there may be no behavior if the geography of the situation makes the behavior impossible; thus *facilitating conditions* are seen as important determinants of behavior. The interpretation of the objective consequences may differ because of genetic/biological influences or because of the previous situation-behavior-reinforcement sequences that the individual has encountered in his or her history, i.e., the individual's *personality*. Personality internalizes the *culture*'s way of perceiving the social environment, called the *subjective culture* of a group. Subjective culture includes *norms, roles, and values*. These internalizations correspond with but are not identical to the group's subjective culture, and form the *social factors* that influence the intention to behave. In addition, previous experiences of the individual with particular behaviors result in *affect* toward the behavior, which in turn are among the determi-

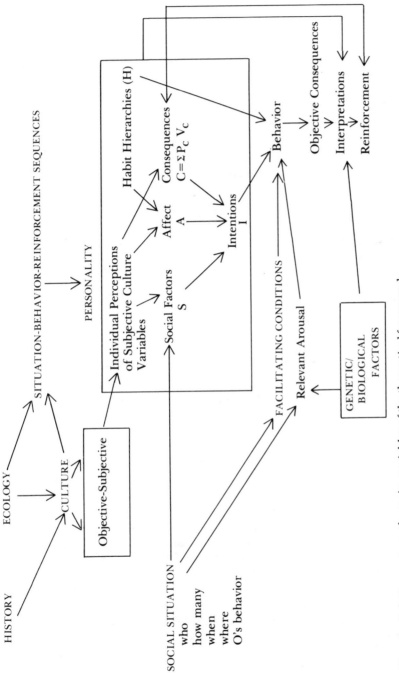

Figure 1. Relations among the major variables of the theoretical framework

nants of intentions. Personality is seen as an outcome of situation-behavior-reinforcement sequences and the subjective culture to which the individual is exposed. This subjective culture reflects the human-made part of the environment, shaped by *historical* and *ecological* forces.

Any behavior can be seen as occurring in a particular situation, which influences the facilitating conditions and the relevant arousal of the person while simultaneously activating specific levels of the social factors. For interpersonal behavior the *social situation* includes particular individuals, in a behavior setting, as well as the other's previous behavior.

One explanation about this figure is important at this time. The arrows show the directions of probable causality. However, there are several bidirectional relationships which are not shown on the diagram (to avoid making it too complex). For example, culture is shown to influence the situation-behavior-reinforcement sequences available in particular ecologies, and such sequences are shown to influence personality. One could make a case also that personality influences culture, since personality, according to our definitions (below), includes values, and values are in part shaped by events independent of culture (such as interactions of biological and ecological factors), and once values have changed in certain directions they increase the probability of behaviors that will in themselves change culture. More specifically, and as an example, in an ecology that happens to have low human densities (for historical reasons), human behaviors that change the environment, such as building a fence, a small dam, or a road, can have a major impact on the reinforcements of a few individuals, who are then likely to acquire an even stronger "mastery over nature" value, which then leads to more ecology-changing behaviors, and to a culture in which ecological change is rapid and valued, and in which social structures are particularly suited to accommodate the change. In a high density culture a person may not be allowed to build a fence or dam and hence will never get a taste of mastery of the environment.

This sketch of the relationships between the major concepts of the framework is probably only vaguely understandable by the reader because I have used so many different concepts and have not defined them. Before presenting and defending the various links, therefore, I will provide some definitions, ordered in the same way as the concepts presented in this outline.

DEFINITIONS

Behavior

Behavior in this essay refers to a broad class of reactions by an organism to any stimuli (internal or external to the organism). It includes *acts* (see below for definition). Some intrapersonal events have both affective and cue-properties, triggering other events. Such events, e.g., thinking, feeling, dreaming, and fantasizing, are considered behaviors.

An important issue concerns which aspect of behavior should be measured: duration, intensity, frequency, latency, probability in certain settings, etc. Other issues concern the validity of self-reports and their relationship to behavioral observations. If we are willing to live with distortions in self-perception, due to forgetting, defense mechanisms, etc., it may be more useful to use the actor's perspective, which includes his or her own past, present, and future behavior, because the observer's perspective includes *only* present behavior (unless a longitudinal study can be done). In measuring behaviors a problem is the coding system. Should one use time intervals as units? What are the behavioral boundaries of units (Newtson, 1976)? How broad or detailed should the coverage be? What kinds of coding errors are frequent, and how can they be controlled? To what extent should we consider sequences of behavior? These and many other questions are discussed by Longabaugh (1980) and will not be covered here, since the present paper does not focus on methodology.

Acts

An act is a socially defined pattern of muscle movements. Specific acts, such as hitting someone, are too numerous and are subject to too many influences to be good primitive terms of a theory. Such acts do not have meaning in themselves but acquire meaning from the social context, particularly the perceived causes of the acts. For instance, "to hit" is very different if it is done accidentally, as a joke, to "correct" a naughty child, or with the intention to hurt. In what follows, acts that include both muscle movements and a minimum of meaning are considered as primitive terms of the theory.

Acts differ in frequency or *probability* of occurrence in a certain setting. In addition, it is useful to consider their *intensity* and *duration*. For example, shaking somebody's hand has higher probabilities in France than in the United States; it may vary in the amount of pressure exerted, and in the duration of the act.

The measurement of acts employs an observational methodology (Longabaugh, 1980). Acts can be recorded on film or video tape, or observed directly, and they can be coded in a variety of systems of differing complexity and elaboration. Video or audio recording provides a replica of the acts, but data can be used only after they are reduced through some sort of coding. The interaction chronograph (Chapple, 1940) provides several indices of the rate (frequency per unit of time) and duration of social interaction. Systems of trait ratings, after observers have followed a series of acts, provide still other procedures. Problems of sampling—who is to be observed, when and where, and what behaviors are to be coded—have to be solved before a replicable system of observations is developed. The Bales (1950), Barker (1963, 1968), Birdwhistell (1952, 1970), and Wright (1967) methods of measurement are representative of those used by psychologists.

Perceived Consequences of an Act (P_c)

Each act is perceived as having some consequences. If the individual perceives an inescapable connection between act and consequence, P_c is close to 1.00; theoretically, if the individual believes that it is *certain* that a particular consequence will *not* follow the act, then P is close to zero. If a person is uncertain about the connection of act and consequence then P_c is about .50.

Methods of measurement of P_c include asking the person to indicate his or her certainty that a consequence will or will not follow an act. A rating scale can be used in which the middle point is labeled "uncertain" and the end points are labeled "certain it will happen" and "certain it will not happen." Another method is to provide individuals with a list of conceivable consequences and ask them to select the consequences they consider to be most likely to follow an act. Then a P_c of 1.00 can be assigned to the consequences that are selected and a P_c of 0.00 to the remaining consequences.

Value of Consequence (V_C)

The affect attached to a consequence can be measured by the evaluative factor of the semantic differential (Osgood, May, & Miron, 1975) when the concept that is judged is the consequence. Another method is to use a set of prescaled, affectively positive or negative stimuli (e.g., going to a good movie or being told by one's boss that one is doing a poor job) and ask the subject to match a particular consequence, on the "pleasant-unpleasant dimension" with one of these prescaled stimuli.

Behavioral Intention (*I*)

Behavioral intentions are instructions that people give to themselves to behave in certain ways. They involve ideas such as "I must do X," "I will do X," and "I am going to do X." One way to measure these is to use a behavioral differential scale (Triandis, 1964b). Many other kinds of procedures can be devised, such as asking, "What do you intend to do?" or "How are you going to reach this goal?"

It is useful to clarify that acts are typically organized into action patterns that reflect particular goals. A *goal* can be stated by an individual as a state of affairs that requires a series of acts for its realization. Acts correspond to behavioral intentions, while goals correspond to "general intentions." General intentions are quite abstract.

Factor analysis is a useful methodology for inferring general intentions from behavioral intentions. The general intention "to show association toward another" may be defined by intentions to show concern, to help, to behave altruistically toward; and each of these can in turn be defined by particular behavioral intentions. For example, the intention to help may take the form of helping someone who has fallen on the floor, or helping one financially. The latter intentions naturally depend very much on the situation.

Obviously, the measurement of intentions can be done with specific scales, in the case of behavioral intentions, and with several scales loading on the same factor in a factor analysis, in the case of more abstract intentions.

Habits

These are situation-behavior sequences that are or have become automatic, so that they occur without self-instruction. The individual is usually not "conscious" of these sequences. *Reflexes* are similar sequences, but they do not have to be learned; habits require learning. Learning is a function of (a) the magnitude of reinforcement, (b) its close contiguity in time, (c) the extent to which the behavior and the reinforcement are associated with each other in different settings or contexts, (d) the clarity of the cue associated with the learning situation, (e) the simplicity of the cues, (f) the familiarity of the cues, (g) the ability of the organism to learn, (h) the confidence of the learner that learning is possible, and (i) the extent to which a variety of others provide reinforcements when a behavior takes place. The well-known relationships of inconsistency of reinforcement to extinction, modeling to learning, and drive state to learning are merely mentioned here to suggest that all of the above factors also have some role in the establishment of habits.

Exactly what is a reinforcement is difficult to define. Premack (1966) argued that "the most probable response of a set of responses will reinforce all members of the set; the least probable will reinforce no member of the set" (p. 132). Presumably such probabilities reflect the previous history of the organism. Thus there are some variations in the extent to which particular individuals find particular events highly reinforcing.

Certain *cognitive schemata*, such as those discussed by Piaget, Abelson (who calls them scripts), and others, are habits, as defined here. They are elicited by patterns of stimuli, and a consequence of their activation often includes a complex sequence of behavior.

When a person has high *ability*, e.g., intelligence, habits are established more easily. For example, a person with musical ability is likely to learn to play the piano (a behavior that starts by being intentional, but becomes automatic) more easily than one with less ability. A person who faces an easy task may develop the habits necessary for doing it more readily than one who has to do a task that is difficult relative to his or her abilities. Thus habits are seen as reflecting not only the learning history of the organism, but also the organism's level of ability relative to the difficulty of the task.

Habits can be measured by the frequency of occurrence of behavior, by subjects' judgments of the likelihood that a behavior will take place in different kinds of situations, and by a subject's response of how frequently she or he has done something. Obviously, none of these measures is ideal, particularly the self-report measures which can be easily distorted because of social desirability. But if several measures converge, it is likely that the common elements are reflecting the construct.

Relevant Arousal (P)

The physiological arousal (P) of the organism that is relevant to the act facilitates the act, and increases its probability. Either high drive or a situation which is relevant to the individual's values may increase the probability of the act.

Facilitating Conditions (F)

A person may have the intention to do something, but be unable to do it; the geography of the environment may prevent the act. Acts that are easy to carry out because they require little expenditure of energy have high facilitating conditions, while acts that are difficult to do because they require much energy have low facilitating conditions. Facilitating conditions are objective factors, "out there" in the environment, that several judges or observers can agree make an act easy to do. The person's perceptions that the act is easy are "internal" factors and would be included in the P_cV_c terms discussed earlier. Of course, there is some correspondence between the F and P_c factors, but the correspondence may not always be high.

Personality

Personality refers to the organized functions of the individual. These include individual definitions and perceptions of each of the elements of subjective culture discussed above. Thus, roles may be examined at the cultural level, but also in the perceptions of individuals; values can be studied across individuals, but also at the level of a single person (an ideographic approach, as outlined by Zavalloni, 1980). Individual differences in cognitive complexity, authoritarianism, anxiety, breadth of categorization, impulsivity, length of time perspective, and so on, can be considered in describing different personality structures.

An important aspect of personality is the *self-concept.* How do people see themselves? Here we can consider attributes that the person uses to characterize the self. Of particular interest here are behaviors that people consider appropriate for themselves. These are self-instructions to behave in particular ways. Methods of measurement can include ratings of whether people believe that they should engage in a particular behavior in a particular situation.

Habit hierarchies are another way to view the personality. Here we are interested in descriptions of what the subject normally does. Some behavior patterns have high probabilities, while others have low probabilities.

Culture

Culture is the human-made part of the environment (Herskovits, 1955). It has both objective aspects (bridges, roads, tools) and subjective aspects (laws, myths, roles, norms, values). A culture is determined by place, time, and language. For example, the British and Americans speak the same language, but live in a different place; the British of 1960 and 1690 lived in the same place but at a different time; the English and French speakers in Quebec live in the same place and time, but speak a different language. In each of these three examples, there is a difference of culture.

In discussing cultures it is important to keep in mind that from a psychological point of view they are complex patterns of schedules of reinforcement. Such patterns can be associated not only with culture but also with other demographic characteristics, such as sex, age, social class, and religion. Obviously, a complete discussion of the effects of culture on psychological variables needs to unconfound the demographic variables from the "purely" cultural, which are traceable to language, place, and time. Furthermore, the within-culture variance on any psychological attribute is often very large. In fact, in many studies, the between-cultures variance is less than the within-culture variance. Also, when hypotheses are tested by using the Human Relations Area Files (Barry, 1980), it is not possible to obtain estimates of the within-culture variance. But despite the fact that the term "culture" is rather gross and imprecise, it is often useful as a "first approximation."

Cultures differ along several important dimensions. (1) One of these is *complexity* (Lomax & Berkowitz, 1972; Murdock & Provost, 1973). Both ancient Roman and modern industrial cultures are considered complex, while certain cultures without written language, roads, and political and social differentiation are considered simple. (2) There appears to be an important distinction between hunting and fishing modes of subsistence on the one hand, and agricultural modes on the other (Barry, Child, & Bacon, 1959). The former are characterized by lenient socialization patterns and little insistence on conformity; the latter employ severe socialization methods and insist on conformity. A parallel distinction, though perhaps somewhat more general, is the notion of *tight* versus *loose* cultures (Pelto, 1968). (3) *Tough* versus *easy* cultures are discussed by Arsenian and Arsenian (1948). Easy cultures are those in which most individuals reach most of their goals most of the time; goals are clear and numerous, and having one goal does not preclude having another. Thus in such cultures most persons have many highly valued goal objects, relations, properties, and means of gratification. Tough cultures are those where the number of goals is limited; goals are unclear; reaching one goal often precludes reaching another; few goals are available to few people; and the large majority of people cannot reach goals. (4) *Modernity* is still another dimension (Inkeles & Smith, 1974). It reflects attributes of socioeconomic development such as the increased amount of education available to most members of the culture, urban rather than rural environments, experience with factory life, and work in modern cooperatives rather than in traditional social settings.

I have selected these dimensions of cultural variations because they appear to have the broadest consequences and hence are most likely to have psychological consequences. There are other analyses of cultures which extract more specific dimensions; for example Smith and Crano (1977) identified 14 factors of variations across cultures.

Combinations of these dimensions are also useful. For example, Boldt (1978) suggests a typology of cultures with two dimensions: simple-complex and tight-loose. The agricultural/pastoral groups are both simple and tight; the hunting/gathering groups are both simple and loose; modern totalitarian cultures are complex and tight; modern pluralistic cultures are both complex and loose.

Dawson (1973) has proposed that when the ecology makes tight socialization more likely, people develop the notion that social structures are stratified; this makes them more amenable to life in modern societies, and hence their attitudes are likely to be more modern.

Subjective Culture

Subjective culture (Triandis, Vassiliou, Tanaka, & Shanmugam, 1972) refers to a human group's characteristic way of viewing the human-made part of the environment. It consists of ways of categorizing experience (see below for discussion of categorization), beliefs, attitudes, ideals, roles, norms, and values.

Norms: Norms are self-instructions to do what is perceived to be correct and appropriate by members of a culture in certain situations. Norms vary in clarity, in the extent to which sanctions for breaking them exist, and in the intensity of feeling attached to them. They can be measured by asking people to rate the appropriateness of a behavior in various situations and the extent to which they tell themselves to act appropriately in these situations.

Norms as an attribute of cultures must be distinguished from personal normative beliefs. In predicting behavioral intentions from norms the appropriate concept should be measured at the personal rather than at cultural/societal levels. Furthermore, particular individuals will be most sensitive to the norms that are characteristic of their reference groups, which may or may not agree with the norms of other members of their culture.

Roles: Roles, like norms, are concerned with behaviors that are considered correct or appropriate. They differ from norms in that they are behaviors appropriate for persons holding a particular position in a group, society, or social system. The usual distinction is between *emitted, subjective,* and *enacted* roles. The first correspond to what group members actually expect and tell other people; the second correspond to what a person perceives as being expected; the third correspond to what a person actually does. Roles can be specific and unique (e.g., Pope) or general (e.g., fathers), and clear or unclear, with sanctions for not doing what is expected being applied consistently or inconsistently. Roles can be measured with the role differential (Triandis, Vassiliou, & Nassiakou, 1968).

Values: These are relationships among abstract categories with strong affective components, implying a preference for a certain kind of action or state of affairs (Triandis et al., 1972, p. 16). The categories reflect abstract terms such as humans, nature, time, human-to-human relationships, action. Thus when a person feels good at the thought that "man should be the master of the universe," this implies the value that Kluckhohn and Strodtbeck (1961) called "man's mastery over nature."

Values refer to concepts that are widely used by social scientists, humanists, and the public. Philosophers deal with them in a subdivision of their discipline called axiology. Modern axiologists have argued that values are not only subjective entities but are also inherent in the structure of reality. In other words, human biology and adaptation to the environment force certain structures of preference for particular situations and states of the world.

The measurement of values has generally corresponded to the concepts that people have used to define and describe them. Spranger's conception of values as economic, religious, theoretical, aesthetic, social, and political led to a measuring procedure developed by Allport, Vernon, and Lindzey (1960). Kluckhohn's (1956, 1959) thorough examination of the concept, historically, philosophically, and cross-culturally, led to the operationalization by Kluckhohn and Strodtbeck (1961).

Values have at least three functions: (a) They are relevant to selectivity in perception by increasing or decreasing the likelihood that a stimulus will be perceived. (b) They influence the interpretation of the outcomes of responses, so that some responses and their outcomes become positive reinforcements while other responses and their outcomes become negative reinforcements. For example, a confirmed equalitarian and an aristocrat who opposes equalitarian principles might be equally likely to perceive a social event in which a high-status person is rejected by a low-status person. The event might be viewed as pleasant by the first and as unpleasant by the second person. If the observer's actions are seen as the antecedents of the event, the event is reinforcing. In short, the extent to which an event is consistent with a perceiver's value structure makes the event pleasant to the perceiver, and pleasant events often increase the probability of acts that are perceived to cause these events. (c) Values provide nonspecific guidelines for the selection of goals. To use an example: A chess player keeps the value "to win" constantly in mind in selecting goals for his or her next move. While that move may in fact lead to a loss, the player at the time the move is made usually thinks that it will lead to a good outcome.

During socialization children note connections among a variety of events and abstract categories loaded with affect from these observations. For example, they note "how nice it is" to heat or air-condition a house, to have houses that are comfortable, to grow crops in the wilderness, etc., and from these, and a myriad of similar observations, they abstract the value orientation that humans *should* control nature. This is an *early* value. Once the value is present it can function as a *late* value to filter new experiences and provide interpretations of experiences. The older child (say, a teenager) hears of a new drug that controls the speed of a woman delivering a baby. Given the person's control-over-nature orientation, the new drug then appears *desirable*. So experiences produce affect, and affects toward many different categories are abstracted to form values, which then are used to interpret new events, and result in "derived affect" toward specific events.

The sequence in time would be as shown in Table 1.

As in the discussion of affect (see below), it is important to recognize that values are formed both directly, as just outlined, and indirectly. The indirect value formation is through other people, and follows the "information"-beliefs-affect-values route.

Social Factors

The individual's internalization of the reference group's subjective culture, and specific interpersonal agreements that the individual has made with others, in specific social situations, constitute social factors that determine behavioral intentions.

There is some correspondence between norms, roles, and values as societal constructs, and individual norms, roles, and values. These individual entities influence the individual's conceptions of behaviors which are appropriate, desirable, and morally correct. Self-instructions to act in particular ways are influenced by such

Table 1
Experiences and derived affect

Experiences →	Affect →	Early Values	Late Values	Interpretations of new events	Derived Affect
e.g., Many specific observations	Feel good in many situations where nature is controlled	The idea "humans should control nature" as a summary of these experiences	"Humans should control nature" as a filter for new experiences	Meanings of new experiences	Feel good about those experiences associated with humans' control of nature

conceptions. In addition, interpersonal agreements are also likely to influence behavioral self-instruction.

Affect

This term refers to the emotional system of an individual. In this essay it will be used in a more restricted sense to refer to the feelings of joy, elation, or pleasure, or depression, disgust, displeasure, or hate associated by an individual with a particular act. As Wundt (1896), Schlosberg (1954), and Osgood (1966) have noted, emotions are structured in three dimensions (pleasant-unpleasant, attention-rejection, arousal-sleep). The view of affect which will be used here refers to the pleasant-attending-arousing corner as opposed to the unpleasant-rejecting-arousing corner of the "emotion solid" (see Triandis & Lambert, 1958, p. 324, for a picture). Operationalization of this construct can take several forms. One can ask an individual to rate the verbal label of the act, on scales such as pleasant-unpleasant, enjoyable-disgusting, exciting-depressing, and joyful-hateful. The average rating on such scales can be used as an index of affect. A more complete measure would use scales, appropriate for each culture, derived from factor analyses of semantic differentials as outlined by Osgood, May, and Miron (1975). Thus separate scales would be used for evaluation (pleasant), potency (attention), and activity.

Another way is to use the Galvanic Skin Responses, obtained when the verbal label, or a photographic representation of the act, is presented together with a very positive or negative word, such as "delightful" or "disgusting." One obtains a strong physiological response when a liked act is combined with an unpleasant verbal cue or a disliked act is combined with a pleasant verbal cue (Cooper, 1959).

Affect toward an object has two different determinants. (1) Attributes or characteristics of the attitude object have affective loadings, and are linked to the object with differing degrees of strength. The sum of the products of the strength of each linkage times the affect attached to each characteristic is an estimate of the total affect toward the attitude object. (2) Classical conditioning processes link pleasant or unpleasant events to the attitude object. The usual laws of learning apply, i.e., the strength of the affect depends on the frequency of linking of the attitude object with the pleasant or unpleasant events, the degree of pleasure associated with the events, the contiguity in time between the presentation of the attitude object and the event, and so on. The distinction between the two kinds of processes is important because the first can lead to a change of affect indirectly, as when a person is "informed" about the characteristics of an object, while the second requires a direct experience of the person with the attitude object.

Ecology

Ecology refers to the relationships between organisms and the physical environment, including climate, physical terrain, prevailing fauna and flora, resources which favor various forms of exploitation for survival, and the extent to which resources are limited or plentiful.

Theories about the link between ecology and social behavior range from those that link climate to social behavior to those that link aspects of the social environment (see below) to behavior. Moos (1976) has provided a good review of both. For example, most riots in Indià occur when the temperature is between 80 and 90°F, and most in America when the temperature exceeds 90°. Other studies link ecology and crime, suicide, mental illness, and other variables. The dimensions of social environments, according to Moos, include the degree of involvement, emotional support, independence, competition, achievement, intellectuality, order, and innovation found in a culture.

The level of emotional arousal is said to be systematically related to climate and weather, in a study by Robbins, DeWalt, and Pelto (1972). The warmer the climate the greater the amount of emotional expression. Classifying societies into warm or cold, depending on the level of the average winter temperature (more or less than 50° F), these authors found that in warm cultures there was greater indulgence of aggression and less aggression socialization anxiety, more permissive sex codes for females, and greater emotional expressiveness. Nationals in warm climates were found to have high homicide rates and those in cold climates high suicide rates. The authors speculate that since humans evolved in the tropics, adjustment to colder climates has required greater involvement of cultural control mechanisms, and such mechanisms tend to regulate both emotions and behavior.

Social Situations

Behavior settings (see below) include social situations, where more than one individual is present. Social situations differ in the extent to which they are private or public and the extent to which they do and do not specify what behaviors are appropriate in them. Adamopoulos (1976) studied the perception of social situations, using an adaptation of the role differential. Subjects were asked to indicate how they would behave, in a given role relationship, in one of thirty social situations. Factor analyses revealed two dimensions: formality-informality (reflecting the public-private character of the situation) and constraining-unconstraining (reflecting the number of different behaviors that can appropriately occur in the situation).

Behavior Setting

Each environment consists of cues that may be connected with acts. Such connections reflect habits (see definition) that people have to behave in particular ways in the presence of such cues. A behavior setting (Barker, 1968) has place-time coordinates, it consists of physical entities and processes, and it evokes particular behaviors. It can be distinguished from what is outside of it, it has structural features, and it exists independently of any particular person's perception of it. For example, a classroom has a particular location and a particular time when the class meets; it also has chairs, walls, and blackboards; and in it people act in certain ways, e.g., talk, listen, write, take notes, and so on. Wicker (1979) defines a behavior setting as "a bounded, self-regulated and ordered system composed of replaceable human and nonhuman components that interact in a synchronized fashion to carry out an ordered sequence of events called the setting program" (p. 12).

Behavior settings are determined by intensive observations of environments. One finds that certain acts happen very frequently or infrequently in certain settings.

Some Other Terms: Attitudes and Beliefs

It should be noted that the framework just presented and the terms that were just defined did not include the term *attitude*. Since the title of the paper does include this term, it is necessary to comment. *Attitude* is a layman's term, and it is not necessary for a rigorous discussion of the links between predispositions to action and behavior. Nevertheless, when communicating with the public we can use this term to include affect, the perceived consequences of an act, the value of the consequences of an act, and the behavioral intentions toward the attitude object. In short, attitude is "an idea, charged with affect, that predisposes a class of actions to a particular class of social situations" (Triandis, 1971, p. 2). It is an imprecise, all-inclusive term. But just because it is both imprecise and all-inclusive, it is useful for those discussions that need not specify more precisely whether one is talking about a behavioral intention, the affect toward the behavior, or what not.

Attitudes depend on *beliefs* (see below for definition) that the person may have, linking two categories of experience.

Beliefs: All humans categorize experience (Triandis, 1964a). Categorization can be inferred from the observation that people give the same response to discriminably different stimuli. Connections between and among categories are beliefs. When beliefs help define a category they act as *criterial attributes* for the category. For example, many systems of government (such as those in Britain, the United States, Denmark, and France) are considered by the public as identical, and are all given the label "democratic." But people have different beliefs about the attributes that such systems *must* have—the existence of at least two parties, voting by a large percentage of the public, etc. The identical label is used by the Soviets for a political system we do not classify as democratic, because they do not require the attribute "two-party system."

Other beliefs concern the antecedents and the consequences of this political system. For example, in many less developed countries people believe that it is necessary to have a revolution in order to have a democracy, and that a consequence of democoracy is instability. The total network of beliefs surrounding a category, including the criterial attributes, is the cognitive component of the attitude toward the category.

Methods for the study of beliefs consist of asking subjects to make probability judgments or true/false judgments (e.g. if you have a democracy you also have a two-party system) or agree-versus-disagree judgments (often using a Likert format) that a statement is true, or to complete sentences of the form "If you have a democracy, then you have . . .", or to select from a list of attributes the attribute that best completes such a sentence.

Under most conditions there is a connection between beliefs and affect. Fishbein (1967a) suggests that affect is the sum of the products of the strengths of beliefs about an object, multiplied by the evaluative aspect of each of these beliefs. Thus, for example, if a two-party system is seen as good, rather than bad, its evaluative component would be positive. The strength of the belief could be viewed as the probabilistic connection that a democracy implies a two-party system. The product of these two quantities can be computed for each belief about democracy. For Fishbein the sum of these products is a measure of the affect toward the concept democracy.

THE ATTITUDE-BEHAVIOR LINKS

The major focus of this paper is on attitudes and behavior. In this section I will introduce the relationships that are most directly connected with these concepts,[3] then I will present the theoretical

3. This conceptualization is the outcome of interactions between Dulany (1962) and myself (Triandis, 1964b), and Fishbein (1967b). It is a third iteration around the same idea, and is offered as an improvement on ideas previously offered by Fishbein and myself (in Triandis, 1971; Triandis, Vassiliou, Tanaka & Shanmugam, 1972; Triandis, 1977) in earlier publications.

framework in more detail. I will try in each case to examine causal chains, working backwards, that is, starting with behavior and ending with ecological, historical, or cultural variables, or particular experiences of the individual prior to the point in time when we examined the individual's attitudes.

The central relationships between attitudes and behavior are reflected in two equations. First, the *probability* of an act's occurrence (P_a) is a function of the sum of *habits* (H) plus *behavioral intentions* (I), multiplied by the organism's *physiological arousal* (P) and by *facilitating conditions* (F).

$$P_a = (w_H H + w_I I)P.F \qquad \text{Equation 1}$$

where P_a is the *probability of the act,* indexed by a number between 0 and 1; w_H and w_I are *weights;* I is a *behavioral intention,* or self-instructon to perform the act; and H is the *habit* to perform the act that reflects automatic behavior tendencies developed during the past history of the individual, such that particular stimuli elicit the act even when the individual does not instruct himself or herself to perform the act. Habit reflects both the individual's ability relative to the task, and past experience, such as rewards or punishments which followed performance of the act. The greater the individual's ability the greater the H. Many behaviors are not under intentional control but occur under habit control. These behaviors involve well-established links between the stimulus situation and complex patterns of behavior. Abelson (1976) has described *scripts,* and Langer (1978) has reviewed much evidence that most ordinary human behavior is under the control of habits. The more frequently the activity takes place, the more people rely on scripts.

Habits are here viewed as including not only patterns of acts under stimulus control, but also patterns of thought, fantasy, or emotion. Nisbett and Wilson (1977) have reviewed evidence that suggests that individuals are unable to give an accurate account of their mental processes. Apparently people cannot report accurately on the effects of particulalr stimuli on higher order, inference-based responses. Thus "mental habits" and "emotional scripts" may well operate, and behavior controlled by such habits and scripts will not be under intentional control.

P reflects the physiological state of the individual, and can be zero when the individual is asleep, and 1.00 when the individual is extremely aroused.

F reflects the objective conditions of the geographical environment which facilitate the act. When these conditions are optimal for the act's performance, $F = 1$; when they are most unfavorable for the performance of the act, $F = 0$. An example of external factors that moderate the intention-behavior link can be found in a study by Davidson and Jaccard (in press). Women provided their behavioral intention to have a child during the next two years, and two years later these investigators checked to see if they did have a child. Those who were subfecund (unable to have the child) depressed the correlation of intention and behavior. The correlation for 244 women was .53 when the subfecundity was not considered, and .62 when it was. This difference, which is statistically reliable at $p < .01$, reflects the operation of the F-component. A woman trying to have a child by *not* using contraceptives is "behaving" just as much as one who actually has a child, and when this is taken into account the correlation of intention and behavior increases.

Thus we have both internal (H, I, and P) and external (F) factors determining the probability of the act. Furthermore, we have factors under the individual's control (I) or not under such control (H, P, F). Acts are often interconnected, as when a goal or plan is activated. Also, information can be used to connect the acts, as happens, for instance, when a person is told how to go from one place to another. Assuming that the person has the intention to go, already established habits are activated to cause the required series of acts. The weights of Equation 1 vary from individual to individual and also depend on the kind of act and the kind of situation in which the act takes place.

In general, when an act is new to a given individual, $w_I = 1$ and $w_H = 0$. As acts occur more and more frequently, there is a shift toward a $w_I = 0$ and $w_H = 1$. Behaviors that are totally automatic, such as walking are generally under the control of H. Many social behaviors, such as the distance maintained between two bodies, touching, looking in the eye, body relational posture, level of voice, and similar paralinguistic behaviors, are mostly under the control of H. Particular acts may be under H-control while others are under I-control. For example, driving for a new driver is under I-control and for an experienced driver mostly under H-control. In a well-integrated personality H and I are consistent, as is the case for nonsmokers who do not intend to smoke, or smokers who intend to continue smoking. But this does not preclude the inconsistent cases, such as the habitual smoker who intends not to smoke.

The second equation states that *behavioral intentions* (*I*) are a function of *social factors* (*S*), the *affect* (*A*) toward the behavior, and the *value of the perceived consequences* (*C*) of the behavior.

$$I = w_S S + w_A A + w_C C \qquad \text{Equation 2}$$

The *W*s are the weights, as discussed above. *S* = the individual's self-instruction to do what is viewed as correct from the point of view of the individual's moral code, and to do what has been agreed to in previous interactions with others. (These weighted self-instructions add algebraically.) *A* = the *affect* attached to the behavior, and *C* = the value of *n* perceived consequences of the behavior, which can be measured by

$$\sum_{i=1}^{n} (P_{c_i} \cdot V_{c_i})$$

where P_{c_i} = the perceived probability that the act will have the consequence i, and

V_{c_i} = the value of the consequence i.

The *social factor* (*S*) reflects the individual's internalization of the subjective culture of the group of people with whom the individual interacts most frequently or which she or he uses as a reference group. Thus the norms, roles, and values of the culture (objectively outside of the individual) have direct connections with the *perceptions* of the norms, roles, and values that the individual uses to judge the appropriateness of social behavior. The individual considers the appropriateness of behavior for himself or herself (the morality factor) and also agreements that may have been made with others concerning how the individual should or will behave.

The *affect* toward the behavior reflects the direct emotional response to the thought of the behavior—is it enjoyable and delightful, or disgusting and unpleasant? Such connections are probably established via classical conditioning, though it may well be that human genetic structure makes some behaviors more enjoyable than others.

The *value of the perceived consequences* of an act reflects the expectations of reinforcement as well as the values of the perceived consequences. It is the usual subjective utility factor that has received considerable support in the literature (see Triandis, 1977).

The affect in equation 1 is different from the affect in equation 2. In equation 1 it is the physiological arousal (*P*) and has minor cognitive aspects (if any); in equation 2 it is mostly cognitive-evaluative, and arousal is a small aspect (if any). The affect in equation 2 is perceived directly as connecting the act to emotion. There is also affect in the C-component, but here the individual has to process information about possible consequences, so that there is not the same *direct* link between act and affect as in the A-component. It is useful to think of the A-component as a "deposit" of previous experiences with the act, and the activation of the A-component as a retrieval of memories about the act from long-term storage. By contrast, the C-component requires an information search, with judgments about probable consequences and the value of these consequences. Such a search operates in short-term memory.

An example may help understand these distinctions. Imagine that a supervisor has been convinced that he must fire one of his subordinates that he likes very much as a person. The *affect* attached to the act (firing) is extremely negative, because of previous associations of the act with unpleasant events. But the *perceived consequences*, in terms of organizational efficiency, are seen as very positive. Thus the A-component is negative, the C-component is positive, and there is much "ambivalence." Now, if the weight of the C-component is higher than the weight of the A-component, the individual will fire the liked subordinate. But at the moment of action, the P (*physiological arousal*) will be very high, and we might expect some of the dominant responses (H-controlled) to occur, which may or may not produce a straight "firing."

As mentioned above, a *behavioral intention* is conceived as a self-instruction to act in a certain way. That such self-instructions will be related to the self-instructions that people give themselves concerning doing what is considered appropriate by others, what is considered appropriate in certain role relationships, what is considered appropriate for themselves, and what has been agreed between the self and others, follows by definition. Thus, at least some of the time, *I* will be a function of *S*.

Positive *affect* implies a physiological condition that the organism wants to maximize, in frequency and intensity. It follows from such a definition that positive affect will lead to self-instruction to do what elicits positive affect. Thus, at least some of the time, *I* will be a function of *A*.

The C-component is similar to subjective utility and implies that humans will instruct themselves to reach situations that have high subjective utility. Thus, at least some of the time, I will be a function of C.

In short, the $I = f(S,A,C)$ is a theorem because it follows from the definitions of terms. A "test" of the $I = f(S,A,C)$ relationship is simply a validation of the *measurements* for the four terms. The greater the multiple correlations when predicting I from S, A, and C, the more valid the measurements. Equation 2 needs testing, however, because it includes a particular function.

The similarity of the present formulation and Fishbein's (see his paper in this volume) requires that the differences between the models be made clear. The most important difference concerns the relationship of behavior to behavioral intention. Fishbein simply states that behavior is some function of behavioral intention. I specify the function and indicate the role of habit and facilitating conditions. Since for many behaviors habit is more important than intention, and often facilitating conditions have a decisive role in reducing the predictability of behavior from behavioral intentions, this part of the formulation is rather different from Fishbein's. Furthermore, equation 1 suggests some rather different avenues of behavior change, such as those of behavior modification (habit change), and changes in the environment to make facilitating conditions more favorable for the behavior. Turning to the second equation, the S-component, in Fishbein's model, has two aspects: our beliefs about what others want us to do and our beliefs about whether we want to do what others want us to do. My conceptualization simply refers to self-instructions to do what others consider appropriate behavior. Others have such conceptions because of norms, roles, or interpersonal agreements. In addition, I include moral considerations, that is, self-instructions to do that which the actor considers morally correct.

The Fishbein conception of "attitude toward the act" considers all salient beliefs that a person has about the act. I make the distinction between beliefs that link emotions to the act, occurring *at the moment of action* (the A-*component*), *and beliefs that link the act to future* conse-quences (the C-component). I think the distinction between beliefs that concern "here-and-now" and beliefs that concern the future is important, because some people live in the here and now and use little or no time perspective, while others live for the future. Further-more, some behaviors have few consequences (e.g., having a cup of coffee) and others have many (e.g., getting married). Also, Fish-bein's definition of attitude toward the act is broader than mine, since it can include *all salient* beliefs, that is, not only consequences of the act but also antecedents of the act. I doubt that antecedents of the act make much difference in self-instruction about how to act (which by definition is a cognitive event that precedes the act). For example, a man who tells us that he voted for the Republican party because his parents voted for the Republican party is not focusing on the antecedents of the vote, but on consequences, such as *"after* voting for the Republican party I will feel good, my parents *will* approve (or *would* approve if alive), or my friends *would* approve that I vote the way my parents did."* To the extent that Fishbein's conceptualization includes salient beliefs that are not having an influence on behavior, it also includes "noise," and hence it is likely to be less effective in explaining or predicting behavior.

These comments point to the fact that the two conceptualizations, even though superficially similar, are quite different. Every one of the terms is different. Many of the competitive tests of the two models, such as that of Jaccard and Davidson (1975), use identical operationalizations (i.e., the same data) to reflect the C-component, and in some cases the A-component. While using the same operationalization is more economical, it is really inappropriate. When measurements reflected the actual definitions of the constructs (such as in Hom's study, 1978) my conceptualization proved somewhat superior to Fishbein's, suggesting that the *additional* distinctions that I propose are worth making (see also Brinberg, 1979). Of course, it is too early to be sure. Much more research is needed to determine the best way to improve these models, and probably some elements of each model will prove superior to other elements and will lead to a better model in the future.

In short, I do not think the $I = f(S, A, C)$ proposition needs testing, in the *usual* sense of "testing a theoretical hypothesis," because it is bound to receive support *some* of the time, in *some* of the places, for *certain kinds* of subjects. The really interesting questions are those that test the function and specify these parameters. Also, for a well-integrated personality the three factors are likely to be consistent: people like to do what others want them to do, what is consistent with their self-concept, and what is likely to be rewarded in the future, and all of these point to doing the same type of behavior in a particular social situation.

Note also that cognitive balance (Heider, 1946, 1958) forces consistency between the affect toward the other person and the affect toward the act. Thus we expect that people will generally enjoy

emitting positive acts toward persons they like and emitting negative acts toward persons they dislike. Consistently with Fishbein's
formulation, and considerable evidence that has since accumulated
(e.g., Davidson & Jaccard, 1975), it is preferable to predict behavioral intentions from the affect toward the act than from the
affect toward the attitude object.

Values, as discussed earlier, have multiple influences on behavior. First, they are explicitly present in the "value of the consequences" term, which reflects the extent to which an individual feels
positive about particular outcomes of his or her actions. For example, "buying a nice home" might be perceived as a consequence
of "saving." Then the act of saving is connected with a positive
value. Secondly, this value is likely to be connected to the broader
and more abstract values discussed earlier, such as the value of "a
comfortable life." Thus a hierarchy of values, from specific to more
abstract, is operating. The more abstract values act as broad and
nonspecific anchors. Different outcomes are "checked" against
these abstract values and the value of each consequence depends on
how well it relates to each abstract value. Third, values can influence
the relative weights of the S, A, and C elements of equation 2. This
will be discussed below.

The affect toward a behavior can be conceived of as having at least
two determinants: (a) indirectly it is acquired by interaction with
others and reflects beliefs about the behavior that are associated
with the behavior, and (b) directly it is acquired through experience
with the behavior and reflects classical conditioning of the behavior
due to previous associations with pleasant or unpleasant events.
Thus the A-component, by definition, overlaps with the C-component. In operationalizing these components it is desirable to
avoid such overlap. This can be done by making sure that no
consequences are included in the measurement of the A-component, and that the measurement focuses on the here-and-now: Is
the act *directly* enjoyable or disgusting, pleasant or unpleasant,
exciting or depressing?

One final point deserves special emphasis. Much of the theory
presented above concerns prediction of an act. However, the two
equations should be applied not only for the particular act but also
for "doing nothing." Ideally, we need to have a list of all plausible
acts, plus "doing nothing," and compute the probabilities of an act
for each and every one of them. Theoretically, that act will take place
that has the highest probability; if "doing nothing" has the highest

probability value (P_a), the prediction is that the person will do nothing.

APPLICATION OF THE TWO EQUATIONS TO THE ATTITUDE/BEHAVIOR RELATIONSHIP

In examining the consistency of attitude and behavior we must remember that attitudes are most routinely measured by specific paper-and-pencil behaviors. So in effect the whole issue is one of relating a particular kind of behavior, such as answering a questionnaire, with another kind of behavior, such as voting. We can apply the same equations to both behaviors.

When answering a questionnaire *anonymously* the subject is probably not concerned with the S-component, and probably does not see clear consequences of the particular act. Thus the A-component is likely to be the most relevant determinant of *I*. Since most questionnaires are novel for the subject, the H-component will be zero, and since the subject can give any answer with equal ease, the F-component is 1.00 for all answers. Thus the two equations collapse so that P_a is simply a function of affect. Also, certain kinds of answers are more satisfying to the subject than other answers. Satisfaction may be derived from "telling it like it is," "expressing one's values," or "telling the truth," though one must not exclude the possibility that for certain subjects playing games with the experimenter might be more satisfying, so that the answers might reflect the opposite of what the subject thinks the experimenter wants as an answer. In the case of questionnaires where the subject is identifiable, both the S- and the C-components can be important. The subject might give an answer that is socially desirable, or try to make a good impression from which she or he might derive benefits in the future.

When responding in the "behavior test" situation, the subject is more likely to be under the influence of the H-, S-, or C-components. Since these components are often not tapped when attitudes are measured, the correspondence between the attitude measurements and the behavior can be low. However, what this tells us is that we should measure behavioral intentions directly, rather than attitudes via Thurstone or Likert scaling. Norms predict behavior better than stereotypes (Bastide & Van den Berghe, 1957), but behavioral intentions are usually the best predictors (Triandis,

1964b, 1977). Furthermore, it tells us that we should not expect any of our attitude measures to predict behavior in those situations where the H-component is the most important predictor of behavior.

However, these conclusions are pessimistic about the possibility of prediction, because in many cases there is consistency across the H and I components, which may also reflect consistency across H, S, A, and C.

When a person is in a novel situation the behavior will reflect the person's perception of the situation, and will be under the control of the S, A, or C factors. But behaviors that were rewarded become habits, and these habits are often consistent with the S, A, and C factors. When there is total consistency among the factors it obviously makes no difference which factor we measure; in such situations we will always find correspondence between our attitude measurements and behavior. It is when the factors are inconsistent that it is important to choose the correct factor to measure. Obviously, if we measure all the factors and correlate them with behavior over a large set of situations, for a given person, we can predict that person's behavior well. Or if we correlate such data across persons we can predict well for a given situation. The point is that we cannot simply pick at random one situation and one person and hope to predict.

All of this discussion so far has assumed that the various factors that predict behavior are temporally stable. This is an assumption which for short periods of time is likely to be valid, but for long periods of time is almost certain to be wrong. Alwin (1973, 1976) has provided an attitude-behavior model that explicitly takes such temporal changes into account. Such a model must be used when long periods of time are involved.

In short, when examining the attitude-behavior relationship we need to consider the extent to which the attitude measurement situation and the behavior measurement situation have common elements. As Dollard (1949) noted thirty years ago, the cues that elicit verbal responses may not be the same as the cues that elicit the behavior. For certain categories of persons, such as neurotics, this might be a particularly serious problem. For persons with poor verbal skills, when the verbal response requires skills (i.e., H is low) the correspondence between the P_a for the verbal response and the P_a for the criterion behavior may be poor because of this complication. By contrast, as Dollard points out, for those people who think carefully before they act, and verbalize their intentions clearly, the prediction may be unusually good.

The point about the similarity between the attitude measurement and the criterion measurement situations has been made by many (Crespi, 1971; Fishbein, 1973; Silverman & Cochrane, 1971). The analysis presented above also suggests why attitudes predict behavior better when beliefs, affect, and behavioral intentions are consistent (Seibold, 1975); when the situation is highly institutionalized and routinized (Crespi, 1971; Seibold, 1975); when the subjects feel certain about their attitudes (in which case the *I*- and *H*-components are likely to correspond) (Fazio & Zanna, 1978; Sample & Warland, 1973; Seibold, 1975); when similar cues are engaged by both the attitude and the criterion behaviors (Fazio, 1969; Liska, 1974; Schuman, 1972); when people feel that their intended behavior will in fact reach their goals (Rosen & Komorita, 1971); when attitudes are clearly conceptually connected to behavior (Fazio & Zanna, 1978); when attitudes can be easily expressed (Brannon et al., 1973); when people are willing to disclose their attitudes, and define the attitude measurement and the criterion behavior situations similarly (Ehrlich, 1969); when attitudes are salient (Brown, 1974); and when the measurements are not taken at very different times (Fishbein, 1973).

The analysis also suggests that there are many situations in which there will be no correspondence between attitudes and behavior (Corey, 1937). For example, we can understand now why Bray (1950) found no correspondence when attitudes toward Jews and blacks were correlated with the degree of conformity in an autokinetic effect situation. Obviously the similarity between test and criterion is very low in that case. In all probability the attitude measurement reflected the *A*-component ("expressing values about Jews and blacks"), while the behavioral criterion reflected the *S*-component ("doing the right thing in this experiment").

The above analysis also suggests, as found by Friederes, Warner, and Albrecht (1971), that when there is consistency between the attitudes of the subject and the subject's group members there will be more consistency between attitude and behavior than when there is inconsistency between the attitudes of the subject and the group members.

Finally, we must also consider the differing thresholds of the verbal and the criterion response. Obviously it is easy to talk and more difficult to act. As Campbell (1963) suggested, the thresholds of the two events may be quite different, producing apparent inconsistencies. Raden (1977) has pointed out there are many kinds of consistency between attitudes and behavior, and in part these might reflect different thresholds. The difference in the thresholds could be expressed as a difference in the level of the F-component of equation 1. The verbal response is often easy ($F = 1$) while the actual behavior is sometimes difficult ($F = $ low).

It is possible to extend this argument to analyze other problems as well. One concern of psychologists is whether it is possible to *simulate* social behavior (Palys, 1978). One can conceptually analyze simulations by examining the extent to which the simulation engages the same components (and to the same probable degree) as the situation that is being simulated. Such a conceptual analysis would help us determine if a simulation is likely to be appropriate. If our analysis suggests that the simulation engages a combination of components that is very different, in weight or level, from the components that are likely to be engaged by the behavior being simulated, we can safely conclude that the simulation would be of little value.

A similar argument can be used to discuss the value of role playing (Mixon, 1972), rather than deception, as a method of testing particular theories. Again, if the phenomenon is mostly due to role-determined behaviors, role playing is an appropriate procedure; but if affect or perceived consequences are the important determinants of the phenomenon, a role-playing study would have limited value.

A similar point was made by Langer (1978) when she pointed out that most ordinary human behavior is under the control of scripts (H-control), but most laboratory behavior is novel and requires thought, so that it is under I-control. Since much social psychology is generated in the laboratories, one wonders about the extent to which it is applicable to most ordinary social behavior.

EMPIRICAL SUPPORT FOR THE EQUATIONS

Since I have summarized the empirical evidence in support of the proposed model elsewhere (Triandis, 1977), I will do so here very briefly. I will mention below in more detail only recent studies which provide further support.

There are two kinds of studies that can be considered in relation to the model described by the two equations: direct and indirect studies. The direct studies have attempted to test the utility of the particular model; the indirect were done for a different purpose but they have used variables similar to those used in the model.

Equation 1: Direct Studies

Landis, Triandis, and Adamopoulos (1978) observed teacher behavior in classrooms during three different periods of time, and classified it into a system of interpersonal behavior categories. The frequency of the behavior at time 1 was correlated with the frequency of the behavior at times 2 and 3. These correlations provided an estimate of the importance of the H-component. Correlations of the order of .42 were obtained. In this study H was the only reliable predictor, because the teacher's intention (I) did not correlate with the frequency of the interpersonal behaviors. It should be noted that teacher behavior is routinized, and has a relatively high base rate.

In contrast, Pomazal (1974), working with the behavior "to give blood," which is neither routinized nor has a very high base rate, found that intention was more important than habit.

Adamopoulos and Brinberg (Note 1) tested the first equation with another behavior that has low base rate: volunteering for a psychological experiment. The subjects who actually appeared for the experiment (overt behavior) tended to indicate several days earlier that they intended to participate. Four levels of difficulty to participate (variations of the F-component) were used. The easiest required the students to be interviewed in their homes on any day of their choosing during a given week; the most difficult required the students to come to the Psychology Building on a specified day at a specific hour that same week. In this case I predicted behavior very well ($r = .59$), but H made no contribution to the prediction. The model further predicts that for the easy (high F) condition the prediction will be best, and it was (.81); for the least easy (low F) condition the prediction from I to behavior should be poor, and it was (.18).

Brinberg (1979), also working with the blood donation behavior, found that the behavior "went but could not get an appointment to donate blood" was predicted with a multiple correlation of .51 ($p <$ .01), and that both intentions times facilitating conditions (FI) and habits times facilitating conditions (FH) had significant regression weights of .4 and .20, respectively. In this case a significant regression weight was obtained for both intentions and habits, though the greater importance of intention than habit is consistent with the results of the other studies, where it was found that volunteering, non-routine, low base-rate behaviors are more under the control of I than H. Theoretically, this is exactly what we expect, since I have argued that as a behavior becomes routinized it comes under the influence of H, but before it is routine it will be under the influence of I.

Equation 1: Indirect Studies

A study by Schachter, Festinger, Willerman, and Hyman (1961) shows the importance of habits in one condition and intentions in another. These researchers instructed half the foremen in a plant to behave in a highly objectionable manner toward their subordinates, while the other half were allowed to continue behaving as usual. Productivity in those units where the foremen behaved objectionably dropped *only* when the workers were learning new jobs; in those cases where the workers did well-learned jobs, there were no changes in productivity. The data are understandable: when the behavior is well-learned it is under H-control, so when the foreman behaves "badly" and the worker becomes dissatisfied, the dissatisfaction which registers on the I-component has no effect, since that component does not control the productivity behavior. By contrast, in those cases where the behavior was not overlearned, and hence the I-component could control some of the variance of the behavior, there was a significant drop in production.

A similar point about the importance of the difference between overlearned (H-controlled) and new behaviors is made by Zajonc (1965) in his discussion of social facilitation effects. When others are present they have an effect, facilitating behaviors that are under H-control and inhibiting behaviors that are under I-control.

Steers and Rhodes (1978) reviewed 104 empirical studies of employee attendance and concluded that attendance is influenced by two factors: (a) attendance motivation and (b) ability to come to work. Careful examination of what is meant by these terms shows

that attendance motivation is an intention to attend; thus attend-
.ance motivation is under the influence of the S-component (pressure to attend, work group norms, personal work ethic, organizational commitment), the A-component (satisfaction with the job
situation), and the C-component (employee values and job expectations, opportunities for advancement). Ability to come to work
includes such factors as illness or accident and transportation problems (F-component).

The literature showing that intention is the best single predictor of
novel behavior is voluminous and cannot be reviewed here. It
ranges from studies in experimental settings (Ryan, 1970) to studies
in organizational settings. An example of the latter is a study by
Mobley, Horner, and Hollingsworth (1978) which investigated
several measures that might be predictors of quitting among hospital employees. The intention to quit did predict quitting, while other
measures, such as job satisfaction, thoughts about quitting, and
biographical information did not. Langer, Blank, and Chanowitz
(1978) present data consistent with this viewpoint.

Equation 2: Direct Studies

Davidson, Jaccard, Triandis, Morales, and Diaz-Guerrero (1976)
examined the fertility-relevant behaviors of women in Illinois and
Mexico City. A number of samples of women from both upper
middle-class and lower-class backgrounds were studied. Multiple
correlations testing the second equation, corrected for shrinkage,
exceeded .6 and often reached .8.

Hom (1978) predicted both the intention to reenlist in the Illinois
National Guard, and the actual reenlistment behavior, from the
model. The intention was predicted with a multiple correlation of
.78 (based on 852 subjects). The actual behavior was predicted with
a multiple correlation of .71. Examining several other models of
behavioral prediction and the extent to which the models correctly
classified those who reenlisted and those who decided not to reenlist, Hom found Equation 2 the most satisfactory, with an actual
error rate of classification of only 15%.

Brinberg (1979) also found considerable support for Equation 2.
Using factor analysis he was able to show that there is an empirical
as well as a conceptual distinction between the A- and the C-
components. Since he obtained data at different points in time he

was also able to assess whether the model could measure "intention change"; in that respect also the data supported the model.

Seibold and Roper (1979) examined the second equation as a predictor of intentions of behaviors relevant to the detection of cervical cancer (visit clinic this year, have a Pap test in the future, have a Pap test in 12 months). Samples included both college students (N = 38) and community women (N = 55), and both minority (N = 23) and nonminority (N = 32) women. The second equation yielded multiple correlations of the order of .7 to .9 for visiting the clinic and having a Pap test in the future, and .6 to .9 for having a Pap test within 12 months. Significant predictors were the S- and A-components. Minority women tended to give more weight to the A- than the S-components; the nonminority women gave weight only to the S-component.

Second Equation: Indirect Studies

Triandis (1977) reviews several studies that show the importance of the elements of the S-component (e.g., the importance of norms, roles, the self-concept [Ziller, 1973], personal norms [e.g., Schwartz, 1977], and other factors), A-component (e.g., Dillehay, Bruvold, & Siegel, 1967), and the C-component (e.g., Mitchell & Biglan, 1971).

It may be useful now to examine what causal chains there are that link the elements of the two equations to other variables, and thus to a broad theoretical framework.

VARIABLES THAT DETERMINE THE WEIGHTS OF THE TWO EQUATIONS

In the discussion that follows the term *weight* will be used repeatedly. A natural reaction of the reader is to think of regression weights. But regression weights have methodological limitations. Specifically, in situations where the predictor variables are intercorrelated, as is most likely to be the case in Equations 1 and 2, these weights tend to be unstable and impossible to interpret. Thus, in what follows, it is wise to think of *weight* as a theoretical construct and not as a statistical one. The factors mentioned in the following pages of this paper do influence the weights that different people will give to the independent variables of the two equations, or the weights that these variables will have for particular behaviors or in specific situations; this should lead to *theoretical* predictions of the results. Empirical investigations will most likely use regression analyses, but when this is done cross-validation is essential, and testing in different situations, for different behaviors, and for different kinds of subjects is needed, to find *consistencies* in the otherwise unstable regression weights. In short, only extensive, parametric studies can result in a meaningful pattern of findings concerning the weights mentioned here.

First, consider one more way in which values can influence the attitude-behavior link: by influencing the weights of the two equations.

> *Theorem 1.* Subjects with values that stress morality, conformity to the views of others, and "doing the proper thing" (being self-controlled, popular, dutiful, loyal, and having a life of social participation) will give more weight to the S-component than will other kinds of subjects.
>
> *Theorem 2.* Subjects with values that stress hedonism ("doing one's own thing," being pleasure-loving, comfort-seeking, independent, cultivating independence from others) will give more weight to the A-component than will other kinds of subjects.
>
> *Theorem 3.* Subjects with values that stress future outcomes (being successful, wealthy, famous, having a life characterized by achievement) will give more weight to the C-component than will other kinds of subjects.

The distinction among persons who emphasize the S-, A- and C-components seems reasonable because of two lines of research. Feather and Peay (1975) performed factor analyses of the values of the Rokeach (1973) instrument. Factor 1 was a contrast between individuals who approve of S-relevant values (being obedient and responsible, having family security, and self-control) versus A-relevant values (leading an exciting life, experiencing mature love, being broadminded and imaginative). Factor 4 contrasted the Rokeach "personal" (A- and C-components) with the "social" (S-component) values. The emphasis was on *social recognition, true friendship, mature love,* and *happiness* versus *world at peace, national* security, and equality. Factor 5 contrasted immediate gratification (A-component) with delayed gratification (C-component), with emphasis on clean, comfortable life, cheerful, pleasure-seeking, courageous, self-respect, and self-control. Factor analyses of terminal values in the Rokeach instrument gave similar patterns, such as altruistic (S) versus hedonistic (A), personal versus social, and self-expression versus safety.

Another line of research is that by England (Note 2), who found businessmen in several countries emphasizing doing what is appropriate, what is fun, and what will produce good results in the future (S-, A-, and C-components).

Some personality variables suggest themselves as relevant: It seems plausible that intelligent individuals will emphasize intentions and will be sufficiently analytical to frequently self-instruct themselves to act in particular ways. Hence the hypothesis:

Hypothesis 1. The greater the individual's intelligence, the greater the weight of the I-component of the first equation.

It is also plausible that neurotics will have less control over their own behavior, so that the H-component will have more weight in their case. Hence the hypothesis:

Hypothesis 2. The greater the degree of neuroticism of the individual, the greater the weight of the H-component.

Individuals who are not dominant, and tend to be submissive, are more likely to instruct themselves to pay attention to social pressures, hence:

Hypothesis 3. The more submissive the individual, the greater the weight of the S-component.

Hypothesis 4. The more authoritarian the subject (as measured by the F-scale), the greater the weight of the S-component (see Kirscht and Dillehay, 1967, for relevant studies).

Hypothesis 5. The more acquiescent the subject (as measured by Couch and Keniston, 1960), the greater the weight of the S-component.

Hypothesis 6. The lower the cognitive complexity of the subject, the higher the weight of the A-component and the lower the weight of the C-component.

It is generally argued in the literature that low complexity subjects are high in acquiescence (Goldstein & Blackman, 1976), have short time perspectives, and are more likely to act impulsively and to seek immediate gratification of their needs. The last hypothesis reflects these arguments.

There is already some evidence (reviewed in Triandis, 1977) indicating that the weights of the two equations vary depending on the type of behavior, type of social situation, and type of person. Gabrenya and Arkin (1979) suggest that when volunteering to perform interracial behaviors, committed individuals place more weight on attitudinal considerations while uncommitted individuals place more weight on personal norm considerations. Snyder (1976) reviews evidence which suggests that individuals high on his self-monitoring scale will pay more attention to the S-component than those low on his scale. Furthermore, he argues that people are rather good at identifying whether they are controlled mostly by the S-component or by another factor. Wicklund (1979) presents similar evidence concerning "self-aware" individuals.

Hypothesis 7. The more formal the behavior, the greater the weight of the S-component.
Hypothesis 8. The clearer the norms concerning a behavior, the greater the weight of the S-component.
Hypothesis 9. The more lasting the consequences of a behavior, the greater the weight of the S-component.

This is so because cultures develop clear norms for behaviors that have consequences. Consider the behavior "to get married" as opposed to the behavior "to have a cup of coffee with." It is clear that the first is more formal, has clearer norms concerning it, and has lasting effects on the individual, while the latter is informal, the norms concerning it are practically nonexistent, and the effects are of short duration. Societies tend to develop clearer norms not only about behaviors that are important in those societies but also for behaviors that have more lasting consequences than for behaviors that do not have such consequences. It is fair to say also that for informal behaviors, where the norms are unclear and the consequences short-lived, the affect toward the behavior is a much more important factor. Thus I think that Rokeach has been correct in arguing that belief similarity is the most important determinant of *friendship* judgments. What most American subjects mean by "friendship" is closer to what most people in Europe and other continents mean by "acquaintance." It is the kind of social relationship found in parties, athletic games, or Saturday-night outings. It has very definite affective components, and people are concerned with maximizing the affect in such situations.

Belief similarity leads to positive affect, and this is reflected in what the subjects tell us. When it comes to other behaviors, however, such as accepting someone into the neighborhood or into one's family (particularly if marriage is involved), social norms play a much larger role. In those segments of American society where norms of racial discrimination still prevail, one is likely to find that race is a larger factor in determining those social behaviors than belief similarity. The results that have been obtained by Triandis and Davis (1965), Dienstbier (1972), and Goldstein and Davis (1972) are consistent with this interpretation. What we call "intimate" behaviors tend to be behaviors that have clear social norms and have important consequences that do last for some time. One often engages in such behaviors after some sort of a formal ceremony (introduction, marriage, invitation). There are definite norms about race relations concerning intimate behaviors, and few norms about casual behaviors. Where norms are clear, there is social pressure, and sanctions are exercised against those who disregard the norms.

Corollary of Hypothesis 8. The more constraining the social situation, the greater the weight of the S-component.

This reflects Adamopoulos's (1976) observation that social situations differ: Some allow only some behaviors to occur (e.g., in church there are few behaviors that are appropriate), and some allow a broad set of behaviors to take place (e.g., a party). Norms tend to be clear and to be supported by sanctions in the case of constraining social situations, and tend to be unclear in nonconstraining situations.

Hypothesis 10. The more private the social situation (rather than public), the greater the weight of the A-component.

Hypothesis 11. The more highly arousing the emotion associated with a behavior, the greater the weight of the A-component.

Hypothesis 12. The more constraining the social situation, the lower the weight of the A-component for behaviors occurring in that situation.

The latter three hypotheses reflect a conceptual analysis of the A-component. Obviously, the stronger the emotions attached to a behavior (as in a traumatic experience or in peak experiences), the more influence will these experiences have on future behavior, and that will result in larger weights for the A-component. It is also obvious that private and nonconstraining situations that provide the individual with more freedom allow for greater enjoyment of the behaviors within them. Public constraining situations often force the individual to act in a highly distasteful manner, as in the "Ridi Pagliccio" aria from the opera *Pagliacci*.

Hypothesis 13. The sum of the probabilities of consequences for a given behavior (ΣP_c) will be correlated, across behaviors, with the weights given to the C-component.

Some environments provide clear relationships between behavior and consequences (e.g., if you mail a letter it arrives at its destination) while others do not (e.g., if you mail a letter it rarely arrives at its destination). When the connections between behavior and consequences are weak, the behavior becomes extinguished, and the C-component is also weak. The observations reported by Triandis, Feldman, Weldon, and Harvey (1975) and Triandis (1976), that lower-class unemployed blacks are characterized by "eco-system distrust," reflect this generalization. This perspective includes the notion that nothing that one does has known and dependable outcomes, as well as less trust in people, suspicion of the motives of others, rejection of authority figures, a sense of powerlessness, and a sense that one must be very careful or one will get into trouble. It is reasonable to assume that this point of view develops when there are few clear consequences for behavior, and the few consequences that have been experienced were negative. In the case where there are few consequences the environment appears to be chaotic, and almost anything is likely to happen. Since the particular urban black unemployed samples are not likely to use the norms and roles of white society, and those norms are not particularly clear, much of the behavior of persons with ecosystem distrust is under A-control (drugs, and other forms of getting a kick).

Hypothesis 14. The more consistent the perceived consequences of an act and the goals and values of the individual, the greater the weight of the C-component concerning this act.

This hypothesis is a formal statement of some of the points made earlier about the relevance of the person's values for social behavior.

Hypothesis 15. The more a social situation allows a relaxed and carefree examination of the consequences of action, the greater the weight of the *C*-component of the acts occurring in that situation

The assumption is made here that people who have the time to think of the consequences of an act are more likely to give a large weight to the *C*-component.

When sufficient time is available, and the decision is important, individuals will engage in a search for the best path toward their goals. Goals reflect values and situational factors. For example, a person who has a high value for "a comfortable life" is likely to consider most important the income received from a job, and will develop job goals where the income will allow the realization of this value. Reaching the particular job goals may be possible through a variety of paths. For example, a person may try to obtain intermediate jobs that provide experience, or obtain a university degree, or join the navy. If the connections between each of these intermediate goals and the final consequences are well understood the person may engage in a search for the best path to the final goal. In addition, if the available information is perceived by the individual to be inadequate, the search may include various information-seeking behaviors, such as reading about the job, interviewing experts, and trying out the job for a limited period of time.

This discussion points to the function of values as *general guides* to action. Just like the chess player who has a general goal (to win), which can be reached by some combination of moves, with the intermediate moves unavailable in the player's cognitive map (except for moves that are very close to the final game), so goals that are consistent with values guide search behavior in a very generalized way.

In analyzing the emergence of goals it must be realized that those goals that are reached only rarely or always are less likely to be part of the *C*-component than those goals that have an intermediate probability of being realized. The sure goal is trivial; the impossible goal is not economical to pursue. As McClelland (1961) has argued, there are individual differences in the tendency to pursue goals of intermediate difficulty, with individuals high in need for achievement being more likely to have such goals than individuals low in need for achievement. Many of the latter choose inappropriate goals (too easy or too difficult) because of fear of failure. Obviously if one selects an easy goal the chances of reaching it are high and hence the chances of failure are low; if one chooses an extremely difficult goal one will not be blamed for failure, since the difficulty of the goal is a much more obvious cause of the failure than the actor's abilities. With goals of intermediate difficulty, however, failure can easily be attributed to inabilities or inadequacies of the actor.

In short, we assume that "search behavior" is guided by values, and involves goals of more or less intermediate difficulty to reach (depending on the individual's need for achievement, as specified by McClelland). Once an individual settles on a few (two or three) "next moves," the influence of the social, affective, and consequence factors discussed above will provide a particular level of strength of intention. For deliberate, unhurried action, that behavior which has the greatest strength of intention is most likely to take place. As already stated, one of the options in such calculations is always the option "to do nothing." Thus, in predicting behavior we need to obtain not only the values of the intentions for particular actions, but also the values for "doing nothing."

THE BEHAVIOR-CONSEQUENCES-REINFORCEMENT SEQUENCE

Behavior has many actual consequences, only some of which are perceived by the individual. A distinction is made here between the *perceived* consequences (P_C) that are anticipated by the individual and the *actual* consequences that occur after the behavior has taken place. The actual consequences are "interpreted"—that is, they are given a desirable or undesirable meaning, depending on how the individual perceives the total situation.

Individuals who consider several values important will be more flexible in interpreting the consequences of an act than those who consider only a few values important. For example, a thirsty individual alone in a desert, digging for water and finding a treasure, will not be reinforced by the discovery as much as one who finds water, or one who can use the treasure to get water. Thus, values interact with the situation to lead to particular interpretations of the consequences of one' actions.

The behavior-consequence-reinforcement sequence is likely to result in revisions of both P_c and V_c. If a particular consequence is not expected, when it does occur the individual is likely to see a higher probability of connection between behavior and consequence; the converse is true for consequences that were expected and did not materialize. Also, the value of a consequence is often different before it is experienced than after it is experienced. In any case, the behavior-consequence-reinforcement sequence does feed back into the person-system.

Einhorn and Hogarth (1978) have presented a model of the judgment-action process which explicitly includes feedback. Judgments of prediction (i.e., P_c) lead to action (i.e., P_a), which results in outcomes. These outcomes feed back directly on to the judgments and to the actions. In addition, the outcomes are coded (i.e., interpreted) and evaluated as coded, and these evaluations in turn also change the value of P_c and P_a. The authors examine the reasons that people show such low levels of ability in making a wide range of different judgments while at the same time they think that they are very good at making such judgments. They offer the above-mentioned model as a means of organizing the relationships between learning and experience.

All of the discussion, so far, has been concerned with the probability of an act occurring once. It is useful, however, to also consider the frequency, intensity, and duration of an act. Frequency must be highly related to probability, though frequency will reflect ecological conditions to a larger extent (e.g., did the act get reinforced?). However, the analysis for probability and frequency is parallel and need not be discussed further. Intensity and duration are probably completely unrelated to frequency and probability of occurrence of an act.

INTENSITY AND DURATION OF ACTS

Obviously for some acts there are no important variations in intensity or duration. They either occur or they do not occur. Some acts occur at a level of intensity which simply reflects individual or cultural differences—for example, handshaking.

Both intensity and duration reflect, in part, the organism's general arousal level. In addition, the degree of superordination of the actor may be reflected in high intensity and duration of superordinate acts (e.g., to criticize extremely and at length). Subordinates, by contrast, act at low levels of intensity with acts of short duration.

Perhaps the most important factor is the actor's perception of whether the act is pleasant or unpleasant for the recipient. For pleasant acts, the intensity and duration tend to increase when the actor likes the target. For unpleasant acts they tend to increase when the actor dislikes the target or feels that the target needs to change behavior. But complications do occur. Farina, Chapnick, Chapnick, & Misiti (1972) found that radicals shocked conservatives with intensive bursts of short duration, while conservatives shocked radicals with intensive bursts of long duration. The interpretation of these data is difficult. Several possibilities come to mind: Radicals are monitoring themselves more than conservatives, and knowing that they are hurting with an intensive shock they make it short. Or radicals are more cognitively complex, and though they dislike conservatives, do not want to wipe them out. Or, radicals are "soft" and empathize more. Or, conservatives feel a "justified indignation" with radicals, because radicalism is seen as inconsistent with the American ethos, so they give them "all they got," while radicals realize that conservatives represent the American ethos and hold back, or show ambivalence about shocking them. Or, conservatives know mostly conservatives, and radicals seem "way out," while radicals know many conservatives and feel more ambivalent about shocking them. Obviously, these points suggest that more research is needed.

These arguments can be summarized in the following hypotheses: When there is no ambivalence about the target of action, actors are more likely to emit acts of greater intensity and duration

Hypothesis 17: when they are more aroused, with an inverted U relationship at very high levels of arousal;

Hypothesis 18: when the act is consistent with norms, roles, and values;

Hypothesis 19: when the affect toward the act is consistent with the affect toward the target; and

Hypothesis 20: when the perceived consequences of the act are uncertain and/or small.

The latter hypothesis reflects the idea that if the consequences are large and certain it would not be economical for the person to expend the additional energy required for a high intensity act of long duration.

FURTHER LINKS: THE CULTURE AND PERSONALITY DETERMINANTS OF ATTITUDES

In discussions of this and subsequent hypotheses, we use the term *culture*, keeping in mind that it often is an imprecise term (see above, p. 206). We postulate that two aspects of the personality of subjects will be particularly relevant to the way the weights of the two equations are going to be used: time perspective and cognitive complexity.

> *Theorem 4.* The greater the time perspective, the lower the weight given to the *A*-component.
>
> *Theorem 5.* The greater the time perspective, the greater the weight given to the *C*-component.

Time perspective is defined here as concern for the events that are to occur in the future, so that the above statements are theorems. Methods for the measurement of the construct include the use of a Thematic Apperception Test (TAT) and the scoring of the responses according to when they occur in time (e.g., now, next year, in ten years).

Time perspective probably reflects (a) education and (b) cultural complexity:

> *Hypothesis 21*: The greater the subject's level of education, the greater the time perspective.
>
> *Hypothesis 22*: The greater a culture's complexity, the greater the time perspective of individuals in that culture.

So far we have examined the links between behavior and some of the terms that are inside the "personality" box of Figure 1. The focus has been primarily on attitudinal variables linking to behavior. Personality variables were seldom considered, but some hypotheses can be proposed that include such variables. In this section we will examine some personality variables linking to the weights of the components of our two equations, and then ask what aspects of the culture, ecology, and history of the individual are likely to result in such personalities. Thus we will move from the center to the periphery of Figure 1.

Research by Inkeles and Smith (1974) shows that economic development and the average level of education of the people in a culture are related to the modernity of the population. Modernity is itself related to a long time perspective, including a positive evaluation of planning behavior.

Schmidt, Lamm, and Trommsdorff (1978) found that the future orientation (time perspective) of German subjects was patterned: men tended to have a longer time perspective in the occcupational and economic sphere, women in the private (family life) sphere. Middle-class subjects had longer time perspectives than lower-class subjects. This study is consistent with the Inkeles and Smith notion that modernity is related to education. It is theoretically consistent with our theory that in those areas where a person has greater concerns (occupation for men, family for women) the time perspective is longer, because to be concerned means to have thought more about a topic. The more one thinks about a topic the more likely it is that one will think not only of the present, but also of the future.

There are numerous hypotheses that follow logically from variations of characteristics of cultures linked to the likelihood of specific behavior in those cultures. Some examples of such hypotheses follow.

> *Hypothesis 23.* The more abundant the resources of a culture, the more associative the behaviors of members of this culture.

Resources are defined, as in Foa and Foa (1974), to include money, goods, services, status, love, and information. Associative behaviors are behaviors that are helpful, supportive, cooperative, and affectively positive. Dissociative behaviors are those that take away resources such as status (insulting), love (hating), information (lying to), money (stealing), or services (denying help). Obviously this hypothesis can be tested only when many other factors, such as the actor's social status and access to resources, are controlled. For example, if a culture has abundant resources but a particular person or group does not have access to these resources, we would not expect this particular person or group to act associatively. On the contrary, because of the operation of social comparisons, we might expect such a person or group to act dissociatively.

Hypothesis 24. The more unequal the distribution of resources in a culture, the more controlling the behavior of those who have more resources.

Controlling behavior includes directing, checking on, criticizing, and rewarding others, as opposed to depending on others to obtain resources.

Hypothesis 25. The higher the level of education in a culture, the more positive the evaluation of planning behavior.

Planning behavior, however, also reflects the success of members of a culture with such behavior. Thus,

Hypothesis 26. The more frequent the disruptions due to revolutions, wars, and other catastrophic events in the history of the culture, the more negative the evaluation of planning behavior.

Data presented and discussed by Triandis and Vassiliou (1972) support this hypothesis.

There is evidence that cognitive complexity is related to low levels of authoritarianism and acquiescence, which are in turn related to high levels of individual conformity. Authoritarianism and acquiescence have been linked to the weights of Equation 2, and cognitive complexity was linked to these weights in previously stated hypotheses.

High cognitive complexity is plausibly related to high cultural complexity. Hence,

Hypothesis 27. The higher the levels of cultural complexity, the higher the levels of cognitive complexity of members of that culture.

The study by Gruenfeld and MacEachron (1975) found that managers and technicians from countries that were more economically developed (or, roughly, more complex culturally) are more likely to be cognitively complex, as measured by the rod-and-frame test. Thus some support for this hypothesis exists already.

However, cultural complexity is probably related to "controlling childrearing" patterns, up to an optimal point. Thus,

Hypothesis 28: An inverted U relationship exists between cultural complexity and controlling childrearing patterns. As cultural complexity increases there are greater needs for control, but at a particular level of complexity no more control is possible or desirable, so that at very high levels of complexity there is again less control in childrearing.

It is plausible that high control in childrearing leads to low cognitive complexity, since children have fewer opportunities to explore the environment. The connection between cultural complexity and cognitive complexity, therefore, will not be strong, since at high levels of cultural complexity it may be reversed.

Certain ecologies make large demands for cooperation among members of the cultures living in them because survival requires cooperative activities. In those ecologies where the demands for cooperation are large we expect more cultural complexity and more controlling childrearing patterns. When the requirements for cooperation are low, childrearing will be more autonomous, and conformity will be less valued. Finally, high population density is related to cultural complexity (Berry, 1976, Table 4.2), presumably because it requires more organization to survive in a densely populated environment. When the requirements for cooperation are high, the culture is also more likely to be tight, and conformity is more likely to be valued. When resources per capita are abundant, there will be greater probabilities that individuals will reach positive outcomes as a result of their behaviors. In such ecologies we expect larger values of P_c.

TYPOLOGY OF SOCIAL BEHAVIOR

I have reviewed elsewhere (Triandis, 1977) evidence suggesting that the basic, universal dimensions of social behavior are four: *association* (to help, to support) versus *dissociation* (to avoid, to attack), *superordination* (to criticize, to command) versus *subordination* (to obey, to conform), *intimacy* (to kiss, to cuddle) versus *formality* (to send an invitation to), and *overt* (to hit) versus *covert* (to hate). Every interpersonal behavior can be conceived as having coordinates on a four-dimensional space defined by these four dimensions. For example, the behavior to "ask for the advice of" may be represented on -3 to $+3$ scales of these four dimensions as a $+2$, -3, $+2$, $+2$; the behavior "to plan to kill" may have the profile -3, $+3$, $+3$, -3.

Ecologies have differential effect on the prevalence of social behaviors. This can be seen in the kinds of childrearing patterns adopted by most socializers in those ecologies and the prevailing personalities that are likely to be found in them. These personality profiles constitute the major inputs to the Habit Component of Equation 1.

The following analysis of the relationships between ecology and personality has to be speculative, because there is as yet too little evidence in this area, which requires large-scale culture and personality research. I simply submit that some of the relationships that I propose are reasonable.

When an ecology/culture is in a privileged position where these resources are abundant, there will be more associative behaviors (see hypothesis 23) not only among adults, but also in childrearing. Cultures with abundant resources are similar to those that Arsenian and Arsenian (1948) have called easy.

Hypothesis 29. The more abundant the resources (the easier the cultures), the more individuals will perceive high probabilities that their behaviors will be followed by positive reinforcements (high P_c for positive consequences).

The opposite case is where behaviors (objectively) are most likely to lead to negative reinforcements. In such cases people will see low probabilities that their behavior will be followed by reinforcements, and in fact they may not even see any pattern in the reinforcements because of differential remembering and forgetting of positive and negative events. Triandis, Feldman, Weldon, & Harvey (1975) and Triandis (1976) found among unemployed blacks such a tendency (see above, p. 235, for details).

An aspect of this broad tendency will be greater external locus of control, as defined by Rotter (1966), in the case of those with limited resources. There is considerable evidence supporting the notion that economic deprivation is associated with external rather than internal locus of control. Cross-cultural differences (e.g., Reimanis, 1977) are in the same direction.

Hypothesis 30. The more abundant the resources (easy culture) the more likely it is that childrearing patterns will be "warm" (that the child will be loved, helped, supported).

The most extreme negative case is that described by Turnbull (1972), in his study of the Ik. Here resource scarcity was extreme. Many parents abandoned their three-year-old children to fend for themselves. There was no love but only the cold reality of survival. When one child was more malnourished than another, parents were likely to snatch the food from the more malnourished child's mouth so that it could be eaten by themselves or the stronger children. "Family ceased to exist" (p. 28). There was no empathy: "Anyone falling down was good for a laugh too, particularly if he was old or weak . . ." (p. 113). When someone died they took away the clothes and shoved the body into a hole. When a child was sick the parents would lock the house and leave and return after it was dead, and then would bury it without ceremony. The burying was done so that the neighbors would not object to vultures coming around and littering the yard, otherwise they would not have bothered to do it.

In other words, where resources per person are abundant, or where limited resources are distributed within a narrow ingroup so that they are in fact abundant per capita, there is warm childrearing. Where they are scarce, childrearing is cold. "Warm" here is used as in Rohner (1975), whose evidence is quite strong that:

> *Proposition 1*: Warm parental relationships result in personalities with little dependence, high self-evaluation, emotional responsiveness, a positive world view, emotional stability (low anxiety), generosity, and nurturance. Cold parental relationships result in personalities where there is hostility, particularly toward peers, dependence, low self-evaluation, little emotional responsiveness, a negative world view, emotional instability (high anxiety), and little generosity or nurturance (Rohner, in press).

In short, it is argued that warm childrearing, which may reflect an aspect of the ecology/culture, leads to warm personalities. Personality is here conceptualized as including a predisposition to behavior (habits) as well as beliefs, expectations of reinforcement, a self-image, affect toward the behaviors, and subjective norms and values as well as particular habits of perception of social situations. When the personality is "integrated," these entities tend to be consistent and to reinforce each other.

It is argued, then, that associative childrearing patterns lead to associative personalities, characterized by both habits and intentions to behave associatively. Behaviors such as little dependence on others, concern for others, emotional responsiveness to others, low anxiety, high generosity, and nurturance are more likely to take place in ecologies that foster such personalities. In parallel to the behavior patterns just mentioned there will be beliefs, and a subjective culture which views the world optimistically will react to others with trust, and with the assumption that they should be helped, as well as with a positive image of the self and others, and a tendency to perceive reality with multiple perspectives. By contrast, dissociative childrearing (child abandoned, rejected) leads to dissociative personalities, characterized by distrust, a negative view of the self and others, and a distorted and restricted or defensive perception of reality.

We have already discussed the requirements for cooperation which characterize certain ecologies, making the imposition of norms and the use of sanctions for norm deviations more likely. It is obvious, for example, that certain kinds of ecologies lend themselves to solitary hunting and fishing while others lend themselves to agriculture. Survival in the former kinds of ecologies often depends on the success of particular individual hunters or fishers. The Eskimo provide a good example of this ecology/cultural situation. In those environments where group action is needed for survival, either in fishing (to poison a river), or in agriculture (to create irrigation systems), we find a much greater emphasis on normative behavior (S-component). There is evidence that ecology influences psychological differentiation and conformity (Berry, 1966, 1967, 1977). In general, cultures where solitary activities are consistent with survival tend to (a) allow children to be autonomous and independent, and (b) want their adults to be self-reliant. By contrast, cultures where group action is needed for survival tend to socialize their children severely, and the level of conformity (in modified Asch-type situations, 1956) tends to be high. Tight cultures (Pelto, 1968) also tend to emphasize conformity.

Childrearing analysts often examine parental behaviors along the two dimensions that have just been described: parents or socializers are seen as *warm* versus *cold* and as *giving autonomy* versus *controlling* the child. These two dimensions of childrearing correspond to the first two of the four dimensions of social behavior just outlined. Furthermore, they correspond to two dimensions of personality discussed by Leary (1957) and many others: Love versus hate and dominance versus submission.

Another important variable is the type of family structure—nuclear versus extended. There is a tendency for very simple cultures to have simple family structures and for cultures intermediate in complexity to employ extended families, while modern industrial, highly complex cultures tend to return to the nuclear family (Blumberg & Winch, 1972). One consequence of extended families is that children are reared by other children (e.g., their older siblings and cousins) to a much larger extent than in nuclear families. Whiting and Whiting (1975) reported that both the nuclear-extended family distinction and cultural complexity are important in understanding the typical behavior patterns of children in their six-cultures project. Children in simple cultures had mothers who were more busy than the mothers of children in complex cultures. When the mothers are busy they assign more child-rearing chores to older children. Thus in simple cultures also there is a tendency for children to be socialized by other children. Children who engage in many childrearing activities tend to be more affectionate and to be more helpful than children who do not. In nuclear families interaction tends to be more intimate than in nonnuclear families. The Whitings provided a 2 × 2 table in which cultural complexity and nuclear versus nonnuclear family structure were the facets, and showed different patterns of behavior in each of these four cells.

It seems plausible that the patterns of childrearing (warm versus cold; autonomous versus controlling) will be related to the major patterns of variation of culture. While the following hypotheses are really guesses, they are worth stating so they will be tested explicitly in the future. It is interesting to ask how these patterns of childrearing are likely to relate to the dimensions of culture that were presented earlier.

> *Hypothesis 31.* The more complex the culture, the more likely are parents to use controlling childrearing patterns, up to an optimal point, after which the less likely they are to use such patterns.

In short, we hypothesize a curvilinear pattern, where the very simple (food-gathering, hunting) cultures use autonomy, the more complex (wet-rice agricultural and lower-class industrial) cultures use control, and the very complex or upper-class (industrial) use autonomy. The logic behind this hypothesis is that when the culture is very simple parents do not need to be concerned about the socialization of the child into the authority system and hence can afford to let the child "do its own thing." In such cultures the adults that emerge from this lenient socialization pattern are well adapted to the ecology. But in more complex cultures children have to learn to do what the boss, chief, or supervisor dictates. Experiencing control early in life makes conformity to authority easier at a later point in life. When an environment is extremely complex, however, as it is for professionals in industrial cultures, there is little advantage derived from conformity to authorities. After a certain point, the valued qualities become creativity and independence, and then the childrearing patterns emphasize autonomy.

Some evidence in support of these arguments is already available. Berry (1967) obtained the expected cultural contrast and Kohn (1969) found that lower-class parents in both Italy and the United States emphasize conformity, while upper-class parents emphasize independence and creativity.

The combination of complexity and abundance of resources leads to a 3 × 3 classification of cultures. The facets of this analysis are not independent, because there is a strong tendency for extremely high complexity to be associated with high availability of resources. Table 2 shows the expected pattern of childrearing in the 3 × 3 classification.

The nine childrearing patterns have been given letter-names. Pattern A approximates the pattern found among the Eskimo and other hunting and fishing groups that have adequate balances in their ecologies between resources and population. Pattern B is typi-

Table 2
Hypothesized relationships of societal complexity and abundance of resources as determinants of childrearing patterns

Resources/Person   Cultural Complexity

	Low	Intermediate	High
	Warm	Somewhat Cold	Warm
Abundant	Autonomous	Controlling	Autonomous
	A	B	A
	Cold	Cold	Cold
Intermediate	Controlling	Very Controlling	Controlling
	B	C	B
Extreme	Abandonment	Abandonment	Abandonment
Scarcity	D	D	D

cal of those agricultural societies that hold the limited-good view and use small ingroups, and of lower-class samples in industrial societies. Pattern A is also typical of successful professionals in industrial societies. Pattern D is typical of societies in a state of famine, such as the Ik (Turnbull, 1972); pattern C is typical of many barely subsisting peasants. Pattern D is also typical of the abandonment of children in highly complex societies where parents "do their own thing" and the children are left to fend for themselves. It is interesting to note that the same pattern (say warm, autonomous) has a different meaning when it is found in a complex rather than a simple culture.

The next set of relationships relates the childrearing patterns just outlined to particular aspects of personality development.

> *Hypothesis 32.* Warm parental patterns result in higher levels of cognitive complexity when combined with autonomous patterns, with resulting emphasis on the C-component, and in lower levels of complexity when combined with controlling patterns, resulting in little emphasis on the C-component.

It is assumed that cognitive complexity requires information, and that warm patterns will be characterized by higher levels of information-giving.

Goldstein and Blackman (1976) found that mothers who rejected the motherhood role (as measured by answers to the Schaefer and Bell PARI instrument) had children who were lower in cognitive complexity (as measured by the Bieri modification of the Kelly REP test) and higher in tendencies toward acquiescence (as measured by Couch & Keniston, 1960).

> *Hypothesis 33.* The rank order of acquiescence (including behavior consistent with norms, conformity, dogmatism, emphasis on the S-component, low cognitive differentiation) will be from high to low for childrearing patterns C, B, D, and A.
>
> *Hypothesis 34:* Ecologies with high population density tend to require people to be sensitive to the needs of their neighbors and hence conformity is more likely; since conformity leads to low psychological differentiation, high population density will also be related to low psychological differentiation.

This hypothesis is supported by data presented by Berry (1976; 1979). Further confirmation of both of these hypotheses requires the collection of multiple measures of acquiescence, conformity, and so on, and studies of the relationship of ecology and childrearing patterns to these multiple measures. A useful index of degree of conformity is the percentage of the population, in a given culture, that is left-handed. Dawson (1974) used several tasks (card dealing, managing chopsticks, writing, using a toothbrush) to determine whether people were left-handed, and found high rates (9 to 11%) of left-handedness in cultures (e.g., Australian Aborigines, Hong Kong boat people, Eskimo) where socialization is permissive, and low rates (0 to 3%) of left-handedness in cultures that use harsh socialization methods (Temne, Hakka Chinese, in Nigeria). He argues that relatively high rates are natural but are suppressed by cultural pressures to conform to a universal cultural ideal, which reflects human biology and considers the right hand the "correct" hand for many activities.

The two major dimensions of social behavior that have been discussed so far (association and superordination) apparently can be synthesized to relate to particular features of culture. The other two dimensions (intimacy, overtness) may or may not be so related. One might speculate that the greater intimacy of behavior in nuclear families, noted above, is crucial. However, one can also argue that in very simple cultures intimacy may be more prevalent than in highly complex cultures because the latter, by definition, involve high levels of role differentiation, and hence formality is required in dealing with people that one meets for the first time. Formality seems more likely to help interpersonal relationships in situations where the basis of the relationship is a person's role (job, social position), while intimacy may be most appropriate in those situations where people have long-term face-to-face relationships. If we put the curvilinear trend between cultural complexity and type of family organization together with the trend toward greater formality in complex cultures, we would expect another curvilinear relationship: the more cultural complexity the more formality, up to a point, after which there will be a reduction in formality.

It is interesting to speculate also about the kinds of cultures that are likely to foster overt rather than covert action. Where norms are numerous, explicit, and clear, people might find it more difficult to conform. One way to appear to conform while not actually doing so is to emit overt actions that follow the norms, while corresponding covert behavior does not. Perhaps in such situations more behaviors are covert than overt. Following the analysis of superordinate behaviors mentioned earlier, we would expect that cultures in ecologies where much cooperation is required for survival will develop more and clearer norms, will be more strict in enforcing them, and also will have more people engaging in covert behaviors.

These thoughts are too speculative to allow the development of hypotheses, but they do suggest some very major lacunae in our research enterprise, and some interesting topics for further research.

SUMMARY AND CONCLUSIONS

A theoretical framework has been developed that relates attitudes, values, and behavior. Variables that function as antecedents of attitudes and values and feedback from the outcomes of behavior are included in the framework. Individual difference variables (such as values, authoritarianism, time perspective, acquiescence, cognitive complexity), situational difference variables (such as the dimensions public-private, constraining-loose, and time pressure), and differences among the type of behavior that is to be predicted are also included in the framework. Attributes of cultures, such as cultural complexity, are related to attributes of persons, such as cognitive complexity. Other hypotheses connect attributes of the culture, such as abundance of resources, to attributes of the prevailing socialization patterns. Hypotheses about the relationship of childrearing patterns to personality variables are also presented. Finally, hypotheses are offered about the relationship between attributes of cultures and attributes of social behavior frequently found in those cultures. Of the 34 hypotheses that are presented some are extrapolations from existing studies, and others appear to be supported directly by some studies. A quick way to summarize the proposed framework is to indicate that attributes of the ecology-culture-society determine attributes of persons, such as attitudes and values, which determine the behaviors of those persons; and depending on the outcomes of this behavior, attitudes and values change.

REFERENCE NOTES

1. Adamopoulos, J., and Brinberg, D. *An examination of the determinants of social behavior.* Unpublished manuscript, Department of Psychology, University of Illinois, 1975.
2. England, G. W. *Managers and their values.* Paper presented at the International Congress of Applied Psychology, Munich, Germany, 1978.

REFERENCES

Abelson, R. P. A script theory of understanding, attitude and behavior. In J. S. Carroll and T. Payne (Eds.), *Cognition and social behavior.* Hillsdale, NJ.: Lawrence Erlbaum Associates, 1976.
Adamopoulos, J. *Perceptual dimensions of the social environment.* Unpublished M.A. Thesis, University of Illinois, 1976.
Allport, G. W., Vernon, P. E., & Lindzey, G. *A study of values.* Boston: Houghton Mifflin, 1960.
Alwin, D. Making inferences from attitude-behavior correlations. *Sociometry,* 1973, **36**, 253–278.
Alwin, D. Attitude scales as congeneric tests: A re-examination of an attitude-behavior model. *Sociometry,* 1976, **39**, 377–383.
Arsenian, J., & Arsenian, J. M. Tough and easy cultures: A conceptual analysis. *Psychiatry,* 1948, **11**, 377–385.
Asch, S. Studies of independence and submission to group pressure: A minority of one against a unanimous majority. *Psychological Monographs,* 1956, **70**.
Bales, R. F. *Interaction process analysis.* Cambridge, MA.: Addison-Wesley, 1950.
Barker, R. *The stream of behavior.* New York: Appleton-Century-Crofts, 1963.
Barker, R. *Ecological psychology: Concepts and methods for studying the environment of human behavior.* Stanford, CA.: Stanford University Press, 1968.
Barry, H. Description and uses of the Human Relations Area Files. In H. C. Triandis & J. W. Berry (Eds.), *Handbook of cross-cultural psychology: Methodology.* Rockleigh, NJ.: Allyn & Bacon, 1980.
Barry, H., Child, I., & Bacon, M. Relation of child training to subsistence economy. *American Anthropologist,* 1959, **61**, 51–63.
Bastide, R., & Van den Berghe, P. Stereotypes, norms, and interracial behavior in Sao Paulo Brazil. *American Sociological Review,* 1957, **22**, 688–694.
Berry, J. W. Temne and Eskimo perceptual skills. *International Journal of Psychology,* 1966, **1**, 207–229.

Berry, J. W. Independence and conformity in subsistence level societies. *Journal of Personality and Social Psychology*, 1967, **7**, 415–418.

Berry, J. W. *Human ecology and cognitive style: Comparative studies in cultural and psychological adaptation.* New York: Sage/Halsted/Wiley, 1976.

Berry, J. W. A dynamic model of relationships among ecology, culture and behavior. In L. L. Adler (Ed.), *Issues in cross-cultural research.* New York: New York Academy of Sciences, 1977.

Berry, J. W. A cultural ecology of social behavior. In L. Berkowitz (Ed.), *Advances in experimental social psychology* (Vol. 12). New York: Academic Press, 1979.

Birdwistell, R.L. Introduction to kinesics. Louisville, KY.: University of Louisville Press, 1952.

Birdwistell, R. L. *Kinesics and context.* Philadelphia: University of Pennsylvania Press, 1970.

Blumberg, L., & Winch, R. F. Societal complexity and familial complexity: Evidence for a curvilinear hypothesis. *American Journal of Sociology*, 1972, **7**, 896–920.

Boldt, E. D. Structural tightness and cross-cultural research. *Journal of Cross-Cultural Psychology.* 1978. **9**, 151–165.

Brannon, R., Cyphers, G., Messe, S., Hesselbart, S., Keane, R., Schuman, H., Viccaro, T., & Wright, D. Attitude and action: A field experiment joined to a general population survey. *American Sociological Review*, 1973, **38**, 625–636.

Bray, D. The prediction of behavior from two attitude scales. *Journal of Abnormal and Social Psychology*, 1950, **45**, 64–84.

Brinberg, D. *The comparison of three attitude models for the prediction of blood donation behavior.* Unpublished doctoral dissertation, University of Illinois, 1979.

Brown, D. Adolescent attitudes and lawful behavior. *Public Opinion Quarterly*, 1974, **38**, 98–106.

Campbell, D. T. Social attitudes and other behavioral dispositions. In S. Koch (Ed.), *Psychology: A study of a science.* New York: McGraw-Hill, 1963.

Campbell, D. T., & Fiske, D. W. Convergent and discriminant validation by the multitrait-multimethod matrix. *Psychological Bulletin*, 1959, **56**, 81–105.

Chapple, E. D. Measuring human relations: An introduction to the study of the interaction of individuals. *Genetic Psychology Monographs*, 1940, **22**, 3–147.

Cooper, J. B. Emotion in prejudice. *Science*, 1959, **130**, 314–318.

Corey, S. Professed attitudes and actual behavior. *Journal of Educational Psychology*, 1937, **28**, 271–280.

Couch, A., & Keniston, K. Yeasayers and Naysayers: Agreeing response set as a personality variable. *Journal of Abnormal and Social Psychology*, 1960, **60**, 151–174.

Crespi, I. What kinds of attitude measures are predictive of behavior? *Public Opinion Quarterly*, 1971, **35**, 327–334.

Davidson, A., & Jaccard, J. Population psychology: A new look at an old problem. *Journal of Personality and Social Psychology*, 1975, **31**, 1073–1082.

Davidson, A. R., & Jaccard, J. J. Variables that moderate the attitude-behavior relation: Results of a longitudinal survey. *Journal of Personality and Social Psychology*, in press.

Davidson, A., Jaccard, J., Triandis, H. C., Morales, M. L., & Diaz-Guerrero, R. Cross-cultural model testing: Toward a solution of the emic-etic dilemma. *International Journal of Psychology*, 1976, **11**, 1–13.

Dawson, J. L. M. Effects of ecology and subjective culture on individual traditional-modern attitude change, achievement motivation, and potential for economic development in the Japanese and Eskimo societies. *International Journal of Psychology*, 1973, **8**, 215–225.

Dawson, J. L. M. Ecology, cultural pressures toward conformity, and left-handedness: A bio-social psychological approach. In J. L. M. Dawson & W. J. Lonner (Eds.), *Readings in cross-cultural psychology*. Hong Kong: Hong Kong University Press, 1974.

Dienstbier, R. A. A modified belief theory of prejudice emphasizing the mutual causality of racial prejudice and anticipated belief differences. *Psychological Review*, 1972, **79**, 146–160.

Dillehay, R. C., Bruvold, W. H., & Siegel, J. P. On the assessment of potability. *Journal of Applied Psychology*, 1967, **51**, 89–95.

Dollard, J. Under what conditions do opinions predict behavior? *Public Opinion Quarterly*, 1949, **12**, 623–632.

Dulany, D. E., Jr. The place of hypotheses and intentions: An analysis of verbal control in verbal conditioning. In C. W. Eriksen (Ed.), *Behavior and awareness*. Durham, NC.: Duke University Press, 1962.

Ehrlich, H. Attitudes, behavior, and intervening variables. *American Sociologist*, 1969, **4**, 29–34.

Einhorn, H. J., & Hogarth, R. M. Confidence in judgment: Persistence of the illusion of validity. *Psychological Review*, 1978, **85**, 395–416.

Farina, A., Chapnick, B., Chapnick, J., & Misiti, R. Political views and interpersonal behavior. *Journal of Personality and Social Psychology*, 1972, **22**, 273–278.

Fazio, A. Verbal and overt-behavioral assessment of a specific fear. *Journal of Consulting and Clinical Psychology*, 1969, **33**, 705–709.

Fazio, R. H., & Zanna, M. P. Attitudinal qualities relating to the strength of the attitude-behavior relationship. *Journal of Experimental Social Psychology*, 1978, **14**, 398–408.

Feather, N. T., & Peay, E. R. The structure of terminal and instrumental values: dimensions and clusters. *Australian Journal of Psychology*, 1975, **27**, 151–164.

Fishbein, M. A behavior theory approach to the relations between beliefs about an object and the attitude toward the object. In M. Fishbein (Ed.), *Readings in attitude theory and measurement*. New York: Wiley, 1967 (a).

Fishbein, M. Attitude and the prediction of behavior. In M. Fishbein (Ed.), *Readings in attitude theory and method*. New York: Wiley, 1967 (b).

Fishbein, M. The prediction of behavior from attitudinal variables. In C. D. Mortensen & K. K. Sereno (Eds.), *Advances in communication research*. New York: Harper & Row, 1973.

Fishbein, M., & Ajzen, I. *Belief, attitude, intention, and behavior*. Reading, MA.: Addison-Wesley, 1975.

Foa, U., & Foa, E. *Societal structures of the mind*. Springfield, IL.: Charles Thomas, 1974.

Friederes, J., Warner, L., & Albrecht, L. The impact of social constraints on the relationship between attitude and behavior. *Social Forces*, 1971, **50**, 102–112.

Gabrenya, W. K., & Arkin, R. M. The effect of commitment on expectancy value and expectancy weight in social decision making. *Personality and Social Psychology Bulletin*, 1979, **5**, 86–90.

Garner, W. R., Hake, H. W., & Eriksen, C. W. Operationalism and the concept of perception. *Psychological Review*, 1956, **63**, 149–159.

Goldstein, K. M., & Blackman, S. Cognitive complexity, maternal child rearing and acquiescence. *Social Behavior and Personality*, 1976, **4**, 97–103.

Goldstein, M., & Davis, E. E. Race and belief: A further analysis of the social determinants of behavioral intentions. *Journal of Personality and Social Psychology*, 1972, **22**, 346–355.

Gruenfeld, L. W., & MacEachron, A. E. A cross-national study of cognitive style among managers and technicians. *International Journal of Psychology*, 1975, **10**, 27–55.

Heider, F. Attitudes and cognitive organization. *Journal of Psychology*, 1946, **21**, 107–112.

Heider, F. *The psychology of interpersonal relations*. New York: Wiley, 1958.

Herskovits, M. J. *Cultural Anthropology*. New York: Knopf, 1955.

Hom, P. *A comparative examination of different approaches to the prediction of turnover*. Unpublished doctoral dissertation, University of Illinois, Urbana, 1978.

Inkeles, A., & Smith, D. H. *Becoming modern*. Cambridge, MA.: Harvard University Press, 1974.

Jaccard, J., & Davidson, A. A comparison of two models of social behavior: Results of a survey sample. *Sociometry*, 1975, **38**, 497–517.

Kirscht, J. P., & Dillehay, R. C. *Dimensions of authoritarianism*. Lexington: University of Kentucky Press, 1967.

Kluckhohn, C. Toward a comparison of value-emphases in different cultures. In L. D. White (Ed.), *The state of the social sciences*. Chicago: University of Chicago Press, 1956.

Kluckhohn, C. The scientific study of values. In *University of Toronto Installation Lectures.* Toronto: University of Toronto Press, 1959.

Kluckhohn, F. R., & Strodtbeck, F. L. *Variations in value orientation.* Evanston: Row Peterson, 1961.

Kohn, M. L. *Class and conformity: A study of values.* Homewood, IL.: Dorsey, 1969.

Landis, D., Triandis, H. C., & Adamopoulos, J. Habit and behavioral intentions as predictors of social behavior. *Journal of Social Psychology,* 1978, **106**, 227–237.

Langer, E. J. Rethinking the role of thought in social interaction. In J. H. Harvey, W. J. Ickes, & R. F. Kidd (Eds.), *New directions in attribution research* (Vol. 2). New York: Halsted, 1978.

Langer, Ellen, Blank, A., & Chanowitz, B. The mindlessness of ostensibly thoughtful action: The role of "placebic" information in interpersonal interaction. *Journal of Personality and Social Psychology,* 1978, **36**, 635–642.

Leary, T. *Interpersonal diagnosis of personality.* New York: Ronald Press, 1957.

Liska, A. Emergent issues in the attitude-behavior consistency controversy. *American Sociological Review,* 1974, **34**, 261–272.

Lomax, A., &Berkowitz, N. The evolutionary taxonomy of culture. *Science,* 1972, **177**, 228–239.

Longabaugh, R. The systematic observation of behavior in naturalistic settings. In H. C. Triandis & J. W. Berry (Eds.), *Handbook of cross-cultural psychology: Methodology* (Vol. 2). Boston: Allyn & Bacon, 1980.

McClelland, D. C. *The achieving society.* Princeton, NJ.: Van Nostrand, 1961.

Mitchell, T., & Biglan, A. Instrumentality theories. *Psychological Bulletin,* 1971, **76**, 432–454.

Mixon, D. Instead of deception. *Journal for the Theory of Social Behavior,* 1972, **2**, 145–177.

Mobley, W. H., Horner, S. O., & Hollingsworth, A. T. An evaluation of precursors of hospital turnover. *Journal of Applied Psychology,* 1978, **63**, 408–414.

Murdock, G. P., & Provost, C. Measurement of cultural complexity. *Ethnology,* 1973, **12**, 379–392.

Newton, N., & Newton, M. Relationship of ability to breast-feed and maternal attitudes toward breast feeding. *Pediatrics,* 1950, **5**, 869–875.

Newtson, D. Foundation of attribution: The perception of ongoing behavior. In J. H. Harvey, W. J. Ickes, & R. F. Kidd (Eds.), *New directions in attribution research* (Vol. 1). New York: Halsted, 1976.

Nisbett, R. E., & Wilson, T. D. Telling more than we can know: Verbal reports on mental processes. *Psychological Review,* 1977, **84**, 231–259.

Osgood, C. E. Dimensionality of the semantic space for communication via facial expressions. *Scandinavian Journal of Psychology,* 1966, **7**, 1–30.

Osgood, C. E., May, W., & Miron, M. *Cross-cultural universals of affective meaning.* Urbana: University of Illinois Press, 1975.

Palys, T. S. Simulation methods and social psychology. *Journal for the Theory of Social Behavior*, 1978, **8**, 341–368.

Pelto, P. J. The differences between "tight" and "loose" societies. *Transaction*, April, 1968, pp. 37–40.

Poincaré, H. *Science and hypothesis*. New York: Science Press, 1905.

Pomazal, R. J. *Attitudes, normative beliefs and altruism: Help for helping behavior*. Unpublished doctoral dissertation, University of Illinois, 1974.

Premack, D. Reinforcement theory. In D. Levine (Ed.), *Nebraska Symposium on Motivation 1965* (Vol. 13). Lincoln: University of Nebraska Press, 1965.

Raden, D. Situational thresholds and attitude-behavior consistency. *Sociometry*, 1977, **40**, 123–129.

Reimanis, G. Locus of control in American and Northeastern Nigerian students. *Journal of Social Psychology*, 1977, **103**, 309–310.

Robbins, M. C., Dewalt, B. R., & Pelto, P. J. Climate and behavior: A biocultural study. *Journal of Cross-Cultural Psychology*, 1972, **3**, 331–344.

Rohner, R. *They love me, they love me not: A world wide study of the effects of parental acceptance and rejection*. New Haven, CT.: Human Relations Area Files Press, 1975.

Rohner, R. P. Worldwide tests of parental acceptance-rejection theory: An overview. *Behavioral Science Research*, in press.

Rokeach, M. *The nature of human values*. New York: Free Press, 1973.

Rosen, B., & Komorita, S. Attitudes and action: The effects of behavioral intent and perceived effectiveness of acts. *Journal of Personality*, 1971, **39**, 189–203.

Rotter, J. B. Generalized expectancies for internal versus external control of reinforcement. *Psychological Monographs*, 1966, **80**, 1 (Whole of No. 609).

Ryan, T. A. *Intentional behavior*. New York: Ronald Press, 1970.

Sample, J., & Warland, R. Attitude and the prediction of behavior. *Social Forces*, 1973, **51**, 292–300.

Schachter, S., Festinger, L., Willerman, B., & Hyman, R. Emotional disruption and industrial productivity. *Journal of Applied Psychology*, 1961, **45**, 201–213.

Schlosberg, H. Three dimensions of emotion. *Psychological Review*, 1954, **61**, 81–83.

Schmidt, R. W., Lamm, H., & Trommsdorff, G. Social class and sex as determinants of future orientation (true perspective) in adults. *European Journal of Sociology*, 1978, **8**, 71–90.

Schuman, H. Attitudes vs. actions vs. attitudes vs. attitudes. *Public Opinion Quarterly*, 1972, **36**, 347–354.

Schwartz, S. H. Normative influences on altruism. In L. Berkowitz (Ed.), *Advances in experimental social psychology* (Vol. 10). New York: Academic Press, 1977.

Seibold, D. R. Communication research and the attitude–verbal report–overt behavior relationship: A critique and theoretical reformulation. *Human Communication Research*, 1975, **2**, 3–32.

Seibold, D. R., & Roper, R. Psychosocial determinants of health care intentions: Test of the Triandis and Fishbein models. In D. Nimmo (Ed.), *Communication Yearbook 3*. New Brunswick, NJ.: Transaction Books, 1979.

Silverman, B., & Cochrane, R. The relationship between verbal expressions of behavioral intentions and overt behavior. *Journal of Social Psychology*, 1971, **84**, 51–56.

Smedslund, J. Bandura's theory of self-efficacy: A set of common sense theorems. *Scandinavian Journal of Psychology*, 1978, **19**, 1–14.

Smith, F. T., & Crano, W. D. Cultural dimensions reconsidered: Global and regional analyses of the ethnographic atlas. *American Anthropologist*, 1977, **79**, 364–387.

Snyder, M. Attribution and behavior: Social perception and social causation. In J. H. Harvey, W. J. Ickes, & R. F. Kidd (Eds.), *New directions in attribution research* (Vol. 1). New York: Halsted, 1976.

Steers, R. M., & Rhodes, S. R. Major influences on employee attendance: A process model. *Journal of Applied Psychology*, 1978, **63**, 391–407.

Triandis, H. C. Cultural influences upon cognitive processes. In L. Berkowitz (Ed.), *Advances in experimental social psychology*. New York: Academic Press, 1964 (a).

Triandis, H. C. Exploratory factor analyses of the behavioral component of social attitudes. *Journal of Abnormal and Social Psychology*, 1964, **68**, 420–430. (b).

Triandis, H. C. *Attitude and attitude change*. New York: Wiley, 1971.

Triandis, H. C. (Ed.). *Variations in black and white perceptions of the social environment*. Champaign: University of Illinois Press, 1976.

Triandis, H. C. *Interpersonal behavior*. Monterey, CA.: Brooks/Cole, 1977.

Triandis, H. C., & Davis, E. E. Race and belief as determinants of behavioral intentions. *Journal of Personality and Social Psychology*, 1965, **2**, 715–725.

Triandis, H. C., Feldman, J. M., Weldon, D. E., & Harvey, W. M. Ecosystem distrust and the hard to employ. *Journal of Applied Psychology*, 1975, **60**, 44–50.

Triandis, H. C., & Lambert, W. W. A restatement and test of Schlosberg's theory of emotion with two kinds of subjects from Greece. *Journal of Abnormal and Social Psychology*, 1958, **56**, 321–328.

Triandis, H. C., & Vassiliou, V. A comparative analysis of subjective culture. In H. C. Triandis (Ed.), *The Analysis of Subjective Culture*. New York: Wiley, 1972.

Triandis, H. C., Vassiliou, V., & Nassiakou, M. Three studies of subjective culture. *Journal of Personality and Social Psychology Monograph Supplement*, 1968, **8** (4), 1–42.

Triandis, H. C., Vassiliou, V. G., Tanaka, Y., & Shanmugam, A. V. *The analysis of subjective culture*. New York:Wiley, 1972.

Turnbull, C. M. *The mountain people*. New York: Simon & Schuster, 1972.

Whiting, B. B., & Whiting, J. W. M. *Children of six cultures*. Cambridge, MA.: Harvard University Press, 1975.

Wicker, A. W. *An introduction to ecologicial psychology.* Monterey, CA.: Brooks/Cole, 1979.

Wicklund, R. A. The influence of self-awareness on human behavior. *American Scientist*, 1979, **67**, 187–193.

Wright, H. F. *Recording and analyzing child behavior.* New York: Harper & Row, 1967.

Wundt, W. *Grundriss der Psychologie.* Leipzig: Engelmann, 1896.

Zajonc, R. B. Social facilitation. *Science*, 1965, **149**, 269–274.

Zavalloni, M. Values. In H. C. Triandis & R. Brislin (Eds.), *Handbook of cross-cultural psychology: social psychology* (Vol. 5). Boston: Allyn & Bacon, 1980.

Ziller, R. C. *The social self.* New York: Pergamon Press, 1973.

Some Unresolved Issues in Theories of Beliefs, Attitudes, and Values[1]

Milton Rokeach

Washington State University

While I have had a long-term commitment to furthering our understanding of the role of beliefs and attitudes in human affairs, I have at the same time, perhaps more persistently than others, deplored the fact that social psychologists continue by and large not to appreciate the importance of values in human affairs—a fact demonstrated by our chief journals and by textbooks in social psychology. I was therefore gratified to learn that the organizers of this symposium had entitled it "Theories of Beliefs, Attitudes, and Values." I gladly accepted the invitation to participate because I felt the occasion would provide me with an opportunity to address myself to several issues that I believe continue to remain unresolved, to attempt to articulate to what extent my earlier formulations (1960, 1968b, 1973) require revision or elaboration, to react to the formulations and findings of others working in this area, and to suggest how a recent interest in attribution theory might lead to new insights in thinking about organization and change in beliefs, attitudes, and values.

Having faith that the confrontation of theoretical differences is a good thing, I would anticipate that the published proceedings of this symposium will provide a stimulus in the next few years for further advances in theory and research in this classical area of social psychology—classical in the sense that an interest in attitudes and related constructs has remained central and constant over many

1. Preparation of this paper was facilitated by Public Health Service Grant No. 1R01 MH29656–01 from the National Institute of Mental Health, and this support is gratefully acknowledged.

years. It was a main topic of study when I was a graduate student in the forties, and I confidently anticipate that it will continue to remain so even as our ever changing and sometimes floundering field moves into the 21st Century.

DEFINITION OF BELIEFS, ATTITUDES, AND VALUES

Satisfying conceptual definitions should go beyond informing us about how they might be operationalized. A conceptual definition should, in addition, inform us about how the concept is distinguishable from, yet related to others with which it is often confused; should specify all the phenomena in the real world to which it is thought to apply; should inform us about functional significance; and finally, should provide us with at least a clue about the conditions under which it will remain stable and undergo change. With these criteria in mind I propose the following interrelated conceptual definition of beliefs, attitudes, and values.

A *belief* is any expectancy concerning existence, evaluation, prescription-proscription, or cause. An *attitude* is a relatively enduring organization of existential, evaluative, prescriptive-proscriptive, and causal beliefs organized around an object or situation, predisposing one to respond (a) preferentially to the object or situation, (b) discriminatingly to all persons perceived to vary in their attitude to object or situation, and (c) differentially to social controls or pressures intended to coerce expression to specified positions toward object and situation. All such preferential, discriminatory, or differential responses are instrumental to the realization of societally originating *values*—shared prescriptive or proscriptive beliefs about ideal modes of behavior and end-states of existence that are activated by, yet transcend object and situation. All such responses—to objects and situations, to people who agree or disagree, and to social controls—are congruent with one another, and are also congruent because they are directed by one's hierarchically organized cognitive system of beliefs, attitudes, and values. This cognitive system will remain stable to the extent that it will maintain or enhance societally originating self-conceptions concerning competence and morality.

The conceptual definitions offered above now provide me with a framework for discussing and elaborating further a number of issues of theoretical and empirical interest that I believe are still unresolved despite much debate. I have organized my remarks under the following headings:

(a) The nature of attitudes,
(b) the attitude-behavior relation,
(c) the broader question of the relation between values, attitudes, and behavior,
(d) attitudes and causal attributions,
(e) the belief congruence principle, and
(f) the effects of cognitive change on behavioral change, and of behavioral change on cognitive change.

THE NATURE OF ATTITUDES

Despite a widespread consensus about the centrality of the attitude concept—a centrality that no longer needs documentation or rationalization—a consensual understanding of exactly what an attitude is continues to elude and challenge us. The rich, multifaceted nature of attitudes is hinted at by Cohen when he defines them as "complexes of ideas and sentiments" (1966, p. 341), and by Smith, Bruner, and White (1956), who conceptualize them as "agendas for action." Such richness and multifacetedness are, however, obscured by those who define attitudes more simply as dispositions to respond affectively to an object or class of objects, and who thus operationalize attitude to mean not much more than a point on a pro–con evaluative scale. Preference for the latter type of definition seems typical of those more interested in pressing on to other questions of theoretical interest, most particularly to questions about the attitude-behavior relation, or the conditions leading to attitude change, or to questions about the validity of one or another consistency theory.

In offering the above interrelated conceptual definitions, I wish to draw special attention to the following:

(a) I believe that an attitude cannot be adequately defined unless we are able to say explicitly not only how it is conceptually differentiated from, but also related to, two concepts in particular: belief and value—concepts that are often employed loosely and interchangeably in discussions about attitudes.

(b) I have expanded my earlier formulation of attitudes (Rokeach,

1968b) as an organization of different kinds of beliefs (existential, evaluative, and prescriptive-proscriptive) to include a fourth kind which in recent years has been a central concern of attribution theory: beliefs about causality. Thus, a person's attitude toward blacks, Nixon, or one's mother includes not only many existential, evaluative, and prescriptive-proscriptive beliefs, but also causal beliefs that assert why and how they got that way and behave as they do.

(c) The target of an attitudinal response is seen to extend far beyond object and situation to two additional targets. It is also a predisposition to make differential, discriminating responses to all persons who may be perceived to have any given attitude toward object or situation, whether similar to or discrepant with one's own. And it is also a predisposition to differentially perceive and respond to formal and informal social control—social pressures from the laws and norms of society and from significant reference persons and groups that are intended to coerce compliance to specified positions toward object or situation. People socialized to conform to a normative, consensually held attitude are less predisposed to perceive or to admit to the existence of social controls coercing conformity; they are thus predisposed to perceive their attitudes as natural, incontrovertible, and arrived at independently by mental reflection, and thus less predisposed to resist or to evade such social control. In contrast, people having attitudes that deviate from normatively held attitudes are more likely to be aware of and perceive such social control; they are thus more predisposed to see the normatively held attitudes as controvertible and as threatening their autonomy, and are thus more likely to resist, or evade, or to entertain resisting or evading or to be ambivalent or in conflict about acquiescing to such social control.

(d) The conceptual definition attempts to make more explicit how the principle of belief congruence is implied whenever we say a person has an attitude (and a belief and value). All preferential, discriminatory, and differential responses are governed by the principle of belief congruence—a greater preference for and comfort with objects and situations, people in general, and social controls or pressures that are congruent with one's belief system.

(e) Only two qualitatively different kinds of attitudes are reaffirmed (Rokeach, 1968b) to be analytically useful—attitude-toward-object and attitude-toward-situation. The concepts "object" and "situation" are abstract concepts or categories (Bruner, Goodnow, & Austin, 1956) that are intended to include all instances or exemplars of object or situation. But the "object" is inherently a static one: it is not doing anything, and we do not know where it is located when it is under consideration, since it has the capability of being encountered in different situations. Attitudes toward such static objects are cumulations and summaries of all that one knows and feels about them, as a result of encountering them in different situations. They represent a person's theories about objects, what they are, how they got that way, and what they are good for. Social scientists have long been interested in such attitudes toward objects because they are assumed to somehow affect, influence, direct, or determine how people will behave toward the objects, *especially* when they are encountered in situations not previously encountered.

In the same way that it is possible to develop attitudes toward objects as a result of encountering them across situations, it is possible to develop attitudes toward situations as a result of encountering various objects within them. For present purposes, the definition of the situation can be restricted to two main components: (a) an ongoing event or activity—something happening without regard for particular objects that might be encountered; and (b) a set of societally or internally originating constraints that set the boundaries on whatever is happening. These may come from limits imposed by one's competence and abilities, or from controls or pressures exerted by societal laws, norms, family, peers, or other reference persons or groups. A person's attitude toward a situation is thus a global summary of all that the person knows, evaluates, and feels about participating in an ongoing event, taking into account whatever the person knows, evaluates, and feels about his or her abilities and about the relevant social controls.

Thus conceived, it is possible to envision a finite rather than infinite number of attitudes that any person can be said to possess. It corresponds to the total number of conceptual categories that the person has developed as a result of encounters with objects and situations, either directly or vicariously.

(f) A full account of what an attitude is should not only attempt to say what it has to do with beliefs and the realization of values, but should also suggest what all these are all for. I have therefore attempted to draw attention in the conceptual definition to the idea that all attitudes, as well as all beliefs and values, are predispositions that serve the function of maintaining and enhancing self-conceptions, which derive in large part from societal demands and focus upon issues of competence and morality. Competence and morality are exhaustive categories: that is, I cannot think of any other ways for society to make demands upon individuals, or for individuals to make demands upon themselves, other than to demand competence and morality. And the proposition that beliefs, attitudes, and values all serve the maintenance or enhancement of competence and morality is seen to be superordinate to Smith, Bruner, and White's (1956) or Katz's (1960) classical functions of attitudes.

(g) One's total organization of beliefs, attitudes, and values should remain stable only so long as it is able to maintain and enhance conceptions of oneself as competent and moral. But if such self-conceptions cannot be thus maintained or enhanced, then one's beliefs, attitudes, or values should undergo change, in a direction that will be more satisfying to self-conceptions.

ATTITUDES AND BEHAVIOR

The controversial issue of the attitude-behavior relationship is too well known to require review here. Social psychologists have reacted to the empirically observed inconsistency between attitudes and behavior in essentially three different ways. First, there are those who would agree with Abelson (Note 1) that "*general* attitudes do amazingly badly in predicting specific behaviors" (p. 21), and would therefore go on to conclude that the attitude concept is not useful.[2] Second, there are those who would go to the other extreme of suggesting that while we still need the attitude concept we should make it far more specific in meaning and measurement. Third, there are those who would come to the rescue of the attitude concept by advocating that additional attitudes or other variables be added to the equation as determinants and predictors of behavior. Let me consider each of these three proposed solutions in somewhat more detail.

First, the Abelson conclusion, from empirical findings such as those reviewed by Wicker (1969) and others, is a conclusion that I

2. A position also taken by Doob (1947) and Blumer (1955) in earlier days.

myself would be unwilling to draw from the same findings. All that can be concluded from such data is that attitudes considered one at a time do "amazingly badly" and, to boot, that it is single attitudes-toward-object that do so "amazingly badly." What these data cannot be claimed to show, because they are typically inadequate, is that attitudes in the plural, or that attitude-toward-object combined with attitude-toward-situation, or that attitudes combined with other variables, are poor predictors. Thus, if it turns out that one particular attitude-toward-object that is under scrutiny by a researcher is indeed a poor behavioral predictor, we need to be assured that other relevant attitudes or variables are not operating. Such assurances are not typically forthcoming.

All the negative evidence concerning the attitude-behavior relation notwithstanding, I suspect that questions that take the form "Are attitudes necessary?" (Abelson, 1972) will be answered in the negative by only a small minority of social scientists. Most social scientists would rather doubt their own intellectual ability to conceptualize the attitude-behavior problem than abandon their basic assumption that attitudes do indeed determine behavior. Thus, to persist in reviewing the evidence concerning the relation between single attitudes and behavior is to raise a straw man—rather a straw person. It seems to me that the more fruitful theoretical problem is not whether attitudes determine or predict behavior but how they do so.

At the other extreme from Abelson is the solution proposed by Fishbein and Ajzen (1975), who advocate abandoning a global conception of attitudes and substituting a conception that could hardly be more specific. Ajzen and Fishbein (1973) call it "attitude-toward-act," and Fishbein and Ajzen (1975) later call it "attitude-toward-behavior"; either way the classical attitude concept is now redefined to mean attitude-toward-performing-a-particular-act-within-a-given-situation-with-respect-to-a-given-object. Consistent with such a reformulation, Ajzen and Fishbein (1977) demonstrate that attitudes do an increasingly better job of predicting behavior when the attitude object, target of action, and situation are increasingly specified. While the precision, specificity, and operationalization of attitude-toward-act leave nothing to be desired, I find myself hesitating to accept such a way of thinking about attitudes for several reasons.

First, when attitude is defined that specifically the total number of attitudes that people can be said to possess would now be increased from the thousands or tens of thousands to a number somewhere in millions or billions, and we would thus have to deal with a much larger universe of attitudes to which our empirical research would have to generalize. Second, when defined that specifically the attitude concept confounds object and situational variables and there is no rule that enables us to count attitudes, to say when we are dealing with one attitude or more than one. Attitude toward buying lead gasoline in a gasoline station, for example, leaves it unclear as to whether it is an attitude we have about lead gasoline, or about engaging in the activity of buying gasoline, or about some combination of such attitudes (Heberlein & Black, 1976).

Third, and perhaps most important, the concept has now become so specific that it would allow us to predict and generalize only to another precise instance of the same act in the same situation with respect to the same object. While undoubtedly representing a gain in precision of measurement and prediction, it paradoxically defeats the very purpose why the attitude concept has been considered so important for so long in the social sciences—namely, that a person's global attitude representing some general predisposition is an important determinant of the person's behavior with respect to virtually all instances or exemplifications of the object in some new, previously unobserved context, or with respect to virtually all instances or exemplifications of the situation regardless of objects encountered within them.[3]

In sum, the challenging theoretical issue was originally posed (LaPiere, 1934; Kutner, Wilkins, & Yarrow, 1952) when an inconsistency was observed between an attitude and behavior. Much theoretical and empirical work has been directed toward explaining such inconsistency. The theoretical problem that continues to plague us is to explain why this inconsistency is more apparent than real. The apparent inconsistency is not dispelled either by abandoning the attitude concept or by reformulating it in more specific terms. Real people in their everyday lives continue to have, *and to*

3. ". . . if we move instead toward measuring a portfolio of more specific attitudes covering every hypothetical combination of specific . . . object and situation, then we're really in trouble . . . . No, I think Ajzen and Fishbein have thrown away the theoretical baby, and with grim determination are clinging to the bath water" (Abelson, Note 1, pp. 22–22). Or, to put it somewhat differently, they have abandoned trying to understand the global attitudes that humans have in favor of improving predictions and producing ever-higher correlations.

phenomenally experience, the same global attitudes they had before we social psychologists came along to study them, and it is these phenomenally experienced attitudes that, I believe, we should try to "capture" and measure because we suspect them of directing single no less than multiple acts, even when the specific object or situation is not an exact replica of ones previously encountered. I believe that the apparent inconsistency can be more persuasively dispelled by supplying the missing data that we typically neglect to elicit from respondents about all the relevant global attitudes that may be activated. Respondents can tell us about such global attitudes that they have, by clinical interview procedures and sometimes more efficiently by questionnaire procedures.

All of which brings me to the third proposed solution. Despite conceptual differences, there is reasonably good consensus that no single attitude toward object can be a sole determinant of behavior (Calder & Ross, 1973; Kelman, 1974; Kiesler & Munson, 1975; Schuman & Johnson, 1976). There is also good consensus that the total situation, or selected features of it, must also be included. Recognizing the importance of the situation, I have previously argued that at least two attitudes, one concerning the object and the other concerning the situation in which the object may be encountered, must always be taken into account when considering the determinants of behavior. But perhaps I should have added that a focus on these two types of attitudes is only a minimum point of departure for a systematic analysis. For instance, a particular minority member to whom we may be asked to react may be not only black, but also male, poor, fat, brilliant, and old. This particular person may thus activate our attitudes towards blacks, males, the poor, the fat, the brilliant, and the aged. Exactly which attitude object are we talking about? In the example given, at least six attitudes-toward-object[4] may have been aroused, and are all thus relevant determinants of behavior.

Similarly with the concept attitude-toward-situation, which may be further analyzable into as many features of the situation as we think relevant. Such a determination would surely include an assessment of how one feels about, wants to or does not want to,

---

4. As already indicated, the term "object" in attitude-toward-object refers to a general conceptual category that includes all instances of a class of objects. It is not, I believe, the specific stimulus or concrete object referred to in the conceptualization proposed in Fishbein and Ajzen's work.

enjoys or does not enjoy, engaging or participating in whatever the activity or event. Others have zeroed in one one or another important feature or component of the total situation. Acock and DeFleur (1972) call it perceived social influence, Kelman (1974) calls it social constraint, Fishbein and Ajzen (1975) call it normative beliefs and motivation to comply with normative beliefs, and Triandis (1971) calls it norms. Disregarding terminological differences, all such formulations attempt to point to the total social situation or to some significant feature of it that should be included in attitude-behavior relation models. We are thus reduced to disagreeing among ourselves mainly about how best to put it.

As I see it, the main problem on how best to put it is that the formulation should attempt to be comprehensive and that the concepts should come from the same universe of discourse. I have always felt that there is something not altogether satisfying or pretty about the notion that behavior is an interacting function of two variables, one of which is attitudinal and the other of which is situational. I prefer on grounds of scientific parsimony for the interacting variables to come from the same universe of discourse. The formulation that behavior is a function of attitude-toward-object interacting with attitude-toward-situation attempts to be systematic in the sense that it is comprehensive, within the same universe of discourse, and takes situational factors into account. Its point of departure is three separate elements that are always present in every attitude-behavior analysis: an object, a situation, and a specified behavior. This formulation moreover proposes that two kinds of attitudes—toward objects and situations—are the major if not sole determinants of behavior, and that "other variables" or "situational variables" need not be brought into the analysis from other universes of discourse to interact with attitudes. Attitude-toward-situation is an attitudinal variable, but it is also a situational variable.

From this perspective it may now be seen that it is not social constraint (Kelman, 1974), or perceived social influence (Acock & DeFleur, 1972), or perceived social pressure (Rokeach, 1960) or norms (Triandis, 1971), or normative beliefs (Fishbein & Ajzen, 1975) that should be entered into our predictive models as interacting with attitude-toward-object, but people's attitudes toward complying with such constraints, pressures, social influences, or whatever we may wish to call it. Thus, while all people in Mississippi may be exposed to powerful social controls against black integration, they will vary in their beliefs about the very existence of such controls and also in their attitude toward complying with them in different situations. It is this varying attitude toward compliance with social control when we engage in any activity we like or dislike that interacts with attitude-toward-object to culminate in some preferential response to some specific object-in-situation.

VALUES, ATTITUDES, AND BEHAVIOR

In my view, the attitude-behavior relation question is a narrow one that can be subsumed under the broader question of the relation among values, attitudes and behavior. As we thus broaden the inquiry, additional questions leap out at us: What about consistency between values and attitudes, and between values and behavior? How are we to coordinate whatever the answers given to such questions with those given to the more classical question of the relation between attitudes and behavior? And why the silence or indifference to questions about the relation between values and attitudes, and between values and behavior?

A meaningful discussion of such issues presupposes at least some willingness to probe into the nature of human values and at least some recognition of the difference between values and attitudes. As Levitin notes, however, such concerns are generally absent from the literature of social psychology: "The empirical investigation of values remains an isolated area within the field of social psychology . . . . In the related disciplines of anthropology, sociology, and philosophy it has received considerable attention . . . . Anthropologists and sociologists for the most part (rather than psychologists) have made the major contributions in the conceptualization of values" (1973, pp. 405–406). Levitin goes on to suggest several reasons why social psychologists have largely ignored values. There is apparently a belief that studying value judgments is outside the realm of empirical investigation and that such value judgments are not amenable to measurement. And "even when the measurement issue is settled in principle, . . . there remains another difficulty related to the nature of values conceived as deep, irrational forces: their resistance to manipulation in laboratory experiments. Unlike more superficial attitudes, values are assumed to be central to the way an individual structures his world and defines himself and thus are not subject to experimental change . . . . This problem seems to have encouraged psychologists to avoid the study of values . . ." (p. 407).

But social psychologists have not altogether ignored the study of values. Value has been variously defined as a "general attitude" (Harvey & Smith, 1977;[5] Schwartz, 1978), a "broader attitude," a "component of attitude," a "valence of all the goals" (McGuire, 1969, p. 151), or as a "bipolar evaluation" (Fishbein & Ajzen, 1975, p. 13). All such conceptions seem, in my opinion, not to do justice to the large philosophical literature on values or to capture the essence of the conceptual difference between values and attitudes. This essence seems better conveyed when we say that humans have thousands of attitudes but only dozens of values, that attitudes are biases and values are metabiases, that humans have reason on many occasions to conceal their attitudes but less reason to conceal their values, that values are deeper as well as broader than attitudes, that values are standards of "oughts" and "shoulds" whereas attitudes are not, that values are determinants rather than components of attitudes, that values transcend objects and situation, that philosophers, theologians, anthropologists, sociologists, historians, and therapists think it more important to understand people's values than their attitudes, that moral dilemmas involve questions of value, that intergroup and intrapsychic conflict involve questions of value conflict rather than attitude conflict, and that different social institutions specialize in inculcating and transmitting different subsets of values rather than attitudes (Rokeach, 1979a).

Such considerations have led me to argue that however central the attitude concept may be to social psychology, the value concept must surely be even more central.[6] And granting the need for a distinctive value as well as attitude concept, we may now move on to ask about value-behavior and value-attitude consistency in the same way that so many others have previously been moved to ask about attitude-behavior consistency. What empirical evidence is

5. They eloquently warn us against the biasing effects of "value orientations" that exist in society and among social psychologists, but they apparently ignore the existence of the similarly biasing effects of value orientations among the people whom social psychologists study. These people are said to have attitudes, and their values are subsumed under the category "general attitudes." Nothing further is then said either about people's values or their general attitudes.

6. And, I will argue in closing this paper, however central the value concept, the self concept is even more central.

there that values, singly or in combination, are related to or predict behavior and attitudes?

In a chapter that I entitled "Values and Behavior" (Rokeach, 1973), I report and summarize a large body of data on the extent to which measures of one or more of 18 terminal and 18 instrumental values in the Value Survey (Rokeach, 1967) significantly predict to various behaviors. These behaviors range from the very specific to the very general—from eye contact with blacks, to returning borrowed pencils at the end of an experiment, to participating in civil rights demonstrations, to church attendance and political activism, to getting along with a roommate, to differences in academic major, to differences in occupation, and, finally, to differences in life style. Quite aside from many theoretically unanticipated significant findings, the findings show that virtually any given value significantly predicts, and predicts best, to various logically related behaviors, and conversely, that any given behavior is significantly predicted by many values. To provide a more specific example, rankings of one value, *equality*, significantly predict in a theoretically expected manner to the following behaviors, listed roughly below from molecular to molar:

(1) Amount of eye contact with blacks (high),
(2) Joining NAACP (high),
(3) Participating in a civil rights demonstration (high),
(4) Political activism (liberals high, conservatives low),
(5) Getting along with a roommate,[7]
(6) Being a professor in the social sciences (high),
(7) Being a police officer, small entrepreneur, or salesperson (low),
(8) Being a hippie (high)

Similarly, *salvation* rankings considered alone significantly predict in theoretically expected ways to such behavior as church attendance, political activism, returning borrowed pencils, being in jail, getting along with one's roommate, and being a hippie, professor, or priest. But *salvation* rankings do not predict to joining NAACP, eye contact with blacks, or participating in civil rights demonstrations.

Conversely, any specified behavior is significantly predicted by

---

7. Significant correlation between *equality* rankings for compatible roommates and nonsignificant correlation for incompatible roommates.

many values. Two examples: (a) Out of 36 values, 10 are significantly related to participation in a civil rights demonstration, and the value *equality* leads the list; (b) Out of 36 values, 12 significantly predict church attendance, and the values *salvation* and being *forgiving* lead the list. Summarizing all such findings: "Over one-third of all the value-behavior relationships are significant—252 out of a possible 684 (Rokeach, 1973, p. 159).

Findings regarding value-attitude relationships parallel those obtained for value-behavior relationships and these are reported in a parallel chapter that I entitled "Values and Attitudes" (Rokeach, 1973). Specific values significantly predict to many theoretically related attitudes. For example, rankings of the value *equality* significantly predict attitude toward Martin Luther King's assassination, attitude toward blacks, the poor, student protest, involvement in the Vietnam war, communism, and church activism; and difference in equality rankings predicts significantly to such more comprehensive attitudes as intrinsic versus extrinsic religious orientation and dogmatism. Rankings of the value *salvation* significantly predict to virtually every type of socially important attitude we studied.

Conversely, specific attitudes are significantly predicted by many values. For instance, conservatism is significantly predicted by 20 out of 36 values (with age controlled) in South Australia (Feather, 1977). Attitude toward blacks is significantly predicted by 21 out of 36 values in a national sample of adult Americans, and attitude toward student protest is significantly predicted by 10. When we ask how many of 36 values predict to 11 important social attitudes we find that 146 out of 396 relationships are statistically significant—again, about a third (Rokeach, 1973, p. 119).

More generally, it is difficult to identify socially important behaviors or attitudes that are *not* predicted by one or more values (Feather, 1975; Rokeach, 1973; Searing, 1978; Williams, 1979). Evidence about such relations comes not only from my Value Survey but from other value measures as well, such as the Allport-Vernon-Lindzey Scale (1960), or the value scales of England (England, Olsen, & Agarwal, 1971) or Gordon (1975). For those interested in tracking down evidence about the predictive validity of these scales, see Levitin's (1973) review in Robinson and Shaver, and Regan and Rokeach (Note 2).

At this point in the discussion, the question may legitimately shift from "Is there consistency between X and Y?" to "How much of the variance of Y can be explained by X?" While empirically it is always a long way to unity of prediction in the social sciences, it is reasonable to propose that more and more of the variance of any specific behavior can be explained as we include more theoretically relevant value or attitude variables in the predictive equation. Thus, Munson and Posner (Note 3) report that 10 values of England's Personal Values Questionnaire (England et al., 1971) correctly predict managerial versus nonmanagerial position 61% of the time in a holdout (cross-validating) sample, and that 10 values of the Rokeach Value Survey correctly predict 71% of the time. Cochrane, Billig, and Hogg (1979) report that compared to a chance accuracy of 25%, 13 values of the Rokeach Value Survey correctly classify 77% of respondents' primary identification with the four main political parties in Britain: Labour, Conservative, Communist, or National Front.

In sum, I would argue that we should now extend the classical question of the attitude-behavior relationship by seeing it as being embedded in the much larger value-attitude-behavior question. Behavior toward one or another object encountered in one or another situation is not only a function of multiple attitudes toward objects and situations, but also of related transcendental values that are activated by objects and situations. Put another way, the objects and situations we encounter have meaning for us not only because of the attitudes they activate within us but also because they are perceived to be instrumental to realization (or to stand in the way of realization) of one or more instrumental values, and of one or more terminal values (Peak, 1955; Carlson, 1956; Rosenberg, 1956; Homant, 1970; Hollen, 1972; Rankin, Note 4). At the same time there are theoretically compelling reasons to anticipate that any one specified behavior in which we might be interested will not be all that highly related to or predicted by any one attitude or any one value, when considered in isolation.[8]

The value-attitude-behavior relation can be pursued by studying not only their interrelationships but also how a change in one of

---

8. Although philosopher Robert Audi does not employ the concept of values or distinguish between attitude-toward-object and attitude-toward-situation, his analysis of action as being a function of multiple beliefs, attitudes, and wants is in many ways similar to my analysis. We "should not expect to make accurate predictions of behavior on the basis of attitude alone . . . . We must . . . assess a much wider range of wants and beliefs than attitude measurements have so far tested . . . . it is not single attitudes, but constellations of attitudes together with various wants and beliefs that determine . . . action" (1972, p. 198).

these affects the others. This issue is discussed further in the last section of this paper.

ATTITUDES AND CAUSAL ATTRIBUTIONS

Generally neglected in theories of beliefs, attitudes, and values, and neglected also in attribution theories, is an analysis of the extent to which existential and causal beliefs are implied whenever we say a person has an attitude, a philosophy of life, a belief system, a political ideology, or a religious or scientific outlook. In all such instances existential attributions as well as causal attributions are made and the two are so closely tied to one another, and tied also to evaluative and prescriptive-proscriptive beliefs, that it is difficult to sort out chicken from egg. Racists, for example, account for the impoverished conditions and performance of blacks by first attributing the existence of certain attributes to them, such as lack of effort or laziness, and by then making causal attributions to explain the existential attributions, such as inferior genes, or God having decreed it that way. Anti-racists would deny such existential and causal attributions and instead typically account for the impoverished conditions and performance of blacks by attributing them to other kinds of personal dispositions, such as low self-esteem, low motivation, or despair, and then causally attributing such dispositions to external social circumstances beyond their control.

A person's cognitive organization of beliefs, attitudes, and values is at one and the same time a "causal understanding model" and a model that can be applied "in the social context of justification of self and criticism of others" (Orvis, Kelley, & Butler, 1976, p. 379). Or, to put it in Jones and Thibaut's terms, such an organization provides the perceiver with a "causal-genetic set" as well as a "value-maintenance set" (1958).

The range or variety of existential and causal attributions that humans make in their everyday life seems to be very wide, as illustrated by the following examples:

(11) Although most people are altogether naive about theories and controversies in the field of genetics, many of them will nonetheless account for certain kinds of performances or behaviors by making causal attributions that rely on such notions as instinct, genes, good and bad breeding, good and bad blood, and good and bad character. The naive commonsense psychologist or intuitive scientist will often bring in such causal ideas when explaining such

phenomena as race differences in intelligence, insanity, crime, drug addiction, mother love, being a great sports star, scientist, or artist, and so on.

(2) American conservatives typically have a negative attitude toward government interference, an attitude that includes beliefs about the existence, causes, and consequences of too much government control. When conservatives inform us that they care more for *freedom* than for *equality* (Rokeach, 1973), we may suspect the presence of existential and causal beliefs about free will, the benefits of individual initiative and free enterprise, why certain people are entitled to have more than others, how it nonetheless happens that some people end up getting more than they deserve, and existential and causal beliefs about the high costs and low benefits of government interference. American liberals, in contrast, have attitudes that include existential beliefs about not enough government control (or the wrong kind of government control) and beliefs about the causes and consequences of such control.

More generally, when we think of conservatives and liberals we think of people who make distinctively different existential and causal attributions, some of which are attributions to the person and others of which are attributions to the environment. Is a liberal one who typically attributes the ultimate causes of action to the environment, and is a conservative more likely to attribute the ultimate causes of action to the person? Whether or not this is so, both conservatives and liberals can be expected to employ their belief-attitude-value organizations an an a priori framework through which they can better understand, predict and control their everyday environments.

(3) Marxists have many attitudes consisting of existential beliefs about the nature of capitalist societies, causal beliefs explaining why different social classes arise and behave as they do, evaluative beliefs representing how good or bad they believe all this to be, and prescriptive-proscriptive beliefs advocating what is to be done. Proponents of socialism, capitalism, and fascism will, of course, disagree with such views, disagree with one another as well, and adhere to alternative attitude organizations of existential, causal, evaluative, and prescriptive-proscriptive beliefs.

(4) The religiously devout, mystics, enthusiasts of astrology, the occult, and mental telepathy will all make certain kinds of existential attributions when explaining certain kinds of behavior—existential attributions that will be unacceptable to naturalists and scientists.

They will then go on to attribute the causes of such existence to extranatural or supernatural forces.

All such examples of existential and causal attributions suggest a taxonomy of "the entire domain of the layman's causal repertoire" (Orvis et al., 1976, p. 354) that would include at least the following:

(1.) *Internal attributions.* In addition to attributing the causes of an action to a person's ability,[9] motivation, attitude, and emotion (to which Heider and others have drawn attention), humans are also prone to attribute the causes of action to free will, instinct, genetic constitution, habit, traits, values, moral character, and the inherent goodness and evilness of humans.

(2.) *External attributions.* Humans are prone to attribute the causes of action not only to features of the situation to which they might react consensually, consistently, and distinctively, as Kelley has suggested (1967), but also to more distal, macroscopic circumstances that convey one or another correct or incorrect idea of natural or social causation, such as attributing cause to evolution, the laws of chance, social circumstances, social circumstances beyond one's control, culture, childrearing practices, the system, the class structure, the power structure, the Establishment, the military-industrial complex, institutional racism and sexism, Big Business, and even to such projective externalizing causes as international Zionism or communism, identifiable or unidentifiable conspirators and persecutors, and electronic interferences (Adorno et al, 1950; Rokeach, 1964).

(3.) *Extranatural and supernatural attributions.* And then there are probably countless millions of "naive psychologists" throughout history who have been prone to attribute existence and causality to extranatural and supernatural forces—the Cosmos, God, guardian angels and saints, the devil, fate, magic, evil spirits, Lady Luck, the heavenly bodies, mental telepathy, clairvoyance, precognition, psychokinesis, and, of special delight to children, the good fairy and Santa Claus.[10]

---

9. Attributing success to a person's ability is to see ability as a cause of success; but what causes ability—personal or environmental factors—is a problem that needs to be pursued further. Judging a person as having failed for lack of ability that is traceable to environmental deprivation may lead to different decisions and behaviors than judging a person as having failed for lack of ability that is traceable to gentic defect.

10. A recent Gallup poll shows that 51% of Americans believe in ESP, and 56% in UFOs (*Spokesman Review*, August 6, 1978). It would be interesting to know from what such existential attributions were inferred.

Thus, over and beyond the determinants of internal and external causal attributions that have been described by Heider (1958), Jones and Nisbett (1972), and Kelley (1967), and of endogenous-exogenous attributions described by Kruglanski (1975), in their accounts of interpersonal relations and person perception there are other transsituational determinants of beliefs about existence and causality that seem to be derived from more distal philosophical, ideological, religious, institutional, societal, or cultural contexts. Countless millions of us are all observers via the mass media of a relatively small number of actors engaged in national and international politics, entertainment, sports, crime, military exploits, etc. As observers we form attitudes and take different sides for and against such actors. Depending upon our attitudes, we perceive existence and what is happening differently and explain them differently, and it is difficult to say whether perceiving existence precedes or follows causal explanation. Cause may be assigned by observers to internal dispositions or to external circumstances depending upon their attitudes, but perhaps equally important as mediators of behavior is whether the internal attributions are rooted in biology or learning, whether internal and external attributions support or oppose the status quo, and whether the external attributions are to natural, extranatural, or supernatural forces. Humans will engage in conflict with one another and even go to war with one another not so much over whether attributions are internal or external, but over which attributions are the more valid. Perhaps more to the point, wars have been fought over *whose* rather than *which* existential and causal attributions are the more valid.

As a result of processes of socialization, persons develop manifold beliefs about existence and causation to account for many kinds of behavior—for instance, about health and illness, poverty, crime, war and peace, death and dying, unemployment, and differences in the performance of various racial, ethnic, and sexual groups.[11] How

11. As social scientists we are accustomed to attributing a person's actions to certain kinds of personal and social circumstances, and most of us would not ourselves dream of attributing such actions to God's will, the movement of the stars, or mental telepathy. We are, moreover, accustomed to attributing a person's action to such internal dispositions as ability and motivation, and we would not ordinarily attribute such actions to a person's genes, blood lines, breeding, free will, or instinct. I am thus led to wonder whether we have created an image of humans rationally processing information much as we ourselves do, and whether the naive intuitive scientists we study thus end up not making causal attributions that we ourselves would not make. Buss (1978) makes a similar point in his analysis of causes and reasons in attribution

do people learn and develop such beliefs about existence and causa-tion?

The path from observable behavior to existential to causal attribu-tion seems problematic. We cannot be altogether sure that causal attributions are inferred from existential attributions and that these are in turn inferred from observable behavior. It is conceivable that the sequence is the other way around, that what we observe and believe to exist is derived or deduced from causal beliefs. It is also conceivable that causal beliefs, like all beliefs, are learned directly through processes of socialization rather than inferred from obser-vation. Two considerations seem to argue against the view that the existential and causal beliefs that enter into attitude organizations are an end-result of a more-or-less rational, ANOVA-like inductive processing of information. First, Nisbett and Wilson (1977) have concluded from a review of literature of cognitive dissonance and attribution studies that:

1. People often cannot report accurately on the effects of par-ticular stimuli on higher order, inference-based responses. Indeed, sometimes they cannot report on the existence of critical stimuli, sometimes cannot report on the existence of their responses, and sometimes cannot even report that an inferential process of any kind has occurred. The accuracy of subjective reports is so poor as to suggest that any introspec-tive access that may exist is not sufficient to produce generally correct or reliable reports.

2. When reporting on the effects of stimuli, people may not interrogate a memory of the cognitive processes that operated on the stimuli; instead, they may base their reports on implicit, a priori theories about the causal connection between stimulus and response. If the stimulus psychologically implies the response in some way . . . or seems "representative" of the sorts of stimuli that influence the response in question . . . the stimulus is reported to have influenced the response. If the stimulus does not seem to be a plausible cause of the response, it is reported to be noninfluential.

---

theory: "In explaining explanations, attribution theorists have uncritically and un-consciously projected their own (causal) explanatory self-image onto laypersons. In this way, attribution theorists have fallen victim to the ideology of causality" (p. 1312).

3. Subjective reports about higher mental processes are sometimes correct, but even the instances of correct report are not
due to direct introspective awareness. Instead, they are due to
the incidentally correct employment of a priori causal theories.
(p. 233)

Second, beyond the question of accurate report is the question of
accurate inference. From a review of an altogether different body of
literature on judgment and decision-making, Fischoff concludes
that "judgment researchers reveal people to be quite inept at all but
the simplest inferential tasks—and sometimes even at them—
muddling through a world that seems to let them get through life by
gratuitously allowing for a lot of error" (1976, p. 421).

Regardless, however, of how competently humans are able to
process information or of the extent to which existential and causal
beliefs are inferred from observation, it is nonetheless undeniable
that people have such beliefs, and it is reasonable to suppose that
they are important mediators of behavior. Where attitude theorists
have assumed that attitudes are central to social psychology because
these are the major mediators of behavior, attribution theorists,
possibly because of the weak empirical evidence for the attitude-
behavior relation, may have focused upon causal beliefs as major
mediators.[12] We are thus left not only with an attitude-behavior
problem but also with an attribution-behavior problem. Unfortunately, however, the empirical evidence for the (single) attribution-
behavior linkage is not much better than the empirical evidence for
the (single) attitude-behavior linkage.

Nisbett and Wilson's proposal that it is the "a priori theories about
the causal connection between stimulus and response" (1977, p.
233) that are the important mediators of judgment and of behavior
comes close, almost full circle, back to the idea that it is attitudes that
are the main mediators. If we conceive of attitudes as organizations
of various kinds of beliefs that include causal beliefs, we may readily
agree with Nisbett and Wilson about the importance of a priori
causal theories as behavioral mediators; but I would hasten to add
that attitudes consist not only of a priori beliefs concerning causal
connections but also of a priori beliefs about existence, and a priori

12. "There is much evidence, then, that attributions do matter. Man's concern with
the reasons for events does not leave him 'lost in thought' about these reasons.
Rather, his causal explanations play an important role in providing his impetus to
action" (Kelley, 1973, p. 127).

evaluative and prescriptive-proscriptive beliefs—in short, attitudes represent a priori theories of existence, cause, evaluation, and prescription-proscription about objects and situation.

All such beliefs organized into attitudes are assumed to be highly interrelated, and this is empirically testable. Four different scales could be constructed to measure attitude toward, say, a specified object, one composed only of existential statements, the second, third, and fourth composed only of causal, evaluative, and prescriptive-proscriptive statements, respectively. But each of such beliefs is so interwoven with and implies the others that it would be difficult to say that any one type of belief is a more important mediator of behavior than any other type of belief. If I were forced to guess, however, I would hypothesize that prescriptive-proscriptive beliefs, that is, beliefs about desirable means and ends to which objects and situations are perceived to be instrumentally related, should be the most central mediators and thus predictors of behavior. Prescriptive-proscriptive beliefs have a more direct self-reference than do the other types of beliefs; they are the standards we constantly employ to judge and evaluate the competence and morality of our own actions. But all this is highly speculative and I hope that others will help resolve the presently unresolved issue of which types of belief are the most important mediators of behavior.

BELIEF CONGRUENCE

As previously indicated, beliefs, attitudes, and values can be conceptualized as hierarchically organized dispositions to respond preferentially, discriminatingly, or differentially not only to objects and situations, but also to people in general, depending upon whether they agree or disagree with us, and also to social controls, depending upon whether they are congruent or incongruent with our beliefs, attitudes, and values. We are thus oriented to respond selectively to a very wide range of social stimuli, in accord with a general principle that I have previously called the principle of belief congruence (Rokeach, 1960). A considerable body of research has been concerned with the role of belief congruence (which, of course, includes attitude and value congruence) as a determinant of preferential responses, and a controversy has arisen over whether and when belief congruence is sufficiently important to override other kinds of congruence, even race congruence, as a determinant of preferential response. This controversy lingers on in the literature of social psychology and continues to remain unresolved.

While the proposition that individuals and groups are attracted to one another on the basis of belief congruence might be "explained" as arising from a need for balance or cognitive consistency (Brewer & Campbell, 1976; Ashmore & Del Boca, 1976) or by reinforcement theory (Byrne, 1969), the proposition that belief congruence is more important than racial congruence cannot thus be explained. Psychological theory is uniformly silent about the priority or relative potency of these inherently confounding variables. Why should similarity on the basis of belief be claimed to be more important even than similarity on the basis of race?

I would prefer to let the whole matter go by agreeing with Ventimiglia that "Cognitive theories explain what is unique in man as a species" (Note 5). Cognitive similarity is important to humans but not to infrahumans because humans distinctively engage in higher-order reflexive symbolic behavior. They define themselves and are defined by others, compare themselves and are compared by others, in cognitive rather than physical terms. Cognitive similarity is a more important criterion of consistency or reinforcement because, we may suppose, this is what is distinctive about being human. Put somewhat differently and possibly provocatively, I suspect it would be easier to condition dogs to dislike all members of any given race, regardless of belief, than to condition humans to dislike them all, regardless of belief.

Widely cited in discussions of the race-belief controversy is the finding by Triandis and Davis (1965) and also by Goldstein and Davis (1972) that belief similarity is the main determinant of preference or discrimination at less intimate levels, whereas race similarity is the main determinant at more intimate levels. There is little reason to doubt the validity of this finding, since not only has it been reported by others, for example, by Stein, Hardyck and Smith (1965), by Mezei (1971), and by Hendrick, Bixenstein, and Hawkins (1971), but also it is consistent with commonsense and everyday observation of the social facts of life in such countries as the United States, South Africa, and Rhodesia. The finding that racial discrimination increases with intimacy is not an issue, but the conclusion drawn from this finding is.

It is perhaps natural to equate intimate social relations with important social relations and to equate less intimate social relations with "relatively superficial or brief contacts" (Berkowitz, 1975, p. 191). Examples often given of more intimate relations are "dating" and "marriage," and examples of less intimate are "being friends with," "going to coffee with," and "working with." Skepticism about the general validity of the priority of belief over race effects then typically takes the following form: "Yes, but what about dating or marrying someone of another race?" It is thus implied or concluded from studies in which social distance measures systematically are employed that belief similarity is indeed demonstrated to count most in trivial or superficial social relations, but race similarity is what really counts in more important or intimate social relations.

It is possible to take exception to such an implication or conclusion. The issues that typically divide white from black Americans, and that typically define individual and institutional racism, are not about such intimate relations as dating and marriage but about such economic and political relations as discrimination in employment, education, and housing. The latter "less intimate" relations are socially as important, and possibly even more important or salient for everyday intergroup relations and conflict than the former. By conceding that belief is the basis of discrimination only in nonintimate areas the impression that is conveyed (unwittingly, I believe) is that racism in nonintimate areas is not only "relatively superficial" but is also qualitatively different from racism in intimate areas, and therefore that their causes and solutions must also be qualitatively different.

A more serious difficulty with the implication or conclusion typically drawn from race versus belief studies in which social distance measures are employed is that no theoretical explanation is offered to account for the switch of criterion of choice from belief to race as we proceed from the less to the more intimate. Why should race be more important at more intimate levels and belief more important at less intimate levels? Does it mean that balance principles or cognitive consistency theories are explanatory only at less intimate, that is to say, only at trivial levels? Does it mean that humans follow the laws of conditioning to race at intimate levels but follow the laws of conditioning to belief as they engage in less intimate relations?

We obviously need a theoretically parsimonious explanation that would not only account for all the empirical findings but one that would also take the mystery out of the observed switch from belief to race as the criterion for discrimination as we move from the less to the more intimate. I believe that all the known facts, those deriving from informal observation of everyday life in the United States and other countries, as well as from all the empirical studies on the race-belief issue, are consistent with the following two assumptions. First, belief is more important than race as a determinant of discrimination at all levels of social interaction—up to and including marriage. Second, the more intimate the social interaction the more it is also likely to be permanent and public (Allen, 1978) and to have far-reaching economic, political, and social consequences; and thus the more likely is it that controls and pressures will emerge from the laws of society, from societal norms, and from significant others to coerce and reward choice on the basis of race, and to suppress, inhibit, or punish choice on the basis of belief. Even genuinely color-blind persons, within whom race may be altogether absent as a psychological consideration, can be confidently expected to discriminate on the basis of race if coercion is strong enough. If social pressure to discriminate on the basis of race is powerful enough, as in the traditional South, Nazi Germany, or South Africa, all people will discriminate on the basis of race, regardless of level of intimacy, attitude toward object or situation, or toward social controls coercing conformity, or psychological preference for belief or race.

Various empirical findings are, I believe, wholly consistent with these two assumptions. In the Philippines, where the social pressures to discriminate on the basis of race are probably weaker than those found in the United States, belief is found to be a more important determinant of choice at all levels of social intimacy—including marriage (Willis & Bulatao, Note 6).[13] Rokeach and Mezei (1966) found that belief is a more important determinant of choice

13. Ashmore and Del Boca (1976) in their review of the research on the race-belief controversy summarize the findings of Willis and Bulatao (Note 6) as follows: "Race was found to be more important than belief for marriage acceptance by Filipino subjects" (p. 92). I believe they have misread Willis and Bulatao's findings: "On the average, belief accounts for about 30 times as much variance as does ethnicity in the friendship ratings, while the corresponding ratio for marriage is about 20" (Willis & Bulatao, Note 6). The difference between the 30-to-1 and 20-to-1 belief-to-race ratio for friendship and marriage is then validly claimed by these authors to provide support for "Triandis' contention that group membership becomes relatively more important as the intimacy of the social relationship increases" (p. 6). While this is true, it does not support Triandis' contention that race is more important than belief as intimacy increases.

even when there are real consequences of such choice—even when unemployed workers believed they were selecting potential work partners. Silverman (1974) found belief to be more important than race even when entering freshmen were led to expect that their roommates would actually be assigned on the basis of their expressed preference. I cannot agree that we have here instances wherein "the actual behavioral consequences of their decisions were relatively minor" (Ashmore & Del Boca, 1976, p. 92)—unless they mean by "minor" anything short of interracial dating and marriage. Silverman and Cochrane (1972) found that white home owners in Lansing "felt more pressure to discriminate against Negroes as members of their families than as potential home purchasers, while perceiving more social pressure to discriminate against Negroes as potential home purchasers than as friends" (p. 263). Summarizing their findings, they report "that as perceived social pressure to discriminate against Negroes increases across a situation, the importance of race as a factor in social choice also increases" (p. 266). Mezei (1971) found that when perceived social pressure from parents and friends to discriminate on the basis of race is held constant, that is, when the confounding effects of perceived social pressure are removed statistically, belief overrides race as a determinant of choice at all levels of social intimacy— including marriage.

Now, Dienstbier (1972) advocates that we dismiss such data as Mezei's on the effects of perceived social pressure on the ground that they are "unfortunately, not free from the alternative interpretation that race prejudice is very real, and that subjects see other people as sharing their prejudice in order to defend their own views and because (as the belief theory suggests) they want to believe that others largely share their beliefs and values" (p. 148). Dienstbier's criticism erroneously implies that proponents of the belief congruence position do not see "that race prejudice is very real." As previously stated, the phenomenon of race prejudice is not in doubt or dispute. What is debatable is the question of what exactly those who discriminate on the basis of race are responding to. The issue is not what is the *response* but what is the *stimulus*. And if we pin down the stimulus, we are probably not identifying the cause of prejudice but merely the eliciting stimulus.[14]

---

14. The cause of prejudice is an altogether different matter—one that must surely be situated in socioeconomic conditions rather than attributed to such psychological variables as belief or race dissimilarity.

Dienstbier moreover suggests that Mezei's subjects had invented or conjured up a set of social pressures that in fact did not exist, in order to defend themselves against their own "race-prejudiced" views. Such a proposal implies that Mezei's subjects were aware of the fact that (a) they had discriminated on race rather than belief on more intimate, and on belief rather than race on less intimate relations, (b) accused themselves or anticipated being accused by others of doing so, (c) felt ashamed or guilty about it, (d) and therefore rationalized or defended themselves against such self-accusations, or anticipated accusations by others, by projecting a set of social pressures onto the external world that did not actually exist. All this seems unlikely, given the social rather than the purely reductionistic, individual origins of discrimination, and given the complex randomized presentation of stimulus persons and social distance measures employed in Mezei's study. And it is also unlikely for another reason as well.

Even if there are methodological flaws in studies that measure perceived social pressure rather than actual social pressure, I believe Dienstbier dismisses the social pressure explanation, which has been employed in a number of studies (Acock & DeFleur, 1972; Mezei, 1971; Silverman, 1974; Silverman & Cochrane, 1972) rather prematurely. There are altogether independent grounds for believing that social pressures coercing people to discriminate on the basis of race are real and pervasive, even if actual social pressure is difficult to measure. Pettigrew has shown (1958, 1959) that prejudice against blacks in South Africa and in the traditional South is more a function of conformity than of authoritarianism. This is but another way of saying that racial discrimination is more a function of social controls or pressures to discriminate on the basis of race than of authoritarianism. The more a response is believed to be to social pressures to conform, the less reason there is to think that it is a response to anything else. Intimate relations between races are routinely discouraged in racist societies by social controls that coerce discrimination on the basis of race, and the existence of social controls can thus explain why discriminations are made to race even if not a soul were so predisposed to respond.

I now go on to consider in some detail a closely related point. Triandis and Davis (1965) bolster their intimate-nonintimate qualification of the belief congruence principle with a closely related qualification, namely, that there are two types of people, the belief-prejudiced and the race-prejudiced. "Some people are particularly sensitive to race (they are 'race' or 'conventionally' prejudiced), but

others are particularly sensitive to belief dissimilarity ('belief' prejudiced). The racially prejudiced show greater prejudice in situations
of intermediate intimacy, and they give some importance to race in
formal (nonintimate) situations. On the other hand, the belief
prejudiced respond only to belief dissimilarity in non-intimate
social situations" (Triandis, 1971, p. 131).

Again, I would suggest, there is a question of theoretical interpretation of such empirical findings. The finding that there are these
two kinds of prejudiced people, or these two kinds of sensitivity, is
one that demands theoretical explanation. Triandis's explanation
that their "relative importance is largely because of differences in
subculture and personality" (1971, p. 133) is not altogether satisfying because the differences are not further specified.

I do not believe that it will be any more possible to provide a
satisfying theoretical explanation for the two types of prejudice or
sensitivity than to provide one for the proposition that the belief
congruence principle applies to nonintimate and the race congruence principle to intimate relations. If a "race-prejudiced" person is
operationally defined as one who (in the absence of social control) is
observed to respond on the basis of race to a stimulus person
varying on both race and belief, we may legitimately inquire: Precisely which beliefs had been attributed to the stimulus person, and
how important was the belief that had been pitted against race?
Would race override belief no matter how central the belief? In most
of the empirical research that has been conducted on the race versus
belief issue little attention has been paid to the question of the effects
of the centrality of the belief that can be attributed to the stimulus
person, and belief is treated almost as if it were as homogeneous a
variable as race.

But beliefs vary in importance, and the "race-prejudiced" person
empirically found by Triandis and Davis (1965) via factor analysis
may be understood to differ from the "belief-prejudiced" person
only in the centrality of belief required to elicit the belief effect. If the
belief that is explicitly linked to race is not sufficiently important for
any given person, a race effect will typically be observed, and that
person will be diagnosed as "race-prejudiced" rather than "belief-
prejudiced." But such a race effect is more apparent than real. It may
mean only that the belief variable that had been employed was not
potent enough to override race for a particular person. We must
assure ourselves that the "race-prejudiced" person, that is, a person

who seemingly discriminates on the basis of race, is not implicitly conjuring up or attributing other central beliefs, attitudes, and values to the stimulus person, over and above those that had been explicitly attributed to the stimulus person. A "race-prejudiced" person, if one really exists, should show a race effect no matter how central the belief, attitude, or value that is being pitted against race.

In a study I carried out in 1967, in collaboration with Judy Goldbaum, which is reported here for the first time, we tried to ascertain whether seemingly "race-prejudiced" persons, that is, persons who exhibit a race effect, could be induced under certain conditions to reveal that they were really "belief-prejudiced" persons, that is, to exhibit a belief effect. This study was carried out with 440 white introductory psychology students at Michigan State University. Of these 440 students, only 10% (46 persons) could be identified as "race-prejudiced," defined as those who indicated that they preferred more as a friend a white person with incongruent beliefs—either about God, or communism, or both—to a black person with congruent beliefs.[15] We then selected for comparison 46 nonracists from the remaining 90% of the students who were exactly matched with the 46 racists on age, sex, state of birth, and belief position on God and communism. We then compared these 46 racists and nonracists, so defined, on their friendship preferences for hypothetical black and white stimulus persons who were varied systematically on four values—honest, clean, intelligent, and responsible. The research design was identical with the one originally reported by Rokeach, Smith, and Evans (1960), systematically employing stimulus persons such as "A white person who is clean," "A Negro person who is clean," "A white person who is not clean," "A Negro person who is not clean," and so on. Each stimulus person was rated on a nine-point friendship scale. All told, 24 stimulus persons were presented. Of these 8 varied on race and belief (God and communism) and, as indicated, we selected the 46 racists and nonracists on the basis of their responses to these for

15. All respondents first stated whether they did or did not believe in God and whether they were pro- or anti-communist. Of these 46 "racists," 8 were "hard-core" racists, preferring whites with incongruent beliefs to blacks with congruent beliefs on both of these issues. The remaining 38 "racists" preferred the belief-incongruent white over the belief-congruent black on only one or the other of these two issues. All of the remaining 440 students were found to be typically "belief-prejudiced," and, less typically, they indicated an equal preference for stimulus persons varying on race and belief.

further comparison. The remaining 16 stimulus persons varied on race and value. Would the 46 "race-prejudiced" persons still prefer whites with incongruent values over blacks with congruent values?

Shown in the upper part of Table 1 are the exact number of white racists and nonracists who preferred as friends blacks with compatible beliefs concerning God and communism. Notice that 34 of the 46 racists had indicated that they preferred more as a friend a white person with incompatible belief in God than a black person who believed as they did (overwhelmingly, they preferred a white atheist to a black believer in God); the comparable figure for nonracists is zero out of 46. Notice also that 21 of the 46 racists had indicated a preference for a white person who disagreed with them about communism over a black who agreed (overwhelmingly, they preferred a white communist to a black anti-communist); and again, the comparable figure for nonracists is zero out of 46. There were no surprises here, though, because racists and nonracists were initially

Table 1

Number of subjects who prefer blacks who agree more than, equal to, or less than whites who disagree

		Black Is Preferred		
		More than white	Equal to white	Less than white
God	Racists	9	3	34
	Nonracists	34	12	0
Communism	Racists	16	9	21
	Nonracists	32	14	0
Honest	Racists	42	3	1
	Nonracists	45	1	0
Clean	Racists	35	7	4
	Nonracists	46	0	0
Intelligent	Racists	30	8	8
	Nonracists	40	3	3
Responsible	Racists	30	6	10
	Nonracists	44	2	0

defined and selected on the basis of their responses to these race-belief stimulus persons.

As we glance further down Table I to the race versus value choices we will notice, however, a dramatic change from these base-line results shown in the upper part of the table: now 42, 35, 30, and 30 out of 46 racists, respectively, prefer an honest, clean, intelligent, or responsible black to a dishonest, unclean, unintelligent, or irresponsible white. The same 46 "race-prejudiced" persons who had indicated they preferred as friends whites with incompatible beliefs about God and communism over blacks with compatible beliefs now overwhelmingly inform us they prefer blacks with compatible values. These racists now seem to be choosing their friends more as the nonracists do.[16]

There are other ways of showing the effects of race versus belief versus value in discrimination. Our research design permits us to compute five different discrimination scores for each subject, as follows:

(1) Race discrimination score (the total amount of preference shown for all white stimulus persons minus the total preference for all black stimulus persons). Here, belief is held constant.

(2) Belief discrimination score (the total amount of preference shown for all stimulus persons with compatible beliefs in God and communism minus the total preference for stimulus persons with incompatible beliefs). Here, race is held constant.

(3) Value discrimination score (the total amount of preference shown for all stimulus persoons with compatible values minus the total preference for those with incompatible values). Here, race is again held constant.

(4) Race-belief discrimination score (the total difference in preferences shown to pairs of stimulus persons in which both race and belief were varied). Here, we cannot tell whether the discrimination is to race or belief.

---

16. But not altogether so. One can still clearly note in Table I some lingering race effects. The centrality threshold has been almost but not completely reached or breached for all racist respondents by the four values considered separately. The findings suggest that there remain additional value connotations in our racial stimuli, over and above the four tapped here, when presented one at a time. For example, how would our 46 racists have responded to a "white person who is dishonest *and* unclean *and* unintelligent *and* irresponsible" versus a "black who is honest *and* clean *and* intelligent *and* responsible"?

(5) Race-value discrimination score (the total difference in preferences shown to pairs of stimulus persons in which both race and value were varied). Here we cannot tell whether the discrimination is to race or value.

Now, if we consider measures 4 and 5 as the dependent variables and measures 1, 2, and 3 as the independent variables, we may ask whether discrimination to racial stimuli (measure 1) or to belief stimuli (measure 2) or to value stimuli (measure 3) is the more closely related to discriminations to the two confounded dependent measures. Tables 2 and 3 show these correlations. Consider first the results shown in Table 2. For the nonracists it is clear that dependent variable 4 (discriminations to stimuli varying on both race and belief) is negligibly correlated with discriminations based only on race (measure 1) and almost perfectly correlated with discriminations based only on belief (measure 2). For the racists, however, we see that discrimination to both race and belief stimuli are correlates of race and belief discrimination, with race discrimination being the somewhat larger correlate. Consider now the results shown in Table 3.

Here we see that for racists and nonracists alike, the dependent measure (measure 5) is uncorrelated with racial discrimination and is very highly correlated with discrimination on basis of value. These data support those shown in Table 1, and both together suggest that people, even those allegedly "race-prejudiced," typically do not make discriminations on the basis of race when confronted with stimuli that vary simultaneously on race and on extremely central beliefs called values.

Table 2

Correlations between discrimination responses when both race and belief are varied (type 4) with race discrimination responses (type 1) and belief discrimination responses (type 2)

Correlations between race-belief difference score and:	Nonracists	Racists
Race difference score	.13	.67
Belief difference score	.99	.51

These data not only suggest, contrary perhaps to common sense, that there may be no such person as a "race-prejudiced" person, that is, a person who uniformly discriminates on color regardless of belief or social control, but also suggest that however important race might be, it is generally far less important than such very important beliefs as those that people have about God and communism.[17] And they moreover suggest that values are even more important. How much more important?

Nelson (1965) obtained an estimate of the amount of variance that can be apportioned to race, belief, and value from another study carrid out at about the same time, in which stimulus persons were systematically varied on all three variables simultaneously—race, belief, and value. One hundred students in introductory psychology courses at Michigan State University responded to such stimulus persons as the following: "An honest (dishonest) white (Negro) who is a pro-communist (anti-communist)." Two races, three beliefs (communism, God, and equal rights) and six values (honest, sincere, tolerant, patient, sociable, and efficient) totaling 48 stimulus persons were thus systematically presented. The findings showed that values, beliefs, and race accounted for 54.4, 39.4, and 6.2% of the variance, respectively. To be sure, these findings were obtained for friendship ratings and once again a question may be raised as to whether they would also hold for more intimate relations. My guess is that they would, but to a lesser extent, if perceived social pressure is present. But if social pressure is absent, or

Table 3
Correlations between discrimination responses when both race and value are varied (type 5) with race discrimination responses (type 1) and value discrimination responses (type 3)

Correlations between race-value difference score and:	Nonracists	Racists
Race difference score	.06	.08
Value difference score	.97	.85

17. Recall that only 10% of our 440 respondents preferred as friends those of the same race having incongruent beliefs on God and communism.

statistically controlled, I would anticipate that the results would be essentially the same for marriage as for friendship since all the known results and informal observations seem to be instigated by belief differences, or by beliefs about social control, rather than demographic race differences.

COGNITIVE CHANGE AND BEHAVIORAL CHANGE

No discussion of value-attitude-behavior relations would be complete if it did not also consider the effects of cognitive change on behavioral change, and the effects of behavioral change on cognitive change. The great majority of experimental studies on attitude change have typically not addressed themselves to such questions and have instead focused their attention mainly elsewhere—on the testing of hypotheses designed to confirm one or another theoretical proposition derived from learning or dissonance or self-perception or attribution theory. The main aim is theory-confirmation (Silverman, 1977) rather than improved understanding of the directive nature of attitudes or of the consequences of attitude change for behavior change. Attitudes are typicallly treated as following rather than determining action, as dependent rather than independent variables—as dependent variables that, as Kelman (1974) has noted, are not much more than cognitive adjustments or epiphenomena. And, as Calder and Ross (1976) have noted: "The major focus of social psychologists has been attitude change. Attitude change can be demonstrated by merely comparing attitude measures; it does not require any serious consideration of the psychological foundations of attitude" (p. 6).

Our discipline, I believe, started out being interested in attitudes and attitude change because these were thought to have important consequences, but it seems to have ended up concentrating its theoretical and experimental attention almost exclusively on studying their antecedents.[18] In contemporary theory and research we may note a curious indifference to or possibly even an evasion of questions about the consequences of attitudes and attitude change.

18. Major exceptions that come to mind are Newcomb's Bennington study (1943, 1967) and his study of the acquaintance process (1961), both of which are field studies that were concerned, in part, with the effects of attitude change on behavior change.

The few studies that have directed attention to this problem have forced Festinger (1964) to conclude that the evidence for the attitude change–behavior change relation is unimpressive, perhaps parallel to and no better than that for the attitude-behavior relation.[19] Theoretically, however, there is about as little reason to expect that any single attitude change should culminate in a behavior change as there is reason to expect that any single attitude should be related to or predict a specified behavior.

The rarity of experimental studies of the effects of attitude change on behavior change, and the unimpressiveness of the few studies that have addressed themselves to this issue, could both be regarded as symptoms of an as-yet missing consensus not only about what attitudes have to do with behavior but also about the functional nature of attitudes. The conceptual definitions of beliefs, attitudes, and values offered at the beginning of this article attempt to go beyond traditional definitions to suggest not only how these concepts are defined but also to provide an account of how they are oganized together to form a cognitive system, what functions attitudes serve for value-realization, and, in turn, what function value-realization serves for self-maintenance and self-enhancement.

Countless objects and situations, about which we develop beliefs organized into attitudes, have meaning for us only insofar as they are perceived to be instrumental to the realization of a relatively small handful of values. These values are cognitive representations of human needs on the one hand and of societal demands on the other. They take the psychological form of prescriptive or proscriptive beliefs about the desirable or undesirable means and ends of action. They are organized hierarchically to serve as standards or criteria (Williams, 1979) that the socialized self—a self born with biological needs continuously shaped by societal demands—employs to judge the efficacy of itself not only as a competent self (Bandura, 1977) but also as a moral self. One or more of such a relatively small number of values are implicated and activated whenever a person is required to act with respect to whatever the

19. Since Festinger's 1964 paper, I have come across a few additional studies reporting on the effects of attitude change on behavioral change (Freedman, 1965; Greenwald, 1965, 1966; Leventhal, 1970). Findings from these studies are mixed and, when added to those reviewed by Festinger, do not warrant revision of the conclusion that such findings generally parallel those obtained for the attitude-behavior relation. In any event, I think it rather extraordinary to find so few attitude change– behavior change studies in the experimental literature of social psychology.

object in whatever the situation. The function of encounter and experience with objects-in-situations is not only to satisfy a need for balance or to revert the self back to some earlier state of balance but also to satisfy self-realization needs; put another way, their function is to satisfy one's need for self-enhancement, *growth*, insofar as possible, and for self-maintenance, *balance*, only insofar as necessary. There is thus a continuous interaction between cognitions about the self, cognitions about what are the desirable means and ends of action, various cognitions (existential, causal, evaluative, prescriptive-proscriptive) about objects and situations, cognitions about one's own behavior, and cognitions about the values, the attitudes, and the behavior of significant others.

Kelman, in his analysis (1974), draws attention to three major types of discrepancy conducive to attitude change: discrepancy between attitude and information about reality, between one's own and significant others' attitudes, and between attitude and behavior. If we broaden the inquiry to also include other types of discrepancy that might be conducive to change, particularly to include discrpancies implicating values and self-cognitions, a much larger matrix of discrepancies can be generated (Rokeach, 1973, pp. 220–221). And, I have argued (Rokeach, 1973), the most important discrepancies, those that are the most conducive to changes that will be persisting rather than ephemeral—to value as well as attitude change, to behavioral as well as cognitive change, in short, to changes that will have the widest and most enduring repercussions in cognitions and behavior—are those discrepancies that deeply implicate and threaten self-cognitions.

Discrepancies that implicate self-cognitions are considered to be the most important initiators of change because they threaten self-maintenance and self-enhancement. Awareness of such discrepancies leads to self-dissatisfaction, and the experience of self-dissatisfaction is seen to be the major mechanism that initiates a process of cognitive and behavioral change. Conversely, self-satisfaction is seen to be the major mechanism that maintains stability in cognitions and behavior. To the extent that people experience consistency between cognitions about themselves and other cognitions—their values, their attitudes, cognitions about their behavior, cognitions about the values, attitudes, and behavior of significant reference persons and groups—they will have no reason not to remain satisfied with themselves as competent and moral people, and therefore their total cognitive system should be stably maintained. But to the extent that they experience a discrepancy (or inconsistency, or contradiction) between self-cognitions and other cognitions, they will experience a sense of self-dissatisfaction about their competence or morality, or at least a sense of self-dissatisfaction that is less than they are willing to tolerate. I believe that it is this phenomenal experience of self-dissatisfaction, which is reportable and measureable, which is the most crucial variable initiating a process of enduring change in cognitions and behavior—in the experimental social psychologist's laboratory, in the clinic, and in everyday life. Thus, in the final analysis, I have come to view the problem of attitude change and behavior change as being ultimately linked to the problem of how changes are brought about in the self.

The preceding account merely summarizes and updates a view of the conditions leading to long-term value, attitude and behavioral change that I have spelled out in more detail earlier (Rokeach, 1973). A fair body of evidence is now available that seems to be consistent with such a formulation and has been reviewed elsewhere (Rokeach, 1979b). The basic paradigm is the same for all such studies: Via the method of self-confrontation, experimental subjects are given feedback designed to increase self-awareness about their own and others' values, and how their own and others' values are related to specified attitudes and behaviors. In this way many experimental subjects discover discrepancies or contradictions implicating their self-conceptions, and the psychological mechanism that is aroused in such subjects is a specific state of self-dissatisfaction that they can identify for themselves.

To summarize the findings from these studies briefly, I can do no better than to quote from the paper (Rokeach, 1979b) in which I have reviewed all the research findings to date:

The effects of self-dissatisfaction with one's values at the end of the treatment on subsequent value change have been investigated in nine . . . studies. All of these studies, without exception, report significant value change as a function of self-dissatisfaction (p. 17)

In 21 out of the 22 studies in which value change was ascertained, the investigators reported significant change in at least one theoretically expected value, in one or more posttests—95 percent. In the nine experiments in which value-related attitude changes were ascertained, significant changes were reported in seven of these, or 78 percent. Finally, value-related behavioral changes were ascertained in 13 of these studies, and significant long-term behavioral effects were reported in six of these, or 46 percent. (p. 18)

The research reviewed here suggests that it is possible to bring about socially-desirable long-term changes in values and in related attitudes and behavior with respect to such diverse issues as racism, ecology, health, and teaching, and that such changes can be brought about by a single experimental session. Messages in such a session may issue forth from a human experimenter, an interactive computer, a closed-circuit television set, or the printed word, and they may reach single or many persons. Variations in the prestigefulness of source (Rokeach, 1973, p. 316), the channel of communication (Sanders & Atwood, 1979), or the personality of the receiver (Rokeach, 1973, p. 307) do not seem to make much difference: long-term effects are reported to occur regardless of such differences. (pp. 24–25)

As I come to the end of this essay, I must content myself with the realization that there are surely other unresolved issues in theories of beliefs, attitudes, and values than those I have selected. I assume that the other participants to this volume will have discussed some of these same issues, will have raised yet others, and will have propoed their own solutions and resolutions. Whatever these may be, I hope that readers stimulated by the various contributions to this symposium will be able to come up with more comprehensive and systematic formulations in the future. The best that I have been able to come up with after having grappled with these unresolved issues over the past few decades is to view attitudes, in the plural, as having everything to do with social behavior, to see attitudes as serving values, to see values as serving the self, and to see all of us striving for the same two things: to hang onto or enhance whatever sense of competence and morality we have been able to accumulate as a result of living in society. And I see signs, at least, of an increasing convergence in the theoretical thinking of social psychologists on the concept of self (Bandura, 1977; Smith, 1978), and in defining at least one of the components in consistency theories as always including self-conceptions (Malewski, 1962; Deutsch,

Krauss, & Rosenau, 1962; Frentzel, 1965; Aronson, 1968; Rokeach, 1968a, 1973; Greenwald & Ronis, 1978).

I therefore arrive at the view that the classical central concern of social psychology that Allport had so ably and effectively drawn to our attention should now be expanded to include the self and the values that are employed as standards of conduct and ultimate strivings, as well as attitudes—in that order.

REFERENCE NOTES

1. Abelson, R. P. *Scripts.* Paper presented at Annual Meetings of Midwestern Psychological Association, May 1978.
2. Regan, J. F., & Rokeach, M. *Personal and corporate values of managers from several levels of an organization.* Unpublished manuscript, 1979.
3. Munson, J. J., & Posner, B. Z. *The use of value paradigms in discriminating job classifications.* Unpublished manuscript, 1978.
4. Rankin, W. L. *Human value conflicts concerning nuclear power.* Paper presented at Annual Meetings of American Psychological Association, Toronto, Canada, Aug. 28–Sept. 1, 1978.
5. Ventimiglia, J. C. *Theoretical convergencies in the two social psychologies: Some comments on the crisis in the field.* Paper presented at the Annual Meetings of the Americal Sociological Association, San Francisco, September, 1978.
6. Willis, R. H., & Bulatao, R. *Belief and ethnicity as determinants of friendship and marriage acceptance in the Philippines.* Paper presented at the Annual Meetings of the American Psychological Association, Washington, D. C., September, 1967.

REFERENCES

Abelson, R. P. Are attitudes necessary? In B. King & E. McGinnies (Eds.), *Attitudes, conflicts, and social change.* New York: Academic Press, 1972.
Acock, A., & DeFleur, M. A. A configurational approach to contingent consistency in the attitude-behavior relationship. *American Sociological Review*, 1972, **37**, 714–726.

Adorno, T. W., Frenkel-Brunswik, E., Levinson, D. J., & Sanford, R. N. *The authoritarian personality.* New York: Harper, 1950.

Ajzen, I., & Fishbein, M. Attitudinal and normative variables as predictors of specific behaviors. *Journal of Personality and Social Psychology*, 1973, **27**, 41–57.

Ajzen, I., & Fishbein, M. Attitude-behavior relations: A theoretical analysis and review of empirical research. *Psychological Bulletin*, 1977, **84**, 888–918.

Allen, B. P. *Social behavior: Fact and falsehood.* Chicago: Nelson Hall, 1978.

Allport, G. W., Vernon, P. E., & Lindzey, G. *A study of values.* Boston: Houghton Mifflin, 1960.

Aronson, E. Dissonance theory: Progress and problems. In R. P. Abelson et al. (Eds.), *Theories of cognitive consistency: A sourcebook.* Chicago: Rand McNally, 1968.

Ashmore, R. D., & Del Boca, F. K. Psychological approaches to understanding intergroup conflicts. In P. A. Katz (Ed.), *Toward the elimination of racism.* New York: Pergammon Press, 1976.

Audi, R. On the conception and measurement of attitudes in contemporary Anglo-American psychology. *Journal of Theory and Social Behavior*, 1972, **2**, 179–203.

Bandura, A. Self-efficacy: Toward a unifying theory of behavioral change. *Psychological Review*, 1977, **84**, 191–215.

Berkowitz, L. *A survey of social psychology.* Hinsdale, Ill.: Dryden, 1975.

Blumer, H. Attitudes and the social act. *Social Problems*, 1955, **3**, 59–64.

Brewer, M. B., & Campbell, D. T. *Ethnocentrism and intergroup attitudes.* New York: Wiley, 1976.

Bruner, J. S., Goodnow, J., & Austin, G. A. *A study of thinking.* New York: Wiley, 1956.

Buss, A. R. Causes and reasons in attribution theory: A conceptual critique. *Journal of Personality and Social Psychology*, 1978, **36**, 1311–1321.

Byrne, D. Attitudes and attraction. In L. Berkowitz (Ed.), *Advances in experimental social psychology* (Vol. 4). New York: Academic Press, 1969.

Calder, B. J., & Ross, M. *Attitudes and behavior.* Morristown, NJ.: General Learning Press, 1973.

Calder, B. J., & Ross, M. *Attitudes: Theories and issues.* Morristown, NJ.: General Learning Press, 1976.

Carlson, E. R. Attitude change through modification of attitude structure. *Journal of Abnormal and Social Psychology*, 1956, **52**, 256–261.

Cochrane, R., Billig, M., & Hogg, M. Values as correlates of political orientations. In M. Rokeach (Ed.), *Understanding human values: Individual and societal.* New York: Free Press, 1979.

Cohen, P. S. Social attitudes and sociological inquiry. *British Journal of Sociology*, 1966, **17**, 341–352.

Deutsch, M., Krauss, R. M., & Rosenau, N. Dissonance or defensiveness? *Journal of Personality*, 1962, **30**, 16–28.

Dienstbier, R. A. A modified belief theory of prejudice emphasizing the mutual causality of racial prejudice and anticipated belief differences. *Psychological Review*, 1972, **79**, 146–160.

Doob, L. W. The behavior of attitudes. *Psychological Review*, 1947, **54**, 135–156.

England, G. W., Olsen, K., & Agarwal, N. *A manual of development and research for the Personal Values Questionnaire*. Minneapolis: University of Minnesota Press, 1971.

Feather, N. *Values in education and society*. New York: Free Press, 1975.

Feather, N. Value importance, conservatism, and age. *European Journal of Social Psychology*, 1977, **7**, 241–245.

Festinger, L. Behavior support for opinion change. *Public Opinion Quarterly*, 1964, **28**, 404–417.

Fischoff, B. Attribution theory and judgment under uncertainty. In J. H. Harvey, W. J. Ickes, & R. F. Kidd (Eds.), *New directions in attribution research* (Vol. 1). Hillsdale, NJ.: Lawrence Erlbaum Associates, 1976.

Fishbein, M., & Ajzen, I. *Belief, attitude, intention, and behavior*. Reading, MA.: Addison-Wesley, 1975.

Freedman, J. L. Long-term behavioral effects of cognitive dissonance. *Journal of Experimental Social Psychology*, 1965, **1**, 145–155.

Frentzel, J. Cognitive consistency and positive self-concept. *Polish Psychological Bulletin*, 1965, **1**, 71–86.

Goldstein, M., & Davis, E. E. Race and belief: A further analysis of the social determinants of behavioral intentions. *Journal of Personality and Social Psychology*, 1972, **22**, 346–355.

Gordon, L. V. *The measurement of personal values*. Chicago: Science Research Associates, 1975.

Greenwald, A. G. Behavior change following a persuasive communication. *Journal of Personality*, 1965, **33**, 370–391.

Greenwald, A. G. Effects of prior commitment on behavior change after a persuasive communication. *Public Opinion Quarterly*, 1966, **29**, 595–601.

Greenwald, A. G., & Ronis, D. L. Twenty years of cognitive dissonance: Case study of the evolution of a theory. *Psychological Review*, 1978, **85**, 53–57.

Harvey, J. H., & Smith, W. P. *Social psychology: An attributional analysis*. St. Louis: Mosby, 1977.

Heberlein, T. A., & Black, J. S. Attitudinal specificity and the prediction of behavior in a field setting. *Journal of Personality and Social Psychology*, 1976, **33**, 474–479.

Heider, F. *The psychology of interpersonal relations*. New York: Wiley, 1958.

Hendrick, D., Bixenstein, V., & Hawkins, G. Race versus belief similarity as determinants of attraction: A search for a fair test. *Journal of Personality and Social Psychology*, 1971, **17**, 250–258.

Hollen, C. C. *Value change, perceived instrumentality, and attitude change.* Unpublished doctoral dissertation, Michigan State University, 1972.

Homant, R. *Values, attitudes, and perceived instrumentality.* Unpublished doctoral dissertation, Michigan State University, 1970.

Jones, E. E., & Nisbett, R. E. The actor and the observer: Divergent perceptions of the causes of behavior. In E. E. Jones, D. E. Kanouse, H. H. Kelley, R. E. Nisbett, S. Valins, & B. Weiner (Eds.), *Attribution: Perceiving the causes of behavior.* Morristown, NJ.: General Learning Corp., 1972.

Jones, E. E., & Thibaut, J. W. Interaction goals as bases of inference in interpersonal perception. In R. Tagiuri & L. Petrullo (Ed.), *Person perception and interpersonal behavior.* Stanford, CA.: Stanford University Press, 1958.

Katz, D. The functional approach to the study of attitudes. *Public Opinion Quarterly*, 1960, **24**, 163–204.

Kelley, H. H. Attribution theory in social psychology. In D. Levine (Ed.), *Nebraska Symposium on Motivation 1967* (Vol. 15). Lincoln: University of Nebraska Press, 1968.

Kelley, H. H. The processes of causal attribution. *American Psychologist*, 1973, **28**, 107–128.

Kelman, H. C. Attitudes are alive and well and gainfully employed in the sphere of action. *American Psychologist*, 1974, **29**, 310–324.

Kiesler, C. A., & Munson, P. A. Attitudes and opinions. In M. R. Rosenzweig & L. W. Porter (Eds.), *Annual Review of Psychology.* Palo Alto, CA.: Annual Reviews, Inc., 1975.

Kruglanski, A. W. The endogenous-exogenous partition in attribution theory. *Psychological Review*, 1975, **82**, 387–406.

Kutner, B., Wilkins, C., & Yarrow, P. R. Verbal attitudes and overt behavior involving racial prejudice. *Journal of Abnormal and Social Psychology*, 1952, **47**, 649–652.

LaPiere, R. T. Attitudes versus actions. *Social Forces*, 1934, **13**, 230–237.

Leventhal, H. Findings and theory in the study of fear communications. In L. Berkowitz (Ed.), *Advances in experimental social psychology.* New York: Academic Press, 1970.

Levitin, T. Values. In J. P. Robinson & P. R. Shaver (Eds.), *Measures of social psychological attitudes.* Ann Arbor, MI.: Institute for Social Research, 1973.

Malewski, A. The influence of positive and negative self-evaluation on post-decisional dissonance. *Polish Sociological Bulletin*, 1962, **3–4**, 39–49.

McGuire, W. J. The nature of attitudes and attitude change. In G. Lindzey & E. Aronson (Eds.), *The handbook of social psychology* (Vol. 3). Reading, MA.: Addison-Wesley, 1969.

Mezei, L. Perceived social pressure as an explanation of shifts in the relative influence of race and belief across social interactions. *Journal of Personality and Social Psychology*, 1971, **19**, 69–81.

Nelson, A. M. *Race, belief, and values as determinants of discrimination*. Unpublished Master's thesis, Michigan State University, 1965.

Newcomb, T. M. *Personality and social change: Attitude formation in a student community*. New York: Dryden, 1943.

Newcomb, T. M. *The acquaintance process*. New York: Holt, Rinehart & Winston, 1961.

Newcomb, T. M., Koenig, K. E., Flacks, R., & Warwick, D. P. *Persistence and change: Bennington College and its students after twenty-five years*. New York: Wiley, 1967.

Nisbett, R. E., & Wilson, T. C. Telling more than we can know: Verbal reports on mental processes. *Psychological Review*, 1977, **84**, 231–259.

Orvis, B. R., Kelley, H. H., & Butler, D. Attributional conflict in young couples. In J. H. Harvey, W. J. Ickes, & R. F. Kidd (Eds.), *New directions in attribution research* (Vol. 1). Hillsdale, NJ.: Lawrence Erlbaum Associates, 1976.

Peak, H. Attitude and motivation. In M. R. Jones (Ed.), *Nebraska Symposium on Motivation 1955* (Vol. 3). Lincoln: University of Nebraska Press, 1955.

Pettigrew, T. F. Personality and sociocultural factors in intergroup attitudes: A cross-national comparison. *Journal of Conflict Resolution*, 1958, **2**, 29–42.

Pettigrew, T. F. Regional differences in anti-Negro prejudice. *Journal of Abnormal and Social Psychology*, 1959, **59**, 28–36.

Rokeach, M. *The open and closed mind*. New York: Basic Books, 1960.

Rokeach, M. *The three Christs of Ypsilanti*. New York: Knopf, 1964.

Rokeach, M. *Value survey*. Sunnyvale, CA.: Halgren Tests, 873 Persimmon Ave., 1967.

Rokeach, M. A theory of organization and change within value-attitude systems. *Journal of Social Issues*, 1968, **24**, 13–33. (a)

Rokeach, M. *Beliefs, attitudes, and values*. San Francisco: Jossey-Bass, 1968. (b)

Rokeach, M. *The nature of human values*. New York: Free Press, 1973.

Rokeach, M. (Ed.), *Understanding human values: Individual and societal*. New York: Free Press, 1979. (a)

Rokeach, M. Value theory and communication research: Review and commentary. In Nimmo, D. (Ed.), *Communication Yearbook III*, New Brunswick, NJ.: Transaction Books, 1979. (b)

Rokeach, M., & Mezei, L. Race and shared belief as factors in social choice. *Science*, 1966, **151**, 167–172.

Rokeach, M., Smith, P. W., & Evans, R. I. Two kinds of prejudice or one? In M. Rokeach (Ed.), *The open and closed mind*. New York: Basic Books, 1960.

Rosenberg, M. J. Cognitive structure and attitudinal affect. *Journal of Abnormal and Social Psychology*, 1956, **53**, 367–372.

Sanders, K. R., & Atwood, L. E. Value change initiated by the mass media. In M. Rokeach (Ed.), *Understanding human values: Individual and societal.* New York: Free Press, 1979.

Schuman, H., & Johnson, M. P. Attitudes and behavior. In A. Inkeles, J. Coleman, & N. Smelser (Eds.), *Annual review of sociology.* Palo Alto: Annual Reviews, Inc., 1976.

Schwartz, S. H. Temporal instability as a moderator of the attitude-behavior relationship. *Journal of Personality and Social Psychology*, 1978, **36**, 715–724.

Searing, D. D. Measuring politicians' values: Administration and assessment of a ranking technique in the British House of Commons. *American Political Science Review*, 1978, **72**, 65–79.

Silverman, B. I. Consequences, racial discrimination, and the principle of belief congruence. *Journal of Personality and Social Psychology*, 1974, **29**, 497–508.

Silverman, B. I., & Cochrane, R. Effects of the social context on the principle of belief congruence. *Journal of Personality and Social Psychology*, 1972, **22**, 259–268.

Silverman, I. Why social psychology fails. *Canadian Psychological Review*, 1977, **18**, 353–358.

Smith, M. B. Perspectives on selfhood. *American Psychologist*, 1978, **33**, 1053–1063.

Smith, M. B., Bruner, J. S., & White, R. W. *Opinions and personality.* New York: Wiley, 1956.

Stein, D. D., Hardyck, J. A., & Smith, M. B. Race and belief: An open and shut case. *Journal of Personality and Social Psychology*, 1965, **1**, 281–290.

Triandis, H. C. *Attitude and attitude change.* New York: Wiley, 1971.

Triandis, H. C. & Davis, E. E. Race and belief as determinants of behavioral intentions. *Journal of Personality and Social Psychology*, 1965, **2**, 715–725.

Wicker, A. W. Attitude versus actions: The relationship of verbal and overt behavioral responses to attitude objects. *Journal of Social Issues*, 1969, **25**, 41–78.

Williams, R. M., Jr. Values. In E. Sills (Ed.), *International encyclopedia of the social sciences.* New York: Macmillan, 1968.

Williams, R. M., Jr. Change and stability in values and value systems: A sociological perspective. In M. Rokeach (Ed.), *Understanding human values: Individual and societal.* New York: Free Press, 1979.

Attitudes, Values, and Selfhood

M. Brewster Smith

University of California, Santa Cruz

*T*he challenge and opportunity to give a coherent
account of oneself as a
psychologist, an *apologia pro vita sua*, is one that can hardly be
refused by any psychologist as a self-regarding person. But I face
serious substantive questions about just *what* account I should give.
I have drifted rather far from the focal concern with opinion-and-
attitude research with which I began, and, since near the beginning,
I have been marginal to the mainstream tradition in experimental
social psychology. Presently I am in the midst of trying to accommodate ambivalent commitments to both humanistic *and* scientific
psychology in the arena of selfhood—that is, personality theory. My
recent APA involvements have made it impossible for me to take a
responsible sidewise look at the current state of research on beliefs,
attitudes, and values. By my schedule of inner readiness, it is hardly
the right time to look back on my earlier investments in the psychology of attitudes. But is there ever a right time?

This essay is in two parts. The first is a venture in metapsychology. After making explicit my discontent with the framing assumptions of recent social psychology, it goes on to develop a perspective
on selfhood as a positive alternative. The second part examines the
psychology of attitudes and values in some historical depth from
this perspective.

A METAPSYCHOLOGICAL STANCE

Before I can talk about how social psychology has dealt with attitudes and values from a perspective that takes the phenomenon of

selfhood seriously, I need first to make explicit my reservations about the metapsychology—the philosophical assumptions, sophisticated or naive—underlying mainstream experimental social psychology in the years since World War II, and sketch the quite different stance that I have come to—which highlights a conception of selfhood. There has been much armchair debate about the "crisis of social psychology," in which, with sharp prodding especially from Gergen (1973), many of these ideas have gained currency. So I can be brief on the critical side. But I cannot appropriately omit the criticism, even if it is old hat by now, because for the most part experimental social psychology seems to be going right on as if the criticisms had never been made.

What Is Wrong With Mainstream Social Psychology?

The main current of American psychology, and post-war experimental social psychology as it joined the mainstream, has always aspired to the goal of cumulative, systematic, ahistorical, unified science, on the model of Newtonian or post-Newtonian physics. True, the grandiose aspirations of American neo-behaviorism were abandoned as premature and unrealistic; general experimental psychology had moved on to the era of mini-theories and models, now predominantly within the quasi-paradigm of cognitive behaviorism, by the time that experimental social psychology emerged with its own mini-theories and models—dissonance theory, equity theory, exchange theory, reactance theory, attribution theory, and the like. But these were all seen ahistorically, usually as pieces of a larger imagined jigsaw puzzle, pieces that with enough reshaping and replacement could eventually be fitted together into a general Newtonian or Einsteinian account. The old goal had not been abandoned; it had simply receded. Cumulative progress toward the receding goal had to be assumed if we psychologists were to justify the activity of our laboratories and the content of our journals.

I can quickly recapitulate the criticisms I have made elsewhere (Smith, 1976) of this way of viewing our common enterprise:

1. After three decades of industrious and intelligent (which is not to say wise) effort, the case for cumulative advance in experimental social psychology remains open to reasonable doubt. Brilliant pedagogical integrations like Aronson's The Social Animal (1976) hold together by selection and conceptual sleight of hand. It has some-

times seemed to me that the near-simultaneous publication of the five-volume Lindzey-Aronson *Handbook* (Lindzey & Aronson, 1968–1969) and the 900-page *Theories of Cognitive Consistency* (Abelson et al., 1968) in fact precipitated the "crisis": without the benefit of a year in jail, no one could get abreast of the field. *Pages* cumulated; what else?

2. So far as the domain of personality and social psychology is concerned, it seems to me to require a heavy dose of dogmatic blindness not to agree with Gergen (1973) and Cronbach (1975) that the central problems and relationships to be dealt with are heavily cultural and historical. The putative ahistorical generalities that have been proposed are either almost empty of specific content or lie very close to the psychophysiological or sociobiological poles. (Harry Triandis [1978] persuades me more than anyone else, but even his cross-cultural universals are not outside human history.) Or, like exchange theory, they are reasonably good fits to the historically given preoccupations of our own society—and thus descriptors of it.

3. The "classic" contributions to our field—studies by Asch (1951), Festinger (1957), Lewin (Lewin, Lippitt, & White, 1939), and the Sherifs (Sherif and Sherif, 1953), for example—that we are proud of and ought to be, have been valuable as exemplifications and demonstrations of important processes and relationships, more than as starting points for cumulative parametric exploration. What cumulates from them is sensitization to and enlightenment about aspects of contemporary human, social process that we had not previously seen so clearly. The attempts at parametric exploration, when they have been valuable, have added to and clarified the enlightenment rather than filling in a firm composite of bricks in a systematic structure.

4. Sensitization and enlightenment for the guidance of human action through enriched understanding are congruent with humane values as we inherit them and continue to reshape and refine them in the dialectic of participant human history. The ideal of an ahistorical science of people, built upon manipulative (and often deceptive) experimentation, and applied through manipulative technology, is a very bad fit indeed.

5. As things now stand, Koch (1976) is surely right that our scientific and applied concerns are best characterized as a diverse family of psychological studies, not as a single, inordinately ambi-

tious but indifferently successful science. Our prevalent ideal self-image as a would-be unified science and profession surely has some productive consequences, pressing us to make useful connections, but it is hard for me to envision its realization in any conceivable run, short or long. Such a view of what we are up to is largely a distraction from what we do well and might be doing better. It is a source of vulnerable pretense and needless self-castigation.

6. At least in personality and social psychology, our masochistic love affair with the physical sciences seems to have led to faddishness, rather than unification. If we are determined to find our models in the harder, more successful sciences, we would do better to seek them in meteorology or biology! But we should make a more serious try to find models that better fit our own historical, cultural, meaningful domain.

A First Look at My Topics

The topics of this essay—attitudes, values, and selfhood—identify facets of social psychology that made it a refuge from and an alternative to the mainstream in psychology during the periods of classical Watsonian behaviorism, the neo-behaviorism of Hull and Spence, and, potentially, the cognitive behaviorism of today. During the first two of these periods, the old *Journal of Abnormal and Social Psychology*, which I once had the arduous honor of editing, was the respectable vehicle for unrespectable psychology. In an early handbook chapter, my teacher Gordon Allport (1935)—a previous long-term editor of the *Journal*—had declared the psychology of *attitudes* to be the central topic of social psychology. So, in a way, it was—with some technology of measurement, the beginnings of a descriptive taxonomy, but little indeed that could pass as theory in the most tolerant sense. Attitude research gave some psychologists in the twenties and thirties an excuse for attending to otherwise excluded topics of cognition and affection, and for involving themselves in social issues: the minimal technology of measurement was legitimizing!

It was Allport, too, who introduced the topic of *values* into American social psychology, bringing back from his *Wanderjahr* in early Weimar Germany a strong interest in the *Geisteswissenschaftliche* (cultural, humanistic) psychology of Edouard Spranger (1928), and a lifetime agenda of defending this interest against and accommodating it to American empiricism. The *Study of Values* (Allport, Vernon, & Lindzey, 1951), a measure of individual differences corresponding to Spranger's ideal *Types of Men*, was the successful product of his accommodation; it kept the topic of values conspicuous in personality and social psychology until Milton Rokeach (1973) gave it a new lease on life.

As for selfhood, after William James's (1890) prescient introduction of the modern treatment of the self and Mary Calkins's (1906) abstract attempt that had no sequels, the concept thus labeled found its home in the sociological wing of social psychology launched by C. H. Cooley (1902) and G. H. Mead (1934)—the symbolic interactionist wing that had little interaction with psychological social psychology until Newcomb and others began to knit the two traditions together. Psychologists including Allport (1943), and Sherif and Cantril (1947), preferred the term "ego." Only recently has "self" returned as a term of choice for socially and humanistically oriented psychologists of personality. Now the term is taking new hold even in psychoanalysis (Kohut, 1971).

In the years immediately preceding World War II, thus, social psychology was the forerunner of a humanistic science that didn't quite happen. So was the psychology of personality under the leadership of Allport (1937), Gardner Murphy (1947), and Harry Murray (1938)—the first two of them strongly identified with social psychology. Kurt Lewin (1951), the acknowledged patron saint and founding father of modern social psychology, also contributed importantly to the psychology of personality. At its inception, Division 8 of the new postwar APA—"Personality and Social"—reflected this common ground of a psychology that sought to be at once scientific and humanistic, an alternative to the behavioristic mainstream. But postwar developments, expanding social psychology exuberantly along scientistic lines and cramping personality psychology into a narrow situationism of experimentally manipulated variables, aborted the promising venture.

As I now reconstruct my own participation since World War II, I see it as an attempt to hold on to the ideal of a personality-*and*-social psychology that is both scientific *and* humanistic—and also relevant to our continually changing perceptions of our human predicament and historically given concerns. But it is not good enough just to regress to my origins with Gordon Allport and Harry Murray. Having raised my objections to the dominant tradition in personality and social psychology, I need now to sketch the grounding of my positive alternative, before recurring to examine attitudes and values from the perspective of selfhood.

An Evolutionary and Historical Perspective on Selfhood

I will not repeat here the perspectives on our social/cultural/ historical human nature that I developed in a recent essay (Smith, 1978d). The relevant gist follows from a broadly evolutionary approach that merges with a historical perspective and even an existential one. I take seriously what we have learned from our colleagues in anthropology about our human distinctiveness as technologists and as symbolizers, as creators and creatures of material and symbolic culture. Two decades ago, Washburn (1959) had speculated that the selective advantages given to early prehuman bipeds by tool-use and tool-making had participated in the evolution of our large brains, and of the behavioral complexities and competences that depend on them. The early date of prehuman tool making (back several million years) and the presently large cortical projection area for the human hands make this interactive view of the role of material culture in human evolution plausible—but by itself it can hardly be sufficient, since there was very little change in tool-making technology over the last million years until, well within the last hundred thousand, our own big-brained species had already appeared after a rapid evolutionary spurt of cranial development.

So it now looks as though precursors of our other distinctive human feature, virtuosity in symbolization, may have played the more central role in selecting us to become biologically human— through the advantages that even primitive symbolization gave in social organization to survive and exploit the competitive ecology of the savannahs in Africa or elsewhere, to use tools to greater effect, and, eventually, to make better ones. Our symbolic functions, too, are built into the brain in ways that must have a long evolutionary history. Certainly, since the dawn of true language among early *Homo sapiens* genetically virtually identical with ourselves—the best conjecture now seems to be as recently as forty or fifty thousand years ago (Harnad, Steklis, & Lancaster, 1976)—it is to symbolization and its consequences that we must turn to understand the emergence of humanness, of selfhood as we take it for granted.

In my APA address (Smith, 1978d) I applied the familiar ideas of

G. H. Mead (1934) in this speculative evolutionary-historical context. Mind, self, and society entail each other and emerge together, he held. Only the quantum leap of attaining true language on what is now the universal human model seems adequate to account for the rapid proliferation of the species beginning about forty millenia ago and the rapid elaboration and diversification since then of what, for a million years and more, had been a remarkably uniform and stable material culture continued by tenuously small populations. I also suggested that our language-given capacity to be social objects to ourselves, to be aware of ourselves and of our mates and kin with forethought and afterthought, brought with it the distinctively human existential predicament as an unwelcome but inherent side-effect: we are all too aware that none of us can avoid miseries and that we must die. Much of the symbolic culture that we have elaborated is intelligible as creative ways of denying or transcending or somehow coming to terms with this disastrous fact, of avoiding or reducing a natural anguish that could otherwise disrupt our lives. In another recent essay (Smith, 1978f), I have followed out that line of thought in an attempt at a bird's-eye view of the human adventure. Here, the idea I want to emphasize and develop is the radical degree to which our symbolic formulations are actually constitutive of our selfhood, as well as of the culturally interpreted world that we inhabit.

G. H. Mead's armchair account of the emergence of reflective selfhood with role-taking and language was essentially unhistorical, both in the framework of the individual life (we are beginning to learn a good deal more about the origins of selfhood in infancy) and in the history of our species. Selfhood as we know it cannot have burst forth in full bloom all at once. We can be sure of that if only because, as the anthropologist Geertz (1973, 1975) shows us, selfhood as *we* know it is substantially unlike selfhood as it is known in Bali, in Java, and in Morocco. Selfhood as *we* know it is clearly only one of very many cultural and historical versions, actualizations of human potentiality.

I have recently found a toehold toward an understanding beyond Mead's schematic generalities in the brilliant but extravagant speculations of Julian Jaynes (1977) about what he calls *The Origins of Consciousness in the Breakdown of the Bicameral Mind*, the mind-boggling title of his recent book. I am not persuaded to accept his grand hypothesis that our predecessors of Homeric times and earlier, even the partially literate Sumerians and Egyptians, were walking automata who hallucinated the voices of the gods. But he makes a strong case, along the way, that the self-consciousness of the Homeric heroes and of the bards who sang about them was different from ours. On this matter, Jaynes's conclusions independently converge with those of the German classicist Bruno Snell (1953) two decades earlier. The English classicist Onians (1951/1973) had offered generally similar analyses.

On close examination, what at first glance seems to be the psychological language of the Iliad does not translate accurately into such terms of our common language as spirit or soul, mind, thought, consciousness, emotion, will, or their reasonable equivalents in the Greek of classical times. In fact, though some of the words (like psyche) that later became psychological occur in Homeric context, Jaynes and Snell agree that for the bards of the Iliad, these words were not psychological at all. When they occur in Homer, they stand rather for concrete bodily organs or functions—like the lungs, the breath, the blood, the stirrings of the gut, the movements of the limbs. For the Homer of the Iliad, there is no subjectivity or introspection. So it follows, as Lionel Trilling (1972) observed, that it would be quite meaningless to speak of Achilles as *sincere*.

Snell traces the emergence of unmistakable subjective reference in the remnants of post-Homeric but pre-classical Greek literature. In justifying the title of his book, *The Discovery of the Mind*, he writes,

The discovery of the intellect cannot be compared with the discovery of, let us say, a new continent. America had existed long before Columbus discovered the New World, but the European way of thinking did not come into being until it was discovered; it exists by grace of man's cognizance of himself. All the same, our use of the word "discovery" can, I think, be defended. The intellect was not "invented," as a man would invent a tool to improve the operation of his physical functions, or a method to master a certain type of problem. As a rule, inventions are arbitrarily determined; they are adapted to the purpose from which they take their cue. No objective, no aims were involved in the discovery of the intellect. In a certain sense it actually did exist before it was discovered, only not in the same form, not *qua* intellect. (vi)

Slightly later in his discussion, Snell goes on to say,

It must be obvious to anyone that we are here using a metaphor; but the metaphor is unavoidable. . . . We cannot speak
about the mind or the intellect at all without falling back on
metaphor. (vi)

In Jaynes's view, too, developed in his introductory chapter in more
abstract detail than I can do justice to here, our consciousness, our
subjective world of inner "space" and serialized biographical
"time," is fundamentally metaphoric, a realm of "as-if." It is a
symbolic construction, historically developed and culturally transmitted.

I fear I have drawn us into a realm of extreme ambiguity, in which
empirical difficulties are complicated by all sorts of philosophic
traps, and I certainly do not regard myself as the all-qualified guide
to lead us firmly forth on the one true path. But I see alternative
directions of interpretation at this point, all the same, and I have a
clear preference between them. The choice depends upon the valua-
tion one puts on metaphor, on "as-if." To use a metaphor to clarify
metaphor, is it half empty or half full? Is consciousness of self *merely*
metaphoric, or is it creatively, comically, tragically, and sometimes
even gloriously metaphoric?

The tradition of positivism would say "merely." My friend and
colleague Ted Sarbin, whose recent contextualist presentation to
this Symposium (Sarbin, 1977) takes radical issue with the positivist
tradition in ways that I find thoroughly congenial, has on other
occasions espoused the "merely" view of metaphor in his analysis
of a variety of psychological problems. According to Sarbin, hypnosis, for example, is not a "real" state of consciousness as implied
by the term "trance"; it is "merely" role-taking that is highly accomplished and imaginative, deep investment in "as-if" (Sarbin & Coe,
1972). Schizophrenia is a myth (a metaphor mistakenly taken as
reality); so is anxiety. Calling psychological concepts metaphors and
myths in this "merely" vein becomes a kind of debunking. It is
implied that we are getting beneath phony appearances to tougher
realities. Yet, I wonder, doesn't this appraisal come down to
whether one evaluates metaphor and myth as half-full or half-
empty?—a distinction that may be more a matter of affective connotation than of conceptual difference, but has important consequences all the same.

To return to the problem of the origins of selfhood, and the light
thrown on them by Snell and Jaynes in complicating and enriching

the Meadian account: Of course I am urging the path, one congenial to artists and humanists, that regards myth and metaphor as creating peculiarly human realities, constitutive of human selfhood and of the humanized, interpreted worlds in which all human beings in fact have lived. Through their symbolic capacities and resources, people early and late have always (that is, ever since they can be described as people) created the *macrocosm* of the world they inhabit and the *microcosm* that characterizes each of its inhabitants. Not surprisingly, there have always been strong symbolic correspondences between their formulations of microcosm and macrocosm. What we learn from Snell and Jaynes, if we take their inherently uncertain findings on this point seriously, is that our own prized version of microcosm, reflexive selfhood with its metaphorical inner space that we think of as "inside our heads" (though Aristotle didn't), may be a much more recent attainment than the crucial, nearly miraculous achievement of true language on which it is built.

The role-taking that Mead said was required for language—ourselves reacting to the signs we produce for our partners in conversation *as if* from the perspective of their receivers—is necessary but not sufficient for generating human subjectivity as we think we know it. The microcosms of the Homeric heroes surely contained "I" and "Me," just as Mead would have it, but reflective inner conversation between the heroic "I" and "Me," if it occurred, would have been severely limited before the "invention" of the metaphorical language of subjectivity that permitted the "discovery" of mind. Alfred Schutz's (1967) brilliant phenomenological analysis of intersubjectivity (which he found congruent with Mead's differently based ideas) applies to Schutz and Mead and to thee and me, but it would not make sense applied to Achilles and Agamemnon. It lacks the universality to which it makes claim (with no empirical basis for doing so). Selfhood is not just a matter of role-taking, of adopting the perspective of a "generalized other"; its structure depends upon specific metaphoric content. This content has its historical origins and partakes of symbolic culture. It takes different shapes in different cultures—and is changing even today, in part under the impact of scientific psychology.

What leads positivists to debunk metaphors and deny the minds and selfhood that people have attained is their commitment to the very special view of the macrocosm that is the product of the physical sciences. There is a perspective on the scientific world view, one that I understand Claude Levi-Strauss espoused at least on occasion, that regards it as only one more mythic macrocosm on all fours with the myriad others. For the unsophisticated person-in-the-street, that is probably pretty much the case: atoms and black holes may be even less real from the commonsense perspective than the angels and hells of former times. Certainly for scientists themselves in their own fields of competence, however, the particular scientific version of the macrocosm that they accept (limited, as they know, by the state of development of the sciences) has a very special status. It is the product of the remarkable cultural invention of scientific inquiry as a collective and public enterprise, with rules of evidence and customs of conceptualization that foster abstract, generalizable, and corrigible formulations. They know, and so do the rest of us, that the scientific macrocosm has paid off by powerful pragmatic tests. Scientific constructs and theories are not brute reality-in-itself, and, as cognitive schemes for selection from the plenum, they have their metaphoric aspect. They are framed and modified under a very different discipline, however, from the formative metaphors of everyday life.

Like everyone else since time immemorial, scientists are uncomfortable unless their macrocosms and microcosms are symbolically consistent. The problem, as it affects the challenge to personality-and-social psychology, arises when scientists set out to construct a new microcosm on the model of the specially privileged macrocosm of the physical sciences. In important respects, this agenda has obviously been productive. We have discovered much that is factual and intellectually, even humanly, important about muscles and nerves and the biochemistry of the brain and body as it related to behavior, and we draw on computer theory and information science for metaphors of mind that fit its phenomena and mysteries a good deal less restrictively than the mechanistic metaphors that previously attracted us.

All the same, the common human microcosms of metaphoric intentionality and subjectivity elude the attempt at reconstruction on scientific macrocosmic lines. It has been a high drama. The first stage of it was the "warfare between science and theology" (White, 1896)—the scientists' successful attempt to establish firmly their own view of macrocosm to replace the religious one that was in tune with ordinary people's prevailing versions of the microcosm. By now the arena of battle has shifted to formulations of the microcosm, our own territory as psychologists and, indeed, as people. A good instantiation of the terms of the debate can be encountered in Skinner's (1971) *Beyond Freedom and Dignity* and Chein's (1972) *The Science of Behavior and The Image of Man.*

From my side of it, the same as Chein's, it is a critical consideration that our personal myths and metaphors of the microcosm, of selfhood, have a standing, a *reality* if you agree with Lewin that what is real is what has effects, that has no parallel on the macrocosmic side. True, our mythic or scientific conceptions of the macrocosm also have subjective reality for us as human actors, but Heisenberg notwithstanding, these conceptions do not change the reality they conceive, except as they guide human actions that alter it. In utter contrast, our metaphors and myths about the microcosm of personhood enter intrinsically into constituting who we are as persons as well as providing the ground for our valuing (the physical macrocosm knows no values) and for our actions towards ourselves and others. As my quotation from Snell caught the point, our metaphors make us who we are, insofar as we care about ourselves.

The tension toward "cognitive consistency" that pushes the scientist to invent a congruent but dehumanized microcosm has its counterpart with respect to the microcosmic worlds of ordinary people. The impressive technological success of the scientific world view has left very many of us bereft of the symbolic support of a congenial, metaphoric world, a macrocosm imagined along meaningful, value-rich human lines and actually believed in. That is a crucial part of what the cultural and personal crises of modernity have been about. Strains toward consistency with the scientific-technological world view that has entered common sense even begin to undermine our views of our own microcosmic selfhood that we formerly took for granted, a trend augmented by the rapid cultural change catalyzed by technological "progress" (which leaves all of us unsure of our footing), and by the depersonalized relationships increasingly characteristic of urban mass society. The problems come close to home as it becomes apparent that psychologists and other would-be scientific theorists of human nature are adding to the problems of living a truly human life as some of their dehumanized, macrocosmically based versions of the microcosm get disseminated in the general culture. It was Hannah Arendt (1958) who observed that the danger is not that the positivist view of human nature *is* true, but that it might *become* true—if people were to come to believe in it. Our vital metaphors may be an endangered species![1]

Naturwissenschaften and/or Geisteswissenschaften

Selfhood, then, is a metaphoric realm. If personality and social psychologists are to study *people* in their relationships, not just human organisms, they must somehow find ways of dealing with this realm on its own terms, not just in imposed terms that essentially deny it. So to assert may seem to be regressing to the old view of Dilthey at the turn of the century that distinguished between the explanatory natural sciences (*Naturwissenschaften*) and the interpretative cultural or mental sciences (*Geisteswissenschaften*), a conception that has since occupied many pages in the literature of social thought. Or an even deeper regression may be suspected—to a distinction shared by Wundt, the founding father of scientific psychology, and Durkheim, the founding father of modern sociology, the distinction between the individual realm of "physiological psychology" and the separate collective realm of *Völkerpsychologie* (or, for Durkheim, sociology), where Wundt placed the study of the "higher mental processes," and has traditionally been criticized for doing so. (From my present perspective, I think he had a point!) Of course, Wundt himself tried to contribute on both sides of this dichotomy.

I believe that the distinction is indeed pertinent, but we need not descend into a regression. Psychology, following Wundt's precedent, has been working on both sides of the fence ever since, and this is both a problem for our field and one of its strengths. By now, many of us do not want to accept the dichotomous choice of either-or: a dehumanized science of people or a disembodied and maybe ineffectual humanism. As I have suggested elsewhere (Smith, 1978b, 1978d), I think we are already partly engaged in a dialectic process which may actually be a better match than dichotomies to the puzzling realities that we are trying to deal with. I shall not elaborate on that suggestion, since it seems to me that there is still much mystification in the conceptions of a dialectical psychology.

1. Shotter (1974) has argued effectively in a more philosophical vein for a congruent metapsychological perspective, making a direct attack on the Cartesian assumptions that undergird positivism and mechanism in modern psychology.

Two of the connotations of "dialectics" do seem to me to give us appropriate directives, however. For one, if the competing and seemingly complementary perspectives can really engage with each other in their continuing conflict, more comprehensive and valuable insights may result. A second connotation with important general implications for social and developmental psychology is advocacy of the sort of radical interactionism-in-process that has been only weakly represented in psychology since the days of John Dewey. (See Riegel, 1976.)

The prescription for a dialectical psychology does seem much easier to pronounce than to carry out. A more conventional strategy, with ample precedent in the psychology of personality, would seek to apply the conceptual and evidential rigor of science to the symbolic phenomena of selfhood closely described in their own terms. This, as I understand it, is essentially the advice that Geertz (1975) gives to his anthropological colleagues when he suggests an ideal interplay between "emic" and "etic" modes of analysis.

Some Linkages to a Metaphoric Conception of Selfhood

My emphasis on selfhood as a symbolic, metaphoric emergent in evolution and history makes ready contact with some notable sources of insight that have as yet been little drawn upon by the academic psychology of personality: proposals from the first great generation of rebel disciples in the psychoanalytic tradition. One such source is Jung's evocative panorama of dynamic archetypes of the collective unconscious (Jung, 1966). The archetypes are constitutive, metaphoric symbols of selfhood that could be fitted quite congruently into the account I began with G. H. Mead but elaborated with the help of Jaynes and Snell—to the extent that they are substantiated by research and scholarship more disciplined than Jung's.

We need not be bothered by the ambiguous and probably unsatisfactory metaphor of the "collective unconscious." Archetypal formations like animus and anima and, indeed, the Jungian Self, may perhaps be based on templates that are passed on genetically: as I see it, this is no longer ruled out as a scientifically acceptable possibility in the light of what we now know about the time frame of human evolution and the inherited basis, for example, of universal language learning in humans. Or, rather, they may be quasi-universals of human culture, evoked as recurrences of symbolic response to universals of the human condition. The rich but untidy Jungian corpus has yet to be mined for testable insights about the role such metaphoric structures play in the transformations and vicissitudes of selfhood. Not surprisingly, students of literature, for whom such "humanistic" speculations have become a stock in trade, have paid closer attention to Jung than have psychologists.

Adler, too, has been relatively neglected, in spite of sedulous efforts by the Ansbachers (1956) over the years. Since, as they point out, he was deeply influenced by Vaihinger's (1925) *Philosophy of As-If*, a metaphoric perspective pervades Adler's psychological thought, especially in his conception of fictional goals. A renewed interest in human subjectivity should turn more of us back to Adler.

I have already echoed major themes in Rank (especially, 1932), in my imagery of microcosm and macrocosm and my taking note of symbolic culture as an accommodation to the human existential plight. For those like me who find Rank's own writings in translation hard to penetrate, Becker's (1973) enthusiastically appreciative overview may prove helpful.

Note that all three of these early psychoanalytic rebels broke with Freud on essentially humanistic grounds—the inadequacy of psychoanalysis to meaning and purpose. As Holt (1972) has pointed out most clearly, Freud had both a humanistic and a mechanistic side, but he insisted heavily on the latter: the abstract constructions of libido theory. It was Freud's insistence on libido theory (as he expounded it in metapsychological terms that were rooted more in the First Law of Thermodynamics than in clinical observations) and, of course, the *group* dynamics generated by a leader who required his followers to be True Believers, that drove Jung, Adler, and Rank out of the fold.

From early in the century, psychologists have always been interested in Freud, though they have always found him hard to digest. The early rebels got initial attention from psychologists, too, but it was soon co-opted by the second generation of "neo-Freudian" rebels in the thirties, whose grounds for revolt depended rather on ripening concerns, shared by many psychologists and anthropologists of the time, about sociocultural factors in the formation of personality and in the origins of personality disorders. Karen Horney (1937), of the neo-Freudian generation, reissued Adler's ideas without attribution, probably for reasons that were compelling in the politics of the psychoanalytic movement. Carl Rogers

(1942) drew substantially on Rank, at one remove via the Pennsylvania School of Social Work. Murray (1938) merged themes from Freud and McDougall with those of Jung, who carried on with his own voice, surviving the opprobrium of involvement in Nazi Germany, but few psychologists besides Murray listened to him. In general, the work of the first generation of psychoanalytic rebels, who were carrying forward diverse humanistic agendas, has received rather little close attention from psychologists of personality. Now that a new generation of Freudians, trained by the earlier generation of Freudian "ego psychologists" who had tried in principle to accommodate aspects of academic psychology ("ego psychology" was the Freudian Counter-Reformation contemporary with the neo-Freudian revolt), are engaged in a project to resurrect and build upon the humanistic side of Freud's own work, the humanistic rebels of the older generation deserve our renewed interest.

A symbolic psychology of selfhood also makes contact with one of the most satisfactory general interpretations of psychotherapy and personality change, one that also takes into account the social psychological literature on attitudes and attitude change: Frank's (1973) *Persuasion and Healing*, which over more than a decade has gone through two editions. Frank draws on Cantril (1950) for his central concept, the person's "assumptive world": the "highly structured, complex, interacting set of values, expectations, and images of oneself and others, which guide and in turn are guided by a person's perceptions and behavior and which are closely related to his emotional states and his feelings of well-being" (p. 27). As befits the problem context with which Frank is concerned, his conception is focused individually rather than collectively, unlike my discussion that followed from Jaynes and Snell. I note it here not only because of its continuity with Adler's "as-if" formulations, but also because of Frank's explicit reference to the psychology of attitudes, in a broad view that brings experimental research together with an examination of coercive persuasion and "brainwashing" (Lifton, 1961). Apart from Rokeach's (1973) experimental work on values, the psychology of attitude change has paid in superficiality for slighting the changes, such as those induced during psychotherapy, which depend upon reconstitution of a person's metaphors of selfhood. (See also Sarbin & Adler, 1970–71.)

Frank's reasonable and informed discussion offered bridges between the laboratory-based formulations of social psychology and the humanly more consequential concerns of the clinician, bridges that I am surprised have not drawn more traffic from social psychologists. Our compartments of thought are sufficiently rigid that it seldom dawns upon us that much clinical psychology *is* social psychology in principle, if not in the way differently specialized psychologists have come to talk about their conceptual problems. The Skinnerian experimental analysts of behavior and the social learning theorists have done better than social psychologists in crossing these arbitrary boundaries, as the booming behavior modification movement attests.

Finally, the general approach that I am urging links directly with attribution theory in recent social psychology, and with its sociological counterpart, labeling theory. As Jones and Kelley extracted it from the richer and still to be fully exploited phenomenological formulations of Fritz Heider (1958), attribution theory took shape as a partly formalized set of guiding ideas—rather different ones stemming from Jones and from Kelley—that provided a useful perspective on a surprising variety of social psychological problems. (See Jones et al., 1972.) One is tempted to dismiss the surge of attribution research in the journals as only another of the fads and fashions that sweep through social psychology whenever a new idea or a new technique appears—a sign of the field's lamentable lack of a reasonably stable and productive guiding paradigm. I think this would be a mistake. The appeal of attribution theory, and its fertility, it seems to me, follow from the fact that the attributionists have been grappling with fundamental symbolic processes by which people assign and therefore create meaning—in the crucial human realm of self and the interpersonal world.

From the angle that I am following here, the power and enduring promise of the attributional approach is especially evident in the way that it has assimilated Rotter's (1966) concepts of internal and external locus of control, which he had developed in the very different context of his social learning theory. In result, we have the beginnings of a psychology of self-concep*tion*, embedded in causal-functional-explanatory propositions about conditions and consequences, that has far more psychological and human interest than the sterile old tradition centering on the self-concept (Wylie, 1961, 1974). The attributional analysis of "locus of control," and De Charms's (1968) slightly different phrasing in terms of people's self-confirming views of themselves as "Origins" and "Pawns," deal frontally with the critical juncture between symbolic-meaningful-interpretative and causal-functional-explanatory modes of conceptualizing human experience and behavior. They deal, as I have put it (Smith, 1978b), with selfhood as the prime arena in which the "self-fulfilling prophecy" becomes a causal mechanism. (See Jones, 1977). They bring together ways of conceiving the task of psychology that, as we have seen, well-respected metatheoretical traditions have insisted *cannot* be joined. The juncture has nevertheless been made, with results that seem to me to give it ample pragmatic justification. An especially promising theoretical-empirical development is Seligman's extension, in attributional terms, of his theory of learned helplessness (Seligman, 1975; Abramson, Seligman, & Teasdale, 1978). We had best readjust our metatheoretical assumptions accordingly.

Attribution theory is concerned with the meanings, the causal interpretations, that the human subject or actor ascribes to the actions of self and others, and their outcomes. Sociologists of the symbolic interactionist tradition have advanced complementary notions about how society at large or particular "Alters" provide or impose meaning for the actor by the labels they apply to the actor and his or her behavior—so-called "labeling theory" (Murphy, 1976). Weinstein's (Weinstein & Deutschberger, 1963) "altercasting" is a cognate conception. The ideas involved seem to me to be the other side of the same coin that attribution theory has been concerned with. The value of these sociological ideas is not diminished by their frequent abuse by both sociologists and psychologists in social criticism, according to which the essence of such problematic phenomena of "deviance" as delinquency and mental illness is exhausted by the condemnatory labels that get put upon the people who exemplify them. Here again, as in the debunking of psychological concepts by labeling them metaphor and myth, I think we need to show more discernment in how we employ some important and useful ideas.

The view of human selfhood as a symbolic production, thus, makes potentially useful contact with a variety of lines of psychological thought that deserve continued exploration. To epitomize the stance from which I will be looking at the topics of attitudes, values, and selfhood in the second part of this paper, I remain committed to the collective strategies of science insofar as they fit the phenomena of human personality and social behavior. For this area, I forego the goal—a mirage, I think—of a structure of universal ahistorical laws on the Newtonian model, and proclaim that a frankly historical and cultural science is greatly preferable to one that aspires to universality but is historically limited and culture-bound by default.

ATTITUDES, VALUES, AND SELFHOOD:
A SELECTIVE RETROSPECTION

My attempt to make sense of where we have been and to try to discern promising and less productive lines of development, opportunities missed or bungled in the past or opening in the present, will not hinge on exact definitions.

Dispositional Concepts in Personality and Social Psychology

I start with the domain of beliefs, attitudes, and values as social psychologists have actually dealt with these and related topics, a traditionally identified area of interest within a subdiscipline, with the usual degree of historical, nonfunctional autonomy fostered by courses and textbooks and academic inertia. When I ask myself, What is the functional job of this traditional area, my answer is that it has the job of developing and elaborating *dispositional* concepts and principles to account for social behavior, in his respect joining the psychology of personality. When I ask myself further, What is our best account of productive grand strategy for so employing dispositional concepts and principles, where else should I turn but to Kurt Lewin's (1951) old formula, $B = f(P,E)$: Behavior is a joint function of the Person and the psychological Environment. Putting aside Lewin's important distinction between the geographical and the psychological environments as not immediately relevant, I want to stress that this familiar formula is in no sense a "law" or an empirical conclusion from research. Rather, it is a declaration of intellectual strategy for the guidance of research and theory-building, and even of social analysis for public enlightenment. It says that if we are going to work with dispositional concepts, we should not expect them to do the whole job; we need to relate them to concepts specifying the situation of action. Of course, we have given lip-service to the strategy much more than we have actually followed it in practice.

Note that it is by no means the only strategy open to us in accounting for social behavior. For instance, radical behaviorism, with its commitment to avoid dispositional concepts entirely, has never accepted it. Skinnerians want to achieve an input-output analysis of behavior under environmental contingency that by-passes inferred dispositions. This is a perfectly reasonable option. It entails two problems, however, from my point of view. One is the empirical, pragmatic question as to whether, in the realm of the complex social behavior of everyday life and politics, we can attain a degree of explanatory power that is at all satisfactory without reference to dispositions of personality, beliefs and attitudes, and the like. I doubt it. The other is metatheoretical but also has its pragmatic aspects: the radical behaviorist account does violence to the conceptions of human personhood that I spent the first part of this essay developing, whereas the dispositional account does not.

A variety of compromise strategies have been tried that also avoid, in one way or another, a direct treatment of person-environment interaction. In the days of Hullian neo-behaviorism, for example, Doob (1947) identified attitude with habit strength. The attitudinal disposition got translated into a little behavior, an "implicit" behavior, a readiness to behave. Building the behavior to be predicted into the disposition from which it was to be predicted might lack theoretical elegance or even acceptability from some points of view (those were the days when it was customary to condemn R-R psychology in contrast with the approved S-R model), but it had some pragmatic justification when psychologists were not geared to deal with P, E interactions effectively.

Nonbehaviorist theories in the functional tradition seem to me to have made a similar accommodation to duck the implications of the Lewinian strategy. Katz and Stotland (1959), for example, wrote of the "behavioral component" of attitudes as complementing the cognitive and affective components. The behavior to be predicted gets built into the formulation of the structure of the attitude itself. Fishbein and Ajzen (1975) deal more satisfactorily with the problem, it seems to me, by introducing behavioral intention as a separate concept that intervenes between attitudes and their expression in behavior, but they give up much of the ambition of the dispositional strategy.

If we turn from the academic theorists to the one arena in which the study of attitudes was being conducted in "field" settings for practical purposes—survey research in the opinion polling tradition—it is quite clear that asking people how they were going to vote or what they were going to buy provided a much better predictor of behavior than could be obtained from any conceptually guided attempt to deal jointly with attitudinal predispositions and situational constraints and pressures. (See Smith, 1954.) But commercial polling had a practical job to do without the scientific obligation to understand or explain. It was quite all right to let people be their own predictors, and skimp this challenge to social science. Angus Campbell and his collaborators at the Michigan Survey Research Center (Campbell, Converse, Miller, & Stokes, 1960), who were committed to such an obligation from a primarily psychological perspective, came forward with their "funnel" causal model to account for the voting act—a kind of conceptual path analysis conceived before the statistical techniques to match this way of thinking were available—in which attitudinal dispositions toward party, candidate, and issues, each with their own determinants, converge in determining voting intention and thus the act of voting. But their research problem, too, did not require them to face up to the P, E interaction.

From where we are now, it seems to me that psychologists who continue to be interested in beliefs, attitudes, and values are almost bound to be committed to the dispositional strategy, whether they are thoughtful about it or not. Within this strategy, beliefs, attitudes, values, self-attributions—the whole family of related concepts—seem to me to fit under the more inclusive rubric of personality. That was the assumption of my early work in the field (Smith, Bruner, & White, 1956), which participated in the "functionalist" episode in the study of attitudes to which I will recur later. It was certainly the assumption of Allport (1935) in his *Handbook* chapter that summarized the pre-modern period of attitude research, and in his book on personality (Allport, 1937) which launched this as a legitimate subfield of academic study. In Allport's treatment, "social" attitudes are coordinate with "personality" traits. Attitudes are dispositions organized around a psychological object—they are attitudes *toward x*; in phenomenological language, they are structural stabilizations of "intentionality." The coherence of stylistic or motivational personality *traits* does not depend upon an object as the focus of organization. The close linkage betwen the two concepts is illustrated in one of the early topics of attitude research.

Measures of such social attitudes as those toward the church, toward war, toward conventional morality tended to intercorrelate positively. Following ideas that were part of the common culture, psychologists therefore extracted a dimension of radicalism vs. conservatism from this clustering—at first informally, then by the laborious new technique of factor analysis. But radicalism-conservatism has no specific object; in other contexts we would regard it as a personality trait. As Allport wrote, *"the more generalized the attitude becomes the more it resembles a trait"* (1935, p. 838, his italics). The two concepts are of the same ilk.

I have gone into this bit of history not for its own sake or because I subscribe to Allport's old version of trait psychology, but to call attention to the basis for a strict parallelism between central methodological issues that have bedogged attitude research and personality research respectively during the past two decades: the attitudes-and-behavior issue, on the one hand, and the trait-vs.-situation issue on the other. Both inhere in the strategy of deploying dispositional concepts, and both find their resolution, it seems to me, in returning with new sophistication to Lewin's formula.

In retrospect, the position of Allport and his contemporaries was vulnerable in both domains. We have seen that social psychologists tended to expect attitudes to predict behavior directly, without taking situations of action into account. The same charge can be fairly made of Allport's conception of personality, a relatively encapsulated or "integumented" (Chein, 1972) one. In spite of Allport's awareness of the essential contribution of other social sciences to understanding a concrete social problem like the nature of prejudice (Allport, 1954), even in his postwar years of involvement in the new Harvard Department of Social Relations he did not find it comfortable to step outside a rather self-enclosed conception of the personality system. Psychoanalytically oriented psychologists of personality did no better, making them, too, vulnerable to the incursions of the behavioral approach with its situational emphasis.

The years since, until just yesterday, have been unfriendly to the dispositional strategy in personality and social psychology generally. In this period, which appears to some of us as a Dark Age for personality research (Carlson, 1971, 1975), the emphasis became overwhelmingly situational, and personality holistically conceived as organized dispositions and processes almost vanished from view. Quite apart from the intrinsic vulnerability of a one-sided dispositional approach, it is easy to reconstruct why. These were boom years for laboratory experimental research in personality and social psychology. The brave new style of research fitted the prevalent ethos of self-confident positivism, and it thrived in the expanding university laboratories where funds were readily available. The publishable results needed for career advancement could be more quickly attained in small laboratory studies than from intensive "explorations in personality" in the Murray (1938) tradition or intensive forays into the personality roots of consequential attitudes and ideology, like the Berkeley studies of prejudice and authoritarianism (Adorno, Frenkel-Brunswik, Levinson, & Sanford, 1950). Observe that in laboratory experimentation, it is situational variables that can be directly manipulated; personality traits can only be measured and selected for, without experimental control.

In spite of the fact that possible trait-situation "interaction effects" could be highlighted according to the logic of analysis of variance that had come to dominate experimental design, the prevalent experimental style encouraged theoretical attention to situational effects singly or in combination, and to "states" rather than "traits" on the dispositional side. If your research is focused on the effects of situational variations that you are laboring to produce, that is what you will naturally come to believe is most important.

The pendulum had swung so far in the situational direction by the seventies that a corrective reaction was obviously called for, and it has happened. There seems no doubt that an interactive view is finally beginning to prevail in personality theory (Magnusson & Endler, 1977). My side comment—my *snide* comment—is: About time! The resurrection of the view that personality and situation interact (as in Lewin's formula) finally legitimizes a dispositional psychology of personality as once again deserving serious attention in research and theory. The same counterswing of the pendulum, I hope, should affect our treatment of attitudinal dispositions. Once some pseudoproblems identified by Smith (1954), Campbell (1963), and Fishbein (1967) years ago are swept aside, the hoary problem of attitudes vs. behavior ought to yield to the interactive treatment.

The Psychology of Attitudes as a Venture in Social Psychological Understanding

My first theme, just concluded, bore upon whether psychology has room for attributing causal significance to the person (by no means inherently an "attributional error," as some writers in attribution theory seem to assume, joining forces with the extreme situationism in personality theory that is becoming outmoded). My second is concerned with the extent to which the psychology of attitudes has been prepared to deal with substantive issues of human meaning, and has actually contributed to a psychological understanding of our participation in current history. If social psychology has dubious claim to success as a "Newtonian" science, how good has it been at the tasks of a historical discipline?

With a few notable exceptions, I will argue, social psychologists have not been at all good at it, because we have not been interested in the assignment. Even Allport (1935) sought to anchor attitudes in the hard-science side of the discipline. His *Handbook* chapter developed what I can only regard as a legitimizing pseudo-history of the concept, linking it to the ideas of the Wurzburg school of experimental psychology such as set and determining tendency but especially *Bewussteinslagen*, which got translated as "conscious attitudes." The word *attitudes* was there, but the issues of the imageless thought controversy had nothing to do with how the concept was to be used by social psychologists.

With the lead of L. L. Thurstone, who initiated formal measurement of attitudes with his article, "Attitudes can be measured" (Thurstone, 1928), attitudes as they came to be measured were narrowly conceived as having pro-or-con *direction*, and maybe also *intensity*, with respect to a social object, but no analyzed cognitive content. (The source of Thurstone's use of the term traces through the sociologist W. I. Thomas, who used it in the methodological introduction to *The Polish Peasant* [Thomas & Znaniecki, 1918] to refer to *any* object-directed personal disposition, with the linked term *value* referring to any object toward which an attitude is directed, a very different usage from Allport's, Rokeach's, and mine.)

If we are seeking a more cogent historical source for a conception of attitude appropriate to a humanized social psychology, one that is congruent with a dispositional view of personality, we should turn back to the brilliant, much maligned, and indeed often wrong-headed psychologist of vitalism and purposivism William McDougall (1921), whose ideas (if stripped of naively hereditarian, racist, and Lamarckian fallacies, some but not all of which were typical of his time) now seem like a remarkably good attempt to develop a psychological framework congruent with the concerns of my metatheoretical introduction. To the extent that McDougall's ideas have survived, it is mainly in their amalgamation with Freudian and Jungian concepts by Murray (1938).

McDougall did not talk about attitudes; his equivalent term was *sentiments*, which he adopted from the Scottish armchair characterologist Alexander Shand (1914), who conceived of sentiments—integrations around a psychological object of readiness to experience the prime emotions—as the building blocks of character: in present language, personality. For Shand, love and hate were prime examples. Love is not a simple emotion, but a readiness to experience joy, fear, anger, etc., depending on the context relating the subject, the loved object, and the environing situation—already a dispositional concept with interactional implications. For McDougall, too, sentiments were the main structural components of personality: in his case, integrations of the "instincts" around objects. Mostly, psychologists today remember McDougall only as an instinct theorist, and condemn him for that. Actually, the famous list of instincts provided only the abstract foundation for his purposive psychology, and emphasized not pre-programmed actions but integrations of cognitive, affective, and conative tendencies (matching Katz and Stotland's [1959] three aspects of attitudes). Minus the imaginary biology, McDougall's "instincts" translate to Murray's (1938) "needs"—in a longer, more comprehensive list, to be sure. The whole emphasis of McDougall's account of people as social beings, however, was not on instincts but on sentiments, which as integrations of instincts also had cognitive, affective, and conative aspects.

An interesting feature of his scheme, which puzzled me when I first encountered it before I had had any contact with symbolic interactionism, was his conception of the *self-regarding sentiment* as the keystone of personality organization, the explicit agency of volition. Now I see it as one more example of McDougall's prescience. Of course it echoes William James's (1890) discussion of the "I" and the "Me," and parallels G. H. Mead's (1934) doctrine that "I-Me dialogue" is the locus of creative self-direction: our symbolic reflexiveness is the source of such contingent human freedom as we enjoy. McDougall's treatment of the will via the role of the sentiment of self-regard in the hierarchy of personality resembles Chein's (1972), in that he sees our ethical evaluation and sanctioning of volitional moral behavior as depending on philosophical determinism. His account of the social development of the self-regarding sentiment, and of the steps in the development of moral volition that accompany it, may be couched in older language harking back to James Mark Baldwin (1897) rather than to Piaget (1932), but the ideas have a distinctively modern ring to readers familiar with Piaget and Kohlberg (1964). (Piaget was himself explicitly indebted to Baldwin, of course.)

McDougall's theory of sentiments was indeed rich and suitable in principle to the description and analysis of actual human lives, though his interests did not lead him in that concrete empirical direction. Murray and Morgan (1945) picked up McDougall's concept for their descriptive, somewhat abortive monograph from the Harvard Psychological Clinic. Both McDougall's ideas and Murray and Morgan's example were sources for the approach taken in *Opinions and Personality* (Smith, Bruner, & White, 1956), though we decided to use the more prevalent termminology of opinions and attitudes.

During the postwar decades,the substantive psychology of attitudes fell on evil days, like those of personality theory—at least in regard to its adequacy for contributing to an account of historical human actors. (I will return to two major exceptions shortly.) One might think otherwise, given the initial burst of interest in attitude change exemplified and stimulated by Hovland, Janis, and Kelley (1953). The focus of their programmatic research is best described, however, by the title of their book: *Communication and Persuasion*. A good deal was learned that is properly sensitizing, if not definitive, about the variables involved in communication effects on beliefs and attitudes. But the dependent variables in their research were given little attention. The beliefs, expectations, and attitudes selected for study were chosen because pilot work had showed that measurable changes in them *could* be produced by very brief communications or minor manipulations in the laboratory. So the topics were mostly inconsequential to the experimental subjects. The measures employed were also ad hoc. The emphasis, like that of postwar experimental social psychology generally, was on discovering lawful relationships of process, not on understanding the psychology of particular classes of attitudes, or the attitudes of particular categories of people.

With the early death of Carl Hovland, interest in persuasive communication, which had been guided by his rough map of the communication process that accommodated research suggested by quite disparate theories about the psychological processes involved,

generally gave way to interest centered on the theories themselves—theories, for example, concerning reinforcement, social
comparison and social judgment, and, especially, cognitive dissonance. If measures of attitude happened to be employed as
dependent variables in the research that followed, that was inci-
dental. Typically, the measures used remained ad hoc. (It is remarkable that sophisticated experimental design and theoretical analysis
were usually accompanied by the most casual and amateurish
psychometrics.) So it has mostly been with the treatment of attitudes in mainstream experimental social psychology, up to this day.

Eddies in the Mainstream: A Substantive Focus

The two major exceptions that stand out aginst this account are, on
the one hand, the Berkeley studies of anti-Semitism and authoritarianism (with them, also, a whole minor tradition of research on
prejudiced attitudes and behavior), and survey research, particularly that focused on political attitudes and the act of voting, on the
other. Each had strong substantive, content-oriented concerns that
fit squarely the conception of social psychology as a historical
science, and in this respect each deviated from the process-oriented,
content-free mainstream. It should be instructive to examine both.

I have thought for some time that the history of research on *The
Authoritarian Personality* (TAP) (Adorno et al., 1950), after its splen-
did beginning, is one of the more scandalous episodes in our discipline, and a recent occasion to re-review that classic together with
Allport's *The Nature of Prejudice* (1954) only confirmed my judgment
(Smith, 1978c). *TAP* reported a major program of interrelated studies, purporting to show first that anti-Semitic attitudes are correlated
with ethnocentrism as a more general attitudinal structure, then
that ethnocentrism in turn is related to an ideology—a psychologically
coherent though, it appeared, logically inconsistent structure of
beliefs—which the Berkeley authors saw as underlying anti-demo-
cratic or proto-fascist political orientations, and finally that the anti-
democratic ideology seemed congruent with a particular defensive
structure of personality, which they accounted for in generally
psychoanalytic terms. The research drew on a rich background of
speculative theory about the origins of German Nazism, as developed by members of the Frankfurt school. It drew upon the techni-

cal resources of attitude measurement, clinical interviewing, and projective techniques. It employed a number of special samples to check the generality of the findings and to provide independent tests of some of the implications of the theoretical structure that emerged. Presenting a serious model of the relationship between family relations in childhood, personality, political ideology, and more specific social attitudes, TAP was a major contribution to social analysis and criticism. It was no small study. Of course, it had major flaws.

What happened afterwards bothers me. To be sure, Rokeach (1960), who got his start at Berkeley in the aftermath of this research, reacted to one of the flaws—the one-sided focus on right-wing authoritarianism—in an appropriately constructive and programmatic way, in his important studies of "dogmatism." But his work stands by itself in this respect. For nearly a decade, social psychologists were fascinated the TAP's technical deficiencies, mostly those of the "F-Scale," the pencil-and-paper measure of fascistic tendencies that emerged from the Berkeley studies but was far from their sole or central focus. By the time that this flurry of methodologically directed activity had subsided (which for a while made the alphabetically first but substantively marginal Theodor Adorno among the most frequently cited though least known names in the social psychological literature), interest had moved in other directions, mostly captured by the wave of laboratory experimentalism, without adequate resolution of the serious substantive claims of TAP, the claims that made it relevant to the social psychology of contemporary history.

The substantive, analytically descriptive research on "authoritarianism," like the experimental demonstration studies of Asch (1951) and the Sherifs (Sherif & Sherif, 1953), did serve a useful sensitization function. People familiar with it are bound to take a different view of such historical episodes as McCarthyism, anti-gay and anti-fluoridation outbursts, and the present reactive yearning for a "Macho" American foreign policy that President Carter is unwilling to present. All the same, I see this stream of research as a missed opportunity to stay with the substantive, essentially historical problem until firmer conclusions could have been drawn.

At almost the same time that TAP appeared, Allport (1954) published *The Nature of Prejudice*, not a theory of prejudice and discrimination but a collation of theories and research bearing on them, judiciously appraised and brought to bear on recommendations about what ought to be done to ameliorate them. This classic of the appled psychology of attitudes and values is currently being revised—more probably, rewritten—by Pettigrew and Kramer. That they need to do so follows from the fact that the historical context has substantially changed over the quarter century (*justice* more than *mutual liking* is now a central value in ethnic relations), and also from the fact that a good deal of relevant research has continued to go on in the years since Selma and *Brown vs. Board of Education*. This work has participated competently in "social psychology as history" along the lines I am urging, but it has been only a minor current in the social psychology of the time. Prestige in the discipline lay elsewhere.

The development of survey research is a clearer success story, paradoxically, but survey research has been essentially marginal to the social psychology of beliefs, attitudes, and values as pursued by psychologists. Survey research is historical and analytically descriptive, and the present interest in developing time series in historical depth is making it an even more powerful instrument for these purposes. But it has been done mainly by sociologists, whose discipline has probably been too dependent on this one channel of data. And even though the founder of the Michigan Survey Research Center which has been the main site of psychological participation in survey research and analysis, Rensis Likert, got his start in academic attitude research (Murphy & Likert, 1938), and subsequent survey analysis at Michigan in the style of Angus Campbell (e.g., Campbell et al., 1960) has developed its own cognitively oriented array of concepts, there has been remarkably little back-and-forth flow of ideas and influence between attitude research and survey research. I cannnot believe that this is a healthy state of affairs. (During the period when persuasive communication was a focal topic for the academics, Hovland [1959] wrote a classic paper that tried to bring the two traditions together. Mostly they have gone their separate ways.)

So the exceptions actually highlight the general thrust of my second retrospective theme: the psychology of attitudes has mostly avoided substantive issues of human meaning, and shown little interest in contributing a psychological perspective to the understanding of people as participants in current history. Yet the challenge has been there all along, and, as we have seen, a variety of relevant technical and conceptual tools have become available. If our field is to earn its keep, we need to develop a more diversified portfolio, instead of putting so many of our eggs in the basket of the process-oriented, law-seeking experimental strategy.

An Example of Conceptualized Interpretation

If we take the "sensitization" function of social psychological research seriously, moreover, we might set higher priority on organizing what we think we have learned about beliefs and attitudes into coherent conceptual maps for the guidance of analytical and critical thinking about concrete social-historical phenomena. In his contribution to this symposium, Triandis (this volume) has presented a rich example, though he conceives of portions of his map more along the lines of Hullian "mathematical" formulations than is to my taste. He wants his map to become a quasi-Newtonian theory.

Quite a while back I developed a conceptual map of this sort—which bears some resemblance to Triandis's—as an outgrowth of trying to apply the "functional" approach of Smith, Bruner, and White (1956) to the psychology of prejudice. I thought it was more intelligibly coherent than Allport's (1954) end-to-end collation of theories and factors in the successive chapters of his book. For a series of concrete problems—McCarthyism and fertility decisions among them—I found the same general map to be a substantial help in my own thinking, calling attention to relationships to be looked for, possibly relevant factors to be considered. It functioned like a check list for me, but—more than a check list—it was organized in a way to suggest paths and levels of explanation. It was useful in my teaching. So I put forth a generalized version of it as a map of how attitudes, personality, and other factors enter into individual political behavior. Since then I have followed its fate with paternal interest and concern.

With the sponsorship of Fred Greenstein (1975), it has had quite a run in the political science literature of personality and politics. Every now and then, I still get requests from odd places to reprint it or to print specially adapted versions—invariably, it seems, from outside the circle of social psychology. Within my own subdiscipline, it seemed to fall with a dull thud—understandably, since it was offered as an aid to social interpretation, not as a quasi-Newtonian theory. My colleagues weren't much interested. I display it here, not just because I can be assured that it will finally get a

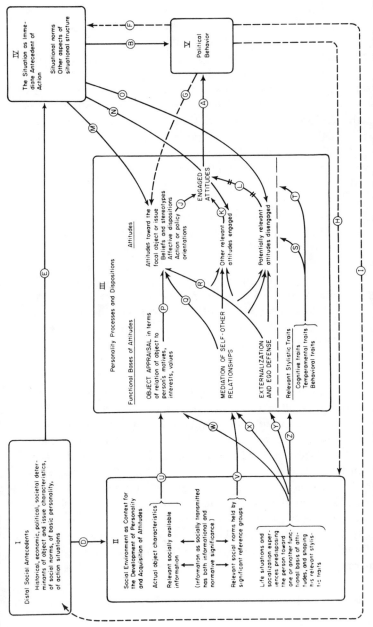

Figure 1. A functional map: political attitudes and behavior in their personal and social context. From Smith, 1968a, 1968b. Reprinted by permission of Harvard University Press from O. Garceau (Ed.), *Political Research and Political Theory* (1968). A slightly different earlier version appeared in the *Journal of Social Issues*, 1968, **24**(3).

psychological audience, but because I think it illustrates several of the points of conceptual strategy that I have been talking about.[2]

For the moment, disregard the tangle of arrows in the fine structure of the map and look only at the five major panels identified by Roman numerals. Personality Processes and Dispositions (Panel III) occupy the center of the stage. The behavioral pay-off is in Panel V, to the extreme right. It is labeled Political Behavior here, but there is no need for the political restriction. Starting with Panel V, the unbroken arrows (marked A and B) that link it with Personality Processes and Dispositions (Panel III) and with the Situation as Immediate Antecedent of Action (Panel IV) represent Lewin's methodological premise: All social behavior is to be analyzed as a joint resultant of characteristics of the person, on the one hand, and of the psychological situation, on the other. To specify the contribution of either requires taking the other into account.

Causal antecedents can be traced back from each of these two panels that show the immediate determinants of action. To Personality (Panel III) a cluster of arrows leads from Panel II, Social Environment as Context for the Development of Personality and Acquisition of Attitudes. Both the environment of socialization (Panel II) and the immediate situation of action (Panel IV) have their own more distal antecedents, represented in Panel I. That is, historical, economic, and institutional factors (Panel I) have an indirect impact on individual behavior—both by shaping the contexts in which socialization occurs and attitudes are learned (Arrow D) and as sources of the features of the immediate situations in which action takes place (Arrow E).

The broken arrows from Panel V reflect the *consequences* of behavior, which may alter the situation in which it occurs (Arrow F), and cumulate across the many actions of many persons to modify the long-run social environments that shape and support the attitudes of each (Arrow H), in the still longer run constituting history and shaping institutions (Arrow I). Arrow G, leading back from behavior to personal dispositions in Panel III, represents the effects that self-committing behavior can have on attitudes, a phenomenon emphasized by Festinger (1957) that has standing in its own right.

I will enter the internal detail of the map only on the right-hand side of Panel III, Personality Processes and Dispositions, to illustrate how the map seeks to clarify the problem of why behavior does not

2. This section is adapted from Smith (1973).

correspond directly to attitudes. Other features of the map are based on the Smith-Bruner-White version of functional theory, accounting for how attitudes arise and are sustained in terms of their role in the person's ongoing psychological economy, or are probably self-explanatory.

The part of the map to which I am calling attention suggests that we cannot take for granted just which of a person's attitudes will become engaged as a co-determinant of behavior in any given situation. Political scientists are probably less naive about this than many psychologists who have been perplexed by the attitudes-and-behavior issue. How people vote for one or another presidential candidate depends, as we know, not only on their focal attitudes toward that candidate but also on attitudes toward alternative candidates, toward party, and toward issues. As Arrows M, N, and O are intended to indicate, the immediate situation of action plays a dual role. On the one hand, it engages with certain of the person's attitudes and leaves in abeyance others that might potentially be engaged; on the other, it serves as a direct co-determinant of behavior, together with the engaged attitudes. An example, again from the political realm: On the floor of Congress, certain of a congressman's attitudes become engaged with the issue under discussion—different ones, very likely, from those that would be engaged in discussion of the same issue with an important constituent. But what he or she says in either situation (and saying is behaving) will depend not only on the attitudes engaged but also on what seems appropriate and likely to be instrumentally effective, given the norms and contingencies of each situation. These complex relationships give us no reason to suppose that people's behavior should correspond in any simple way to their attitudes on a single focal issue or toward a single focal object—the same conclusion reached by Fishbein and Ajzen (1975) though by a different route.

Any map is a simplification, and likely a falsification, too, with trade-offs like those involved in projecting the globe on a flat page. The psychology of attitudes represented in my map is rooted in the functional perspective to which I was committed. The functional point of view is a kind of bastard cousin of the strictly causal-explanatory approach, and it has its pragmatic justification for many psychological as well as biological purposes in the empirical adaptedness that is a salient feature of evolution and development. It can be seen as a way-station toward a more adequate causal analysis, as it has been in physiology, or it may be given an ambiguous quasi-teleological interpretation. What is clear, however, is that while my map has an explicit place for the role of values in what we called the "object appraisal" function of attitudes, it has no way of representing the sort of reflective, symbolic view of selfhood that I was urging in the metatheoretical first part of this essay—for attitudinal orientations such as "Origin" vs. "Pawn" that are constitutive of the self as actor and as reflexive object. Perhaps it could be jockeyed with to accommodate this more humanistic orientation; perhaps not.

Values in the Perspective of Selfhood

So far, my retrospective has dealt mainly with the psychology of attitudes. I will deal much more briefly with the topic of values, on which I have recently had a fuller say in my Allport Memorial Lecture (Smith, 1978e). Rokeach (this volume) has given searching attention to the concept in his paper for this Symposium.

I find Rokeach's approach to values generally congenial. His stress on rather punctiform instrumental and terminal values—*single* beliefs—has surely paid off, though it seems to me to be tied to his own particular measuring instrument, a simple and surprisingly powerful one. (Before I had seen his results, I would not have expected findings so impressive and internally coherent from such a barebones schematic measure.) All the same, Rockeach's concepts as embodied in his instrument still seem to me only one among various possible approaches. Think, for example of Morris's (1956) much more complex "paths of life," which I am not advocating as preferable. At this stage in our enterprise I am not enamored of definitions, but I continue to like Kluckhohn's (1951), which seems to me more general and flexible than Rokeach's. Rokeach's definition is congruent with it in the most essential respects. According to Kluckhohn,

> A value is a conception, explicit or implicit, distinctive of an individual or characteristic of a group, of the *desirable* which influences the selection from available modes, means, and ends of action. (p. 395)

I agree with Rokeach that the distinction between the desirable and the merely desired, the preferable and the preferred, is difficult to maintain in practice and in empirical research, since the pull toward consistency is so strong that it makes us likely to desire what we regard as desirable, and to regard as desirable what we in fact desire. But the history of moral and ethical thought is replete with instances in which this consistency breaks down, and these instances are humanly important and psychologically interesting. It breaks down for both saints and sinners. In social commentary (Smith, 1978a), I have been particularly concerned with the presently visible tendency for our "conceptions of the desirable" to collapse into mere preferences, what we want—now!, a response, I think, to our modern situation in which for many of us our values are no longer legitimated by a symbolic macrocosmic order. As our criteria or standards for choice lose the phenomenal quality that Heider (1958), following Köhler (1938), referred to as "objective requiredness," our commitments to them are likely to falter, and values that have become mere preferences cease to provide the microcosmic anchor needed for a firm sense of identity, meaning and order in the conduct of our lives. I speak as a resident of California!

Values, like attitudes, I agree with Rokeach, have a cognitive core. I don't mind calling both concepts instances of the broader class of *beliefs*, as Rokeach does, so long as we remember that both are integrations that involve much more than cold informational content. The contemporary cognitive psychology of "information processing" is not yet in a position to deal with them.

Beliefs and attitudes as we commonly use the concepts are human phenomena, symbolically elaborated in ways that depend upon our shared linguistic symbol systems. But they have obvious counterparts or precursors at the prehuman animal level in behavioral expectancies (Tolman, 1932) and "canalizations" (Murphy, 1947)—preferences, appetites, and aversions. Animals as well as people can learn about the world and take it into account, and what animals, like people, learn and take into account may be organized around objects, though not around ideal, imaginary, metaphorical, or abstractly conceptual ones. In contrast, values, as standards or criteria of the desirable linked to the experience of "ought," are uniquely human. Like the elaborated symbol systems on which they depend, they are social emergents that require continuity of culture and human association in community.

Yet, with Kluckhohn, I would not restrict the concept to *shared* prescriptive or proscriptive beliefs as Rokeach does. It can be quite true, and I think it is, that we would not have standards for the desirable without social experience (initially the approval and disapproval, then the explicit requirements and prohibitions of parental caretakers), just as we would have little experience of selfhood if we were raised inhumanly as isolated animals. All the same, on this social foundation persons can and do develop value standards of their own that are not wholly shared. It is fine for some purposes to focus on the standards that *are* shared. For other purposes, including some involved in the psychology of personality, the restriction would seem to be hampering.

Values are a major, constitutive ingredient of selfhood, along the lines suggested in the first part of this essay. Some time ago (Smith, 1963), I sketched a historical, developmental sequence according to which, in the first case, that of stable, traditional societies, the requirements of the parents (given "objectively" in the nature of things from the perspective of the infant) merge seamlessly into macrocosmically sustained values. In such societies, which were the universal human setting until very recently, everyone "knows" what is right and proper in each of the finite array of life situations that the culture recognizes, and has no occasion to question why. (If there *is* questioning, there are mythic answers.) Rapid socio-cultural change in the modernizing West offered tempting alternatives and also imposed stricter demands (for capital accumulation, as Fromm's [1941] neo-Freudian-Marxist analysis would have it); so new provisions emerged for the "internalization" of values, along lines such as those formulated by the Freudian superego, still with macrocosmic support (the "Protestant Ethic" *was* rooted in Protestantism, after all!). In our contemporary "post-industrial" society, the imperatives for self-discipline have slackened and the macrocosmic props have also also eroded. Now we find some people's values anchored neither in macroscopic myth nor in unthinking "introjection," but in principled self-commitment—but vulnerably so, ever at risk of relapsing to mere preferences. Existential philosophy expresses and explores aspects of this predicament.

Even this schematic account should suggest correspondences with the historical characterology of Riesman (1950), based on Fromm (1947), and with Kohlberg's (1964) developmentalist ideas about moral judgment, which have the drawback of being unhistorical and I fear culture-bound in essential respects. My hope is to persuade you that an appropriate psychological treatment of values requires a historical and cultural perspective not only in regard to the *content* of the values to which people adhere (the main focus of

Rokeach's research, as I understand it), but also in regard to the *way* in which people adhere to them (which has been Kohlberg's main concern—Smith, 1969).

How Can Psychology Participate in the Dialectic of Values?

Psychologists study values; they also participate in the advocacy of values, often without being aware of doing so. A prime example is their use of evaluative concepts like "maturity," "personal soundness," "mental health," or "self-actualization" in personality theory and in framing the goals of professional practice. In my Allport Lecture (Smith, 1978e), I examined a number of attempts by psychologists (including ones by Maslow [1954] and by Loevinger [1976]) to provide an empirical, "scientific" justification for choice among values in this area of special psychological relevance. I concluded that it can't be done: as many philosophers have held, no magic bridge between facts and values is to be found. All the same, I further concluded that we *can* participate legitimately, *as psychologists*, in the ongoing discourse or dialectic about values, in which, in our fluid, unstable culture, values get transmitted, differentiated, and sometimes transformed. Indeed, we have been participating all along, although sometimes unwittingly and under the false colors of supposed "value-neutrality."

I used Allport's (1954) classic on *The Nature of Prejudice* to illustrate actual ways in which psychologists participate in the dialectic of values without the need to claim access to a magic bridge that they do not have. In this careful, wise, and humane work, infused with democratic values as conceived in the context of his time, Allport drew upon the resources of psychology and social science primarily to *clarify causal and means-end relationships*—how best to proceed to attain already valued goals Beyond that, however, his close examination of the nature and manifestations of bigotry surely made many of his readers more thoughtful and self-critical about ways in which they too had played the bigot unthinkingly: a role of *sensitization* that can lead to the emergence of new values, and a role of *encouraging Socratic self-confrontation* that can lead to the reordering of the reader's values toward more inclusive self-chosen patterns of consistency. (Rokeach's [1973] research has focused on these processes.) And Allport's own example of scrupulous fair-mindedness was surely a cogent contribution to the dialectic of values—*modeling* has a role in the dialectic, too. According to my conception of social and personality psychology as a historical discipline that also *participates* in history with its own specialized resources for augmenting human reflectiveness and self-direction, the example is a cogent one.

The Self?—and Selfhood

To bring this long excursion to a close, I return to the theme of *selfhood* as a historical, cultural, creative project in symbolization. When, long ago, I agreed to participate in this symposium, I offered "Attitudes, Values and The Self" as my working title. By the time I was writing my APA address (Smith, 1978d), I had come to realize that my proper topic was selfhood, as criterial features of the human condition—reflexive self-awareness prime among them. *The* self then seemed much too concrete a term for my purposes. But as I mulled and stewed about what I would do for this essay, I still held to the hope and expectation that I would somehow be able to sort out my thinking so as to resurrect a concept of "the self" as one of a family of concepts in the domain of selfhood. I stuck to the old title nearly to the bitter end. But I couldn't make a go of it, as I discovered at the cost of unusually painful writer's block. Now I attribute the snarl not to my incapacities but to the nature of the problem. (Healthy attribution, that!) I now think that I started with the wrong heading.

There are a number of terms in the domain of selfhood that give me no trouble, or seem potentially useful. There is the *person*, the actual, concrete participant in symbolically construed and governed social relations. There is *personality*, the psychologist's formulation or construction of the person, a construction of organized processes, states, and dispositions (beliefs, attitudes, and values among them). There is Erikson's (1959) rich but slippery concept of *identity*—some trouble, here, to disentangle and pin down the meanings. There is a set of terms in the reflexive mode—*self-perceptions* and *attributions, self-concepts, self-theories* (Epstein, 1973)—in which the prefix "self-" implies reflexive reference but does *not* imply a surgically or conceptually separable object of reference—other than the *person*. People—persons—may reify "I" and "Me," but psychologists shouldn't, except as they recognize the causal-functional importance of people's own reifications. There is Jung's (1966) elusive *Self-as-archetype*—an ideal of integration to be approached, perhaps a template for integration, a symbolization of it, to guide the process of "individuation." I don't see a place for *the self* in such a list. It is not a term that designates an entity or agency, except in usages that treat it as synonymous with the *person*—in which case one or the other term is superfluous.

Yet there *are* contexts in which "self" is employed in near synonymy with "person" that seem to me more justifiable. We may talk about transformations of the Greek self from Homer to Euripides, or of the Western self from Shakespeare to Proust, Pynchon, or R. D. Laing. We may talk of the fragmentation of self in role-differentiated modern society. When we use such locutions, we are emphasizing the symbolic, *self-referential* aspect of being a person (with the reflexive prefix having its usual sense as interpreted above), with the implied reminder that self-referential features in which we are interested are somehow constitutive of the person as social actor. We are not talking about an entity, conceptual or otherwise, that is distinguishable from the person. If it makes sense to talk about a fragmented or divided self, the fragmentation/ division is a metaphor of metaphors: a characterization of the metaphoric symbol system that partly constitutes us as persons.

So I draw back in what I think are significant ways from the language of William James and George Herbert Mead, which I began by taking for granted. Selfhood, person, and personality remain my key terms.

Conclusion

In the first part of this essay I developed a metatheoretic basis in which selfhood is proffered as the proper concern of a personality and social psychology that is at once scientific *and* humanistic in its aims. In doing so, I gave voice to my misgivings about the recent preoccupation of the field with the model of the physical sciences, calling rather for a view of its historical character and its potential value as a mode of participating in human history. I exemplified a historical approach and sought a kind of justification of it in a speculative account of the evolutionary and historical emergence of selfhood, an account that was nevertheless grounded on an empiri-

cal base. I proposed that a view of selfhood as substantially constituted by vital metaphors of culturally transmitted symbolism is
congruent with a variety of existing clusters of theoretical insight,
some of them presently neglected by the personality and social
psychology of the mainstream, some of them (like attribution
theory) near the center of the main current. Divergences among
contemporary theorists, I suggested, partly hinge on whether they
take a positive or a pejorative view of the role of metaphor in
selfhood.

In the second part, I applied the perspective thus developed to the
topics of this symposium, in a retrospective, evaluative look at the
recent history of our discipline. I applauded what seems to be our
present belated rediscovery of the Lewinian principle that psychological dispositions, whether beliefs, attitudes—or personality, are
relevant to the explanation of behavior only when they are taken
jointly in interaction with formulations of the situation of action.
The rediscovery should relegitimize the psychology of personality,
the context in which a substantive psychology of attitudes belongs. I
decried the inadequate attention that mainstream social psychology
has given to the substantive understanding of attitudes, where a
view of the discipline as historical might expect it to make more of a
contribution. And I resurrected an old conceptual map, an outgrowth of my earlier participation in functional attitude theory, to
illustrate, among other things, a legitimate role for social psychology in clarification and social interpretation that we have largely
skimped. My brief treatment of values, differentiating my approach
from Rokeach's, again emphasized a historical-cultural perspective
on people's ways of relating to value standards, conceived as important ingredients of selfhood. It also took a quick look at how psychologists can legimately participate in the modification of values—
again from a perspective that regards psychology and psychologists
as *participant* in history, not merely studying history with or without
the knowledge that that is what they are doing.

And I ended, as I do here, with the discovery that my search for
the self as the hero of this adventure was misguided. The hero, if
there is one, is the *person*, whose selfhood is a cultural gift and a
historical and personal achievement. From the point of view of this
essay, psychology has a potentially proud role to play in people's
enacting of their further history, through contributions it can make
to collective and individual self-understanding and therefore to
collective and individual self-direction.

REFERENCES

Abelson, R. P., Aronson, E., McGuire, W. J., Newcomb, T. M., Rosenberg, M. J., & Tannenbaum, P. H. (Eds.), *Theories of cognitive consistency: A sourcebook*. Chicago: Rand McNally, 1968.

Abramson, L. Y., Seligman, M. E. P., & Teasdale, J. D. Learned helplessness in humans: Critique and reformulation. *Journal of Abnormal Psychology*, 1978, **87**, 49–74.

Adorno, T. W., Frenkel-Brunswik, E., Levinson, D. J., & Sanford, R. N. *The authoritarian personality*. New York: Harper, 1950.

Allport, G. W. Attitudes. In C. Murchison (Ed.), *A handbook of social psychology*. Worcester, MA.: Clark University Press, 1935.

Allport, G. W. *Personality: A psychological interpretation*. New York: Holt, 1937.

Allport, G. W. The ego in contemporary psychology. *Psychological Review*, 1943, **50**, 451–478.

Allport, G. W. *The nature of prejudice*. Cambridge, MA.: Addison-Wesley, 1954.

Allport, G. W., Vernon, P. E., & Lindzey, G. *A study of values: A scale for measuring the dominant interests in personality* (Rev. ed.). Boston: Houghton-Mifflin, 1951.

Ansbacher, H. L., & Ansbacher, R. R. (Eds.), *The individual psychology of Alfred Adler*. New York: Basic Books, 1956.

Arendt, H. *The human condition*. Chicago: University of Chicago Press, 1958.

Aronson, E. *The social animal* (2nd ed.). San Francisco: W. H. Freeman, 1976.

Asch, S. E. Effects of group pressure upon the modification and distortion of judgment. In H. Guetzkow (Ed.), *Groups, leadership, and men*. Pittsburgh: Carnegie Press, 1951.

Baldwin, J. M. *Social and ethical interpretations in mental development: A study in social psychology*. New York: Macmillan, 1897.

Becker, E. *The denial of death*. New York: Free Press, 1973.

Calkins, M. W. A reconciliation between structural and functional psychology. *Psychological Review*, 1906, **13**, 61–81.

Campbell, A., Converse, P. E., Miller, W. E., and Stokes, D. E. *The American voter*. New York: Wiley, 1960.

Campbell, D. T. Social attitudes and other acquired behavioral dispositions. In S. Koch (Ed.), *Psychology: A study of a science* (Vol. 6). New York: McGraw-Hill, 1963.

Cantril, H. *The "why" of man's experience*. New York: Macmillan, 1950.

Carlson, R. Where is the person in personality research? *Psychological Bulletin*, 1971, **75**, 203–219.

Carlson, R. Personality. In *Annual Review of Psychology*, 1975, **26**, 393–414.

Chein, I. *The science of behavior and the image of man*. New York: Basic Books, 1972.

Cooley, C. H. *Human nature and the social order*. New York: Scribners, 1902.

Cronbach, L. Beyond the two disciplines of scientific psychology. *American Psychologist*, 1975, **30**, 116–127.

De Charms, R. *Personal causation: The internal affective determinants of behavior*. New York: Academic Press, 1968.

Doob, L. The behavior of attitudes. *Psychological Review*, 1947, **54**, 135–156.

Epstein, S. The self-concept revisited: Or a theory of a theory. *American Psychologist*, 1973, **28**, 404–416.

Erikson, E. H. Identity and the life cycle. *Psychological Issues*, 1959 (Whole No. 1).

Festinger, L. *A theory of cognitive dissonance*. Evanston, IL.: Row, Peterson, 1957.

Fishbein, M. Attitudes and the prediction of behavior. In M. Fishbein (Ed.), *Readings in attitude theory and measurement*. New York: Wiley, 1967.

Fishbein, M., & Ajzen, I. *Belief, attitude, intention and behavior: An introduction to theory and research*. Reading, MA.: Addison-Wesley, 1975.

Frank, J. D. *Persuasion and healing* (Rev. ed.). Baltimore, MD.: Johns Hopkins University Press, 1973.

Fromm, E. *Escape from freedom*. New York: Farrar & Rinehart, 1941.

Fromm, E. *Man for himself: An inquiry into the psychology of ethics*. New York: Rinehart, 1947.

Geertz, C. *The interpretation of cultures*. New York: Basic Books, 1973.

Geertz, C. On the nature of anthropological understanding. *American Scientist*, 1975, **63**, 47–53.

Gergen, K. J. Social psychology as history. *Journal of Personality and Social Psychology*, 1973, **26**, 309–320.

Greenstein, F. *Personality and politics: Problems of evidence, inference, and conceptualization* (Rev. ed.). New York: Norton, 1975.

Harnad, S. R., Steklis, H. D., & Lancaster, J. (Eds.). *Origins and evolution of language and speech. Annals of the New York Academy of Sciences*, 1976, **280**.

Heider, F. *The psychology of interpersonal relations*. New York: Wiley, 1958.

Holt, R. R. Freud's mechanistic and humanistic images of man. In R. R. Holt & E. Peterfreund (Eds.), *Psychoanalysis and contemporary science*, **1**, 3–24.

Horney, K. *The neurotic personality of our time*. New York: Norton, 1937.

Hovland, C. I. Reconciling conflicting results derived from experimental and survey studies of attitude change. *American Psychologist*, 1959, **14**, 8–17.

Hovland, C. I., Janis, I. L., & Kelley, H. H. *Communication and persuasion*. New Haven: Yale University Press, 1953.

James, W. The consciousness of self. In *Principles of Psychology* (Vol. 1). New York: Holt, 1890.

Jaynes, J. *The origins of consciousness in the breakdown of the bicameral mind*. Boston: Houghton-Mifflin, 1977.

Jones, E. E., Kanouse, D. E., Kelley, H. H., Nisbett, R. E., Valins, S., & Weiner, B. *Attribution: Perceiving the causes of behavior.* Morristown, NJ.: General Learning Press, 1972.

Jones, R. A. *Self-fulfilling prophecies: Social, psychological and physiological effects of expectancies.* Hillsdale, NJ.: Lawrence Erlbaum Associates, 1977.

Jung, C. G. *Two essays in analytical psychology* (2nd ed.). Princeton, NJ.: Princeton University Press, 1966.

Katz, D., & Stotland, E. A preliminary statement to a theory of attitude structurre and change. In S. Koch (Ed.), *Psychology: A study of a science* (Vol. 3). New York: McGraw-Hill, 1959.

Kluckhohn, C. K. Values and value orientations in the theory of action. In T. Parsons & E. Shils (Eds.), *Toward a general theory of action.* Cambridge, MA.: Harvard University Press, 1951.

Koch, S. Language communities, search cells, and the psychological studies. In J. K. Cole & W. J. Arnold (Eds.), *Nebraska Symposium on Motivation 1975* (Vol. 23). Lincoln: University of Nebraska Press, 1976.

Kohlberg, L. Development of moral character and moral ideology. In M. L. Hoffman & L. W. Hoffman (Eds.), *Review of child development research* (Vol. 1). New York: Russell Sage Foundation, 1964.

Köhler, W. *The place of value in a world of facts.* New York: Liveright, 1938.

Kohut, H. *The analysis of the self.* New York: International Universities Press, 1971.

Lewin, K. *Field theory in social science: Selected theoretical papers.* New York: Harper, 1951.

Lewin, K., Lippitt, R., & White, R. K. Patterns of aggressive behavior in experimentally created social climates. *Journal of Social Psychology,* 1939, **10**, 271–299.

Lifton, R. J. *Thought reform and the psychology of totalism: A study of "brain-washing" in China.* New York: Norton, 1961.

Lindzey, G., & Aronson, E. *The handbook of social psychology* (Rev. ed.). 5 vols. Reading, MA.: Addison-Wesley, 1968–1969.

Loevinger, J. *Ego development.* San Francisco: Jossey-Bass, 1976.

Magnusson, D., & Endler, N. S. (Eds.). *Personality at the crossroads: Current issues in interactional psychology.* Hillsdale, NJ.: Erlbaum, 1977.

Maslow, A. H. *Motivation and personality.* New York: Harper & Row, 1954.

McDougall, W. *An introduction to social psychology* (14th ed.). Boston: Luce, 1921.

Mead, G. H. *Mind, self, and society.* Chicago: University of Chicago Press, 1934.

Morris, C. *Varieties of human value.* Chicago: University of Chicago Press, 1956.

Murphy, G. *Personality: A biosocial approach to origins and structure.* New York: Harper, 1947.

Murphy, G., & Likert, R. *Public opinion and the individual*. New York: Harper, 1938.

Murphy, J. Psychiatric labeling in cross-cultural perspective. *Science*, 1976, **191**, 1019–1028.

Murray, H. A. *Explorations in personality*. New York: Oxford University Press, 1938.

Murray, H. A., & Morgan, C. D. A clinical study of sentiments. *Genetic Psychology Monographs*, 1945, **32**, 3–311.

Onians, R. B. *The origins of European thought*. New York: Arno Press, 1973 (originally published 1951).

Piaget, J. *The moral judgment of the child*. New York: Harcourt, Brace, 1932.

Rank, O. *Art and the artist: Creative urge and personality development*. New York: Knopf, 1932.

Riegel, K. F. From traits and equilibrium toward developmental dialectics. In J. K. Cole & W. J. Arnold (Eds.), *Nebraska Symposium on Motivation 1975* (Vol. 23). Lincoln: University of Nebraska Press, 1976.

Riesman, D., with Denney, R., & Glazer, N. *The lonely crowd*. New Haven: Yale University Press, 1950.

Rogers, C. *Counseling and psychotherapy*. Boston: Houghton-Mifflin, 1942.

Rokeach, M. *The open and closed mind: Investigations into the nature of belief systems and personality systems*. New York: Basic Books, 1960.

Rokeach, M. *The nature of human values*. New York: Free Press, 1973.

Rokeach, M. Some unresolved issues in theories of beliefs, attitudes, and values. In H. E. Howe, Jr. & M. M. Page (Eds.), *Nebraska Symposium on Motivation 1979* (Vol. 27). Lincoln: University of Nebraska Press, 1980. (This volume)

Rotter, J. B. Generalized expectancies for internal versus external control of reinforcement. *Psychological Monographs*, 1966, **80** (1, Whole No. 609), 1–28.

Sarbin, T. R. Contextualism: A world view for modern psychology. In J. K. Cole & A. W. Landfield (Eds.), *Nebraska Symposium on Motivation 1976* (Vol. 24). Lincoln: University of Nebraska Press, 1977.

Sarbin, T.R., & Adler, N. Self-reconstitution processes: A preliminary report. *Psychoanalytic Review*, 1970–71, **57**, 599–616.

Sarbin, T. R., & Coe, W. C. *Hypnosis: A social psychological analysis of influence communication*. New York: Holt, Rinehart, & Winston, 1972.

Schutz, A. *Phenomenology of the social world*. Evanston, IL.: Northwestern University Press, 1967.

Seligman, M. E. *Helplessness: On depression, development, and death*. San Francisco: W. H. Freeman, 1968.

Shand, A. F. *The foundations of character*. London: Macmillan, 1914.

Sherif, M., & Cantril, H. *The psychology of ego-involvements: Social attitudes and identifications*. New York: Wiley, 1947.

Sherif, M., & Sherif, C. *Groups in harmony and tension.* New York: Harper, 1953.

Shotter, J. What is it to be human? In N. Armstead (Ed.), *Reconstructing social psychology.* Harmondsworth, England: Penguin Books, 1974.

Skinner, B. F. *Beyond freedom and dignity.* New York: Knopf, 1971.

Smith, M. B. Comment on the "implications of separating opinions from attitudes." *Public Opinion Quarterly,* 1954, **18**, 254–265.

Smith, M. B. Personal values in the study of lives. In R. W. White (Ed.), *The study of lives: Essays on personality in honor of Henry A. Murray.* New York: Atherton, 1963.

Smith, M. B. A map for the analysis of personality and politics. *Journal of Social Issues,* 1968, **24** (3), 15–28. (a)

Smith, M. B. Personality in politics: A conceptual map with application to the problem of political rationality. In O. Garceau (Ed.), *Political research and political theory: Essays in honor of V. O. Key, Jr.* Cambridge, MA.: Harvard University Press, 1968. (b)

Smith, M. B. Morality and student protest. In M. B. Smith, *Social psychology and human values.* Chicago: Aldine Press, 1969.

Smith, M. B. Encounter groups and humanistic psychology. In K. Back (Ed.), *In search for community: Encounter groups and social change.* Washington, D.C. and Boulder, Colo.: American Association for the Advancement of Science and Westview Press, 1978. (a)

Smith, M. B. Humanism and behaviorism in psychology: Theory and practice. *Journal of Humanistic Psychology,* 1978, **18**, 27–36. (b)

Smith, M. B. Landmarks in the literature: The psychology of prejudice. (Retrospective review essay on T. W. Adorno et al., *The authoritarian personality,* and G. W. Allport, *The nature of prejudice.*) New York University, *Education Quarterly,* 1978, **9** (no. 2), 29–32. (c)

Smith, M. B. Perspectives on selfhood. *American Psychologist,* 1978, **33**, 1053–1063. (d)

Smith, M. B. Psychology and values. *Journal of Social Issues,* 1978, **34** (no. 4), 181–199. (e)

Smith, M. B. What it means to be human. In R. Fitzgerald (Ed.), *What it means to be human.* Rushcutters' Bay, Australia: Pergamon, 1978. (f)

Smith, M. B., Bruner, J. S., & White, R. W. *Opinions and personality.* New York: Wiley, 1956.

Snell, B. *The discovery of the mind: The Greek origins of European thought.* Oxford: Blackwell, 1953.

Spranger, E. *Types of men: The psychology and ethics of personality.* Halle: Max Niemeyer Verlag, 1928.

Thomas, W. I., & Znaniecki, F. *The Polish peasant in Europe and America* (Vol. 1). Boston: Badger, 1918.

Thurstone, L. L. Attitudes can be measured. *American Journal of Sociology*, 1928, **33**, 529–554.

Tolman, E. C. *Purposive behavior in animals and men.* New York: Century, 1932.

Triandis, H. C. Some universals of social behavior. *Personality and Social Psychology Bulletin*, 1978, **4**, 1–16.

Triandis, H. C. Values, attitudes, and interpersonal behavior. In H. E. Howe, Jr., & M. M. Page (Eds.), *Nebraska Symposium on Motivation 1979* (Vol. 27). Lincoln: University of Nebraska Press, 1980. (This volume)

Trilling, L. *Sincerity and authenticity.* Cambridge, MA.: Harvard University Press, 1972.

Vaihinger, H. *The philosophy of "As if": A system of the theoretical, practical and religious fictions of mankind.* New York: Harcourt, Brace, 1925.

Washburn, S. Speculations on the interrelations of the history of tools and biological evolution. In J. N. Spuhler (Ed.), *The evolution of man's capacity for culture.* Detroit, MI.: Wayne State University Press, 1959.

Weinstein, E., & Deutschberger, P. Some dimensions of altercasting. *Sociometry*, 1963, **4**, 454–466.

White, A. D. *A history of the warfare of science with theology in Christendom.* New York: Appleton, 1896.

Wylie, R. C. *The self concept.* Lincoln: University of Nebraska Press, 1961.

Wylie, R. C. *The self concept* (Vol. 1, rev. ed.). *A review of methodological considerations and measuring instruments.* Lincoln: University of Nebraska Press, 1974.

Subject Index

ability, 204, 238
abortion, 19, 25–26, 29, 32, 34–35,
    39, 51–53, 171–172
action
    and attitude, 160, 184, 191
    consequences of, 149–152, 162,
        202–203
    contemplation of, 148–149
    context of, 126, 128
    defined, 119, 201–202
    determinants of, 336
    discrepant, 148, 153–184
    dynamics of, 138, 142–152
    induced, 174–178
    intensity and duration of,
        238–240
    measurement of, 202
    process of, 147–149
    surpassing, 153, 185–192
    types of, 120–121
adaptation-level formula, 22
adolescents, 36–37
    see also children
affect
    and behavior, 218–219
    defined, 211–212, 215

affirmative action, 48–49
Africa, 310
aggression, 9
American Statistical Association,
    14
anima/animus, 318
approach and avoidance
    tendencies, 174–178
Arab-Israeli conflict, 122–126, 133
archetypes, 318
ASA Footnotes, 14
assimilation and contrast effects,
    46–56
attitude(s)
    and action, 160, 184, 191
    anchoring effects of, 23, 24
    assimilation-contrast effects,
        46–56
    and behavior, 67–69, 196–197,
        215–226, 266–271, 326, 327, 337
    and beliefs, 84–87, 93, 98, 339
    bipolar, 32–35, 48
    and causal attributions, 276–282
    character of, 191–192
    child-bearing, 109–111
    concept of, 4–5, 17, 56

Author Index

359